天 THE EAST-WEST CENTER—formally known as "The Center for Cultural and Technical Interchange Between East and West"—was established in Hawaii by the United States Congress in 1960. As a national educational institution in cooperation with the University of Hawaii, the Center has the mandated goal "to promote better relations and understanding between the United States and the nations of Asia and the Pacific through cooperative study, training, and research."

Each year about 2,000 men and women from the United States and some 40 countries and territories of Asia and the Pacific area work and study together with a multinational East-West Center staff in wide-ranging programs dealing with problems of mutual East-West concern. Participants are supported by federal scholarships and grants, supplemented in some fields by contributions from Asian/Pacific governments and private foundations.

Center programs are conducted by the East-West Communication Institute, the East-West Culture Learning Institute, the East-West Food Institute, the East-West Population Institute, and the East-West Technology and Development Institute. Open Grants are awarded to provide scope for educational and research innovation, including a program in humanities and the arts.

East-West Center Books are published by The University Press of Hawaii to further the Center's aims and programs.

RURAL
DEVELOPMENT
IN BANGLADESH
AND PAKISTAN

RURAL DEVELOPMENT IN BANGLADESH AND PAKISTAN

Edited by
Robert D. Stevens
Hamza Alavi
Peter J. Bertocci

AN EAST-WEST CENTER BOOK
The University Press of Hawaii
Honolulu

Manufactured in the United States of America

Designed by Penny L. Faron

Library of Congress Cataloging in Publication Data
Main entry under title:

Rural development in Bangladesh and Pakistan.

Revised papers presented at a Research Workshop on Rural Development in Pakistan, held at Michigan State University, June 21–July 28, 1971, under the sponsorship of the Asian Studies Center.
    "An East-West Center book."
    Includes bibliographies and index.
    1.   Bangladesh—Rural conditions—Congresses.
2.   Pakistan—Rural conditions—Congresses.
I.   Stevens, Robert Dale, 1927–   II.   Alavi,
Hamza, 1921–   III.   Bertocci, Peter J.
IV.   Research Workshop on Rural Development in
Pakistan, Michigan State University, 1971.
HN690.6.A8R87   309.2'63'095491   75–17807
ISBN 0–8248–0332–9

CONTENTS

Preface   vii

PART I. RURAL DEVELOPMENT IN BANGLADESH

1. Rural Development in Bangladesh: An Introduction   3
   Peter J. Bertocci

2. Stability and Change in Landholding and Revenue
   Systems in Bengal   9
   Philip B. Calkins

3. The Administration of Rural Reform: Structural
   Constraints and Political Dilemmas   29
   Elliot L. Tepper

4. East Pakistan's Agricultural Planning and Development,
   1955–1969: Its Legacy for Bangladesh   60
   Charles M. Elkinton

5. Comilla Rural Development Programs to 1971   95
   Robert D. Stevens

6. Introduction and Use of Improved Rice Varieties:
   Who Benefits?   129
   LeVern Faidley and *Merle L. Esmay*

7. Experience with Low-Cost Tubewell Irrigation   146
   Khondaker Azharul Haq

8. Social Organization and Agricultural Development
   in Bangladesh   157
   Peter J. Bertocci

PART II. RURAL DEVELOPMENT IN PAKISTAN

9. Themes in Economic Growth and Social Change in
   Rural Pakistan: An Introduction   187
   Robert D. Stevens

10. The Historical Context of Pakistan's Rural Economy   198
    Harry M. Raulet

11. Rural Self-Government in Pakistan: An Experiment in
    Political Development through Bureaucracy   214
    Muneer Ahmad

12. Agricultural Growth and Planning in the 1960s   232
    Parvez Hasan

13. Relationships between Technology, Prices, and
    Income Distribution in Pakistan's Agriculture:
    Some Observations on the Green Revolution   242
    Carl H. Gotsch

14. The Adoption and Effects of High-Yielding Wheats
    on Unirrigated Subsistence Holdings in Pakistan   270
    Refugio I. Rochin

15. The Development of Pakistan's Agriculture: An
    Interdisciplinary Explanation   290
    Shahid Javed Burki

16. The Rural Elite and Agricultural Development
    in Pakistan   317
    Hamza Alavi

17. The Green Revolution and Future Developments of
    Pakistan's Agriculture   354
    Carl H. Gotsch

Glossary   383
Index   389

PREFACE

Rural development experiences in Bangladesh and Pakistan provide a major opportunity to examine the evolving interrelationships between technical, economic, political, and social change. Over the last quarter of a century, these experiences have occurred in the context of a series of national development plans and the onset of the "green revolution."* These rural development efforts have had mixed results. In recent years Pakistan's Punjab has broken international agricultural records through very rapid rates of growth in wheat production. However, current social and political trends in rural areas of Pakistan suggest considerable uncertainty about future agricultural development and increased rural conflict. To the east, the continuing touch-and-go struggle of the Bengali people to increase rural welfare raises grave questions about national economy viability in agriculture and reasonable political stability.

These papers provide the first in-depth study of the problems and processes of rural development, up to 1972, in the two regions of the former nation of Pakistan. The analyses are set against the backdrop of historical change and the emergent social and political structures. They are undertaken in widely varying resource contexts, from the irrigated and unirrigated regions of low rainfall and relatively low population density in Pakistan to the monsoon agricultural regions of high rainfall and exceedingly high population density in Bangladesh. They include details of significant technological developments behind the green revolution in South Asia. The papers aid the student of development to gain insight into how different sets of strategies are rooted in, and interact with,

* The term "green revolution" refers to the recent large-scale development of high-yielding varieties of wheat, rice, and other grains, whose introduction into developing countries has greatly increased crop yields and food production.

historical, but changing, social structures. Attention is focused on evaluating the results of successful strategies as well as on understanding unintended outcomes. In doing so, these papers provide essential knowledge of the lessons of past economic developments at a critical turning point in South Asian history. In accomplishing these tasks they point to major rural development issues of the 1970s in these two large Asian nations and provide guidelines for future planning.

Fundamental questions of economic and cultural change are explored in these two important agricultural regions of the subcontinent, which have shared a common colonial history and until recently the same administrative and political structures. The questions taken up in these studies include the extent to which social structures are flexible and responsive to technical and economic changes, alternative roles for the civil bureaucracy in rural development, the extent of the impact of government policies and planning on rural development, the unexpected social effects of private and governmental agricultural development achievements, the extent to which rural income disparities are increasing, and the impact of original experiments in institutional change on government programs.

Three general themes emerge: of agricultural stagnation and geographically limited spurts of growth in each nation; of the need for political and administrative change to accompany social, economic, and technological developments; and of the importance of the interrelationships between social structures and the distribution of the benefits of technical and economic progress in rural areas.

Most of the authors represented in this volume were active participants in rural development programs in these nations in the 1960s. They have sought to analyze past developments, both as a guide to future rural strategy in these nations and for the lessons these experiences may provide for other developing nations. Despite notable successes, uncertainty is so great about the future directions of these large rural areas of South Asia that questions keep arising as to whether these national and rural social systems will be able to change themselves rapidly enough in an evolution-

ary manner, or whether economic and political events will occur so
rapidly that revolutionary change will ensue.

The following political events provide a time frame for the
analyses that follow. In August 1947, Pakistan attained independence from Britain as a result of the partition of the subcontinent
with India. The new nation led by Governor General Mohammed
Ali Jinnah comprised the predominantly Muslim areas in Bengal
(East Pakistan) and all or parts of five regions in the northwestern
area of the subcontinent, the Punjab, North-West Frontier Province, Kashmir, the Sind, and Baluchistan (West Pakistan). A decade later, in October 1958, after a series of short-lived governments,
the army in a bloodless coup installed General Ayub Khan as
president of Pakistan. Ayub Khan ruled for ten years until he
resigned under pressure in March 1969. General Yahya Khan,
commander-in-chief of the army, then became president and presided over elections in December 1970 that gave a sweeping victory to Sheikh Mujibur Rahman's Awami League in East Pakistan
and a decisive victory to Zulfikar Ali Bhutto's Peoples' Party in
West Pakistan. A few months later, on March 26, 1971, as the result
of a constitutional crisis over the powers of the central and provincial governments and a mass attack launched by the Pakistan Army
upon the Awami League, students, faculty, Hindus, and others in
East Pakistan, an independent Bangladesh was declared. Warfare
ensued between the Pakistan Army and the Mukhti Bahini guerillas. On December 3, 1971, the Indian government ordered her
troops to advance on Dacca, and on December 16, the Pakistan
Army in East Pakistan surrendered. Pakistan's disastrous losses led
to Bhutto's being sworn in as president of what remained of Pakistan (West Pakistan). On January 10, 1972, Sheikh Mujibur Rahman
returned in triumph to Dacca to become the first prime minister of
the nation of Bangladesh.

Four major needs led to this volume and the preceding research workshop, which refined the analyses. The first was the
often-noted relative dearth of scholarship available on Bangladesh
and Pakistan, particularly as compared with material on the more
accessible and popular areas of the subcontinent, such as India. A
few studies are available on the general economic and political

development of Bangladesh and Pakistan, but relatively little scholarly work treats rural development.

The second need was for more analysis of rural social and economic change, in view of the dominance of rural people and of agricultural production in national economic life. In 1965, more than 57 percent of the Gross Domestic Product (GDP) of East Pakistan originated in agriculture. In West Pakistan where other economic activities had grown more rapidly, agriculture remained in 1965 by far the most important industry, originating more than 35 percent of the GDP. All manufacturing industries together originated less than 13 percent of West Pakistan's GDP in 1965.

The importance of rural areas in these nations is shown also by the proportion of population residing in them. The rural population, which depends directly or indirectly almost entirely on agricultural and associated rural economic activities, was estimated for both "wings" of Pakistan at 85 percent of the total population in 1965.

The term "rural development" is used in this volume to encompass the whole range of technical, economic, political, and social changes related to private and governmental efforts to increase the well-being of rural citizens. As agriculture is the dominant economic activity in rural areas, a large share of the scholarly work properly has focused on this sector, a distribution reflected in this volume. Other fields of rural development include the whole range of the technical and social sciences, especially such fields as water technology, administration and government, political development, and community social and cultural change.

The third need was professional: to integrate the research results of different disciplines into a reasonably consistent understanding of significant trends in rural development. As rural development involves many interrelated economic and cultural changes, the strengths of different professional tools and approaches can provide a more general analysis upon which we may have greater confidence. The workshop was a first attempt to assemble a group of scholars representing an appropriate range of social science disciplines to focus on problems of rural development in Pakistan. The authors in this volume, although they sometimes come to different conclusions on major issues, are, to an extraordinary degree, in general agreement about the major changes that are underway in rural areas of Pakistan and Bangladesh.

A particular professional challenge was presented by the fact that although the two areas were under one governmental and administrative structure, two very different rural development outcomes occurred due to large differences in the physical environments and cultural settings. The bringing together of the two experiences in one volume thus provides a broader understanding of rural development processes.

The fourth need relates to the timing of these papers. With the resignation of Ayub Khan in 1969 many observers concluded that an important phase in South Asian history had passed. It was an appropriate time therefore to examine past successes and failures with an eye to guides for future action. The authors represented in the volume recognized they were writing at a watershed moment in the history of South Asia.

One result of these papers is to underline a conclusion about the process of economic change and rural development around which there appears to be growing consensus and of which Bangladesh and Pakistan today are outstanding examples, for if, indeed, we were slow to grasp the by now obvious point these studies highlight, the experience of these areas drives it home with considerable force. They demonstrate most vividly that the process of change and development in the new states, with their traditional social structures and pluralistic political cultures, is more likely to accentuate conflict than to moderate it. These papers emphasize the continual dilemmas, between the constraints of economic choice and the demands of political management, and between the decisions needed to stimulate economic growth and the accommodations required to ensure distributive justice. At the national level, the experience of these peoples in the 1960s suggests in this latter connection that when the gap between growth and equity widens—or is perceived to have widened beyond acceptable levels—ensuing conflict may tragically vitiate the gains of development itself. This, perhaps, is the central lesson of this development experience to date.

The studies presented here are grouped under the geographic

headings of Bangladesh and Pakistan. In doing so the quite different cultural and resource conditions of the two regions are recognized. The word Pakistan is employed for the western wing of the former united nation to reflect current political boundaries, except when the context of the discussion applies to the period August 1947–December 1971. During this time period Pakistan refers to both wings. Bibliographical citations employ the national designation existing at the time of publication.

Most of the papers in this volume were delivered in draft form at a graduate Research Workshop on Rural Development in Pakistan, held at Michigan State University, June 21–July 28, 1971, under the sponsorship of the Asian Studies Center. As it happened, the workshop occurred three months after the military actions began in March 1971 in East Pakistan. At times this led to a highly charged atmosphere. However, the discussions, which examined in depth certain of the fundamental issues in rural development in both regions, served to illuminate to both Bengalis and Pakistanis the interrelationships of social and economic development, which were minimally related to or influenced by the passions of the moment. And although the printed word can convey only partially the authors' sense of urgency, no one present at the Michigan State University workshop when the papers were first delivered and who participated in the animated, but intensely serious, discussion that they suscitated, can doubt the saliency of the underlying concerns to which they were directed.

The editors express their appreciation for the contributions of all the participants in the workship, including the twenty graduate students, Bengali, Pakistani, and American, and especially to the participating professionals, only some of whom are represented in this volume. Without the intense interchange, the revised papers offered here would have been much wider off the mark.

Gratitude is expressed to the Ford Foundation for the financial aid that made the workshop and the writing of this volume possible. Additional support in the final editing of the manuscript was provided by the Title 211-d grant to the Department of Agricultural Economics, Michigan State University, by the U.S. Agency for International Development.

Particular thanks are expressed to Professor William T. Ross, director of the Asian Studies Center; to Professor Harry L. Case for editorial advice; and also to the staff of the Asian Studies Center, including particularly Dorothy Doane for administrative and general support during the workshop. We have appreciated the cheerfully offered editorial aid of Addiann Hinds and Nancy L. Stevens, and secretarial services of Sylvia Anderson, Colleen M. Heron, Diane Hutchinson, Julia McKay, Patti Stiffler, and Marilyn Wilcox. We appreciate also the careful and thorough work of Mrs. Aileen Brothers who prepared the index.

PART I
RURAL DEVELOPMENT IN BANGLADESH

1

Rural Development in Bangladesh: An Introduction

Peter J. Bertocci

Emerging as an independent nation in December 1971, Bangladesh presented a composite picture of all the extremes of poverty and underdevelopment in the Third World. So stark appeared the problems confronting the new state that some world political leaders and not a few development specialists predicted Bangladesh would remain a perennially aid-dependent international "basket case" for some time to come. The underlying concerns that have buttressed this gloomy outlook are not difficult to perceive. They lie in the country's inadequately productive ecosystem and in the legacy it has inherited from the systems of agricultural management and rural public administration of past centuries.

Bangladesh's 75 million people inhabit 55,000 square miles of low-lying deltaic terrain, which is itself the product of one of the world's greatest riverine systems. Its rice agriculture, supplemented over the past 150 years by jute as a major cash crop, is dependently attuned to the late spring and early summer monsoon rains, upon whose uncertain arrival and duration is based the productivity of these two growing seasons, responsible for 90 percent of the rice output and nearly all that of jute. The winter season, given the lack of rain and effective irrigation technology, has not until recently begun to figure importantly in the country's agricultural production.[1]

Intense rural population densities, approaching 2,000 persons per square mile of cultivated area in some regions, have produced great pressure on the land. Coupled with customs of inheritance that stress individual ownership and equal division of landed property, demographic growth has contributed to postage-stamp farm sizes, whose average in 1961 was scarcely more than three acres, a classically minifundist land tenure pattern further characterized by high degrees of plot fragmentation. Technologically, farming in Bangladesh corresponds to the widely accepted Shultzian dictum concerning "traditional agriculture," in which "farmers have long ago exhausted the productivity of the state of the arts at their disposal" (Schultz 1965: 30). The tools of agriculture in Bangladesh, while admirably adapted by preindustrial standards to the refinements of economic life on the Bengal Delta, can no longer carry the day with respect to feeding an immense and rapidly multiplying population. Thus, while the country is everywhere quite fertile and potentially waterable by the continuing benevolence of the great rivers that traverse it, the vagaries of its monsoon climate ensure that, without greater technological mastery of the environment, years of barely adequate crop production will continue to be interspersed by those that bring the threat of hunger and the menace of natural disaster. The peasants of Bangladesh are the human actors in a traditional agricultural ecosystem that long ago reached stasis in its capacity to produce.[2]

Systems of agriculture are, of course, part and parcel of larger rural cultural systems and, in complex societies, subject to influence and often domination by the demands of state systems. In the main, the collection of papers in this volume addresses itself to some of the key elements of both cultural and state systems as they have diachronically shaped the background of Bangladesh's "rural development" to date. More specifically, the stress in several of the papers is on factors of economic policy-making and political administration of the rural areas over a reasonably long period of time. Thus, this section begins with Calkins' discussion of the parallels and continuities of both the Mogul and the British land revenue administrations. Calkins shows the roots of rural Bengali cultural models of land use and land control, which continue to influence rural response to development efforts. Tepper analyzes the impact of both British and Pakistani approaches to rural administration, suggesting that here again the "cultural models" of political control of the countryside, which the Bangladesh leaders have inherited, will in all likelihood be adapted to the present-day requirements of rural development. Elkinton's paper assesses the halting steps toward agricultural development begun in East Bengal under

Pakistani rule. These papers emphasize that the evolution of rural development in present-day Bangladesh has as its background context the control of East Bengal by structures of state power whose decision-making centers have been outside the region for the better part of at least four centuries. Thus, policies affecting East Bengal's agricultural development cannot be separated from the fact that they were made, in different times facing different needs, with reference to the requirements respectively of the Mogul, British, and Pakistani state systems and the elites who controlled them.

Two general themes emerge from among the many more specific ones raised in this collection of essays on Bangladesh. One constant reverberation is that which underlines the relative lack of decentralized, cohesive social organization in the countryside, a point worth careful note when one considers the need for organization in rural development. Paradoxically, however, the other theme suggests that, despite this legacy of a comparatively autonomous and inelaborate social structure in the rural areas, Bengali peasants have been able to organize themselves or be organized in manners signaling a quite positive response to opportunities for agricultural progress. Thus, the reader will perceive a contrast between two "traditions" in the rural political economy of Bangladesh: an indigenous organizational tradition of long standing, which has reflected diffuse, dyadic, and relatively weak modes of social integration coupled with minimal, and usually negatively perceived, extensions of state power to the rural areas (See Bertocci 1970: 105–137), and a more recent, partially imported modern tradition of effective, centrally controlled management of agricultural innovation.

Surely evocative of the first theme is the documentation of the relative neglect, by no means benign, of East Bengal's rural hinterlands, coupled with a history of intense land competition dating from at least the 1700s. Calkins' account of the Mogul and British revenue systems suggests that both tended to allow considerable economic and political power to devolve to the bottom levels of complex and, over time, increasingly elaborate land taxation hierarchies. Hence, he argues, East Bengal's land system has tended for a long time to be quite competitive and unstable, a point later picked up in Bertocci's essay, which focuses in part on how today's small-scale-farming Bengali peasantry, which inherits that land system and the cultural models for economic action it presents, might react to the green revolution once it begins to take widespread hold. Tepper's essay points to the paradox of an "atomized" countryside whose social organization has long been "segmented, diffuse, and in flux," yet overridden by the centralized and highly structured British administrative system with its "linch-pin" focus at the district level. This disjuncture was only partly, and in the end ineffectively, resolved by Ayub Khan's decentralizing efforts, via the Basic Democracies scheme, to create a power base among an emerging rural elite. Elkinton's contribution again begins with the theme of neglect, this time with specific reference to East Bengal's agriculture, to whose serious development little attention was paid until the mid-1960s. The author chronicles down to 1970 the fits and starts, and mixed achievements, of the reversal of this de-emphasis on agriculture. Thus, major contributors to the current problems facing Bangladesh are the cumulative social and economic impact disjointed systems of land control and rural administration, combined with belated and halting attacks upon agriculture's problems commencing only in the 1960s.

Contrasting with this picture of disorganization and neglect as painted by several of the essays is the second general theme, which stresses remarkable achievement, especially organizationally, during the latter half-decade of rural development in East Bengal's "Pakistan period." This general theme suggests that Bengali farmers can and do respond to appropriately organized and comparatively well-managed efforts at agricultural and rural development. The relative successes in this area, serving as counterpoints to Bangladesh's dismal legacy of "rural development" efforts, point, moreover, to possibly fruitful departures for the future. Stevens' outline and evaluation of the development system of the Academy for Rural Development at Comilla—the product of more than ten years' concerted experiment—gives the essential background necessary to the understanding of what appears to have been adopted as one, perhaps *the*, path to integrated rural development by Bangladesh's present Awami League regime. The basics of the

Comilla cooperative system and its allied programs in training, irrigation, new seed diffusion, and education are described by Stevens. Bertocci, in the first part of his essay, suggests some of the ways in which the relative success of the Comilla strategy—as well as some of its potential pitfalls—finds its nexus in the indigenous social organization of the Comilla countryside. The ability of small-scale farmers to benefit from the green revolution, at least as diffused in the context of Comilla-generated programs, is dramatically documented in the essay by Faidley and Esmay. Haq's more technical paper outlines the successes that are possible, as well as the problems yet to be overcome, in diffusing pump and tubewell irrigation systems using the labor-intensive and cooperative organizational methods developed at Comilla. Together, then, these papers center on the very specific and relatively successful developmental legacies that are likely to remain the backbone of Bangladesh's approach to rural development in the 1970s.

As seen from the collective vantage point of these essays, Bangladesh presents to the scholar and development practitioner alike both paradox and contrast. The more dismal, larger, historical picture, marked by a decline toward ecological disaster at the village level and fuelled by the neglect, "atomization," and competitively induced socioeconomic fragmentation over three successive periods of colonial rule, is contrasted with the more hopeful partial successes of comparatively recent years. At this political turning point following the attainment of independence, it remains to be seen to what extent Bangladesh and its people can build on the potential its successes have unearthed so as to lay to rest the legacies of its uncertain past.

Peter J. Bertocci is an assistant professor of Anthropology, Oakland University, Rochester, Michigan. He is a social anthropologist with an interest in the political and economic development of the South Asia cultural area. His field research in Comilla in 1966–1967 led to a Ph.D. in Anthropology from Michigan State University in 1970.

NOTES

1. The standard references on East Bengal's rural economy are Rashid (1965), Ahmad (1968), and Ahmed (1965).

2. For at least a partial picture of the ecological situation in Bangladesh, the reader might consult Parrack (1969) for relevant comparative purposes.

BIBLIOGRAPHY

Ahmad, Nafis
    1968. *An Economic Geography of East Pakistan.* 2nd ed. Oxford: Oxford University Press.
Ahmed, Kalimuddin
    1965. *Agriculture in East Pakistan.* Dacca: Ahmed Bros. Publications.
Bertocci, Peter
    1970. "Patterns of Social Organization in Rural East Bengal." In *Bengal East and West*, edited by Alexander Lipski, pp. 105–137. South Asia Series, Occasional Paper No. 13. East Lansing: Asian Studies Center, Michigan State University.
Parrack, Dwain W.
    1969. "An Approach to the Bioenergics of Rural West Bengal." In *Environment and Cultural Behavior: Ecological Studies in Cultural Anthropology*, edited by Andrew P. Vayda, pp. 29–46. New York: Natural History Press.
Rashid, Haroun Er
    1965. *East Pakistan: A Systematic Regional Geography and Its Development Planning Aspects.* Lahore: Sh. Ghulam Ali and Sons.
Schultz, Theodore W.
    1965. *Economic Crises in World Agriculture.* Ann Arbor: The University of Michigan Press.

2

Stability and Change in Landholding and Revenue Systems in Bengal

Philip B. Calkins

Most writing about the history of nineteenth- and twentieth-century Bengal rightly has been concerned with change over time. Historical changes, however, can be of many types. Historians often have divided their descriptions into categories, perhaps too conveniently called social change, economic change, and cultural change, but they have also suggested, partly in response to the social scientists who are encroaching upon their world, that significant historical changes need not be associated with processes of modernization, even in periods described as modern. This paper is a preliminary exploration of one aspect of the subject of change and stability in Bengal in the seventeenth, eighteenth, and nineteenth centuries.

Our view of a society is determined to a considerable extent by our understanding of the processes of change that are part of it. Thus, if we attribute major changes in social or economic organization to technological, ideological, or administrative innovation, we imply not only a view of how change occurred at that time but also a view of how change did or did not take place prior to the advent of the innovation. In studying nineteenth- and twentieth-century South Asia, it is a temptation to attribute changes to innovations introduced by the British (or at least from the West), and in many cases the attribution will be correct. Occasionally, however, it may lead us to assume that society was more static than it actually was prior to the establishment of British rule, and consequently it may also obscure the fact that processes of change were operative during the nineteenth, or even the twentieth centuries, which were independent of, or only partially dependent upon, the existence of

British rule and the introduction of aspects of Western culture.

Much attention has been given to the concept of modernization and, more recently, to the ways in which "modern" factors have
been utilized in South Asia in what are termed traditional ways.
Both of these conceptual frameworks are useful for historians of
nineteenth- and twentieth-century South Asia, but they should not
be exclusively so, and should not draw attention away from other
possible explanations of historical change that may be relevant for
both the British and pre-British periods. It is likely that some
aspects of British and pre-British Bengal were more similar than is
often supposed, and that the similarities do not necessarily suggest
that pre-British Bengal was on the verge of modernity but rather
that the effects of some British innovations were not as great as they
may appear to have been. The hypotheses upon which the argument depends are that pre-British society in Bengal was far from
static, and that many of the kinds of changes that took place in
pre-British times were similar to changes that occurred during the
nineteenth and twentieth centuries. Thus, there were similar patterns of both change and stability in British and pre-British Bengal.

Similarities between the Mogul and British Land Revenue Systems

The subject of British administration in the late eighteenth and
early nineteenth centuries, and particularly of land revenue administration, is one where both the innovative nature of British
institutions and the novelty of their effects may be subject to considerable doubt. Although many historians have said that the
British administrative system of the early nineteenth century was
based largely upon that of their Mogul predecessors, still much has
been written to suggest that the British system was responsible for
major changes both in landholding patterns and in the revenue
system. In the case of Bengal, it cannot be doubted that the changes
in patterns of landholding, employment, and economic investment
that followed the establishment of British supremacy were significant, but it is also significant that these changes sometimes
followed patterns that were not new to Bengal. At most, some
changes in landholding patterns depended upon the imposition of

extraordinary pressure from the top of the system, and, although the British monopoly of power made it possible for them to apply more pressure than had earlier rulers, a similar response to the application of administrative pressure can be traced during the Mogul period, and perhaps in pre-Mogul times as well. Other changes may have occurred not so much in response to British activity as to the fact that they were part of more or less regular cycles and patterns of landholding that existed at least during the seventeenth, eighteenth, and nineteenth centuries.

Various arguments have been advanced concerning the innovative effects of the Permanent Settlement of Bengal by the British in 1793. It has been said that the introduction of the institution of privately owned land, which was uncompromisingly enforced in law by the British, led to a vast turnover in land ownership or control. Also, the people of Bengal are said to have been unaccustomed to, and did not desire to be governed by, written regulations, which tended to be more rigid in enforcement and less open to alteration than was the earlier system of customary understandings between tenant and landholder. It has also been argued that the Permanent Settlement gave an unfair advantage to the zamindar, whose position was secure, while that of the cultivator became more tenuous as pressure on the land increased and opportunities for earning extra income in domestic industries declined. On the other hand, we are told that many zamindars were unable to survive the first few years of the Permanent Settlement, since they were unable to make the change from collectors of customary payments to "punctual tax-gatherers" (Sinha 1967:102–104). The Permanent Settlement was a failure, then, in the sense that it did not achieve the goals intended for it, partly because of changes in circumstances that were not foreseen by those who planned it, and partly because of the planners' lack of detailed information regarding land tenures and land control.

This simplified view is not intended to summarize all that we know about the Permanent Settlement, although it is clear that a much better understanding of its effects should develop as more detailed local studies are made. What is important here is that parallels for most aspects of this explanation of the Permanent Settlement can be found in the history of the administration of

Bengal during the tenure of the Mogul dewan (finance minister) and governor, Murshid Quli Khan, during the first quarter of the eighteenth century. In addition, a comparison of the landholding system in Bengal during the seventeenth and eighteenth centuries with the system established by the Permanent Settlement suggests that there were many similarities in the processes of change, as well as in the basic structure of the landholding system, before and after 1793.

Although the circumstances that led to Murshid Quli Khan's reform of the revenue system of Bengal were somewhat different from those that led to the Permanent Settlement, many of the methods he utilized and the results he obtained were quite similar. Appointed dewan of Bengal shortly after 1700 by the Mogul emperor, Aurangzeb, with the hope that increased revenues could be raised in that province to support Aurangzeb's war against the Marathas in South India, Murshid Quli Khan rapidly became the most important administrator in Bengal. Except for a period of two years from 1708 to 1710, he retained his power until his death in 1727. First as dewan and later as nazim (governor), he carried out the reforms that were to form the basis for revenue assessment and administration until the British conquest after 1757.[1]

It is possible that Murshid Quli was thinking in terms of the development of a semi-independent government in Bengal even before Aurangzeb's death in 1707, and certainly by the time of the death of Aurangzeb's successor, Bahadur Shah, in 1712, his policies were oriented toward the achievement of that goal. Partly as a result of this policy, and partly because he had been sent to Bengal originally to bring about an increase in revenue collections, Murshid Quli was anxious both to enhance his collections from the zamindars, who controlled most of the land of Bengal, and also to organize a secure and stable landholding system. In order to accomplish his goal, Murshid Quli followed a carrot-and-stick policy with the zamindars. He encouraged efficiency in collection by rewarding those zamindars who were able to deliver the increased sums that he demanded, and by punishing those who were not. His rewards often took the form of opportunities for successful zamindars to acquire the rights to more land, while his punishments usually consisted either of physical harassment and sometimes imprisonment or else removal of a zamindar from his zamindari. Although it is difficult to determine exactly the amount by which Murshid Quli was able to increase collections, it is clear both that they were increased, and that one result of his policy was to create a number of very large zamindaris and generally to substitute a landholding system that consisted of a relatively small number of landholders who held relatively large areas of land from the Mogul government for an earlier system in which there had been a relatively large number of smaller landholders.[2]

Both the intent and the effects of Murshid Quli Khan's policy bear resemblances to the Permanent Settlement, which was established by the British three-quarters of a century later. Although there was no guarantee of permanent ownership of lands under Murshid Quli's system, he did offer a reasonable degree of security, government support, and official status to those zamindars who established their ability to meet the revenue demand. In the case of such enormous zamindaris as Burdwan and Rajshahi, the result must have appeared to be quite permanent to the beneficiaries of this policy. Similarly, for those zamindars who failed to meet the revenue demand and who consequently lost part or all of their zamindaris, the result was probably as unpalatable as it was for those zamindars who suffered a similar fate after the Permanent Settlement.

Like the Permanent Settlement also, the enhancement of the revenue collections after 1700 was accomplished, at least in part, not by increasing the official level of the revenue demand but simply by insisting that the amounts already legally demanded should be paid in full.[3] Thus, while the argument that the British upset the revenue system of Bengal by substituting a strictly enforced legal system for a customary system that was only loosely enforced may have some validity, it must be modified by the proviso that they were not the first administrators in Bengal to adopt such a policy, and that the customary system that they upset was not one that had been consistently in force during the previous century. In the cases of both Murshid Quli Khan's policy and of the Permanent Settlement, one effect of the demand that the revenue be paid in full, and of the subsequent battles for control over the revenue collections, was a large-scale turnover among the zamindars and intermediate collectors. During Murshid Quli Khan's time, the battle was waged, to some extent, under what must have been novel conditions, since the terms set by Murshid Quli Khan placed an increased emphasis upon the ability of the participants to collect revenue and to send it up the hierarchy of the revenue system. The efficient administrator had an advantage, then, but since the use of force by zamindars was by no means absent the advantage did not always prove decisive. By the time of the Permanent Settlement, custom may have changed enough for the preference for efficient administrators to be more pronounced, but the evidence of complaints lodged by zamindars at the time, and by historians since then, suggests that the weight of custom was still heavily in favor of zamindars who had held their lands for at least two or three generations.

The shift toward a preference for more efficient revenue administrators can be seen more clearly in relation to another aspect of both Murshid Quli Khan's revenue arrangements and those of the Permanent Settlement. In both cases, the ultimate effect was not to establish the permanent landholding rights of a relatively small aristocracy exclusively; for, beneath the more visible surface layer, which was occupied by the official landed proprietors, the land continued to be divided among a large number of undertenants, who exercised the most effective control over the land and the collection of the revenue.

Evidence provided by the "Risala-i Zira'at," a mid-eighteenth century description of the pre-British land revenue system,[4] and by British observers (especially John Shore) suggests several generalizations about the organization of the revenue system and the behavior of those who participated in it. First, the system contained large numbers and many levels of intermediate revenue collectors. In terms of the actual control that they had over the land during the early eighteenth century, probably the most important group of intermediate landholders and revenue collectors (i.e., those who had a right to a share of the produce of a plot of land, but were not zamindars, ryots, nor landless laborers) were those who were interposed between the village level and the pargana level. There is little agreement among the sources as to the titles that were held by *tarafdar*, *ta'aluqdar*, and *mustajir* or revenue farmer.[5] What is

ment of *patni ta'aluq*s and was responsible for their particular legal form, neither the functional phenomenon that they represented nor the causal factor that inspired their creation was new to Bengal.

Changes in the Size of Zamindar Holdings

The above comparisons demonstrate some of the most obvious similarities between the land revenue systems of Mogul and British Bengal, and particularly between Murshid Quli Khan's administrative arrangements and those of the Permanent Settlement. No doubt a detailed examination of local systems would reveal even more similarities. One conclusion we might reach is that many of the goals of the two ruling groups and the methods available for implementing them were similar. Perhaps more significant, however, is the likelihood that the similarities between the Mogul and British systems depended largely upon a continuation of similar landholding patterns and styles of political and administrative behavior from one period to the next. The parallel cannot be extended too far; the fact that the Permanent Settlement was permanent made some difference, although the ways in which it differed from Murshid Quli Khan's settlement were less significant during the first decades than they were later. Probably more important than its permanence was the fact that the greater concentrations of power that the British could muster limited the extralegal or illegal options available to competitors within the landholding system, and encouraged a shift toward the use of law courts as dispute-settling mechanisms. However, the change may not have been as great as many historians have thought.

Clearly, the distinction between a pre-British customary system and a British system based upon well-defined and enforced laws is often obscured when particular comparisons are made. The distinction breaks down partly because the British system continued to utilize much that was customary. More significant reasons for its failure, in terms of the examples given above, are that either the Mogul system could produce effects similar to those attributed to the more legally oriented and better-enforced British system or that some landholding patterns were relatively independent of the actions of either the Mogul or the British rulers. Thus there appears to have been a considerable amount of continuity in the landholding system in the eighteenth and nineteenth centuries, and a striking element of that continuity was the existence of mechanisms for change that were part of the landholding system and that functioned under both the Moguls and the British. These mechanisms for change, as well as both the legal and customary aspects of the relationships between participants in the landholding system, may provide a fruitful area for future comparative studies, for they may lead to a better comprehension of both political and social factors as they pertain to the landholding system of Bengal.

One possibility is that a view of zamindaris in Bengal, as subject to relatively regular cycles of rise and decline (increasing and decreasing in size), may suggest explanations of both the effects of administrative action and the nongovernmental mechanisms for change within the system. The simplest argument for the existence of zamindari cycles is that zamindari families, like many other families, may have had a tendency to lose either their interest in or talent for administrative activity in the second or third generation after a zamindari had been built up by a particularly energetic or fortunate individual.

Zamindaris were, of course, normally hereditary, but the advantages of hereditary status were limited. Examples can be cited from many times and places, both in India and elsewhere, to demonstrate that hereditary title to land did not provide a permanent guarantee of ownership or control. In Mogul India, armed rebellion or failure to pay the revenue demand were considered to be legitimate reasons for removing a zamindar. Normally, however, a prejudice in favor of the existing zamindars operated because it was politically expedient to recognize existing titles and local political structures, and because of the presumption that the zamindars' knowledge of local conditions put them in a better position to run their zamindaris than newcomers. Consequently, a good deal of aberrant behavior was allowed before zamindars were removed.[8]

In periods that might be considered as times of crisis, however, zamindars might be removed with much less compunction. Murshid Quli Khan's tenure as dewan and governor was such a time, as was the period when Mogul rule in Bengal was consolidated a century earlier. The years immediately before and after the Permanent Settlement might be considered to be another, and although it can be argued that the ultimate effect of the Permanent Settlement was to prevent land from changing hands at the zamindari level, the immediate effect was the reverse. Because of the increase of either military or financial pressure on the landholders of Bengal, it is likely that more land changed hands during these periods than at other times, although the relative paucity of information about the landholding situation during much of the seventeenth century makes this conclusion tentative.

It is difficult to determine whether the apparent change in the rate of turnover of land rights (or at least of zamindari rights) from the late seventeenth to the early eighteenth century was due partly to the introduction of new factors into the administrative or land-holding system after 1700, or whether it simply resulted from an intensification of competition in areas of conflict and among types of functionaries similar to those of the seventeenth century. Certainly there was competition between zamindars for control of territory before the eighteenth century, and that competition must have been responsible for the turnover of zamindari rights in many cases.

The competition that could exist within a zamindari may, however, provide more significant comparisons for the seventeenth, eighteenth, and nineteenth centuries. The eighteenth-century evidence for this competition among intermediate collectors, and between intermediate collectors and zamindars, is extensive. At least some of this kind of competition existed prior to the eighteenth century, however, for we have some evidence of the acquisition of parganas by particular zamindars.[9] It is also clear that competition existed between intermediate collectors in the nineteenth century.

Thus it appears that while the eighteenth century included two periods of unusually intense competition between landhold-ers, which produced a marked turnover in landholding rights at the *sadr* or zamindari level, large parts of the seventeenth and nineteenth centuries were similar in that competition was less intense and tended to produce a proportionately larger turnover of landed rights below the zamindari level. During both the seven-teenth and nineteenth centuries, zamindari assessments were relatively light, and so there was less pressure on the zamindars from above.

Several questions are important for an understanding of how the landholding system functioned throughout the three centuries, and particularly in the seventeenth and nineteenth centuries. Why did the competition exist, and how intense was it? How did participants compete with each other, and what factors determined success in the competition? Finally, were there factors that tended to maintain a balance within the system so that internal change could continue without causing a change in the nature of the system?

The competition within the landholding system of Bengal depended upon the existence of a reasonable number of competitors, a status hierarchy that was malleable enough to allow changes of position, and the availability to participants of modes of behavior that would result in changes in economic position and/or status within the officially recognized landholding hierarchy. Although competition is a feature of most land systems, some features of the landholding system of Bengal created conditions that tended to encourage certain forms of competition.

The land of the Bengal delta is utilized primarily for growing rice, and much of it is, and has been, highly productive. Consequently, not only can a relatively high population density be supported but relatively small areas can support large numbers of people who do not cultivate the land. The relatively high concentration of surplus produced in many areas of Bengal has tended to create opportunities for dividing up the land revenue into shares, both vertically (between superiors and inferiors) and horizontally (between those of equal status in the revenue hierarchy). In addition, the fact that zamindaris in Bengal usually concentrated power in one individual, or at most in one nuclear family, tended to make them more vulnerable than those Rajput zamindaris of North India, which were based upon a clan system of landholding, since the base of support tended to be narrower in Bengal.

Thus the number of participants with distinct, separate interests (not joined by clan or other strong ties) tended to be relatively large, and tended to be stratified in an elaborate hierarchy of revenue collectors in areas where productivity was high. In addition, the hierarchy was often so flexible that two intermediate landholders might each be in an inferior relationship to the other with respect to the rights for different plots of land. Thus the system of stratification was both complex and, at times, without clearly defined levels for participants.

Since there were fewer large zamindaris during the seventeenth century, the hierarchies of intermediate landholders within the greater number of smaller seventeenth-century zamindaris were probably somewhat less elaborate than they were during the eighteenth and nineteenth centuries. However, the nature of the relationship between land and crops, the fact that zamindars found it difficult to increase revenue collection in the early eighteenth century, and the few seventeenth-century references that we have, all suggest that there were considerable numbers of intermediate collectors in the seventeenth-century revenue system. A reasonable hypothesis, then, would be that the seventeenth century featured a relatively greater amount of competition between participants within the landholding system, who were of equal or near-equal status (particularly at the zamindari level). The history of zamindaris such as that of Burdwan suggests, however, that competition between inferiors and superiors was also important.[10]

Even for the eighteenth century, the details of conflicts between specific participants at the level of intermediate collectors usually are not available, although the generalized descriptions supplied in the "Risali-i Zira'at" and in British sources indicate that such conflicts were common. As indicated above, several means of acquiring increased wealth through additional revenue rights were available to intermediate collectors, and, although more difficult, it was also possible to effect a change in one's official status (from a lower level of intermediate collector to a higher level, or from intermediate collector to zamindar). During the eighteenth century, however, it appears to have been more common for a zamindar to acquire zamindari rights to additional lands than it was for an intermediate collector to acquire zamindari rights.

We may conclude that, although eighteenth-century conditions probably increased the amount of competition, it is evident that conditions that would promote competition existed in the seventeenth century as well. The fact that most of the competition took place at a level where its particulars were not recorded may be especially important: this unrecorded competition was probably responsible for the turnover of land rights at the highest or zamindari level. The various devices for undermining the authority of a zamindar, which are described in eighteenth-century sources, could be utilized for years without any mention of them appearing in the official records. Similarly, a zamindar could alienate revenue rights to part of his land to intermediate collectors for good administrative reasons, without the fact being recorded in the kinds of records that have survived. Only when things went wrong, and the zamindar lost part or all of his revenue rights, might the fact be recorded. In the seventeenth century, as in the nineteenth, therefore, we can expect to find both the alienation of zamindari rights and competition between intermediate collectors.

Again, the hypothesis suggests a comparison with the Permanent Settlement and its effects. After the initial failures of some zamindars to meet the revenue demand following the Permanent Settlement, a situation developed that was more like the seventeenth than the eighteenth century. Under the Permanent Settlement, the revenue demand of the zamindars was fixed, and so they could take advantage of increases in the amount of revenue that they could collect from cultivators and undertenants. Similarly, although the revenue demand was not fixed legally in the seventeenth century, it appears that it was rarely enhanced, even though inflation probably decreased the value of the rupee considerably.[11] Therefore, seventeenth-century zamindars were also in a position to profit from a widening disparity between the value of what they could collect and the value of what they had to pay.

Despite their increasingly favorable financial position, however, many nineteenth-century zamindars alienated the revenue rights to parts of their zamindaris. Thus competition could continue below the zamindari level (and, in some cases, continued also at the zamindari level, despite the Permanent Settlement). Similarly, seventeenth-century conditions appear to have been more conducive to competition below the zamindari level, since zamindars could alienate a substantial portion of their revenue rights without endangering their positions, because of the relatively low level of the revenue demand.

In both the seventeenth- and nineteenth-century cases, there appears to have been a tendency toward the proliferation of intermediate landholders, probably for both administrative and political reasons. Alienation of a portion of the revenue rights was a customary and relatively easy way to get the revenue collected. It also provided a means of supporting political followers in some cases. Certainly, intermediate collectors were in a position where it often would be advisable for them to support the zamindar from whom they held their rights in the land, throughout the period under discussion. In the seventeenth century, it was also often the case that the intermediate collectors were of the same caste as the zamindar, and that they or their ancestors had helped to settle the land and to establish the zamindari.

The existence of the similarities and continuities in the revenue and landholding systems outlined above should not be taken as an indication that nothing new happened in the nineteenth century. Rather, my argument has been that many of the keys for understanding the modern agrarian system of Bengal can be found in earlier periods, even though the imposition of the British Raj and exposure to economic and other pressures from the modern West did affect agrarian relationships. Especially during the last thirty or forty years of the nineteenth century, we can identify a number of changes that appear to have set the scene for the present day. Increases in population, moneylending activities, the growth of cash crops, enhanced governmental control over local administration, and a growing sense of community on the part of the Muslim ryots of East Bengal, all were important factors.

During the last quarter of the nineteenth century, it is likely that, at least in some parts of Bengal, population pressure had become great enough so that competition drove up the price of land rights. Thus, rights in the land became more difficult to obtain and required a relatively larger capital investment. As a result, ryots and intermediaries began to look more toward moneylending and cash-crop farming as sources of additional income. Both of these activities could be practiced with any amount of capital. This extension of economic activity produced new economic hierarchies, parallel to and often interlocked with the landholding hierarchy.

Perhaps the most significant change in late nineteenth-century agrarian society was the growing awareness within Muslim and lost-caste Hindu society of separate, collective identities. And of course, at the very end of the century, the establishment of local councils and the beginnings of an electoral process pointed the way toward a much greater development of Islamic identity in the twentieth century. Thus it is likely that changes in the economic sphere in the late nineteenth century tended to promote further the development of class differentiation and group identification, which was due primarily to Muslim revivalist movements and to increased governmental activity at the local level.

By 1900, however, neither the development of class consciousness among cultivators, nor the development of Islamic identity among Muslim cultivators, had progressed very far. The zamindari system still prevailed, and the traditional elements of agrarian society continued to be of primary significance.

Philip B. Calkins is assistant professor of History at Duke University. He received his Ph.D. from the University of Chicago in 1971. His research has been on Mogul history, with particular focus on Bengal.

NOTES

1. For a general account of Murshid Quli Khan's career, see Karim (1963:15–60).

2. Grant's account of the records for the Mogul revenue assessment of Bengal up to 1728 indicates that it was only during the eighteenth century that some zamindaris became so large that the assessment was organized around them, rather than on the basis of territorial units that had been defined by the Moguls (Grant 1917:176–191).

3. The figures that Shore gives for the annual revenue collections in Bengal from 1700 to 1721 indicate that the collections did not surpass the mid-seventeenth-century level of assessment until 1711, and that most of Murshid Quli Khan's increase in the revenue collections had been effected by that time (Shore 1788:539–540).

4. The author of this description of the pre-British administration and revenue system in Bengal is unknown. The manuscript was written circa 1760, and it is clear that the author had had experience in the administrative system he describes ("Risala-i Zira'at" 1760).

5. For example, see "Risala-i Zira'at" (1760:fol. 4b) and West Bengal Government Archieves (1788:243–244).

6. "Risala-i Zira'at" (1760:fols. 12b, 14a); Shore (1789:40–42); and Glazier (1873 and 1876:20–21).

7. Hunter (1894:I, 35) and Sinha's statement (1967:104) that one-third to one-half of the landed property of Bengal changed hands within twenty-two years after the Permanent Settlement again suggest a parallel with the first quarter of the eighteenth century.

8. Thus, many of the zamindars who resisted Mogul rule in the early seventeenth century were allowed to retain their lands after they had capitulated, and, although many zamindars who defaulted on their revenue payments a century later were imprisoned by Murshid Quli Khan, many of them did not lose their zamindari rights, and were released by his successor (Raychaudhuri 1969:63–69; Gladwin 1788:35–37, 74–75).

9. The growth of the zamindari of Burdwan after 1660, for example, must have been at the expense of other zamindars (Chatterjee 1967:225–256).

10. The founder of the Burdwan raj did not hold the title of zamindar at all, but rather was a local revenue official (Chatterjee 1967:255–256).

11. Only one complete new revenue roll was drawn up in the seventeenth century (Grant 1917:182). Also the *nasaq* form of assessment, which was used in Bengal, was at least semipermanent, the same assessment figures being used year after year (Habib 1963:213–219). The increase in the revenue assessment of Bengal was much less than the increase in most provinces of the empire during the seventeenth century, and it is likely that the value of the rupee declined sufficiently to offset any increase in taxation (Calkins 1972:90–92, 316–322).

BIBLIOGRAPHY

Calkins, Philip B.
　　1972. "Revenue Administration and the Formation of a Regionally Oriented Ruling Group in Bengal, 1700–1740." Ph.D. dissertation, University of Chicago.
Chatterjee, Anjali
　　1967. *Bengal in the Reign of Aurangzib*. Calcutta: Progressive Publishers.
Firminger, W. K.
　　1917. "Minute of 18 June, 1789," In *The Fifth Report from the House of Commons on the Affairs of the East India Company*, edited by W. K. Firminger, vol. 11, pp. 56–59. Calcutta: R. Cambray & Co.
Gladwin, F.
　　1788. *A Narrative of the Transactions in Bengal*. Calcutta: Stuart and Cooper.

Glazier, Edward G.
    1873 and 1876. "The Statement of the Collector of Rangpur in 1786."
        In *A Report on the District of Rungpore*, edited by E. G.
        Glazier, 2 vols. Calcutta: Government of Bengal, Misc. Official
        Publications.
Grant, James
    1917. "Historical and Comparative Analysis of the Finances of Ben-
        gal." In *The Fifth Report from the House of Commons on the
        Affairs of the East India Company*, edited by W. K. Firminger,
        vol. 11, pp. 176–191. Calcutta: R. Cambray & Co.
Habib, Irfan
    1963. *The Agrarian System of Mughal India*. Bombay: Asia Publish-
        ing House.
Hunter, W. W.
    1894. *Bengal Manuscript Records*. vol. 1. London: W. H. Allen & Co.
Karim, Abdul
    1963. *Murshid Quli Khan and His Times*. Dacca: Asiatic Society of
        Pakistan.
O'Malley, L. S. S.
    1914. *Murshidabad*. Bengal District Gazetteers, vol. 32. Calcutta:
        Bengal Secretariat Book Depot.
Raychaudhuri, Tapan
    1969. *Bengal under Akbar and Jahangir*. Delhi: Munshiram Man-
        oharlal.
"Risala-i Zira'at"
    1760. "Risala-i Zira'at." Edinburgh University Ms. 144. Edinburgh,
        Scotland.
Shore, John
    1788. "Minute on the Rights and Privileges of Zamindars." Board of
        Revenue Proceedings, 2 April, 1788, vol. 127. Calcutta: West
        Bengal Government Archives.
Sinha, N. K.
    1967. *History of Bengal*. Calcutta: University of Calcutta.
West Bengal Government Archives
    1788. "Board of Revenue Proceedings." Records of the Government
        of Bengal, vol. 128, 2 April. Unpublished. Calcutta: West Ben-
        gal Government Archives.

3

The Administration of
Rural Reform: Structural Constraints
and Political Dilemmas

Elliot L. Tepper

The Muslim districts of Eastern Bengal have emerged once again as a distinct and distinctive entity, bearing social and political features marking them collectively as a "developing area" with its own problems of political destiny and economic growth. These problems are particularistic, and stem in large measure from events peculiar to the region. Yet to the degree that other former colonies are rural, agrarian, overpopulated, and poor, they will share some of the dilemmas of development that beleaguer this troubled province. Indeed, the former East Pakistan may provide a valuable case study, for it combines these attributes to an extraordinary degree. The present rulers of East Bengal, regardless of ideology or intention, face a formidable set of constraints. They also inherit a formidable set of problems, and dilemmas in meeting these problems. This chapter will consider some of the constraints, problems, and dilemmas of rural development in East Bengal.[1]

Legacies of Colonialism and Neglect

The relative absence of institutionalized groups, and the difficulty in creating them, is at the heart of the province's development problems. Recent field research begins to indicate that in an overwhelmingly rural province with a large, densely settled population, the creation of such groups becomes a critical task for any government seeking rural transformation. Even though my comments here must be expressed very tentatively, this is an aspect of the problem of rural development that seems both crucial and virtually unexplored in a developmental context.

The British Inheritance

East Bengal is a rural hinterland. It is an overwhelmingly agricultural, nonurban area, which seems to have served as a periphery for distant urban centers for almost all of its existence, or at least since it stopped being a region of Buddhist educational activity and became instead an agrarian outpost of the Muslim empires. Even the urban center of Dacca lost its significance with the advent of British influence, and the corresponding decline of Dacca muslin, and the growth of Calcutta as the Bengali imperial capital. When the British abandoned their attempts at direct rule in Bengal and acquiesced instead to indirect rule (as did the Mogul emperors before them),[2] the contemporary fate of the rural regions became set. The Permanent Settlement of 1793 turned over to a private landlord class, a "landed gentry" in British eyes, much of the responsibility for governing eastern and northern Bengal. Thus vast, inaccessible regions of the delta were confirmed, or perhaps reconfirmed, as a colonial outpost, a hinterland serving the interests of the expanding regional metropole of Calcutta and the more distant metropole overseas.

The hinterland status of the rural Muslim region led to its perennial neglect, with deleterious long-term effects. As a hinterland, East Bengal underwent a prolonged period of what may be called institutional atomization. The formal institutions of government were kept to a minimum. The continued abdication to private landlords of revenue collection duties led to a truncated form of the usual British imperial control apparatus, the district collectorate. Even by British standards, therefore, the "nerves of government" were foreshortened. The ingenious mechanism of successive conquerors, district administration, has passed on to the new states of South Asia the very sinews, or infrastructure, of statehood. In East Bengal, the formal infrastructure was kept to a minimum. The private bureaucracy of the zamindars, a mystery never fully penetrated by the British, was an ad hoc arrangement that must have varied from estate to estate and that ultimately therefore was a dispersed and ephemeral form of organization. As a British report once concluded, East Bengal was not so much badly administered, it was underadministered. The region passed on to Pakistan a legacy of "administrative starvation" (Government of Bengal 1915:16).

Indigenous Rural Social Organization

THE COLONIAL IMPACT   The "institutional atomization" carried over to informal, or traditional, forms of political and social control as well. The relative paucity of British institutional arrangements was not compensated by a vigorous network of indigenous institutions. It is not simply that Metcalfe's famous "Village Republics" failed to flourish in East Bengal.[3] Rather, the Permanent Settlement proved pernicious to autonomous, nongovernmental channels of decision-making and social control.

The de-institutionalization of East Bengal was documented by British official reports, even as the process was occurring. A full century ago the effects of the Permanent Settlement of 1793 were being felt, as noted in the annual Bengal administration report of 1871.

> . . . in the plains of Bengal . . . these institutions seem to have been very much weakened even anterior to British rule and in the last one hundred years of British rule and the Zaminaree theory of property, they have almost disappeared. It cannot be said that in more important provinces of this administration there are absolutely no self-government institutions. Some traces yet remain: some things are in some places regulated by village Panchayats and by headmen, elders. But more and more, the Zamindary agent supplants the old model and the landlord takes the place of indigenous self-rule. (Government of Bengal 1873:44)

The same report comments on the weakness of official institutions as well, and tellingly summarizes the human and governmental implications of peripheral status:

> Many things done by tahsildars (village revenue officials and bookkeepers) in other parts of India are not done at all and many things we should know from them we do not know. . . . it has happened that in the province we have held the longest . . . we have less knowledge of or familiarity with

the people than in any other province, that British authority is
less brought home to the people, that the rich are less re-
strained and the poor and weak less protected than elsewhere,
and that we have infinitely less knowledge of statistical, agricultural and other facts. (p. 44)

Contemporary scholarship bears out these earlier conclusions.
Recent field investigators reinforce the view that rural social and
political organization is segmented, diffuse, and in flux. The
"atomization" that seems to have occurred under the British colonial regime and the Permanent Settlement was enhanced even
further by Partition turmoil, and the rather sudden removal of the
Permanent Settlement in 1950, due to the zamindari Abolition Act.[4]
While the old zamindari social order produced a measure of institutional atrophy, it endured for an extended period, and led to its own
order of sorts, a prop for social relations that was dramatically removed. As indicated earlier, that social order has not been given
adequate research—another by-product of indirect rule and hinterland status within the British Empire in India. But since Independence the rural scene has begun to receive attention. While the
picture is not yet clear, it seems likely that one fundamental answer
to the area's problems of rural development will ultimately lie in
discovering a means of bringing into existence some *viable* rural
organizations.

RURAL SOCIAL STRUCTURE   The dominant fact of rural life
seems to be its dispersed, diffuse nature or, to continue a theme, its
atomization. Even geographically, high population density and deltaic flooding have produced a scattered, rather than clustered or
nucleated, settlement pattern in much of East Pakistan (Rashid
1965: 355–357) and a social system has emerged that corresponds to
this "scattered" pattern. As Bertocci has shown in his pioneering
study (Bertocci 1970), while individuals apparently have a clear
perception of what village (*gram*) is their own, that mental entity is
not a corporate unit territorially and may have little to do with the
externally recognized "village," which often was labeled and
placed on a map for revenue and administrative purposes by government officers.

The mental village entity of the rural Muslim offers no great locus of identity and cohesion to replace the physical village entity. Traditional authority structures apparently have decayed. The Muslim status-hierarchy never acquired the rigidity of the Hindu caste system although it acquired castelike characteristics.[5]

However, despite a strong tendency for converts to continue occupational group endogamy and for all groups to enforce commensal practices, the classification system did not evolve into a true counterpart to the fourfold division in Hinduism. The occupational categories were never fully equivalent, nor were marriage practices followed rigidly. Moreover, mobility was apparently much more fluid within Islam in East Bengal, despite the dynamism that has been perceived within the Hindu caste system.[6] Increasing wealth and shifting fortunes of the Mogul empires merged with the absence of enforced occupational heredity and an egalitarian ethic to make the fourfold division unworkable within Islam. An Urdu proverb illustrated the unworkability: "The first year we were butchers, the next Sheikh; this year if prices fall we shall become Syeds" (Karim 1956).

With the pseudocaste system declining in meaning, a class system was elaborated. At first families simply were considered either high born, *sharif* (or *asraf*), or low born, *atraf*. As the older aristocracy lost power and influence and a Muslim middle class emerged, the *atraf bhalamanus* 'atraf made a gentleman' appeared. The 'lowest of all class', the *arzal*, apparently is equivalent to the lowest Hindu castes and retains the ritual and social opprobrium of those castes.

Presently the authority structure is confused. Vestiges of a pseudocaste system still remain, but the quasi-class system has been found more useful by one investigator.[7] Another investigator comments on the absence of a caste system[8] and others find that class, not caste, is a prominent feature (Rahim 1965), or find no present trace of castes.[9] And yet another finds a mixture of traditional and emerging elements competing for authority (Rashiduzzaman 1966:191–200). On balance, this last view seems likely to be the most common rural phenomenon. Ascriptive authority has been undermined, but not replaced. The hereditary charisma of the erstwhile aristocracy retains vestiges of its former ability to command deference. This ability was originally gained by being a functionary in the Mogul apparat, a descendant of the Prophet, an "original Muslim" rather than a Bengali convert, and/or hereditarily wealthy. The coming of the British, which coincided with great population increases and rapid expansion of Islam in East Bengal, removed the first and much of the last element; inflation of claims in the middle two drained them somewhat of authority-conferring potency. Removal of the British and many Hindus at Partition further shook the rural authority structure, and opened the way for the present mingling of old and new claimants to legitimate authority. Traditional authority, new political authority, and wealth seem to be the factors involved in the present makeup of rural social organization.

Both religion and kinship patterns segment "village" life and contribute to its nonvillage characteristics, to the diffused nature of rural existence. Islam, of course, does not rely on a centralized hierarchy with parish-church affiliation at the bottom. Religious leaders of varying degrees are numerous in East Bengal, but the degree depends on religious training and local prestige rather than hierarchical appointment. Mosques also abound but their location depends upon the presence of a wealthy patron, factional disputes between patrons, or other local exigencies rather than on the existence of discrete and "deserving" villages, or of a diocese, areal subdivision imposed by religious authorities. Many ceremonies are celebrated together by traditionally defined social entities, but this group of common mosque attenders may or may not be from a single village grouping, and disputes over the location of a celebration is a common cause of factional division. The tendency for religious observance to segment rather than unify village life is reinforced by its dispersed and localized nature, which leads to an intimate connection between religious celebration and local private sponsorship. Sponsorship of religious activities is a prime source of gaining and sustaining local-level prestige, but it is a relatively costly undertaking. It naturally falls to traditional elites, or would-be competitors with some wealth, to foster various celebrations, which leads just as naturally to extreme localization of religious practices. Individual religious leaders may gain sufficient following to become independent rather than institutional charisma, and is therefore also a form of localization of a nonvillage religion.[10]

VILLAGE POLITICAL ORGANIZATION   Kinship practices become important for present purposes in regard to the formation of lineage patterns, which in turn affect the nature of local authority structures in rural Bengal. Marriage ties, for example, have no regularized function in enforcing either village endogamy or village exogamy, unlike other areas of the subcontinent (Karve 1965). Marriages in traditional Muslim Bengal may be either inside or outside the village (Beech et al. 1966). Family patterns are predominently nuclear, extended, and monogamous, rather than joint and polygynous as might be found in an area where territorial and village cohesion is given higher prominence.[11] Yet it is the family that provides a major organizational nucleus for political and social action. In a land of dispersed villages, there is no village headman, no centralized village authority. There is, however, a hierarchy of family groupings and in the past this hierarchy has provided a form of governing process, or at least adjudication of local disputes.

The peasant homestead (*bari*) is the locus of a patrilineal extended family divided into household units of usually nuclear, or, not uncommonly, joint family structure (Rahim 1965:5). The available information suggests that in much of East Bengal, clusters of homesteads are united loosely under the traditional leadership of the locally more wealthy and influential men, variously known as *sardars* or *matabbars*. These little homestead groupings—known in the Comilla area, at least, as *reyai* or *reai*[12]—constitute indigenous political units whose leaders act as a court of first resort in the resolution of local conflicts. Often these homestead clusters are socially recognized "local villages," even though they may not be officially so recognized by official organs of local government. In some areas of East Bengal, the *sardars* and *matabbars* of several contiguous such homestead clusters form a kind of "council of elders" for the whole area covered by the groupings they represent. The functions of these leaders are related primarily to the settlement of disputes and little else. Such a council of elders is largely one of social control; ". . . its latent function is formally to channel political relations between the prestigious *sardars* and groups they represent when these relations are thrown into open conflict." (Bertocci 1970:3). The effect of this system is twofold. Local political matters remain personalized but institutional, under the aegis of traditional authority and wealth. And political authority, like the village settlement pattern itself, tends to be dispersed.

This view of local political authority further reinforces the picture of a diffuse pattern of social interaction for much of the population in East Bengal. Moreover like other aspects of rural life, the *reyai* system apparently has undergone a decline. While one researcher found and documented its activities (Bertocci 1970), another researcher, in the same general geographical area (Comilla Thana), found that "this traditional social organization has now a nominal existence" (Rahim 1965:7). The diffuse, overlapping, and battered rural institutions combined with the intricacies and complex layering of land tenure encouraged by the zamindari system, and the all-pervasive problems of population density and food shortages, help clarify the nature of the problems of rural development. This is not to imply that individuals are normless, unguided by social custom or economic constraint. The point is not that Eastern Bengal exists habitually in a state of anomie, but rather that it seems to exist in a state of unusual institutional fragmentation, that this is a population that appears inherently little organized on a large scale and lacking in extensive institutional foci of rural life.

Until much more is known about the process of community formation, or until the process itself produces a "natural" change in the existing situation, the formal institutions of rural government retain a high, and perhaps a disproportional, degree of interest. Even though originally imposed by an outside power, the present apparatus is well entrenched. In the relative absence of an alternative mechanism of response and control, perhaps this is not surprising. As truncated as they are, the inherited modalities available for rural development may now be considered a part of the local scene; indeed, it is one more legacy of the colonial era that district administration and a series of local councils seem now to be fully "indigenous." They have acquired a legitimacy that is difficult to ignore, a permanency that is one of the facts of rural life.

Although the history and substance of both these "indigenous" legacies generally are known and understood, perhaps it would be useful to review some of their characteristics salient for a discussion of rural development.

The Government System

DISTRICT ADMINISTRATION   The district collectorate system as originally evolved by Mogul and British practice was skillfully designed to provide the basic framework for imperial occupation and stable rule. After subdividing a region or an empire into provinces, the land was further subdivided into units, the districts. Upon this bedrock the governance of the area rested. A corps of specially trained officials, loyal to the central power and usually not from the area, was placed in charge of a district. Each officer was given nearly absolute authority. Within the guidelines of the center, the district was ruled by a plenipotentiary, an agent of the center expressing the sovereign's will throughout the periphery. Frequent transfers, a well-organized central bureaucracy, and well-trained district officers could maintain large areas with minimum staff. The duties of revenue collection and maintenance of law and order, the historic functions of the district official, required intimate knowledge of local affairs, and when well established and running smoothly, this system facilitates an intensive amount of information collection at the bottom, and relatively easy control from the top. The mediator and linchpin was the district officer, the focus of the expression of national intent and of the capacity to act at the local level.[13]

East Pakistan inherited such a system, but one modified in important ways. The districts established by Cornwallis at the end of the eighteenth century, as part of his efforts to tighten British rule in India, were designed, or forced, to take account of the situation in rural Bengal at the time. This meant coming to terms with the large zamindari estates that emerged into prominence in the period just prior to British usurpation of the Mogul's position (Calkins 1970). The result in East Bengal was fewer, and therefore larger, districts; and as noted above, the collectorate was without the subordinate revenue staff that elsewhere nurtured the viability of district administration. The combination left this portion of the Bengal Presidency with a firmly established but restricted collectorate. Creation of a new subordinate post, the circle officer,[14] partially remedied the situation, but still left the Muslim districts as a holding operation, a strong superstructure with weak underpinnings.

LOCAL COUNCILS   In the absence or impairment of "traditional" forms of self-rule, the local government imposed (or "introduced") within the formal political system takes on great significance. Local government in Bengal has been, from its inception, closely bound to rural administration. The closeness of the link varied over time.

The first local councils were groups of local notables, entirely appointed (nominated) by the district officer, to perform unpleasant tasks of civil government. The *chaukidari panchayats* established in 1870 (Village Chaukidari Act, Act VI of 1870, Bengal Code) were created to assess and collect taxes to support the village watchmen; the district road committees established a year later (District Road Committees Act, Act of 1871, Bengal Code) were created to assess and collect taxes to improve the district roads. A person appointed to the chaukidari panchayats could be fined 50 rupees for refusing to serve. The district road committees were chaired by the district officer. The identity with rural administration was nearly absolute.

Attempts to divorce local government from rural administration were affected and ultimately hampered by administrative imperatives. In 1882, Governor-General Lord Ripon issued an important statement on rural self-government.[15] The rationale and fate of the resolution have been almost paradigmatic.

Ripon wanted a network of local councils, with the most important council to be at the subdivisional (subdistrict) level, or even lower at the thana level; the district was considered too large for effective councils. Membership was to be at least three-fourths elected, and the chairman was to be elected as well. The councils were to be training grounds in citizenship, rather than immediate improvements on the efficiency of rural administration. But even for Ripon, the long-range goal was to facilitate the functioning of the rural bureaucracy, by creating quasi-autonomous local organizations to absorb some duties of government:

> The task of administration is yearly becoming more onerous. . . . The cry is everywhere for increased establishments.

The universal complaint in all departments is that of over-
work. Under these circumstances it becomes imperatively
necessary to look around for some means of relief; and the
Governor-General in Council has no hesitation in stating his
conviction, that the only reasonable plan open to the government is to induce the people themselves to undertake, as far as
may be, the management of their own affairs; and to develop,
or create if need be, a capacity for self-help in respect of all
matters that have not, for imperial reasons, to be retained in
the hands of the representatives of Government. (Government of India 1882: Paragraph 6)

Ripon's councils were never established. Although a bill to implement the resolution was introduced into the Bengal Council,[16] the
act that emerged (Government of Bengal 1885) was substantially
altered, with effects that remain visible and relevant to contemporary East Pakistan. The act established a potentially powerful council at the district level, a powerless coordinating council called a
union committee in any village or group of villages. Only the district board was made mandatory. The local boards and union committees were discretionary. Indeed, the act permitted ample scope
for use of discretionary powers by the district officer, who could and
did fail to establish lower councils, continue to appoint members to
the councils, and maintain personal control of the district board by
assuming its chairmanship. When the president of Pakistan at a
much later date sought to initiate an extensive but controlled system of local government, he could draw upon well-established
local precedent.

There is, however, an alternative precedent, based upon more
recent experience prior to Partition. During the dyarchy period, the
two decades between 1920–1940, local councils were reinvigo-
rated. The reforms instituted by the 1919 Village Self-Government
Act (Government of Bengal 1919) gave local councils deep roots in
the countryside. It is likely that the interwar experience remains as
a standard of legitimacy for rural self-government, just as parliamentary democracy, a concept firmly instilled during the same
period, remained a standard for the national political arena.

In more detail, the precedent consists of an active district

council, with an elected nonofficial as chairman, a weak intermediate council at the subdivision level, and a universally established, popularly elected union council.[17] The councils were based
on a franchise restricted by a land-owning qualification, and suffered perennial limitations due to lack of funds. In addition, they
are far from the original concept promoted just prior to the reforms,
which, as did Ripon, held that the union and not the district councils should be "the real working bodies," and that creating a strong
district council "started local self-government at the wrong end
(Government of Bengal 1915:123). These councils too were intended to take power away from the district, and vest it in much
lower union, thana, and subdivisional councils. But while these
hopes were again frustrated, the district councils displayed a capacity for leadership despite limited authority and funds—and the
absence of the district officer as chairman. The councils, particularly the district councils, came into their own during the dyarchy
reforms, an example that has not been forgotten.

Moreover, the dyarchy councils apparently were received
with enthusiasm by the voting population, perhaps due in part to
the absence of alternative channels of expression. Seats on all the
councils at all levels were hotly contested, and turnout was consistently high. Rural Bengal demonstrated a taste and facility for political activity, when given an opportunity. Other observers since
have shared N.C. Roy's observation at the time: "The interest of the
people in local elections has turned out to be immense. The Ben-
galees are now impregnated with politics" (Roy 1936:25).

Problems of Rural Development

After Independence, Pakistan remained domestically a
quasi-colonial state. Quite apart from external relations, the country's leadership pursued an evolutionary course at home, introducing piecemeal changes without radical rejection of the past. The
predominant tendency was to adapt rather than destroy the basic
structures of statehood inherited from the colonial period. The present leadership in Bangladesh encounters problems created by the
provinces' hinterland legacies. If the future leadership seeks to
improve the countryside, and involve it in the process of emerging

nationhood, it will need to devise responses to some hard-core problems of rural development. Some closely interrelated problems may be capsulized rather briefly.

Introductory Comments

The absence of organized, broad-based rural groups is a primary stumbling block for any efforts at local reform. While this phenomenon is difficult to adequately conceptualize or document, it apparently underlies much of the usual neglect and governmental helplessness in the countryside. Some suggested reasons for rural social disorganization, or compartmentalization, have been alluded to earlier. Whether correct or not, in a formal sense there is a marked absence of institutional foci in rural East Bengal, and a long history of failed attempts to create new ones. This problem faces all governments with limited resources and a large rural population: how can the governors reach and affect the governed; how can the ruled make their will and needs known to the rulers? In a situation of a near vacuum institutionally, in terms of government or indigenous instruments of aggregational expression, the universal problem is rendered particularly acute.

The bureaucratization of reform efforts, and the cost of bureaucratization, is another problem inherent in rural development efforts. Although there have been some notable private endeavors aimed at rural uplift— "rural reconstruction"—these ad hoc schemes faded quickly. Given the nature of rural existence, only programs with government support, and built into the government's district machinery, can hope for sustained success. Rural development, as an effort by government, warrants a detailed examination, since its potential and limitations are so crucial to such a large proportion of the population.

Rural development may be viewed as compensation for the pattern of entrenched but circumscribed administration found in East Pakistan. No government as yet has chosen to destroy the reliable prop of statehood perfected over centuries of changing forms of governance. Rural development is a means of tinkering with that system, an attempt to ameliorate its defects, to augment its effectiveness. Governments in South Asia increasingly have become concerned with the well-being of the governed. In the age of nationalism since the turn of the century, and in the period since Independence in 1947, that concern has come increasingly to the fore. While there is clearly a limit to what government action alone may achieve in the South Asian setting, there also is clearly a perceived obligation for governments to assume a great role in instigating change. In Bangladesh the role of government is especially critical because of the negative effect the Permanent Settlement had on indigenous rural institutions. Where government is likely to be most active, where population pressure is densest and the need for change the greatest, the institutions of government have been weakest. The various strands of rural development found in Bangladesh have their counterparts throughout South Asia. But in East Pakistan, rural development by governmental reform played an especially crucial function in expanding the potential for successful economic and social transformation.

Agricultural reorganization in the context of Bangladesh is a form of rural development. Not only does it cater to the greatest source of manpower and potential productivity, but it is an attempt by government to amplify its restricted mofussil operation; it is an attempt by government to escape the strictures of the Permanent Settlement and affect the social and economic milieu in which almost the entire population of rural Bengal lives. The Agriculture Department and other agencies of the imperial and postimperial systems is an additional segment of rural administration, with important implications for local reform.

Agricultural Department Problems

The troubled existence of the Agriculture Department is therefore instructive. For much of its history, it had suffered from the general weakness of rural administration in Bengal: repeatedly, it was shown to be among the most understaffed in British South Asia; its effective penetration remained restricted to district levels at best. This is a by-product of the neglect of rural Bengal, reinforced by the Permanent Settlement and by the lack of trained Muslim personnel. But the Agriculture Department in East Pakistan met also with another legacy from the Cornwallis era and the colonial period. District administration, stretching back in time perhaps as far as Akbar, was the linchpin for government operations. The bureaucratic apparatus, centering on the person of the district officer, seemed ill-suited to comfortably accommodate parallel lines of authority in the form of the regular civil service (the district officer) and the separate nation-building agencies (the district agriculture officer). It seemed equally ill-suited to accommodate parallel conceptions of government services: the generalist approach, embodied in the Indian Civil Service and its lineal successor, the Civil Service of Pakistan, versus the technical approach, embodied in the Agriculture Department. The clash of structural and conceptual approaches resulted in highly skilled generalists and technicians segmenting their valuable and scarce resources into an uneasy, rigid compartmentalization; both remained restricted in impact by the intrabureaucratic tensions and by the unshakably district-level orientation of rural administration.

Governments from Akbar through Ayub had centered their rural government at the district level and in the district collectorate. The result for nation-building agencies such as the Agriculture Department was tension, insecurity, and limitation of effectiveness. In East Pakistan, the problem as usual was compounded. The occasionally promising results of some government agriculture programs served as poignant indicators of the potential rewards if the structural bottleneck could be eliminated. That bottleneck centers in the district. Rural development in Bangladesh, in the form of the regular district administrative apparatus, retains the historical legacy of being bereft of an intensive network below the district (due to the service provided by zamindars, in lieu of a collectorate staff) and of being internally divided within the collectorate by competing parallel hierarchies and concepts of organizational procedure.

Cooperative Organization Efforts

Cooperative societies were an early and important attempt to resolve the difficulties embedded in orthodox rural administration. Although sponsored by the "nation-building" technical staffs, cooperatives were considered a separate component of rural development. They were attempts to create at or near the village level numerous small groups capable of absorbing the expertise and financial resources that the government allotted to agriculture. Cooperatives contain attractive attributes. They aggregate producers in the villages and focus on credit absorption and generation. They, thus, in the East Pakistan context, provided the manifest function of permitting the district-level nation-building agencies to enhance their effectiveness below the district, in a manner critically affecting the agriculture conditions of the area. They aimed to provide the latent and reinforcing function of inducing a social as well as economic renovation of the village through the alteration of outlook and temperament produced by individuals joining together for mutual self-improvement. Hence, since their introduction to South Asia in 1904, cooperatives, as an appendage of government operations and as initiators of would-be social movements, have been the objects of sustained official and private hopes.

In practice, the cooperative societies movement repeatedly has fallen short of the hopes it engenders. The effects in part have been organizational. Staffing and financial shortages normal to agencies dealing with the large populations found in rural South Asia are habitually compounded, typically enough, by the additional administrative weakness in rural Bengal under the British, and by the lack of Muslim personnel in the cooperative department opting for Pakistan at the time of Partition. In part the defects have been conceptual, as seen in the continued debate in the former East Pakistan over whether cooperatives should be village or union based, single or multipurpose in function.

The Cooperatives Department encountered an additional problem in encouraging a social movement through bureaucratic means. There is inherent tension in the competing goals of a performance-oriented bureaucracy and a voluntaristic-oriented social welfare philosphy. Social movements are neither inherently orderly, nor subject to easy inducement upon official directives. The Weberian-rational bureaucratic model, in its South Asian incarnation, has shown itself in the Cooperatives Department to be statistics conscious; the tension repeatedly, perhaps inevitably, has been resolved in favor of a strong paper superstructure and a weak organizational base. Bureaucratic pressure to produce visible results, combined with relatively limited departmental funds and a capital-starved agrarian economy, leads to the subversion of the social welfare motives, and of the cooperative structure itself, in favor of ephemeral organizations confined to the absorption of un-redeemable credit. The manifest and latent attributes of coopera-tives continue to call forth extensive effort and high aspirations. The clash of concepts, norms, and procedures in an economy of intense scarcity and want continues to inhibit the cooperative societies movement.

Rural Reconstruction and Uplift

"Rural reconstruction," or "rural uplift" combines agricultural reform and a proselytizing spirit into an emotive broad-based appeal for total rural change. It has been expressed in a number of guises, in an honorable tradition including Tagore and Gandhi, Brayne and Hatch, the Bengal Department of Rural Reconstruction, Village-AID, and even the Agricultural Development Corporation. The purpose underlying this component of rural development is to move outside the normal channels of rural administration and create the conditions for a penetrating pervasive change in the moral and human climate of the rural population. All the projects of "uplift" or community development seek to reorient government actions, to break down (or sidestep) compartmentalization. Re-peatedly, the answer to the bureaucratic bottleneck has been seen as the creation of an ad hoc bureaucratic entity with the alleged authority to coordinate the activities of the orthodox administration. In addition, there typically is an attempt to create a new cadre of officials below the district level, charged with the specific task of combining government services and making them available to the rural populace. The urge to jump the boundaries of regular ad-ministration and to provide to villagers a "friend, philosopher, and guide" runs deep within the tradition of rural reconstruction.

In its most familiar forms, rural reconstruction seems now to have run its course. The impulse that guides it remains. Indeed, the desire to renovate the countryside, to bypass routine channels, to alter the spirit and enlist the enthusiasm of the village population undergirds much of the broader process of rural development. But the efficiency of a "super agency," whether as a corporation, de-partment, or series of coordinating committees, has been brought decisively into question. The concept of a change agent, a jack-of-all-trades, a catalyst, has been brought to the verge of disrepute. Extraordinary bureaucratic entities with diffuse idealistic philosophies repeatedly encounter ordinary bureaucratic entities with well-defined notions of orderly procedures, and mundane preoccupation with self-preservation and measurable results. The difficulties of the Cooperatives Department, noted above, were magnified in rural reconstruction agencies such as Village-AID to the exact degree that they claimed superiority of authority over the regular administration, and laid emphasis upon a revitalization and "movement" philosophy. The internal tension in norms and procedures between the civil service and nation-building agencies prompted, but did not readily permit, a third set of competing concepts and approaches. The civil service, in the form of the district collectorate in rural areas, will not easily yield its traditional claims to penultimate authority within its jurisdiction; development bloc areas and development officers were a direct challenge to that authority. The nation-building agencies, particularly the crucial Agriculture Department in Pakistan, would not easily concede that the technical expertise they possessed could be bettered by simple techniques and emotive appeals for voluntary participation in rural uplift; the multipurpose village-level workers, with their rudimentary training and determined search for "felt-needs," constituted an affront to the authority and principles of the nation-building departments. In the face of these and many other problems, it was the regular administration that prevailed. As a separate approach to rural local reform, community development, in its East Pakistani variant as rural reconstruction, seems to have ended. The Village-AID program was its last pure manifestation.

Ayub's Reforms and the Dilemmas of Rural Development

Ayub Khan introduced reforms that directly affected the process of rural development. His reforms were surprisingly evolutionary in some ways, and sharp departures from past policies in other ways. There is no need to review here the familiar background and outline of Basic Democracies, nor is space available for a detailed analysis of Ayub Khan's reforms in operation. However, there are several features of his system that may be given briefly, before the old era fades from memory and the new hardens into permanence.

The New Local Government System

Ayub returned to the predyarchy period for the philosophy and form of his local government system. Basic Democracies was not *sui generis*, but showed unmistakable resemblance to the type of local government established during the earliest, most paternalistic, period of British experimentation. Under Basic Democracies, the district council remained preeminent; the intermediate council (the thana council) initially had little purpose to fulfill; the lower councils remained restricted by lack of funds. Most noticeably, the councils were tied closely to district administration: originally, membership even on the union councils could be filled by appointment; the thana and district councils were at least half officials (government officers); and both higher councils were chaired by representatives of the collectorate. The district officer regained *de jure* control of the district council, in clear contrast to the dyarchy reforms that remained in effect for a full half century prior to Basic Democracies. In 1962, Ayub would have agreed with a British report from the prenationalist period: "We deem it essential that the [local self-government] movement should be completely under the eye and hand of the district authorities" (Great Britain 1909:240).

Basic Democracies sacrificed participation in favor of coordination of scarce resources. If a choice had to be made between democracy and (economic) development, as Ayub apparently thought, then economic development clearly came first. The structure of the thana and district councils was designed to facilitate the coordinated use of the government's human and material resources by bringing together elected representatives and members of the nation-building departments under the guidance of district officials. This can be viewed as a way to resolve some of the dilemmas and problems of rural development. It makes "development" the duty of regular government agencies and local councils, rather than of a special ad hoc cadre as in the unfortunate earlier experiments just before and after Partition, thus reducing the opposition, or reluctance, of the rural bureaucracy. It also potentially reduced the structural and methodological tensions between the collectorate

generalist and nation-building specialist (and competition between the departments as well). The council system was the first to
actually implement in a pragmatic fashion a direct attack on the
problems of fragmentation and coordination. Opponents can argue
the cost was too high; Ayub could argue that the system combined
democracy and development.[18] But if there was an imbalance, the
choice was deliberate.

Basic Democracies inaugurated the first significant shift away
from overcentralization at the district level. Perhaps to everyone's
surprise (except the head of the Academy for Rural Development—see note 18), the thana council emerged as a major component of Basic Democracies, and thus as a major new feature of East
Pakistan's development efforts. The precedent had been decidedly
negative; the subdivisional council established in 1885 and maintained in 1919 had been feeble. There was little reason to suspect
that the first council at the lower, thana, level would differ. Yet due
to the Rural Public Works Program, increasing funds and
decision-making were siphoned downward from the district to the
thana councils.

In the first year of the provincial works program, the district
councils were allocated 50 percent of the total funds, deliberately
shorting the lower councils in the fear that they would be unable to
properly absorb large sums of money. Thereafter, however, the
percentage allotted to the thana councils steadily increased, from a

TABLE 1. Rank Order of Works Program
Allocations to Basic Democracies Councils, 1962–1967

	Five-Year Average 1962–1967 (%)	*1966/67 (%)*
Thana Councils	37.7	58.1
District Councils	26.4	15.0
Union Councils	21.0	13.0
Municipal and Town Councils	2.6	6.0
Experimental Projects	2.1	4.3

SOURCE: Adapted from Thomas (1968:86). Based on official annual report figures.

low of 6.5 percent in 1962/63 to a high of 58.1 percent in 1966/67 (Table 1). The final average for the five-year period, ranked in order of total allocations, shows the dramatic reversal of a well-entrenched tradition; the figures from 1966/67, the most recent year available, underscore the five-year trend.

Despite regular recommendations to the contrary, the district has remained the primary focus of rural politics and administration in Bengal since at least the early British period, when Lord Cornwallis tightened the reigns of company rule. Even the Basic Democracies Order left district authority more or less intact. As the figures indicate, the thana indeed came into its own under the works program. The potential for facilitating development that is built into the thana council has been tested and found reasonably effective. A critic of the Rural Public Works Program complained that this was "merely a devolution of authority from the District Magistrate to the Circle Officer, who is the kingpin of the Thana administration" (Sobhan 1968:152). If completely true, this would have been a fulfillment of a long-sought goal. "Merely" decentralizing government from 17 districts to 413 thanas would have marked a breakthrough in the long search for governmental effectiveness. The decentralization was by no means complete but to some degree the ruler and ruled in East Pakistan were brought into more intimate contact. For that period, enhanced interaction between government and citizen resulted in a major "rural reconstruction" effort.

Political Results of the Reforms

Basic Democracies shifted power to a rural elite, away from urban centers. The most unique, nonevolutionary aspect of Basic Democracies was the use of local councils to alter the basic formulae by which the state was governed. Ayub used the Basic Democrats as an electoral college to choose the head of state and the national and provincial assemblies. This had the effect of politically decapitating the urban centers and institutionalizing rural notables as important actors in the national arena. Perhaps this too is a throwback, in intent, if not form, to the paternalistic days of British rule. Ayub succeeded, through a locally novel device, in achieving what Cornwallis sought and failed to achieve: creation of a relatively stable and politically pliant landed gentry. The novelty of the device, and the resurgent potency of urban elites, will certainly end the electoral functions of local government, and return the rural councils to matters of merely local concern.

Dilemmas for the Future

If the new leaders of Bangladesh seek continuity with the past, rural administration and local government probably will sink comfortably into familiar patterns, and the evolutionary tinkering will resume. The dilemmas that will reappear have been built into the discussion above, and can be recapitulated briefly.

Development-or-democracy very possibly will seem again to be a valid dichotomy as it apparently was for the Ayub regime. Unimpaired centralization of authority remains the hallmark of the district collectorate; even further centralization of control can be urged, to ensure efficiency rather than fragmentation in use of resources. (This argument holds for all development-first theories, regardless of organizational form.) Yet there seems to be little need for such pessimism. The performance of local councils during the interwar period indicates that the simple expansion of popular demand and popular authority enhances, to a degree, the normal operations of government agencies. The interwar councils had limited funds and limited franchise, yet dramatically expanded their scope.

A second dilemma relates also to the structure of district administration. The historic "pull to the district"—centralization of activities at the district level—has only recently and tentatively been broken. The thana council became, perhaps briefly and unexpectedly, crucial to Basic Democracies as a development mechanism. Authority and funds were devolved to collectorate and line agency personnel, and to elected representatives. Abolition of Basic Democracies could lead to abolition of the thana council, at least as an operative council; the legacy of earlier precedents and the attraction upward to the districts likely will prove stronger than potential benefits of decentralization.

Only a very conscious effort will prevent the resurgence of the district to full authority and prestige, to the detriment of the efficacy of government capacity, and of local influence as well. Yet the full thrust of both rural administration and local government has been to move the locus of activities closer to the rural populace, below the district. It is a token of the "administrative starvation" of East Bengal that the government's network of services remains primarily clustered in a handful of district headquarters. Equally, it is the outpost nature of the region that consistently has thwarted efforts to make local government "start from the bottom up, rather than the top down"; paternalism and the appeal of stability have outweighed the desire for extensive local involvement. If future regimes gamble on enhanced local participation through reasonably powerful local councils, then the gamble should be extended one step further: devolution of real authority from district to thana councils. No other single step, within the existing framework, would do more to stimulate effective enhanced demand on the government for resources, and the reciprocal rapid expansion of the rural bureaucracy to meet the demand. The logic of evolutionary tinkering, if that is the course of the postconflict leadership, points to a popularly elected, tax-supported council at the thana level in East Bengal.

A third dilemma of rural development departs from the nature of district administration. Rather, the issue relates to the role of the rural population in shaping the politcal destiny of the country after the end of military rule in Pakistan. The electoral role of local councillors will disappear, regardless of the form that local councils may assume. Whatever the corrupting effect of the electoral college on individuals, local councils, and the party parliamentary system, it did have the effect of giving unprecedented importance to the rural sectors of the country. When the electoral college lapses, will the rural stake in the national arena lapse as well? The dilemma in this case arises due to the absence of viable village-based structures in East Bengal. Without such party structures, the return of party politics and of nonnational rural councils can mean the loss of a rural voice in the formation of the revamped polity. Can urban-based politics accord a significant, participatory role for the non-urban population, to replace the faulty, unacceptable mechanism of Basic Democracies?

If local councils are given a new life, the ready political response historically associated with rural electoral politics may provide the base for the emergence of viable party activities beyond the moffusil rural towns. This could have a salutary effect on stimulating a responsive local bureaucracy (unless it reacts negatively, a form of passive resistance) and give organizational strength to rurally based political party leaders. But this would first entail a gratuitous and strong commitment by urban-based political party leaders.

Summary and Conclusion

Rural development is a process of government, rather than a program or agency. It is an attempt to restructure the government's relationship with its nonurban population. The need to rely on government to take action combined with the need to adapt existing governmental moffusil institutions leads to thorny problems of rural development. In the absence of private organizational capacity for innovation and change, all rural development becomes "governmentized," assumed as a duty of the government; this leads to reliance on the district gridwork to implement rural change. Yet attempts to alter the rural apparatus has both historically and recently proven difficult. The perceived necessity for unrestricted authority in the collectorate causes fragmentation and tension for even the line agencies, the nation-building departments, as the separate but parallel hierarchies conflict philosophically and methodologically—a problem that is greatly accentuated for additional ad hoc "reconstruction" agencies inserted into the district apparatus.

Centralization, as well as fragmentation, is inherent in district organization, and therefore in local tradition as well. Rural development requires reform of the government machinery, and a vigorous local government. The frequently made observation requires, it is further said, decentralization from the collectorate, and a system of local government with power close to the "grass roots"; yet reform efforts within the government, and by the government, seem always to end with reinforced potency at the district level. There is an inexorable "pull to the district" that makes deviation not only in a sense "illegitimate" as noted earlier, but also ineffectual.

There may yet emerge significantly altered conditions in rural Bangladesh. The basic "givens" of rural life suggested in the open-

ing paragraphs may change; the demands of independence could
be a crucible that reformulates the social and political institutions
of rural life, and of the government as well. But if not, the future
must evolve from the givens of the past. Then the potential for rural
development will turn upon two central problems. To what degree
will any government sacrifice the sinews of stable rule, the balky
but reliable district apparatus, for the sake of rural decentralization
and democratic participation at the local level? Without reforms,
the capacity for responsive and responsible rural government will
remain circumscribed; with reforms, the leadership may perceive
its own security, and the skeleton of an uncertain state, in jeopardy.

Related to this, but more broadly, is the problem of development and participation. While the rural citizenry remains unor-
ganized and poor, what can be done to keep the nonurban sector of
the population from fading once again into political and economic
obscurity? Under either a closed or open political system, the most
serious problems of rural development still remain the problems
stemming from neglect and unimportance. In the third and fourth
decades since Partition, and in the initial years of liberation, a central problem of rural development will be to prevent the virtual
reversion of 85 percent of the population to an ignored hinterland
status.

Elliot L. Tepper is assistant director, School of International Affairs,
and assistant professor of Political Science, Carleton University,
Ottawa, Canada. He received his Ph.D. in Political Science from
Duke University in 1970 and carried out field research in
Bangladesh from 1964 to 1965.

NOTES

1. This analysis is partly based on Tepper (1966).
2. The impact of Mogul administrative practice in Bengal is somewhat
controversial, but it seems clear that the Todar Mall's measurement and
assessment reforms were never fully implemented in the eastern districts.
For a recent and concise statement of Mogul organization in Bengal, see
Calkins (1970:794–500). He notes, *inter alia*, "The political structure in
Bengal was somewhat peculiar, however, because almost all the land was
controlled at the local level by indigenous landholders, who were called
zamindars. These zamindars played an unusually important role as re-

venue collectors and keepers of the peace. Over time a group of larger and stronger zamindars began to emerge to take over more of the responsibilities of government." See also the volume edited by Frykenberg (1969).

3. Indeed there is reason to doubt that such village republics flourished anywhere in the subcontinent: ". . . Metcalfe wrote hopefully of the 'little republics' which he had found flourishing in the country between Agra and Delhi, in the twilight between the Moghal and the British administrations, assuming them to be a general phenomenon. In fact in that region, they had been born (or re-born) of the necessity for a defense organization against raiders from the neighboring desert. They were confined to quite a small area. In the north especially, panchayats tended to be based on caste and religion and rarely covered the whole community." (Hicks 1961:46)

4. More technically, the East Bengal Code, State Acquisition and Tenancy Act, Act 28, 1950, East Pakistan. The words "East Pakistan" were substituted by a general ordinance in 1960.

5. Perhaps this can be explained historically. The province was the last stronghold of Buddhism in India; the Hindu revival was slow to advance, and was influenced in the reconversion process by Tantric practices (Beech et al. 1966:7). The personalistic and less-Brahminic version of Hinduism was thus not entrenched at the time of the Muslim conquest (circa 1200). On the other hand, at least 70 percent of the Muslims in Bengal were converts from Hinduism, many lived in areas where Hinduism remained strong (Hindus until very recently formed over 18 percent of the East Pakistan population), and most still live in areas where Hindus dominate socially and economically.

6. For a discussion of the dynamic aspects within village-level caste systems, see Srinivas (1962).

7. F. R. Khan (1962:226) noted a "caste-spirit" and "Muslim caste-like groups" in the village he studied, but ranked these groups into a simple high-born and low-born hierarchy:

A. High Muslim: Khan (Pathan) or   Khandkar
B. Low Muslim: 1. Shek   4. Kulu
                        2. Shikdar   5. Nikuri
                        3. Mondol   6. Bediya

8. The absence of caste is attributed to "the absence of superior middle tenure holders (a class which generally patronized and helped in the settlement of these groups), the predominance of Muslims and the proximity of the town which has most of the service needed by the villagers." This

comment implies that caste is considered by the author to be a Hindu phenomenon exclusively (Qadir 1960:56).

9. A class system is found based on wealth. A local saying is quoted that reflects the new situation: "Nowadays if one's economic situation is good, one's family status is also good" (Bertocci 1970:26–27).

10. Reference here, of course, is only to Islamic practice. Hindu practices in a "quasi village environment" are even less well documented. All comments about local-level religious organization in East Pakistan are tentatively made and open to dispute and revision when further information becomes available; few areas of research are so fruitful or so ignored. Comments here are based upon the village studies listed above, particularly Bertocci (1970), plus Zaidi (1961 and 1963).

11. The critical difference between extended and joint families in regard to land is that while members of extended families may own contiguous property, joint families share ownership of property. In Muslim practice as manifested in East Bengal, primogeniture and Hindu influence combine to provide joint ownership between father and eldest son as long as the father lives, and perhaps joint ownership among brothers for a short time after the father dies, but then property reverts to nuclear family ownership (Beech et al. 1966:4–7). It is interesting to note that in the Dhanishwar study there was strong support for the joint family as an ideal but also wide recognition of its defects (Qadir 1960:100–109). The author concludes, "In spite of all the honest support for the system, it is apprehended that its foundation is becoming weaker due to the changing value judgment as a result of the present educational system. . . . Many respondents blamed wives of the brothers for causing break [sic] in the joint family system." East Pakistan still has more joint families than West Pakistan, but this probably is due partially to the Hindu minority in East Pakistan.

12. Bertocci (1970:8) writes that the word is probably Arabic in origin from the root meaning "protégés", those who are under the protective domain of others. This might indicate that the *reyai* system is Muslim in origin, and an alternative to the Hindu caste panchayat. Rahim (1965:5) suggests that the *reyai* might once have included kin groups only.

13. The literature on "district administration" is rather extensive. The overall pattern of British imperial control is given by Tinker (1966). One of the most detailed examinations of the collectorate is given by Khera (1964). Of the work focusing specifically on East Pakistan, see Hoque (1970), which is part of the continuing examination of administrative patterns by the National Institute of Public Administration in Dacca. See also Muhith (1967, 1968).

14. The "circle" referred to a circle (grouping) of unions, the lowest administrative subdivision. The post was created out of awareness, from firsthand knowledge, of East Bengal's administrative weakness, which resulted from the first Partition in 1904 (Government of Bengal 1915; Anisuzzaman 1963).

15. The Resolution on Local Self-Government of 1882. The resolution first appeared in Government of India (1882).

16. The contents and an analysis of the bill are provided in the *Bengal District Administration Committee Report* (Government of Bengal 1915:81–82).

17. Apart from official reports, which are somewhat inaccessible, there is surprisingly little information about this important phase of local government in Eastern Bengal. The authoritative general source of information is Roy (1936).

18. Union councils, after a short time, were completely elected on the basis of universal suffrage; the elected chairmen of the unions sat as members of the thana council, which in turn chose the elected representatives of the district councils. Indeed, the first suggestion for the "coordination councils" apparently did not come from Ayub, but from Akhter Hameed Khan, the man most prominently associated with rural development in East Pakistan (Mohsen 1963:87).

BIBLIOGRAPHY

Anisuzzaman, Md.
    1963. *The Circle Officer*. Dacca: National Institute of Public Administration.
Beech, Mary Jane; Be⁻tocci, Peter J.; and Corwin, Lauren A.
    1966. "Introducing the East Bengali Village," pp. 1–18. In *Inside the East Pakistani Village—Six Articles*. East Lansing: Asian Studies Center, Michigan State University.
Bertocci, Peter
    1970. "Patterns of Social Organization in Rural East Pakistan." In *Bengal East and West*, edited by Alexander Lipski, pp. 107–137. South Asia Series, Occasional Paper No. 13. East Lansing: Asian Studies Center, Michigan State University.
Calkins, Philip B.
    1970. "The Formation of a Regionally Oriented Ruling Group in Bengal, 1700–1740."*Journal of Asian Studies* 29,(11):799–806.
Frykenberg, Robert E., ed.
    1969. *Land Control and Social Structure in Indian History*. Madison: University of Wisconsin Press.

Government of Bengal
   1873. *Bengal District Administration Committee Report, 1871–1872.*
       Calcutta: Bengal Secretariat Press.
   1882. "The Resolution on Local Self-Government." In *Supplement to
       the Gazette of India*, 20 May 1882, pp. 747–753.
   1885. "An Act to Extend the System of Self-Government in Bengal."
       Act III of Bengal Code.
   1915. *Bengal District Administration Committee Report, 1913–
       1914.* Calcutta: Bengal Secretariat Press.
   1919. *Act V of Bengal Code.*
Government of East Pakistan
   1950. *State Acquisition and Tenancy Act.* Act 28, East Bengal Code.
Government of India
   1882. "The Resolution on Local Self-government of 1882." In *Sup-
       plement to the Gazette of India*, 20 May, pp. 747–753.
Great Britain
   1909. *Department of the Royal Commission upon Decentralization
       in India.* Vol 1. London: H.M.S.O.
Hicks, Ursula K.
   1961. *Development from Below.* Oxford: Clarendon Press.
Hoque, Abunasar Shamsul
   1970. "District Administration in East Pakistan: Its Classical Form
       and the Emerging Pattern." *Administrative Science Review*
       4:21–48.
Karim, A. K. Nazmul
   1956. *Changing Society in India and Pakistan.* Dacca: Ideal Publica-
       tion.
Karve, Irawati
   1965. *Kinship Organization in India.* Bombay: Asia Publishing
       House.
Khan, Fazlur Rashid
   1962. "The Caste System of the Village Community of Dhulandi in
       the District of Dacca." In *Sociology in East Pakistan*, edited by
       J. Owen. Dacca: Asiatic Society of Pakistan, pp. 205–231.
Khera, S. S.
   1964. *District Administration in India.* Bombay: Asia Publishing
       House.
Mohsen, A. K. M.
   1963. *The Comilla Rural Administration Experiment: History and
       Annual Report, 1962–1963.* Comilla: Pakistan Academy for
       Rural Development.

Muhith, A. M. A.
    1967. "Political and Administrative Rules in East Pakistan's Districts." *Pacific Affairs* 40 (Fall and Winter 1967–1968):324.
    1968. *The Deputy Commissioner in East Pakistan*. Dacca: National Institute of Public Administration.
Qadir, S. A.
    1960. *Village Dhanishwar*. Comilla: Pakistan Academy for Rural Development.
Rahim, S. A.
    1965. *Communication and Personal Influence in an East Pakistan Village*. Comilla: Pakistan Academy for Rural Development.
Rashid, Haroun Er
    1965. *East Pakistan: A Systematic Regional Geography*. Lahore: Sh. Ghulam Ali & Sons.
Rashiduzzaman, M.
    1966. Election Politics in Pakistan Villages." *Journal of Commonwealth Political Studies* 4:191–200.
Roy, N. C.
    1936. *Rural Self-Government in Bengal*. Calcutta: University of Calcutta Press.
Sobhan
    1968. *Basic Democracies, Works Program, and Rural Development in East Pakistan*. Dacca: Bureau of Economics, Dacca University.
Srinivas, M. N.
    1962. *Caste in Modern India and Other Essays*. Bombay: Asia Publishing House.
Tepper, Elliot L.
    1966. Changing Patterns of Administration in Rural East Pakistan. South Asia Series, Occasional Paper No. 5. East Lansing, Mich.: Asian Studies Center, Michigan State University.
Tinker, Hugh
    1966. "Structure of the British Imperial Heritage." In *Asian Bureaucratic Systems Emergent from the British Imperial Tradition*, edited by Ralph Braibante et al., pp. 23–87. Durham: Duke University Press.
Thomas, John W.
    1968. "Rural Public Works and East Pakistan's Development." Ph.D. dissertation, Harvard University.
Zaidi, S. M. Hafeez
    1961. "Brief Case Studies of Village Factions." *Journal of the Paki-*

stan Academy for Rural Development 6:26–35. Also available in *Inside the East Pakistani Village—Six Articles,* pp. 69–87. East Lansing: Asian Studies Center, Michigan State University.
1962. "Psychological Methodologies in Community Research." In *Sociology in East Pakistan*, edited by John E. Owen, pp. 14–26. Dacca: Asiatic Society of Pakistan.

4

East Pakistan's Agricultural Planning and Development, 1955-1969: Its Legacy for Bangladesh

Charles M. Elkinton

From Benign Neglect to Top Priority

Pakistan's three successive five-year development plans, covering the period 1956 to 1970, exhibited rapidly improved planning capability. A long-term perspective plan covering twenty years to 1985 provided a useful broad framework within which to construct successive five-year plans. This impressive overall planning effort benefited from a decade-and-a-half of competent assistance from the Harvard Advisory Group (HAG) and a rapid increase in the number and the competence of indigenous planning personnel. The place and need for annual development plans were finally recognized during the third plan period. East Pakistan first produced annual plans for FY(Fiscal Year) 1968 and FY 1969.

During the 1950s, including the First Plan period, East Pakistan played a relatively minor role in the planning process and was accorded a relatively minor share of development resources. This is indicated by the increased flow of public sector development expenditures to East Pakistan from about 20 percent of the national total for the First Plan to some 38 percent for the Second Plan and about 50 percent of the Third Plan allocations.

The total public sector development allocations to East Pakistan accorded to the agricultural sector for each of the first three five-year plans and the share of the total are shown on the following page.

The determination of sectorial allocation of development resources is eternally a knotty problem for any developing country because it usually involves sociopolitical issues and complicated sector analysis. At the margin of development investments, what choice of additional inputs at a given level would produce a higher

TABLE 1. Development Allocations to the Agricultural
Sector in the First Three Plans (millions of rupees)

Five-Year Plan	Total Allocation	Allocated to Agriculture	Agr. % of Total
First Plan (1956–1960)	1,231.1	228.6	19.0
Second Plan (1961–1965)	5,550.5	966.6	17.0
Third Plan (1966–1970)	14,390.0	2,124.0	14.8

SOURCES: Data for First and Second Plans are from GOEP (1966), Table 16.3. Data for Third Plan are from Government of Pakistan (1966).

net social per capita product? Family planning? Additional fertilizer? A new jute factory? Or another addition of kilowatts of electrical power?

East Pakistan's rural sector accounted for some 95 percent of the population and about 95 percent of the value of exports including raw and processed agricultural products, which also provided about 70 percent of the annual gross domestic product (GDP). In view of this relative importance, it is not surprising that there always has existed a high correlation between the year to year annual movement of the GDP and the annual index of agricultural production. Until FY 1967/68 the government of Pakistan assumed a relatively relaxed posture vis-à-vis agriculture; a sort of benign neglect prevailed. One important reason for this was the easy availability of food grain and vegetable oil imports from the United States Public Law 480 (PL480) program. These import purchases were made with rupees and most of the funds generated were in turn made available to finance economic development projects. Thus, it is not surprising that development planning officials, indigenous and expatriate alike, did not undertake comparative cost and advantage studies of Pakistan's agricultural resources and crops and were relatively unconcerned about the lack of agricultural production progress in both the East and West wings. There was, however, some concern about the social and political consequences, especially in East Pakistan, that might be generated by increasing rural unemployment and deepening poverty, and this concern led to the introduction of a massive rural works program to offer seasonal employment and to develop sorely needed rural infrastructure.

The United States Agency for International Development (USAID) made available to East Pakistan for rural works, between 1968 and 1969, 104.3 crore of rupees; 86.7 crore as grants and 17.6 crore as rupee loans on favorable repayment terms. At the official exchange rate of 4.76 rupees to $1.00, 104.3 crore is equal to $210 million.

The relatively relaxed attitude of Pakistani planners toward agricultural development came to an abrupt end in 1967. In that year U.S. food grains (wheat most notably) were in short supply relative to domestic and foreign sales commitments. Pakistan officially was notified that the United States could not supply the requested quantities and that a significant part of the tonnage to be made available would have to be corn and corn sorghum. Pathans of the North-West Frontier Province of West Pakistan did not object to corn since it has been a traditional part of their diet. East Bengalis, on the other hand, viewed corn and sorghum as completely foreign and distasteful foods.

A reassessment of Pakistan's minimum food grain needs led the government of Pakistan to commit about $75 million equivalent to world market food grain suppliers to fill the country's deficit. Having approved these commercial imports, the president of Pakistan promptly called a meeting of provincial governors, ministers, and top economic planning officials. At this and succeeding sessions, it was agreed that Pakistan could no longer afford to depend on the United States for food grain supplies on concessional sales terms to supply the country's deficits. The president requested his officers to prepare, on a crash basis, plans for increasing Pakistan's wheat and rice production to the self-sufficiency level in the shortest time and by 1970, if possible. The initial plans provided for rapid introduction of the short-stemmed high-yielding varieties of wheat from Mexico and rice from the International Rice Research Institute (IRRI). Also, provision was made for a sharp increase in fertilizer supplies through expanded imports and, in the longer term, expanded indigenous production.

West Pakistan had renowned success in the use and rapid adoption of Mexican wheat and IRRI rice, together with expanded use of other necessary inputs and grain support prices. Food grain self-sufficiency was achieved by the end of 1969. Food grain production increased in tonnage from a 6.5 million average between

1961 and 1965 to 9.4 and 9.8 million tons in FY 1968 and FY 1969 respectively.

East Pakistan's plans for quickly achieving self-sufficiency in rice production relied heavily on rapid and successful adoption of IRRI No. 8 and No. 5 (otherwise designated as IR-8 and IR-5), which had proven to be highly successful in West Pakistan and parts of India. In addition, plans were drafted and steps taken to expand fertilizer imports and production and to increase low-lift pump irrigation for the boro rice crop, including IRRI No. 8. Unfortunately, IRRI Nos. 8 and 5 had certain limitations. The East Pakistan climate, plant diseases, and limited supply of controlled irrigation proved less than optimum for these imported varieties. Thus, the East Pakistan food grain deficit continued at over 1 million tons in 1969, and 1.5 million tons in 1970 (Table 2).

Agricultural Sector Plan—A New Initiative

In light of the worsening food-grain-supply situation, the East Pakistan Planning and Development Department, in cooperation with other concerned agencies, in 1968, undertook the preparation of a thorough agricultural sector development plan. Although this

TABLE 2. East Pakistan Food Grain Imports and Average Minimum Price of Rice

	Food Grain Imports (000 tons)	Average Annual Minimum Provincial Retail Rice Prices (rupees per maund)
1960–1964 (Annual Ave.)	662	25.1
1964/65	735	25.0
1965/66	875	29.7
1966/67	1,076	38.8
1967/68*	644	34.6
1968/69	1,029	38.6
1969/70	1,500	N.A.

SOURCE: Government of East Pakistan Food Department.

*1968 was a record-breaking crop year with a reported crop of 11 million tons.

plan had shortcomings, it was by far the most analytical and definitive agricultural development plan ever produced in East Pakistan. The United States Agency for International Development Mission in Dacca concurred in most of the problem assessments and in general with the quantified and costed actions recommended. However, the mission felt that the plans had used population growth estimates that were too low and rice production estimates that were on the high side. Thus, rice production targets were too low to fill prospective requirements.

An elaborate study with recommendations for nationalizing the jute industry from production to marketing and exports was also made by the Government of East Pakistan (GOEP) Planning and Development Department. This study noted that jute production had remained almost static and that East Pakistan's dominant position in world raw jute trade had declined sharply during the past two decades.

Two other important agriculture subsectors that were given relatively less analysis and program attention were fisheries and tea. Expansion of fish production could make a significant contribution to increasing East Pakistan's protein consumption. The Fisheries Department with expatriate help identified the major technical, institutional, and resource constraints to expanded output, but these findings and recommendations remained, for the most part, unimplemented.

Expanding tea consumption outstripped production so that net tea imports came to prevail. Political as well as economic factors were alleged to be major constraints on expanded output. Both tea and jute policies and development plans were of special interest and were subject to some degree of control by the central government, and thus East Pakistan's ability to plan and program production, marketing, and export improvements was abridged.

Input Shortfalls

East Pakistan's annual plans for FYs 1969 and 1970 proposed to achieve agricultural production goals by sharply increasing the supply of important input factors, including high-yield varieties of grain and jute and continued input subsidies to assure farmers a favorable cost-return ratio. The 1970 plan also noted the increasing constraints on development resources and thus the necessity of using the following criteria for project selection: preference for projects in the penultimate stage, quick-yielding projects, aided projects, agricultural supply industries (such as fertilizer production), family planning, and malaria eradication.

The FY 1970 plan projected a 12.8 percent increase in rice production and calculated the quantity of inputs together with their response coefficients, which would give incremental outputs to achieve the targeted rice outputs. The same general planning process was used as was used in preparing the FY 1969 production goals. The official input-output records for the crop of year 1968/69 showed an average or better than average crop year with respect to the influence of climatic factors. Thus it is of interest to note FY 1969 production experience relative to planned output targets for that year (Table 3).

TABLE 3. Targets and Realized Production and Inputs, FY 1969 Plan

	Plan Production Targets	Production Realized	Difference
Rice (millions of tons)	11.50	11.10	−0.40
Jute (millions of bales)	7.00	5.80	−1.20
Sugarcane (millions of tons)	8.00	7.00	−1.00
Tea (millions of lbs.)	68.00	62.00	−6.00
Potato (millions of tons)	0.75	0.75	——
Oil Seeds (millions of tons)	0.18	0.20	+0.20
	Plan Input Targets	Inputs Realized	Difference
Fertilizer (tons)	375,000	278,000	−97,000
Low-lift Pumps (acres irrigated)	698,000	515,000	−183,000
Plant Protection (acres)	993,000	800,000	−193,000

SOURCES: GOEP 1969*a* and 1970*b*. Rice and jute production data from Government of East Pakistan FY 1969 official production report.

The shortfall of almost 100,000 tons of fertilizer, 183,000 acres of low-lift pump irrigation, 193,000 acres of plant protection lacking, plus an informally reported shortfall in acres of IRRI rice, account for most of the deficit in crop output.

Further, there is strong evidence that the official estimates of the 1965 to 1969 rice crop were on the high side by an annual average of about three-fourths of a million tons. These errors led, in turn, to underestimates of grain import needs and to inflated grain prices (See Table 2). The sources and magnitude of these errors as well as corrective action is discussed in a later section.

Required Improvements in Planning, Statistical Methods, and Finance

In 1969, the government of Pakistan decided that the country's economic planning operations could henceforth be performed adequately without further expatriate, that is, Harvard Advisory Group, assistance. This judgment seemed quite reasonable to me as it related to the central government's Planning Commission, which had developed an impressive indigenous planning competence.

On the other hand, the East Pakistan Planning and Development Department, which had a few well-trained economic planners, was still seriously deficient in trained manpower relative to the momentous tasks ahead. Concerned East Pakistani officials voiced the opinion that the elimination of expatriate planning assistance to the East Pakistan Planning and Development Department was premature. However, the central government's decision on this matter prevailed. Had this decision continued in force, it would have then been urgent to expand assistance to East Pakistan in the training abroad of economists who had promise of becoming competent development planners and program evaluators. After Independence, however, several highly trained Bengali development economists, who had previously been associated with the Institute for Development Economics in Karachi and who had fled the country during 1971, returned to take up posts in the new Bangladesh government's planning commission. Moreover, other foreign-trained development specialists in institutions outside of Dacca have been offered positions in various sections of the planning apparatus. Thus, central planning in Bangladesh seems as well served by competent professionals as is possible at the moment. The need for training more specialists to serve at the various district levels, as well as in development institutions such as the Academy for Rural Development at Comilla, will continue.

Adequate and reliable statistics available on a timely basis are a *sine qua non* for effective and efficient development planning. East Pakistan, starting from an almost unbelievably low base, made considerable progress in developing useful series of technical and economic data. The U.S. Department of Commerce, Bureau of Census, under an AID financed agreement, made available to East Pakistan some twenty man-years of advisory service for the development of statistical institutions, capabilities, and a useful series of economic data. This input together with a participant training program helped East Pakistan to make a useful start in the development of this critical capability and service. However, only a relatively modest beginning was made in this important field in East Pakistan while the developed countries have undergone tremendous technological advance in data collection and processing. The US-AID mission to East Pakistan unfortunately found it necessary to close out the statistics project in 1969. The action was taken in part because it was clear that progress in strengthening statistical institutions and services was slowing down as a result of tightness of overall development funds and also because of the relatively low priority accorded statistical services by controlling officials of the East Pakistan government. I believe that the government of Bangladesh should ask a team of able but disinterested outsiders to reevaluate the country's existing statistical institutions, organizations, trained manpower, and methods and to make recommendations for further development and growth of this basic service.

Within the constraints of the limited number of trained planning officers and insufficient high quality and timely socioeconomic statistical series, the Development Planning Department staff and cooperators from other nation-building departments and a few expatriates surprisingly produced two impressive annual plans and a few good sector and subsector studies. With increased resources and related improvement noted above, East Pakistan's planning was in a position to achieve excellence ". . . we presently lack in statistical information on perhaps one-half of the economy. . . . In all probability it is likely that our lack of knowledge impedes our ability to devise suitable programmes to stimulate development in this half of the economy" (Rabbani 1968).

Among the more serious statistical deficiences have been faulty methods for making annual estimates of rice production. Since the annual value of rice output accounts for more than one-third of the gross domestic product, progress made to improve these estimates will be reviewed in the next section.

Rice Production Estimates

Past failures in agricultural planning, food grain import decisions, and in restraining rice inflation have resulted in part from large annual errors in rice production estimates. East Pakistani agricultural production data from 1947 to 1965 were based on a system of "subjective" estimates. From 1965 onward, the same method was employed on all crops except for the aman and aus rice crops and jute. Since 1965, annual estimates of these crops have been in transition to an "objective" method of crop estimation and reporting (Larson 1969).

TABLE 4. Official Reported Rice Production 1947–1969 (millions of tons)

	Aus	Aman	Boro	Total
"Subjective" Sample Estimates				
1947/48 to 1960 ave.	1.7	5.4	0.3	7.4
1960/61 to 1964/65 ave.	2.4	6.8	0.5	9.7
1965/66	2.9	6.8	0.6	10.3
1966/67	2.7	5.9	0.8	9.4
1967/68	3.1	6.8	1.1	11.0
1968/69	2.7	6.9	1.6	11.2
"Objective" Sample Estimates–Aus and Aman				
1965/66	2.9	5.9	0.6	9.4
1966/67	2.7	5.7	0.8	9.2
1967/68	3.1	6.3	1.1	10.5
1968/69	2.7	5.7	1.6	10.0

SOURCES: "Subjective" Sample Estimates are from Government of Pakistan 1969. "Objective" Sample Estimates are from Larson 1969.

The subjective method was based on annual reports of acreage and yield changes by the extension field staff of the directorate of agriculture. As a starting point, this method used the 1944–1945 census of Bengal for benchmark crop acreages and a rather vague so-called normal yield. These were "opinion-type" estimates and were not based on any probability sample of farms or field plots.

The "objective" crop acreage yield survey was based on the annual collection of acreage information from a probability area sample of about 5,000 area segments or cluster of plots—each five acres in size. Crop-cutting experiments to obtain yields were carried out annually on a subsample of some 2,700 aman plots, 2,000 aus plots, and 1,700 jute plots (Table 4). Sampling errors for estimates at the provincial level were estimated to be about 1.0 to 1.5 percent for yields, 2.0 to 2.5 percent for acreage, and 2.5 to 3.0 percent for production (Larson 1969).

Because the growing of boro crop rice was spotty and irregular over the countryside, the general purpose sample survey was not applicable. Thus, for this crop, the traditional "subjective" crop-reporting system still continued.

Financial Constraints

Agriculture accounted for about 20 percent of East Pakistan's Second Plan development expenditures and, aside from rural works, this figure declined to 12.4 percent of total outlay during the first three years of the Third Plan (Table 5). If rural works expendi-

TABLE 5. Average Annual Development Expenditures for Second Plan Period and First Three Years of Third Plan Period (in crores of rupees)

	Second Plan	Third Plan
Infrastructure	40.8	83.4
Social Services	25.2	34.9
Food and Agriculture	18.9	33.8
Industry	9.6	28.1
Total Annual Average	94.5	180.2

SOURCES: Data for the Second Plan are from Government of East Pakistan 1965. Data for the Third Plan are from Government of Pakistan, "Consortium Memorandum."

tures are added in, the agricultural share increases to 18.5 percent.[1]

In addition to the direct fund outlays to agriculture, there were expenditures on infrastructure, industry, and social services, which benefited farmers and thus would have contributed to agricultural development.

The question as to whether agriculture's share of total development funds was "fair" or "adequate" is difficult to assess in general terms. There are related but unanswered questions as to opportunity costs and prospective net returns from alternative investments in a meaningful time frame. However, Government of East Pakistan officials declared, "In keeping with the revised Third Plan Strategy, topmost priority has been accorded to the agricultural development program which includes the attainment of self-sufficiency in food grains and expansion of jute, tea, sugar cane, oil seeds and other crops" (GOEP 1969c).

Given the highest development priority for agriculture in general and food grains most explicitly, the question arises as to whether all possible policy, financial, institutional, and program measures were adopted that would achieve the stated self-sufficiency goal. A selected few of the more important existing deficiencies for policy and program are discussed in later sections of this chapter. Thus, reference will be made here only to financial constraints.

Floods destroy up to 5 to 10 percent of East Bengal's rice crop on an average of about every third year. The feasibility of limited but significant projects to partially correct this problem was determined, but rupee and foreign exchange resources were not adequate to carry on all feasible projects.

Rural works for the development of sorely needed rural infrastructure and relief of rural unemployment only received an average annual input of 15.8 crores during the four years from 1966 to 1969. East Pakistani officials and expatriates alike who had been closely associated with this program agreed that 25 to 30 crore of rupees could be effectively employed annually on this program, especially since the Thana Irrigation Program had been added to other rural works. Further, I personally urged the government of Pakistan (GOP) and GOEP officials, in FYs 1967, 1968, and 1969, to speed up the process of alloting funds to the rural works program.

The program was seasonal, mostly carried out between mid-November and the end of March; funds in hand were required several months in advance of initiating projects in order that commitments could be made for labor and materials. Bureaucratic red tape and perhaps some disinterested officials regularly held up the allotment of funds and thus delayed the start-up date of the annual works program, a malpractice that should be corrected if the program is to continue as part of Bangladesh's overall agricultural development strategy.

These few examples plus other related considerations point up the problems faced by the East Pakistan government because of the limitations imposed on it due to lack of control over the preparation and approval of periodic development plans and the allotment of funds for achieving development plan goals. Even though now an independent Bangladesh will have complete autonomy in these matters, it will still have to face up to major issues relating to increasing public revenue and stimulating private savings and investments. Reduction of the high cost of government revenue collections and positive measures to encourage private savings should be given priority consideration.

One further important consideration relating to the financial problem was the two-decade average annual transfer from East to West Pakistan, of an equivalent of some $50 to $100 million of financial resources, foreign exchange and rupees combined, as a Pakistani economist's study and a balance of payments study by a competent American economist convincingly document.[2] East Pakistan received an estimated one-third of all Pakistan foreign assistance since 1953 and this has totaled some $1.2 to $1.5 billion. It is likely that over two decades East Pakistan transferred financial resources to the West roughly equal to all foreign assistance it received. As the events of 1971 showed, this was a serious economic matter for East Pakistan and a complicated political problem that contributed to the dissolution of the nation.

Rural Works and Inflation

The rural works program was started province-wide in FY 1963, and an annual average of 15 crore rupees were allocated to this program between FYs 1963 and 1969. The question of the inflationary impact of the program was frequently raised. An analysis of the price and living-cost effects of the works program is lacking, but some of the related magnitudes suggest that the price impact was not great and that the additional rupee supply was sorely needed. East Pakistan's money supply, currency plus demand deposits, was only 14.0 percent of the gross domestic product between 1963 and 1968. The comparable West Pakistan figure for the same period was 26 percent. The works input amounted to about 5 percent of the money supply between FY 1963 and 1968, but these funds were dispersed widely in an undermonetized countryside. East Pakistan's per capita income averaged 293 rupees and, assuming an average of six persons per family, reflected an annual average family income of some 1,800 rupees. The average annual works input per family was about 14 rupees; average annual wholesale prices increased 3.5 percent per year and consumer prices about 3.9 percent between FYs 1963 and 1968.

The rupee inputs for rural works were generated by imports of PL 480 food grain and vegetable oil. From 5 to 10 percent of East Pakistan's grain supplies and about 25 percent of oil supplies were imported. Rice demand had a price elasticity of –0.5 and the income elasticity was probably somewhat above 1.0; thus, the increased grain supplies offset in large measure the rice price effects of increased income.

Finally, recognition was given in the East Pakistan Annual Plan of FY 1968 to the need for monetary expansion to stimulate domestic development; an unprecedented Rs. 75 crore (about 30 percent) expansion of commercial bank credit was indicated as necessary to achieve the investment goal in 1968/69.

Priority Agricultural Programs, FYs 1972 through 1975

The Setting

Increased food production should share with population control the highest priority in Bangladesh's development plans. As previously noted, food production in the former Pakistan province during the three planning periods from FYs 1956 to 1969 has not kept up with population growth. Failure to close the food grain gap in the near future will widen the underconsumption gap or alternatively will necessitate large and continuous annual imports from abroad, which in turn will deprive the economy of foreign exchange sorely needed for import of industry production goods and needed consumer commodities.

Agricultural programs must be concerned initially with short-term measures, that is, things to be done that can influence greater production in the immediate future. The major constraints to early achievement of food grain self-sufficiency are obviously population growth and the physical difficulties of Bangladesh's geography. Other constraints are also important. Chief among these are: (1) uncertainty in obtaining the finances for importing an adequate supply of inputs on a timely basis; (2) an inadequate number of trained personnel to assist farmers with efficient use of modern inputs; (3) frequent recurrence of floods and other natural disasters, which regularly cause a 5 to 10 percent loss of food grain; (4) an underdeveloped and inadequate agricultural credit system; (5) an inadequate extension and research service; (6) completely inadequate marketing institutions and facilities; (7) lack of hydrological information about the country's surface water and groundwater; and (8) inadequate or weak management and operation on the part of most development agencies. Factors favorable for short-run agricultural growth are: (1) favorable economic incentives; (2) input subsidies and a large flow of rupees to the rural sector, which reduce the urgency for major improvement in agricultural credit in the short run; and (3) present planning-policy emphasis on agriculture. Finally, Bangladesh normally has a suitable climate for year-round production, good rice soils, and undeveloped water resources, giving the province natural advantages in rice production.

Technical Inputs

FERTILIZER   East Bengali farmers annually increased their use of fertilizer by an average of 23 percent during the year 1965 through 1968. This increase took place despite serious floods during the period. Unfortunately, in FY 1969, fertilizer nutrient use only reached 108,000 tons, a mere 10 percent above FY 1968. In the annual plan, the GOEP projected for FY 1970 an increase of 25,000 nutrient tons; equivalent to a 23 percent advance. This annual rate of increase seems reasonable if supplies are available and if distribution facilities are improved. East Pakistan had two urea plants in 1970 with a combined capacity of about 190,000 nutrient tons, and two triple phosphate units with a capacity of 70,000 tons. If these can resume near-capacity production in the near future, the prospect is that Bangladesh may produce enough fertilizer (except potash) to satisfy a demand increasing by 20 percent per year in FYs 1972 and 1973.

After FY 1973 there is a promising prospect that IRRI high-yielding rice seed, especially adapted to East Bengali conditions, will be generally available for use on the aman crop and possibly the boro crop. Rapid introduction of high-yielding varieties after FY 1973 would, of course, require sharply increased fertilizer use. Bangladesh either must bring another fertilizer plant on production stream in FY 1974 or prepare to again import annually increasing amounts of fertilizer thereafter. Construction of another large natural gas urea plant should be started as soon as possible.

The East Pakistan Agricultural Development Corporation (ADC) was responsible for fertilizer distribution, moving fertilizers from import points and internal factories to interior depots, usually to thana centers. From these points (413 thanas), sales to farmers were handled by local distributors; there were some 18,000 local sellers reported in 1969. This system appears to have functioned reasonably well in increasing fertilizer nutrient use by farmers from an average of 4.3 thousand tons annually between 1955 and 1959 to an annual average of 75,600 tons from 1965 to 1969.

However, there were unsolved problems, as is indicated by the wide differerence in fertilizer sales and use between districts. In FY 1968, a good crop year, five districts, with 21 percent of the cropped area of the province, purchased (and presumably used) 50 percent of all fertilizer distributed. The six lowest districts with 36 percent of the crop area took only 14 percent of the fertilizer. Six other districts, having 43 percent of crops, took 36 percent of the fertilizer supply. The lowest six districts in fertilizer use had fewer local fertilizer sellers than did the higher-use districts.[3] They also have fewer access roads and year-round waterways than do the higher-use districts. These and any other contributing reasons for the low fertilizer intake should be fully investigated by the

Bangladesh government with a view to taking needed action to remove the more serious constraints.

Finally the anticipated increase in availability and use of high-yielding seeds from FY 1973 onward will make necessary a sharp increase in fertilizer availability and use. In view of the problems of distribution discussed above, there would have been some doubt as to the East Pakistan ADC's capacity to service adequately the enlarged distribution role. Before the crisis of 1971, the GOEP had invited province-wide private distributors of petroleum products to consider also taking on fertilizer distribution and sales. Prior to the outbreak of the crisis, an agreement between the GOEP and private companies had not been reached. Fertilizer production and imports were both within the public sector in East Pakistan and there was a subsidy of some 50 percent on fertilizer sales to farmers. Private companies with potential capability to handle fertilizer production indicated that the GOEP proposition was unattractive because of the large prevailing public sector role in fertilizer production, import, and sale. In view of this, the Bangladesh government might well plan for the future transference of all phases of fertilizer production, import, and distribution to the private sector. There is a precedent for this move in West Pakistan, which benefited greatly by moving these important functions to the private sector.

PLANT PROTECTION   The urgency in developing plant protection capabilities lies in assuring the import of an adequate supply of pesticides on a timely basis. Import requirements during FY 1969, FY 1970, and FY 1971 cost annually about $4.5 million and an annual average need of $6 million for the period FY 1970 through FY 1975 was anticipated.

Plant protection application to crops in the past has been carried out by the GOP (10 spray planes), by the GOEP (2,148 field sprayers), and increasingly by private farmers with pesticides and spray equipment supplied by the Department of Agriculture. This system was much less efficient than the ADC fertilizer program and is not likely to be adequate for the present needs of the Bangladesh farmer. Further, it was highly subsidized and it may be hoped this cost to the previous government could be discontinued or sharply reduced over the new country's first planning period.

Information on import requirements, of both kind and quantity, of stocks on hand, and on area distribution are quite unreliable. Proper projection and accounting procedures were greatly lacking in East Pakistan and a complete reorganization of the plant protection division is required for Bangladesh. Stocks normally are moved out from the provincial and district areas to thana storage where accounting becomes difficult because of the number of thanas (413) and the level of staff in charge. Surveys should be made on stocks on hand to determine amounts and quality. Also, a pesticide standardization committee should decide the actual materials that are required for importation.

The commendable GOEP targets were: (1) to take over aerial spraying from the GOP in order to ensure more timely and adequate coverage; (2) intensify extension-service training of farmers in the identification of need and proper use of pesticides; and (3) transfer responsibility for imports, distribution, and use of pesticides to the private sector during the Fourth Plan period. Unfortunately private companies in East Pakistan appeared less interested than those in the West in assuming responsibility for pesticides and in fertilizer distribution. The GOEP had expressed a desire for expatriate assistance in effecting these changes, and the new Bangladesh government may wish to request similar assistance.

SEEDS Improved high-yielding seeds are of paramount importance to countries seeking an accelerated agricultural growth rate because of their high payoff record in terms of increased productivity and expanded output. Recognizing this, the GOEP in 1967 declared a "Grow More Food" policy and had high hopes of achieving a technological breakthrough in rice output by achieving widespread and rapid adoption of International Rice Research Institute varieties. In FY 1967 the GOEP imported 500 maunds of IRRI seed No. 8 and experimented with this quantity on 2,000 acres (GOEP 1967a:13). This test revealed that IR-8 generally produced good results under controlled irrigation and optimum utilization of other essential inputs.

On the basis of the 1967 experience, the GOEP made available 69,500 maunds of IR-8 seed to apply to 240,000 carefully selected irrigated acres of the boro and early aus crop of FY 1968. An assessment of this crop in mid-season revealed some of the problems associated with the IR-8 crop:

> Although early plantings, particularly those without adequate applications of fertilizer, suffered some set-backs due to cold spell and crop disease, on the whole the performance has been satisfactory. However, it may be pointed out that utmost efforts are to be made to evolve new paddy varieties to suit the different local conditions and such efforts will not be confined only to selected irrigated areas. (GOEP 1968a:13)

Thus, it was discovered that this imported seed, even under carefully controlled production conditions, was subject to photosensitive limitations and disease vulnerability in the East Bengal environment. The decision to press on with the development of modified and new varieties tailored to the local environmental conditions was indeed wise. In the meantime, while new varieties were being evolved, it was decided to encourage continued expansion of the acreage in IR-8 and IR-5 on controlled-irrigation lands. This was done in the belief that these varieties would, on the average, at least double and maybe triple the per-acre yields as compared with local boro varieties.

As of the 1969 crop year, low-lift pump irrigation was practiced on 420,000 acres, and other mechanical irrigation, mostly tubewells, may have raised the acreage total to about 550,000 acres. Traditional hand-irrigation methods were used on more than 1 million acres. Accordingly, the planning target for IRRI varieties was raised to over a half-million acres in FY 1969 and about 700,000 acres in FY 1970. How nearly these targets were approached is not yet known but the reported acreage of the boro crop in 1969 was 480,000 acres larger than in 1968 and 525,000 acres above 1967.[4] The reported average yield in 1969 rose by two maunds per acre over the previous year. The expanded boro acreage reflected expanded availability of irrigation, which also influenced yields. Before the advent of IRRI varieties, the yield of the boro crop had been increasing steadily for several years and reached 16.3 maunds per acre in 1967. In 1968 and 1969 the average per-acre yields rose to 19.8 maunds and 21.8 maunds respectively. *If* the half-million-acre IR-8 target for 1969 had been actually realized, it could have, with a favorable season, accounted for a large part of the increase in average yield and also much of the half-million-ton increase in output. Unfortunately the acreage and yield of the aus crop declined so that the aus crop decreased almost 400,000 tons; the aman crop officially was reported almost 100,000 tons over 1968 and the 1969 total rice crop was reported to be 170,000 tons above 1968.[5]

The preliminary record of experience with IR-8 and IR-5 in use on the boro and aus crops suggests that it has made a useful contribution to boro output under controlled irrigation and near optimum use of associated inputs. Having at hand no better alternatives, the GOEP properly took the risk of encouraging these strains. On the other hand, these imported varieties still appear vulnerable to a cool and low-photo-index winter as well as to East Bengal's virile plant disease strains. Accordingly, it is highly desirable and urgent that progress made in 1970, when IR-20 was successfully grown on some 200,000 acres, be continued in seeking to modify imported strains and in developing other new, high-yielding varieties for each of Bangladesh's three rice crops.

Indeed, the GOEP had recognized these needs and in 1969 USAID brought to Dacca a seed improvement adviser who had experienced outstanding success in improved seed development in other countries. Early in 1970 he elaborated a comprehensive plan for new seed distribution to Bengali farmers, aiming at maximum use of ADC facilities, including twenty-two seed multiplication farms and several thousand registered seed growers. The plan envisioned usage of the already existent Agricultural Development Estate program, involving the formation of cooperatives, the supply of credit, and the development of a marketing system. It was thought that the development of an effective seed growers' association would be ideally feasible in connection with a program under way for the multiplication of IRRI No. 532–E–576, that is, IR-20, which had been planted over 500 acres in 1969 to provide seed for further testing and increase during the 1970 aman season.[6]

IRRIGATION   Because of the frequency and destructiveness of monsoon floods (major damage every third year and less destruction about every other year), the GOEP was appropriately giving major emphasis to dry-season winter-crop irrigation. In FY 1969 mechanical irrigation was used on about 420,000 acres and indigenous irrigation on about 1 million acres. During FY 1969 some 11,000 pumps were in use and the target for FY 1970 was 19,000 pumps, which would irrigate almost 1 million acres (GOEP 1969*a* and 1970*b*). This area plus the area irrigated by Water and Power Development Authority (WAPDA) tubewells and local irrigation methods were planned to bring the total irrigated area to about 2.1 million acres, approximately 9 percent of the total crop acres of East Pakistan. Actually, there was a shortfall in pumps and tubewells in use and the mechanically irrigated area probably fell far short of 1 million acres.

There were two limitations to the success of this ambitious program: the first, a shortage of trained people to keep the pumps running; and the second, a question as to the adequacy of surface water in some areas to match the irrigation necessitated by draught. A visiting International Bank for Reconstruction and Development (IBRD) team (FY 1970) expressed concern about surface water availability, and, because of this concern, the team remained noncommittal about providing financing for an additional 18,000 pumps requested by the GOEP. The problem of trained mechanics is discussed in the extension section of a report on this strategy.

The GOEP arranged through several aid donors for the importation of low-lift pumps sufficient to raise the total supply to the 24,000-pump level. Unfortunately, these engine and pump combinations came from several West and East European aid donor countries, and thus parts would not have been interchangeable and maintenance problems would have been difficult.

The Thana Irrigation Program (TIP) was started experimentally in ten thanas in FY 1967, and, from the good results of this trial, it was decided in FY 1968 to embark on a province-wide thana irrigation program as a part of the rural works program. This program not only had the overriding merit of expanding total crop acres, but also would thoroughly involve local people directly in the planning and execution of the program.

The GOEP hoped to reach the target of 4 million acres as soon as possible, but uncertainties about the supply of winter surface water and the amount, location, and quality of groundwater would

have to be removed. Studies and investigations of these water
supplies will require several years. West Pakistan investigated,
with United States Geodetic Survey (USGS) help, the groundwater
of the Indus Plain for almost ten years before embarking on a comprehensive tubewell program.[7]

Newly independent Bangladesh will have to solve other problems in this area. As irrigation programs expand, required funds
from the public sector may rise. Once again economic development
priorities must be evaluated. If water supplies prove to be adequate, the TIP perhaps should be deemed equally as important as
fertilizer, quality seeds, thermal power or other infrastructure, or a
new industry plant. A further persistent problem is the matter of
operation and maintenance of engine and pump equipment and the
procurement of spare parts. Training assistance of this type should
be provided in greater quantity.

Economic Incentives

East Bengali farmers, including the great majority who are
illiterate, have long since demonstrated that they shift the use of
their resources in response to changes in price/cost relationships.[8]
Thus, positive economic incentives must be given the highest
priority in the effort to induce farmers to undertake the technological breakthrough, which is in progress and which must be accelerated. The GOEP recognized the importance of incentives as indicated by large subsidies on fertilizer, irrigation, plant protection,
and improved seeds, as has the government of Bangladesh. Fertilizer and low-lift pump irrigation were formerly subsidized about
50 percent; improved seeds about 20 percent; plant protection,
flood protection, and large-scale WAPDA irrigation projects at 100
percent. Before the emergence of Bangladesh, the USAID mission
shared the view of the GOEP that these subsidies should be continued well into the Fourth Plan period and then be gradually
reduced as production approaches the target level and as a modern
credit system is organized, adequately financed, and readily available to serve the needs of farmers.[9] Support for this general approach may well continue, should the new government in Dacca
wish to adopt it.

In addition to subsidies, and of equal or greater importance, is the current and prospective ratio of rice prices to the prices of commodities other than food. The prospect for Bangladesh over the next three to five years is that this favorable price ratio for farmers will continue because of the deficit food grain position, which still hovers between 2 to 3 million tons of shortfall in rice production each year.

A multiple correlation analysis measuring the movement of retail rice prices as related to changes in the per capita availability of food grains indicates that a 10 percent change in food grain availability per capita would cause a 20 percent change in price at the retail level (HAG 1970). It appears to the writer that a rice price support program will not be necessary nor appropriate as long as Bangladesh is a deficit rice area relying on imports to supply up to 10 percent of the annual supply. On the other hand, it would be prudent to prepare a standby price support system in the event relative price changes do jeopardize achievement of agricultural objectives. In the past, annual smuggling of rice to India also tended to inflate East Pakistani rice prices, and this problem continues for Bangladesh. The GOEP established a compulsory rice purchase plan within five miles of the border to inhibit smuggling and to acquire a portion of the rice supplies needed for the ration shops, which operated to assure low-income groups a supply of food grains at below cost, a form of consumer's subsidy (GOEP 1964, 1965, 1966, 1967*b*, 1968*b*). During FY 1969, the government paid between Rs. 27 and 28 to these areas and sold through the ration shops at Rs. 29+. Also rice was purchased at the regular market price throughout the province to supplement the border purchases made for the ration shops. These purchases only amounted to an annual average of 39,000 tons during the year from 1960 to 1968.[10]

The high price of rice makes it essential that there be a jute price support program to stimulate production, with a view to stabilizing international prices and retaining foreign markets. The GOEP program for jute price stabilization during the year 1968 and 1969 appears to have succeeded in eliminating the wide seasonal fluctuations that had prevailed in previous years. But a significant increase in output would also depend on making available subsidized inputs and extension advisory services, just as has been done for rice. The 5 percent rise in the wholesale price of rice in the years just prior to the crisis of 1971 is clear evidence of the importance of food grain shortages resulting from excessive summer floods and limited imports,[11] even under normal conditions.

Virtually all the farmers were exempt from the agriculture income tax. Land taxes were fairly nominal at an average of Rs. 5.90 per acre, including land revenue, development and relief tax, education taxes, and Basic Democracies assessment. Thus the tax payments by farmers were mostly in the form of excise taxes on commodity purchases, and various fees and stamp taxes. It had been the intention of the GOEP not to increase taxes on agriculture while the "Grow More Food" campaign was in force. Thus it is obvious that taxes were not a disincentive to changing technology in agriculture. On the other hand, the GOEP planners hoped that an agricultural green revolution would create taxable income, and it would be reasonable for their successors in Bangladesh to expect the same.

Agricultural Credit

Agricultural credit in East Pakistan mainly included taccavi loans, Agricultural Development Bank (ADB) and Agricultural Development Corporation supervised loans, and private moneylenders—the latter furnishing 90 percent of the rural credit at annual interest rates of 50 percent to 100 percent.[12] To expect government or commercial credit agencies to service East Pakistan's small annual operating loans to over 6.2 million farmers on 6 to 7 percent interest is unrealistic. Therefore, before any farmer credit program can be workable in Bangladesh, 12 percent to 15 percent interest, or a combination of interest and service charges as is done in some developed countries, must be accepted. It is too large a program for the government to provide this credit, and commercial banks will become involved only on a remunerative basis. Supervised credit with a large percent being offered in kind could perhaps be best to assure proper credit use. Private sector banks should be approached to plan and cost out a project of this size. ADB-ADC experiences in this field were not successful because of poor servicing by the loaning agencies. A profit motive is apparently necessary to make this type of operation successful.

The GOEP planned in 1970 to provide Rs. 100 crore for assistance to the rural economy to finance agricultural modernization (GOEP 1970*b*). This input was to include Rs. 80 crore of institutional credit and subsidies for inputs plus Rs. 40 crore for rural works. The Rural Works Program fell far short of the Rs. 40 crore contemplated in the early plans for FY 1970. Thus, the total rupee inputs probably fell somewhat short of Rs. 100 crore. If the Rs. 100 crore level had been realized, it would have amounted to almost 10 percent of the gross value at factor cost of total agricultural output. Only 25 percent of the Rs. 100 crore input would have created farmer indebtedness. This is a favorable factor for rapid acceleration of farmer adoption of new technology, especially fertilizer and irrigation, during an initial period, for example, three or four years. On the other hand, this sytem of financing agricultural growth is a major drain on government financial resources, and thus the Bangladesh government must reorganize and modernize farm credit institutions in order that an effective credit system can replace subsidies as early as possible.

The need for accomplishing this has already been recognized by the GOEP authorities who expressed a strong interest in introducing an agricultural credit guarantee fund concept in East Pakistan to assist farmers in their purchase of low-lift pumps and tubewell equipment, and perhaps later on to cover fertilizer purchases. The AID Provincial Office worked closely with local bank officials and the GOEP Planning and Development Department to adopt this scheme to meet East Pakistan's tradition-bound and inadequate agricultural credit system. It is especially promising as a technique of getting private bank resources involved in the agriculture credit program. If adopted by the new government, this revised credit system should be put in full operation as soon as possible, in order to meet the needs that will arise from the contemplated use of greater quantities of fertilizer, pumps, and improved seeds and pesticides, and also to permit some reduction in inputs subsidies.

Perhaps the most promising long-run contribution to a solution of the farm credit problems is the organization and method of the

Academy for Rural Development at Comilla. The credit cooperatives in this system encourage and put much emphasis on farmers'
savings as an integral part of the credit program. As the farms progressively modernize, this approach should contribute greatly to
expanded rural credit. While this basic organization is being set up
in additional thanas, it will, of course, be necessary to proceed with
improvement of the other farm credit institutions and resources
noted above.

Agricultural Research

East Pakistan's agricultural research facilities and capacity
were described in 1969 by the leader of a USAID-financed Agricultural Research Review Team as virtually nonexistent (Parker et al.
1968). The new capital uprooted the traditional agricultural research facilities and it may not have been possible for these
facilities to be replaced and made fully functional before the end of
the then-scheduled Fourth Plan period. This project was in operation and staff training underway but more funds would have to have
been provided for an earlier and a more adequate program. The
limited research personnel in the Ministry of Agriculture had been
undertaking nominal adaptive trials of seeds with alternative practices. The Ford Foundation-assisted Rice Research Station was
constructed and functioning by FY 1970, and it has already made a
solid contribution to the development of IR-20 and other new
strains.

East Pakistan Agriculture University at Mymensingh had a
group of some seventy newly trained young agriculture scientists,
who were expected to begin to produce meaningful research
within the next three to five years had they been given the necessary rupee funds for research, additional research facilities, and the
technical guidance of senior expatriate research advisors, including
several resident senior advisors and short-term visiting advisors, as
needed. A USAID contract with a Georgia University consortium
to provide this assistance was postponed in 1971 by East Pakistani
hostilities.

This foreign input is also required to engender the psychology
of success. It has been wisely said that "enthusiasm is often under-

rated in agricultural development. As happened in West Pakistan, one major accomplishment touches off others within a research service. Years of little or no progress have weighed heavily on the whole agricultural research establishment of East Pakistan. One breakthrough, one success would lead to others, and the research service would begin to contribute the way it should" (Hill and Borlaug 1968).

From the above, it is obvious that Bangladesh's agricultural production progress during the next five years will have to rely to some extent on basic research done in areas with a somewhat comparable climate and ecology, such as the Philippines or other Southeast Asian countries. In addition to this, of course, the adaptive trials involving domestic and imported seed together with varying quantities and varieties of fertilizer, insecticides, and other inputs will be useful—in fact, essential. Presumably the Ford Foundation will continue its support of rice research and the introduction of IRRI varieties.

A relatively modest USAID input of rupees for initiating specific projects at the Agriculture University is desirable. This would be only supplementary to rupees for research, which must be made available by the Bangladesh government. The USAID contribution would be essentially for demonstration purposes. The development of basic and applied research at the university is essential, partly because of the long delay in the development of the research facilities of the Pakistan Ministry of Agriculture. Plant scientists agree that "no country should undertake wide scale introduction of high yield expatriate seed without having available adequate facilities and a substantial corps of plant breeding and related science personnel with the capability to keep up with production problems which multiply on a geometric basis as new and high yield varieties are introduced." [13] Thus, East Pakistan would have been introducing the IRRI varieties at great risk if the Ford Foundation had not provided the minimum necessary research facilities and personnel.

Evidence of this is the limited area and seasonable periods where and when IR-8 and IR-5 may be grown. While under certain conditions these varieties produce yields comparable with those achieved in West Pakistan, the scope for these varieties actually has proven less than optimum. These varieties have not been as disease and insect resistant as are local varieties. During the monsoon, IR-5 and to a certain extent IR-8 are photoperiod sensitive and must be sown late in winter as they are not cold resistant. Varieties now on test show much improvement in disease and insect resistance and in not being strongly photoperiod sensitive in this area. It will, however, be two to three years before enough seed is available, even though these varieties proved successful in province-wide trials.

Agricultural Extension and Training

The FY 1969 USAID-provided Extension Review Team concluded in part that the GOEP Extension Service was badly organized, inadequately trained, and underfinanced. The team made specific recommendations for correcting each of the major deficiencies. The GOEP showed a strong initial interest in the recommendations of the team, and in FY 1970 had the report under study in preparation for interagency discussions intended to arrive at agreement on the recommendations and preparation of plans for implementation. It appeared to the visiting mission that even if the government accepted and implemented the team's report, the effect of these improvements would not have been reflected in production much before 1975. This is because basic institutional changes and enlarged budgets for this kind of service came to fruition slowly in East Pakistan. For Bangladesh, an effort must be made to expand and accelerate the training of key advisory personnel to develop a capability to install, service, and maintain irrigation facilities, and to advise farmers on the efficient use of irrigation water. The urgency of additional training is indicated by the sharp increase in the available supply and planned expansion of the use of low-lift pumps.

Facilities for pump operator training were available at twenty-five zonal workshops over the former Pakistani province. Sixteen zonal shops had facilities for mechanic training, and some 6,000 pump operators and approximately 200 mechanics were trained in FY 1969. To operate the 19,000 pumps that were contemplated for FY 1970, an additional trained corps of 12,000 operators and 600 mechanics was going to be needed. Also required was a corresponding increase in trained personnel who could guide farmers in the proper use of irrigation water. Official reports on the extent to which these inputs were realized in FY 1970 are not available as of this writing, but informal reports indicate that there may have been a significant shortfall in pumps used and an even greater deficit in the training of personnel. In 1968, fourteen training courses were held at twelve locations, and 309 trainees participated. Two USAID advisers, one irrigation and one extension specialist, assisted in the organization and carrying out of these training activities, together with the preparation of instructional materials. A second adviser on irrigation methods reported for duty in December 1968. The emphasis has been on the training of instructors, with a goal of accelerating the training program in keeping with the expansion in pumps and mechanically irrigated areas.

Flood Control

East Bengal's periodic floods, cyclones, and droughts cause tremendous economic loss. A recent instance was the November 1970 tidal bore that wracked vast but still uncounted havoc on human and animal life, crops, and property. The excessive summer floods of 1969 destroyed an estimated 600,000 bales of jute and a substantial acreage of aus crop rice.

The boro or "winter" rice crop is free of floods but is necessarily based on irrigation, the increase of which is retarded by mechanical problems and potentially by limited surface water and groundwater resources during the winter months. This crop reached 2 million acres and may eventually reach 4 million acres out of Bangladesh's 22 million acres of crop land.

Thus increased flood protection for the aus and aman crop is considered to be essential. Expatriate hydrologists have stated that comprehensive water resource management in East Bengal would require cooperative efforts among the riparian countries of the Ganges, Brahmaputra, and Meghna rivers. Since there are no feasible reservoir sites in the country, except Karnaphuli, regulation of the rivers would require major water storage structures near the headwaters of the river systems. The international agreements necessary to create comprehensive river management appear to be possible only in the indefinite future (International Engineering Company 1964).

About 2.5 million acres were receiving flood protection and GOEP studies indicated that it was technically and economically feasible to extend flood protection to some 5 million acres by 1980. After the 1968 flood, the GOEP prepared and sumitted plans for an annual outlay of Rs. 110 crore for fifteen years. This plan was designed to protect 16.8 million acres, of which 13.9 are cropped. There is serious question as to whether the East Pakistan Water and Power Development Authority could, even with optimum foreign assistance, have managed a program of the magnitude proposed. On the other hand, increased flood protection is of such paramount importance that Bangladesh and aid donors should undertake as much of the proposed activity as is technically and economically feasible.

Bangladesh Academy for Rural Development

The activities of the (now Bangladesh) Academy for Rural Development at Comilla, discussed in more detail elsewhere in this volume, made a valuable contribution to rural development in a generally traditional countryside. So successful was the "Comilla Approach" regarded that in FY 1969 a formal proposal was made to extend the academy's projects of comprehensive rural organization and development to all 413 thanas of East Pakistan, and the GOEP in 1969 set up a high level interagency committee to consider this. Unfortunately the proposal came at a time of increased budgetary constraint and interagency jealousies, which combined to delay approval of this important proposal. However, the writer notes with approval that the "Comilla Approach" seems likely to be given high priority in the rural development strategy of Bangladesh as it evolves during the 1970s.

Conclusions

The policy of the government of East Pakistan, restated periodically during the 1967–1970 period, was to achieve self-sufficiency in the production of food grains, to expand jute production and exports, and to increase the output of oil seed and other crops that would upgrade the diets of East Pakistani consumers.[14] Studies made of various aspects of the agricultural sector indicate that East Bengal has soil, water, and climatic resources sufficient to attain the stated objectives even for a substantially increased population. Also the studies indicate that rice and jute, as well as some other important crops, have a comparative advantage, especially on farms that have adopted the new high-yielding seed technology.

With some additional numbers of adequately trained personnel, including expatriate services and a substantial upgrading of statistical services, the Bangladesh development planning establishment should be capable of producing first-rate periodic plans. As soon as possible, annual estimates of rice crops should all be based on an "objective" probability sample.

A shortage of public financial resources for development was a chronic and critical problem for East Pakistan. Private savings and investment have continued at a distressingly low level, that is, some 10 to 12 percent of the provincial annual product. This is about one-half the rate that has been realized in West Pakistan. One important consideration related to this problem has been the average annual transfer from East Pakistan to the western wing of millions of dollars of financial resources, foreign exchange, and rupees, as competent economists convincingly demonstrated. East Pakistan received an estimated one-third of all Pakistan foreign assistance since 1953; this totaled some $1.2 to 1.5 billion. Indications are that East Pakistan transferred financial resources to the West over two decades roughly equal to all foreign assistance received by East Pakistan.

Although the problem of disparity in allocation of domestic and foreign-supplied resources between the two wings of Pakistan has now disappeared, it is nonetheless important for Bangladesh to raise far more public revenue from its economy than was ever done while East Bengal was part of a united Pakistan. An obvious start should be made by cost-reducing measures in the revenue collection sector. Also, there appear to be promising opportunities for inducing a substantial increase in private savings and investments. Proposals in this area are beyond the scope of this paper, yet the topic is most important to the future development of the Bangladesh economy, including the agricultural sector.

Bangladesh inherits most of the development-oriented institutions needed to administer development programs and projects. However, most of them have a history of being limited by weak management systems and in some cases archaic practices, for example, accounting methods and personnel policies. Most of the government agencies had able men at the top, some are outstanding, but the top layer was always far too thin, a problem that is likely to continue in the short run. Expatriate assistance to help in the revision and modernization of management and in the training of personnel appears to be the most promising course of development action. A major program of upgrading agricultural research and training extension personnel for field service to promote modern agricultural technology must be given high priority.

Economic incentives for farmers appeared to be adequate in 1971. Improved seed and fertilizer prospects seem to be generally favorable for the near future, but the potential deficits that now threaten Bangladesh could slow down development unless rapid efforts are made to expand in this whole area. Irrigation development was off to a good start under the aegis of TIP, and targets can be reached with adequate further training of personnel and confirmation that the winter water supply will be available and adequate.

The development of agricultural credit facilities and the entrance of private bank resources plus expansion of the Comilla Farmer Credit Cooperatives appear to be the most promising solutions to the farmer credit problem.

Periodic flood damage to Bangladesh's crops is of such a magnitude that if not dealt with it may jeopardize achievement of agricultural production goals. Only 2.5 million acres of land achieved protection but it may be feasible to double the protected area over a five-year period. This would involve a series of limited area projects and *would not* include comprehensive river management based on headquarters reservoir construction.

Finally, with respect to agricultural development institutions, the Comilla comprehensive rural organization approach to modernizing all aspects of farm production and rural life appears most promising, and it is urged that Bangladesh make available the policy determination and financial resources to introduce this proven system to all its thanas.

Charles M. Elkington was director of Agriculture in the USAID mission, Dacca, 1967–1970. He received his Ph.D. in Agricultural Economics in 1947 from the University of Wisconsin, and in addition to being a faculty member of Washington State and Iowa State universities, he served in many U.S. government roles overseas. He was with the USAID mission in Pakistan from 1961 until his retirement in 1971.

NOTES

1. Rural works accounts for 11.2 crore out of the 33.8 crore total for food and agriculture.
2. Mahbub-ul-Haq (1963:100) and John H. Power (1963:205). Roger Norton notes that during 1967/68 East Pakistan's estimated import of shipping and military services, plus its export of capital to the West Wing, amounted to Rs. 2005 million (1969:5, 23).
3. The lowest fertilizer-using districts were Jessore, Pubna, Sylhet, Khulna, Barisal, and Faridput. The high-use districts were Chittagong, Hilltracts, Bogra, Comilla, and Dacca.
4. During FY 1971, less than 3 percent of East Pakistan's total cropped area—under 600,000 acres—were under new varieties. [Ed. note]
5. The more reliable "objective" estimates of FY 1968 and 1969 rice production show a 1969 decline of 600,000 tons in the aman crop, as well as a 400,000-ton decrease in the aus crop. A half-million ton decrease in the 1969 crop, below 1968, appears consistent with rising rice prices and larger import needs.
6. For more detail on IR-20 in 1970, see Rochin (1971). Despite production setbacks due to the civil war and its aftermath, the new government in Dacca is highly attuned to the role that new varieties, along with increased efficiency in their dissemination, must play in the country's agricultural development. Accordingly, its first annual development plan, launched in July 1972, envisioned bringing 3.5 million acres under production with the new high-yielding varieties. The "Comilla Approach" to "integrated rural development" appears to have taken precedence over the former ADC-oriented approach, discussed above as a major strategy in the diffusion of agricultural innovations, including the new varieties. Eighty-three thanas were covered by the Comilla program in 1972/73, and, via gradual rephasing and cumulative addition of new acres, coverage of 410 thanas is targeted for the end of 1977 (Bangladesh Embassy 1972). [Ed. note]
7. Even after the effects of the civil war, Bangladesh was able to irrigate

a little over 1 million acres during 1971/72, or about 5 percent of its total cropped area. The Thana Irrigation Program, pioneered at Comilla, played a key role in this effort. [Ed. note]

8. GOEP 1969*b*: section on farmers' supply response to relative change in prices of raw jute and aus crop rice.

9. Rabbani, in a paper on "An Approach to the Fourth Plan Formulation in Pakistan," said, "Another important policy area will be the level of subsidy on agricultural inputs during the Fourth Plan and the timing of its gradual reduction" (1968:11).

10. Government of Pakistan (1969:128) and unpublished reports of the Government of East Pakistan.

11. As indicated in his preliminary discussion of the approach to the Fourth Plan, Ghulam Rabbani, chief economist, Planning Department, Government of East Pakistan, attached importance to rice price policy. He stressed the need to study the effects of rice pricing on key output variables in formulation of policy during the plan (1968:11; Appendix, p. 8).

12. Taccavi loans are administered by the Agriculture Department. These loans are, in part, of a "relief" nature, i.e., they are provided to assist farmers who have suffered losses from floods or other disasters with purchases of inputs, food, etc. The repayment rate on these loans is low and begins late.

13. This was recently emphasized by the research team visiting Pakistan in 1968 and has been documented and emphasized by Dr. Borlaug and other plant scientists.

14. As indicated in the annual development plans for FY 1969/70, this government also gave high priority status to the Family Planning Program and its objectives.

BIBLIOGRAPHY

Bangladesh Embassy
  1972. *Bangladesh*. (News Bulletin) Vol. 2, no. 15 (July 28) and no. 25 (Dec. 15). Washington, D.C.: Bangladesh Embassy.
Government of East Pakistan (GOEP)
  1964. *Statistical Digest of East Pakistan*. Dacca: East Pakistan Government Press.
  1965. *Statistical Digest of East Pakistan*. No. 3. Dacca: East Pakistan Government Press.
  1966. *Statistical Digest of East Pakistan*. Dacca: East Pakistan Government Press.
  1967*a*. *Economic Survey of East Pakistan 1966–1967*. Dacca: East Pakistan Government Press.

1967*b*. *Statistical Digest of East Pakistan*. Dacca: East Pakistan Government Press.

1968*a*. *Economic Survey of East Pakistan 1967–1968*. Dacca: East Pakistan Government Press.

1968*b*. *Statistical Digest of East Pakistan*. Dacca: East Pakistan Government Press.

1969*a*. *East Pakistan Annual Development Plan FY 1969*. Dacca: Planning and Development Department.

1969*b*. *Monograph on the Jute Economy*. Dacca: Planning and Development Department.

1969*c*. *Economic Survey of East Pakistan FY 1969*. Dacca: East Pakistan Government Press.

1970*a*. *Agricultural Sector Paper in the Annual Plan*. Dacca: Planning and Development Department.

1970*b*. *East Pakistan Annual Development Plan FY 1970*. Dacca: Planning and Development Department.

Government of Pakistan

N.d. "Consortium Memorandum" on the Third Five-Year Plan.

1966. *The Third Five-Year Plan 1966–1970*. Karachi: Government of Pakistan Press.

1969. *Year Book of Agricultural Statistics*. No. 7, January, Rawalpindi.

Haq, Mahbub-ul

1963. *The Strategy of Economic Planning: A Case Study of Pakistan*. Karachi: Oxford University Press.

Harvard Advisory Group (HAG)

1970. "East Pakistan Food Grain Supplies and Prices." Unpublished paper (FY 1970), which includes multiple correlation analysis of retail rice prices and analysis of the availability of food grains. Dacca: East Pakistan Planning Department.

Hill, F. F., and Borlaug, Norman

1968. *Report to President Ayub Khan*. Karachi: Ford Foundation.

International Engineering Company

1964. *Master Plan Report to East Pakistan Water and Power Development Authority*. San Francisco: International Engineering Company.

Larson, D. G.

1969. *Government of East Pakistan Crop Estimate Statistics*. Dacca: USAID.

Norton, Roger

1969. "Some Aspects of Interwing Resources Transfers in Pakistan."

Manuscript reproduced by the Asia Bureau, Agency for International Development, Washington, D. C.

Parker, Frank, and Associates
1968. "A Report on Agricultural Research in Pakistan." Manuscript reproduced by the Asia Bureau, Agency for International Development, Washington, D. C.

Power, John H.
1963. "Industrialization in Pakistan: A Case of Frustrated Take-off?" *Pakistan Development Review* 3(2):191–207.

Rabbani, A. K. M. Ghulam
1968. "An Approach to the Fourth Plan Formulation in Pakistan." Mimeographed. Dacca: Planning and Development Department, Government of East Pakistan.

Rochin, Refugio I.
1971. "Farmer's Experiences with IR-20 Rice Variety and Complementary Production Inputs: East Pakistan Aman 1970." Report to the Government of Pakistan and the Ford Foundation, January 1971 (Revised May 1971). Rawalpindi: Ford Foundation.

5

Comilla Rural Development Programs to 1971

Robert D. Stevens

... The crucial feature of traditional agriculture is the low rate of return to investment in agricultural factors of the type that farmers have been using for generations. ... In order to transform this type of agriculture a more profitable set of factors will have to be developed and supplied. To develop and to supply such factors and to learn how to use them efficiently is a matter of investment—investment in both human and material capital. (Schultz 1964:8)

Introduction and Background

This paper focuses on the nature and status in 1971 of six major rural development programs originating at the Academy for Rural Development in Comilla, Bangladesh. Due to their importance in the progress of work at Comilla, more detailed analysis has been presented of the Agricultural Cooperatives Federation and the Thana Training and Development Center Program. Four other programs are examined briefly: the Rural Public Works Program, the Thana Irrigation Program, the Women's Program and Family Planning, and the Rural Education Program.

A consensus among economists is that the social and economic transformation of low-income developing societies is dependent upon the continuous flow into agriculture of investments in modern technology with high economic returns. Less emphasized in the literature about economic growth from traditional agriculture are the associated institutional changes required in this transformation. The elaboration of a large number of new or modified institutions accompanies rapid economic growth or may be induced by economic change (Hayami and Ruttan 1971). These nonmarginal economic changes are in the public, quasi-public, and private sectors.

After 1947 with the withdrawal of the British, a major change in the role of governmental systems occurred on the South Asian subcontinent, which sought to shift primary emphasis from law and order, and tax collecting to developmental activities. How to modify or create more effective governmental and other institutions at the local level for more rapid economic and social development was a task facing the two wings of Pakistan and the academy in the late 1950s.

An exceedingly complex set of questions are involved in determining how to go about changing institutional arrangements so as to aid in accelerating farmers' investments in modern technology in the varied cultural, economic, and technical environments in different parts of the low-income world. One extreme strategy is to attempt to assure that highly productive agricultural technology is available in the society and then encourage private entrepreneurs to come forward and make the investments that will result in accelerated growth. Another extreme strategy is based on the assumption that government has the most knowledge about new agricultural technology and therefore knows best how to and is most able to rapidly develop agriculture. This approach often has included the unproved assumption of large economics of size in agriculture and has involved the complete reorganization of rural society into large collective or communal farms, such as in the well-known cases of the USSR, Yugoslavia, the People's Republic of China. Both these extreme strategies have had serious shortcomings from an economic as well as other points of view. In contrast, the well-documented, less-extreme national strategies for accelerating agricultural growth in small farm agriculture in Japan (Johnston 1966; Ohkawa et al. 1970), Taiwan (Hough and Ness 1968; Shen 1970), and earlier in Denmark (Skrubbeltrang 1953) have had considerable success. Currently in the developing nations, a number of carefully worked-out approaches and experiments are underway, attempting to accelerate the economic and social transformation of rural society without the mistakes of attempting to directly transplant foreign models. The rural development programs developed at the Pakistan (now Bangladesh) Academy for Rural Development are one set of these experiments. The Swedish aid work at the Chilalo Agricultural Project in Ethiopia is another (Nekby 1971). A different approach was followed in the Puebla Project in a rainfed area of Mexico (Myren 1970).

The Environment of the Comilla Rural Development Programs

The physical environment of the academy is presented in detail in a number of studies (including Muyeed 1969), as well as in many academy research publications. A salient feature of the environment is the owner-operated rice farm with an average landholding of 1.46 acres. The overwhelmingly dominant rice crop is grown in all three seasons, aus, aman, and boro, under a tropical monsoon climate with an extensive summer rainy season involving flooding of much of the land and a rainless winter season. Rice occupies about 90 percent of the cropped acreage. The average cropping intensity was 1.6 in 1968.

The social environment and background of the activities at Comilla have been documented and described in many academy publications and have been summarized as well (Raper 1970; Stevens 1972; Asian Studies Center 1974). In brief, rural development programs in Comilla were developed by a new type of rural training institution, the Academy for Rural Development, charged with providing members of the government administration with improved knowledge about how to increase the rate of social and economic development in rural areas. When the academy began in 1959, its staff consisted of ten professionals, only two of whom had Ph.D. degrees. the expertise of this faculty was primarily in the social sciences, education, psychology, sociology, economics, and political science.

Methods Used in Developing Programs

Bold experimental and pilot fieldwork were fundamental to the wide-ranging impact of the programs discussed below. Pilot activities were conducted by the Academy for Rural Development in one thana (county) containing 107 square miles and, in 1961, 217,297 people. These rural development programs were strategies for the involvement of the people of the area. They were designed to provide a way in which farmers and others could gain increasing access to meaningful economic, political, and social activities. The activities have been the result of careful experimentation in the local cultural environment. Continuing research and evaluation of programs have been reported in academy publications.

These development programs, it should be stressed, were limited largely to improved organizational activities focused on supplying more profitable new technology to farmers, including the provision of training to insure the required investment in human capital for productive use of the new technology. In this process, academy personnel undertook a great deal of local testing of crops and farm equipment. The academy was not assigned the task of developing new and more profitable agricultural technologies, although at least one important technological change was pioneered by the academy—the hand-digging of tubewells.

The methods used in the rural development programs developed out of a need of the academy at its establishment in 1959. In an early statement, Akhter Hameed Khan, the first director of the academy and dominant figure in the development of the programs at Comilla, said:

> Our training activities have been formulated around these rules: that training should be supported by research; that training should be supported by experimental efforts to test theories and find workable procedures. . . . When we began work, the first serious problem was that the instructors had no experience in rural development. Whatever knowledge they had was of an academic nature. The instructor in rural business management had only the experience of having managed to get himself out of the village! Our ignorance could not be removed by reading books. The number of surveys of this part of the world is very small and most of these are about India. But even these only described things as they exist. We were here to try to discover things as they should be and then plan the training accordingly. (Khan 1963:1)

In 1960, experimental and pilot activities were facilitated when Comilla Thana was designated as a development laboratory in which programs and administrative experiments could be undertaken by the academy. Although villagers were the primary target group of the experimental programs, some urban citizens in the city of Comilla were benefited, particularly by the cooperative credit activities.[1]

With respect to the overall goals of the rural development programs, Dr. Khan's view in 1963 was:

> What we are trying to evolve here is a pattern for the future administration of East Pakistan at the Thana level. This is our primary aim. We are not engaged in a little experiment. It is by no means an academic exercise or simply a research project. It is an attempt to find out what can be done to bring about the soundest and quickest economic and social development all over East Pakistan. (Khan 1963:12)

This approach led to the elaboration of various experiments and pilot programs, six of which are examined below. The relationship between the pilot programs at Comilla and the resulting province-wide programs are taken up in appropriate places later in the paper.

Comilla-Type Agricultural Cooperatives

Beginning with experimental activity in 1959, a new system of cooperatives was developed in Comilla Thana to take the place of the largely defunct union cooperatives. This section focuses on evaluation of the Comilla agricultural cooperatives after ten years of development, by analyzing the economic effect of the cooperatives on farmers, examining the financial condition of the agricultural cooperative federation, and by assessing the social impact of the cooperatives. More detail is provided about this program as it was the first one established and it helped set the pattern for subsequent programs of heavy involvement of village people associated with appropriate training.

Approach and Organizational Growth

Central to the success of the cooperative program was the general methodological approach used.

From August, 1959, the Academy has been closely observing the working of plans and programs in the 80-square mile Comilla Thana V-AID area. We have attended regularly the fortnightly conferences of the V-AID workers and listened attentively to their views and the view of the officers. We have also invited selected groups of successful farmers, teachers, office bearers of the cooperatives, artisans and others. We have made case studies of all these groups and carefully recorded their opinions and suggestions and published these in the shape of small monographs.

The Academy has taken this area as a laboratory for social and economic research and experiments because we believe that such experiments and researches are necessary in order to put substance into our training programs and make them realistic. It is also the best use of the talents of the team of experts at the Academy. . . .

We think that we are now in a position to initiate an experiment in agricultural and economic development which may be very significant. Briefly the chief objective of this experiment would be to promote the formation of small cooperative groups of farmers who would adopt improved methods, implements and machines. A small group cooperative would aim to become self-sustained. The members would learn to save and collect their own capital and invest it in better farming. (*A New Rural Cooperative System for Comilla Thana* 1961:64)

From this approach, a cooperative system was developed consisting of small village credit cooperatives run by villagers, and a central cooperative at the thana level, which was responsible for promoting new agricultural technology and providing the necessary agricultural supplies, extension training, credit, and the supervision of record keeping. The requirement that a village select three individuals who were to be their own cooperative leaders and who would receive training at the academy made unnecessary the injection of outsiders into the village cooperative scene. As a result of this approach, the Comilla cooperatives have been based upon natural social groupings (Bertocci 1970).

From early experimental work with village cooperatives in 1959 (Rahim 1961; Stevens 1967a), the number of cooperatives grew among farmers and other groups. By June 1969, there were 301 village agricultural cooperatives and a central agricultural cooperative federation in Comilla Thana (Table 1). Membership in this federation included 11,673 villagers, or an average of 37 members per society. The average loan issued was $53 while savings and shares equaled about $30 in an area where per capita incomes were estimated at $100. Even more rapid development of village cooperatives occurred in three other thanas, each a great distance from Comilla, and in the seven additional thanas of Comilla District (Table 1). In view of the dismal history and the great difficulties faced by cooperatives in developing societies, the record of growth and performance of the voluntary cooperatives in Comilla Thana over an eleven-year period was an incredible achievement.

The program content of the cooperatives is focused on the provision of loans and agricultural inputs to farmers. The loans provide the primary source of income for both the central agricultural cooperative federation and its associated village primary

TABLE 1. Status of Comilla-Type Agricultural Cooperatives, 1970

Agricultural Cooperatives System	Average Number of Cooperative Societies per Thana	Average Number of Cooperative Members per Thana	Average Shares and Savings per Member	Average Loan Issued per Member	Overdue Loans over Total Loans (%)
Comilla Thana 1960/61–1968/69	301	11,673	$28.98	$52.71	2.0 more than 1 year
Three External Thanas 1963/64–1968/69	229	5,873	10.34	57.75	4.4 (2.5 more than 1 year)
Seven Comilla District Thanas 1965–Nov. 1970	196	5,620	19.53	54.60	9.5

SOURCE: *A New Rural Cooperative System for Comilla Thana* (1970:18) and Khan 1971.

cooperatives. In 1968/69, 60 percent of these loans were for two- or three-years' duration (*A New Rural Cooperative System for Comilla Thana* (1970:27).

The new technology content of the cooperative programs has been a fundamental element of success. The major technologies provided by the cooperative organization include: (1) The introduction and operation of low-lift water pumps beginning in 1959 (*A New Rural Cooperative System for Comilla Thana* 1961; Mohsen 1969). (2) The pilot development of low-cost hand-dug six-inch tubewells begun in 1962, including necessary operational supervision, maintenance, repair, and parts supply. (This development of intermediate technology in Bangladesh is the most outstanding original technical contribution of the Comilla programs and is examined by Haq in chapter 7.) (3) Pilot and adaptive research beginning in 1960 on the use of four-wheel, 35-horsepower tractors for rice and other crops. In ten years a great deal of experience had been gained with these tractors, but it is fair to say that, although 6,154 acres were cultivated by seventeen tractors by 1969, a solution has not yet been found to the economic operation of this size of tractor in agriculture in the Comilla area (Faidley 1973). (4) Adaptive research and testing of new crop varieties and animals with the assistance of Japanese, Danish, and United States technicians. In 1966, the first IRRI varieties of rice available for use in East Pakistan were tested and promoted (Bari 1969; Kazi 1969). (5) Adaptive research, supply and promotion of agricultural inputs including particularly chemical fertilizers, pesticides, and improved seeds. (6) A number of storage and processing activities employing new technology, especially cold storage plants, dairy processing, and rice milling. Although the academy as a social science institution was lacking in technological expertise, it succeeded in obtaining, through foreign assistance and Pakistan government agencies, access to technically competent individuals.

The academy's need for outside technical knowledge points to an important weakness in its original concept. The experience of the work at the academy shows that social scientists working in rural areas of developing nations are at a great disadvantage if they lack effective access to high quality agricultural and other technical knowledge. An institution of this nature either requires a few highly competent individuals trained in fields of agricultural technology or a workable way to gain regular access to such persons located in other agencies.

Economic Impact on Farmers

The economic effect of agricultural cooperatives on farmers is difficult to measure because of the joint relationships between the credit and the other activities for the supply of modern inputs to agriculture. Although the results presented below are not all due to cooperative activity, there is little doubt that a major share of the economic impact is due to this work. The impact is measured by the extent of farmer coverage and the effect on production and income. Some concluding comments focus on employment, income distribution, and land tenure issues.

When examining the economic impact of the cooperative program for farmers, it is useful to distinguish cooperative members from others. In Comilla Thana, in 1968/69, 37 percent of the farmers were cooperative members. An average of 22 percent were members after five years of cooperative activity in seven other thanas of Comilla District (Khan 1971).

Due to the lack of farm management studies in the Comilla area, economic benefits can only be measured indirectly in terms of changes in inputs and yields. For winter rice, Faidley and Esmay concluded that within five years almost all farmers, both cooperative members and other villagers, had adopted high-yielding winter rice varieties, which on the average more than doubled rice yields for both groups (see chapter 6). The growth of purchased inputs was significant for winter rice. In 1966, cooperative members used commercial fertilizers at the rate of about $4 per acre on unimproved rice varieties; in 1970, with almost 100 percent use of improved rice varieties, commercial fertilizer increased to more than $16 per acre among cooperative members (chapter 6, Table 8). It is particularly significant that nonmembers of cooperatives were able to purchase and apply almost the same amount of commercial fertilizer per acre for this crop. Thus, in spite of the fact that cooperative membership was limited to less than 40 percent of the farmers, other farmers were able to obtain large quantities of fertilizer and seed directly or indirectly from the cooperatives.

Other evidence of economic gains by cooperative farmers based on unpublished data gathered by Rahim show that, by 1969, a control group of farmers outside Comilla Thana had increased yields by only 10 percent as compared with 98 percent for Comilla cooperative farmers. An estimate of net family assets showed an increase of 19 percent for the control group as compared to an increase of 61 percent among Comilla cooperative members (Thomas 1971a).

An estimate of direct benefits of cooperative credit was obtained by assuming conservatively that one-quarter of an average farmer's debt was shifted from a 60 percent interest rate to the effective interest rate of 17.4 percent possible through cooperatives. Such a change increases annual net income by some thirteen dollars (Stevens 1967b). For farmers with per capita annual incomes of one hundred dollars this is an appreciable gain.

In conclusion, there is little doubt that in Comilla Thana the small village cooperatives and their thana-level cooperative federation had considerable economic impact on a majority of villagers by increasing their income. The two groups least benefited were the very small farmer, the approximately 20 percent of the village families with less than one acre of land, and the landless laborers representing some 19 percent of the families.

The Economic Stability of the Cooperative Federation

By 1970, after ten years of development, the Comilla cooperative system had demonstrated its administrative and financial stability. In this section, credit arrangements are outlined followed by analysis of financial progress and problems.

In the noninflationary environment of the 1960s in East Pakistan, loans were obtained by the members of the village cooperatives at an interest rate of 10 percent plus a service charge of 5 percent per annum. Of the 10 percent interest, 2 percent was paid back to the village cooperative society to build its own fund, 4.5 percent was paid to the financing bank as interest and 1 percent was paid to the village cooperative manager as his commission. The thana-level association retained 2.5 percent to meet its own costs.

The 5 percent service charge was used for salaries of the village accountants, who maintained the accounts of the primary societies, and to provide traveling allowances to the village cooperative managers, the village model farmers, and the chairmen of the primary societies, as well as to members of the managing committee of the central association. An allowance to the thana officers for teaching classes also was paid from the service charge.

The amount of the loans to a village cooperative was dependent upon the sum of its savings and shares. In the 1968/69 accounting period, savings and shares amounted to 35 percent of the loans.

Shares purchased by farmers obtained a 5 percent dividend in 1968/69. A fixed 4 percent interest was paid on cooperative members' savings accounts.

Central to any successful credit cooperative is loan repayment experience. Comilla-type cooperatives have had manageable amounts of overdue loans and bad debts (Table 1). Although further effort is required to reduce overdue loans, other data on the rapid growth of membership, savings accumulated by members, loans issued and realized all point to financial and organizational health. Financial success is indicated by continuing asset growth. The profit and loss statement for 1968/69 showed a net loss of about 1 percent on the total income of the agricultural cooperative federation. The expenditures in this account include about 5 percent of the total income for agricultural extension activities. An important question is whether the cooperatives should have to carry the whole of this technical education cost (*A New Rural Cooperative System for Comilla Thana*, 1970).

From the point of view of the national treasury, the Comilla cooperative system was an immense step forward. Loans of the *taccavi* type through the old union multipurpose cooperative societies, which had been mostly captured by local notables, had annual loan repayment rates of only about 40 percent. No other formal organizations have been able to reach large numbers of small farmers with significant amounts of credit in rural areas of Bangladesh.

Strong evidence that the Comilla cooperative system held further promise came from the approval, in the fall of 1970, of the Integrated Rural Development Program by the central government of Pakistan. Administered by the Department of Agriculture, this program was to establish an agricultural cooperative federation and village cooperatives on the Comilla model in all 413 thanas within a nine-year period. This program has been given high priority by the Bangladesh government and is currently (January 1975) being implemented with a target coverage of 413 thanas by 1977.

The magnitude of the projected investment per thana was $21,000 in annual recurring administrative and training costs, including $15,430 for training and extension and $5,570 for salaries, as well as an annual disbursement of loan funds to each thana of $210,000 for five years. Complete repayment of the loan fund was planned for twenty-five years. The single capital grant for buildings, transport, and office equipment was $42,000 per thana (Government of Pakistan 1970).

Social Impact

Social impacts of the cooperatives, although difficult to document precisely, appear in a number of ways. In many villages, the cooperatives are still too young (three to five years) to have had a major influence on the social system. However, in a number of instances, the village cooperative manager has been asked to participate with traditional leaders in settling disputes.[2] A further development reported by one instructor is that when villagers want to get things done, they now go to the village cooperative manager rather than to the traditional leaders or the elected union councillor.[3] There is little question about the impact of the cooperatives on the agricultural information system. Research in the thana shows that village cooperative members adopt new practices earlier and have higher proportions of adoption in all time periods (Rahim 1963, 1965, 1968).

With respect to educational impact, the weekly training of model farmers from the village cooperatives at the thana headquarters is a major educational input. This training is reinforced by subsequent discussion in the villages, often aided by written lesson material. The cooperatives also have supported literacy classes for men, women, and children.

The impact of cooperative activities has been positive on

employment rates. Most of the changes in agriculture have been employment creating, particularly the major increase in winter crop acreage due to irrigation. The cost and returns studies provide estimates of additional labor used with the new high-yielding varieties (Rahman 1967). It is recognized that there has been some displacement of hand irrigation by low-lift pumps and of animal plowing by tractor cultivation, but the net effect on employment of these two changes appears to have been positive.

With respect to the impact of cooperative activities on values, Schuman, in a pioneering social-psychological study, found that Comilla cooperative farmers had a statistically reliable increased belief that their own efforts can overcome obstacles and realize goals, as compared with control groups in other parts of East Pakistan (Schuman 1967).

The impact of the Comilla activities on government and politics should be considered together. The strong impact of Comilla on certain government programs such as rural works and irrigation is discussed below. Despite this, however, Governor Monem Khan continued to take a negative view of the academy and its activities during the mid-sixties.

Thana Training and Development Center

Introduction and Problem Situation

Just as the returns to investment on a farm are dependent upon the level of management performance, at the thana or county level, the quality of government program operations and management greatly influences the return to government programs. Involved here are issues of institutional or nonmarginal change in an administrative system. The return to program investment is dependent both on the productivity of the specific project activities and on the rate of adoption.

The changed concepts and institutional arrangements for local government organization embodied in the Thana Training and Development Center program represented equally fundamental departures from past operating procedures as did the new cooperative system. Together these programs were the progenitors of other programs, including the four programs analyzed in the latter part of this paper.

This analysis is focused on factors affecting the rate of adoption of programs at the thana level. Such factors include: confusion and conflict among programs; lack of necessary coordination, especially in ensuring availability of required program supplies; also ". . . part of the trouble was that the nation-building departmental officers were not yet ready to plan with the local people and to report to them directly" (Mohsen 1963); and, departmental officers were not able to gain needed participation by villagers in programs.

Government program performance at the thana level in East Pakistan was generally poor in 1959, consisting of independent departmental activities (Agriculture, Cooperatives, Water, etc.), which in a larger number of cases provided low or negative returns. In the early exploratory analysis of problems in the thana, the Comilla academy concluded that a solution to these problems required three kinds of coordination: coordination of different departmental programs at the thana level; coordination of departmental efforts with those of the next lowest level of government, the unions; and coordination between the different unions (Mohsen 1963:12).

At about the time the academy was undertaking its exploratory analysis, the Ayub Khan government of Pakistan established the five-tiered Basic Democracies system of government in October 1959. From the point of view of improved governmental management at the local level, the five-tiered Basic Democracies system was a significant departure from the past history of governmental organization in which the lowest effective governmental unit had been the district, with an average population in East Pakistan of more than two million. The new system added two lower levels of government: the thana and union levels. A union council was elected at the lowest level. A union in 1961 had an average population of 12,544 in East Pakistan. The new system also established a thana council at the next level above the unions and below the district. Thana council membership comprised the elected chairman of each union council, plus government officials (25 percent) and appointed members (25 percent). (For more details, see chapter 3.)

Since in the previous government organization, the district

level, particularly in the person of the deputy commissioner, retained most of the decision-making power and control of funds and personnel, the question was posed as to what powers and activities were appropriate for the new lower levels of government. As it turned out, the Rural Works Program became one major area of successful activity of the thana and union councils with 71 percent of the works program allocations going to these levels of government in 1966/67 (Pakistan Academy for Rural Development 1968). The works program demonstrated that certain kinds of activities, such as road building and water-control earthworks, could be effectively carried out by these new lower levels of government.

Experimental Pilot Activities in Rural Government

In spite of the success of the public works program, there remained many questions about how to improve the management of government programs at the thana level. The history of the academy's experimental activities for the development of improved rural administration is contained in six annual reports (*Annual Report* 1963–1969).

Experimental activity for the development of improved rural government began in 1960. These activities by the academy faculty led to a 1963 proposal for the establishment of an experimental Thana Training and Development Center. In 1964, the concept was accepted and funds were allocated for province-wide elaboration in all the nonurban thanas of East Pakistan (*Annual Report* 1964). By 1970, most thanas in the province were using development centers similar to that piloted at Comilla.

The concept of the Thana Training and Development Center includes the following major objectives (see also Figure 1):

(1) one physical location at the thana level for all major nation-building department offices
(2) a small adjacent adaptive research and experimental farm
(3) housing for government officers sufficiently attractive to encourage them to stay in the thana for many years
(4) physical facilities for adult- and farmer-training classes— the training center

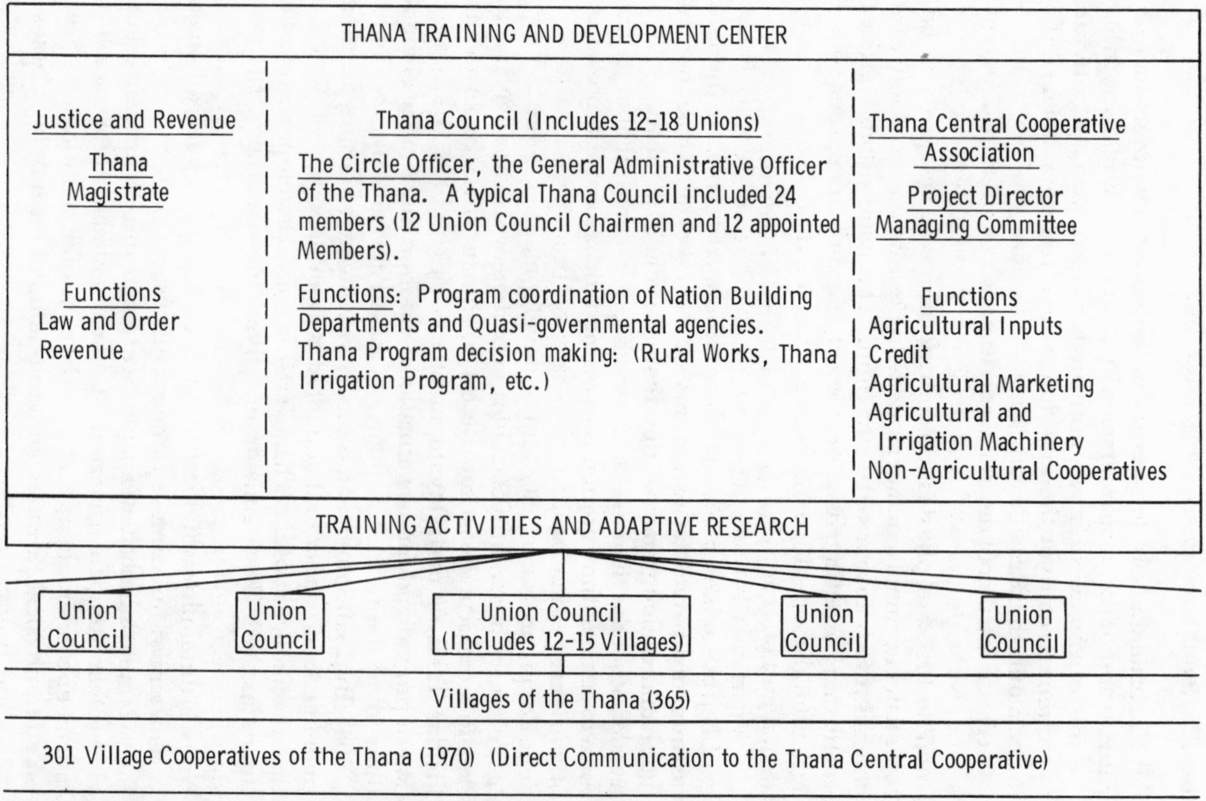

THANA TRAINING AND DEVELOPMENT CENTER

Justice and Revenue

Thana Magistrate

Functions
Law and Order
Revenue

Thana Council (Includes 12-18 Unions)

The Circle Officer, the General Administrative Officer of the Thana. A typical Thana Council included 24 members (12 Union Council Chairmen and 12 appointed Members).

Functions: Program coordination of Nation Building Departments and Quasi-governmental agencies. Thana Program decision making: (Rural Works, Thana Irrigation Program, etc.)

Thana Central Cooperative Association

Project Director
Managing Committee

Functions
Agricultural Inputs
Credit
Agricultural Marketing
Agricultural and Irrigation Machinery
Non-Agricultural Cooperatives

TRAINING ACTIVITIES AND ADAPTIVE RESEARCH

| Union Council | Union Council | Union Council (Includes 12-15 Villages) | Union Council | Union Council |

Villages of the Thana (365)

301 Village Cooperatives of the Thana (1970) (Direct Communication to the Thana Central Cooperative)

Figure 1. The Thana Training and Development Center System, Comilla, East Pakistan, 1970.

(5) Enough land for additional activities as needed such as warehouses, machinery repair shops, a bank, and so forth
(6) an effectively functioning thana council, including elected representatives from the unions and representatives of the nation-building departments
(7) a central cooperative association to serve farmers.

The first five physical objectives were relatively easy to accomplish once decisions were made to allocate the needed works program funds to purchase and build. The more difficult task of establishing an effectively functioning thana council and a sound agricultural cooperative organization has required years of experimental and pilot activity.

A particularly difficult continuing challenge in Comilla Thana has been the achievement of effective cooperation in developmental programs between the administrative and elected members of the thana council under the leadership of the general administrative officer of the thana—the circle officer. A second challenge has been to activate the training component of the center. Examination of five changes made in Comilla through June 1969 provide evidence of progress.

First, as a result of the pilot experiences in Comilla Thana, greatly increased allocation of funds was made to the thana councils for the Rural Works program and the Thana Irrigation Program. These programs represent a major increase in thana council functions.

Second, although the Basic Democracies order for the first time required departmental officers to report their activities to the thana council, as well as through the usual departmental routes to their superiors, the establishment of this important new relationship between government officers and the representative thana council did not develop easily. In Comilla, through hard work, a certain amount of increased communication was achieved between the two groups, but the *Tenth Annual Report* of the academy concludes that attendance in the thana council by these officers leaves much to be desired, and that up to June 1969 the circle officer had no administrative control over departmental officers in the thana (Khan and Hussain 1963:15). Mohsen commented, "Activating the departmental officers seemed to be more difficult than mobilizing the people"(Mohsen 1963:18).

Third, the success of the thana council in providing a forum for effective coordination of the programs in the different unions became very clear in the development of rural works program plans. Instead of receiving comprehensive plans drawn up in district or higher offices that had little possibility of implementation and no genuine support from local leaders, the new approach started the planning process for works programs from the village level. Finally, after many meetings including appropriate departmental officers and other technical experts, a thana rural works plan was approved with implementation steps included—implementation steps that could be carried out. Preventive health and crop- and animal-disease plans were developed in a similar manner. In this way, the required coordination of activities in different unions was achieved.

Fourth, successful operation of the thana training center was achieved through a wide variety of training classes and activities for many categories of the rural population, including women, union council members, farmers, bricklayers, religious leaders, and so forth. In 1968/69 in Comilla, forty-nine training programs were organized with an attendance of 2,226 persons. In many of these programs, departmental officers assumed new roles as teachers, thereby increasing contact with rural people and their practical problems.

Fifth, considerable experimentation continued in Comilla on appropriate administrative relationships among the three major parts of the Thana Development and Training Center (Figure 1). By 1970, in Comilla and other areas, the circle officer apparently had been accepted at least in principle as the chief administrative officer in the thana.[4] However, recent actions of certain departments and officials counter to this administrative model indicate continuing problems (Thomas 1971; Khan 1971).

Evaluation

How may the increased economic and social returns to the use of government funds as a result of improved organization and institutional relationships be evaluated? In Comilla Thana, as in most areas, a number of major variables changed along with changes in government organization. The joint products are difficult to separate. Little data on governmental performance levels are available and experimental controls are not possible. The following judgments are, therefore, made.

From an economic point of view, the returns obtained from both the Rural Public Works Program and the Thana Irrigation Program were dependent upon the Thana Development and Training Center's organization and concepts. Without the center and its training activities, these programs would have either failed completely or would have provided much lower returns.

In social terms, the most important result has been the new and improved relations between government officers and villagers. "Undoubtedly, the most wholesome influence is that of the new relationship between officers and villagers . . . . There is guidance and supervision without undue subordination. There is trust arising from mutual knowledge . . . . They have now a realistic view of government and its agencies . . . . but as human agencies with limited resource, established for their benefit, and solicitous of their loyalty" (Khan and Hussain 1963:15).

Subsequent support of the Comilla rural development model by the World Bank in its East Pakistan Action Program provided additional evidence of the economic and social soundness of the Thana Training and Development Center's organizational system (Thomas 1971*a*).

Rural Public Works Program

As the personnel of the Academy for Rural Development interacted with other government officials in the thana and the villages, the academy staff became more directly aware of the extent of annual crop damage caused by floods. In particular, flooding affected the ability of farmers to repay cooperative credit. Raper indicated that in one area south of Comilla town, for five years in succession prior to 1961, the spring rice crop had been severely damaged and the late summer rice crop often had to be transplanted two or three times before the seedlings could keep ahead of the rising flood waters (Raper 1970:107). There was continual pressure to do something about the flooding.

In 1961, Richard B. Gilbert of the Harvard Advisory Group asked the director of the academy if he could organize public works programs in the villages to increase employment and income, using wheat as part payment for wages under the PL 480 program. Discussion in the thana council in October 1961 ended with approval of a proposal for a thana-wide pilot public works program. As a result, twenty-one schemes for irrigation and drainage and three schemes for flood control were submitted by eleven union councils early in 1962. By the end of the year, 35 miles of canals had been cleared and 14.5 miles of embankments and roads had been constructed to help control floods. This included the construction of two water regulators and twenty-three culverts.

The success of this pilot program led the Department of Basic Democracies and Local Government to authorize funds for a program to be carried out in many parts of East Pakistan in 1962/63. The Comilla academy participated in the training of government officials for the expanded operation. A *Manual for Rural Public Works* was written, which explained the procedures used in the rural works program. Evaluations of works program activity were also undertaken (Pakistan Academy for Rural Development 1963a, 1965; Sultan 1966)

The works program was increasingly supported by the government in East Pakistan. Its success led to a rural works program in West Pakistan as well. Thomas provided a summary of Rural Public Works Program accomplishments in East Pakistan for the years 1962–1968 as follows: Roads, hard-surfaced and dirt, new, 21,895 miles; repaired, 118,371 miles; Embankments, new, 3,743 miles; repaired, 7,595 miles; Drainage and irrigation canals, new, 9,031 miles; repaired, 9,966 miles; Community buildings including schools, 9,584. This activity is estimated to have created a total of 173 million man-days of employment or 40 million annually. The total works program allocations for the period were 196 million dollars. Thomas concludes that the rural works program was remarkably successful in providing a major increase in infrastructure facilities in rural areas. In benefit-cost terms he estimated a 57 percent return to funds invested in the program (Thomas 1968, 1971b).

Thana Irrigation Program

In spite of heavy rains and floods during the summer, water is short for crops in the dry winter season in which less than two inches of rain falls per month from November to February. Hence, irrigation is necessary for most crops during this season. The initial approach to winter irrigation involved use of the accumulated water in ponds and rivers through low-lift mechanical pumps. It was soon recognized, however, that available surface water in many areas was used up quickly during the dry season. Experimental activity in the use of tubewells was therefore undertaken.

The early experience with these activities is reported in a number of publications (Rahim 1961; Pakistan Academy for Rural Development 1963b; Rahman 1964). Data on the growth of irrigation activities and the problems faced are documented in the annual reports of the academy and by Raper. Basic problems in these programs relate to reducing the costs of the tubewells, assuring the continuous operation and repair of the tubewell pumps and engines, and assuring payment for the wells. The cooperative system analyzed earlier provided a solution to these managerial problems.

The experiments and pilot operations at Comilla led to decisions in 1968 to launch the province-wide Thana Irrigation Program. The target of the first year, 1968/69, was to distribute and operate 11,500 low-lift water pumps for irrigation, and for the East Pakistan Agricultural Development Corporation to sink 700 tubewells of 6-inch diameter. The evaluation report states that 10,852 low-lift pumps were used in the 1968/69 season and 638 tubewells were sunk, of which nearly 200 went into operation during the year (Mohsen 1969:21).

By the end of 1970/71, the Thana Irrigation Program had placed 26,000 operating pumps in the field capable of irrigating 1.3 million acres. Due to the thana-level organization and training approach used, farmers were persuaded to pay part of the irrigation cost. The magnitude of this organizational success based on the Comilla experience is better gauged by the fact that the East Pakistan Water and Power Development Authority in twenty years had only been able to irrigate 94,563 acres at immense cost, and that after a nine-year effort the Agricultural Development Corporation had only fielded 3,900 pumps (Thomas 1971a). Subsequently the

Bangladesh government has allocated major additional resources to the Thana Irrigation Program.

Women's Program and Family Planning

> One cause of our misery and poverty is that we keep our womenfolk at home guarded over constantly. We keep them indoors, We have almost imprisoned them. We do not educate them, and because they are confined, they cannot educate themselves; so they are nearly all illiterate. They are timid. And so long as the women are uneducated, development can hardly be expected in our country. (Khan 1963*a*:2)

Following this philosophy, the academy developed a Women's Program, whose basic aims have been well summarized:

> The women's program is intended to bring women out from the physical and psychological seclusion that has withheld their productive energies from the mainstream of development. They are to learn how to get about independently and with dignity, how to earn small sums of money through a variety of economic activities convenient to their household obligations, and how to enrich the health and social life of their families. (Luykx 1970:363)

In attempting to provide more opportunities for women, exploratory conversations between village men and women and academy staff resulted in the decision to develop a series of training programs for women at the academy. These commenced in 1962 and have continued to date. Training classes have included such subjects as child care, maternity diseases, family planning, literacy, sewing, spinning, poultry raising, gardening, sanitation, first aid, and silk-screen printing. More specialized training programs were also developed for midwives. Economic activities of the program for women commenced with the provision of hand-spinning machines in 1963. Other economic activities have included sewing and weaving, poultry raising, and the use of wheat in diets, which led to training in family nutrition. In the 1968/69 year, thirteen different training groups involved 304 women in classes of seven to fifty days (Annual Report 1970; Ahmed 1969). In 1969, women's programs patterned after those at Comilla were introduced by the Agricultural Development Corporation in three experimental farm project areas in different parts of East Pakistan.

In association with the women's program, an experimental family planning activity was undertaken in 1962, with support from the Provincial Department of Health. This pilot, rural family-planning program had three parts: action, promotion, and research. The research was partly supported by the Population Council and included technical assistance by a number of overseas researchers. Valuable lessons were learned from the villagers' responses to different approaches used in providing both materials for family planning and in teaching the use of family-planning devices. These research results were of particular value in a Muslim rural society where there was considerable uncertainty about the acceptability of family planning. Effective promotional techniques developed at the academy involved the creation of songs about family planning, which were sung in local markets and on government radio (Raper 1970:172–185; Annual Report 1970:85–88; Mannan 1968).

Action elements of the program were integrated with the national family-planning scheme in 1965, under the administrative control of the thana family-planning officer. Research and experimental program activities have continued with a view to using the family-planning activities in Comilla Thana as models for the rest of the province (Raper 1970:183–185).

Rural Education Experiments

In 1959, the academy estimated that only one-fifth of the population over five years of age in Comilla Thana was literate. The academy undertook four experiments in education beginning in 1961. They were: (1) the introduction of a "rural bias" (farm-life-related education) in the rural schools through a pilot school project; (2) the establishment of "feeder schools" in villages with cooperative societies (these were one-teacher village schools for small children and adult illiterates); (3) the training of village women to teach adult literacy classes in the villages and to teach small children in government primary schools; and (4) the school-plant improvement project.

In 1969, the status of these programs was as follows. The pilot school project had evolved into a youth club program in all the sixty-nine primary schools in the thana, with a membership in 1968/69 of 5,720 students. Teachers, however, were reported to be reluctant to participate in the youth club programs without additional pay. The feeder school program had become an imam (religious leader) teacher program. The imams were given training in literacy methods at the academy. In 1968/69 they taught 136 classes to 4,227 students, and operated literacy classes for 2,875 adults.

The women's program included sixty-eight female literacy classes in which 2,375 women were enrolled. School-plant improvement became part of the Rural Public Works Program in 1964. Under this program, a large number of classrooms were built and repaired in Comilla Thana (*Annual Report* 1970:75–81; Muyeed 1966; Bhuiyan 1968).

As of 1971, the experiments in rural education in Comilla Thana had had some success and were continuing. However, the Department of Education and other units of government had not yet seen fit to adopt these activities as models for broader programs. Whether this was due to the limited success of these experiments or to a lack of understanding of their usefulness is not clear.

Conclusions and Generalizations

A majority of rural citizens have benefited through increased income from the academy's experimental and pilot activities at Comilla. Also through the Thana Training and Development Center under the Basic Democracies sytem of elections, and the agricultural cooperatives, villagers increased their political and social involvement in planning and local decision-making. As a result, economic and social benefits of the Comilla programs have been widespread.

The generalizations about the experience at Comilla that follow are in three parts— those concerning experimental programs generally, those focused on agricultural cooperatives, and those related to the development of rural government.

The literature on economic growth from traditional agriculture has placed little emphasis on the associated institutional changes required in the agricultural transformation. A large number of new or modified institutions are essential for rapid economic growth. These nonmarginal economic changes occur in the public, quasi-public, and private sectors. In Pakistan, a major change required of the main governing system was a shift in focus from law-and-order and tax-collecting activities to developmental activities.

In this chapter, six major programs of the Academy for Rural Development in Comilla were examined. The promising women's program and rural education experiments were presented briefly. Up to 1971, they had had only limited national impact. The Thana Irrigation Program and the Rural Public Works Program were also discussed only briefly, as there is a considerable literature available about these nationally adopted programs. Major focus in the chapter was placed upon the new type of agricultural cooperatives and the improvement of rural government through the Thana Training and Development Center. Conclusions about the possible usefulness of these three experiences for other nations follow.

Comilla Experimental Development Programs

The following points about the work at Comilla in developing programs appear fundamental to their success.

1. A large number of exceedingly valuable pilot and experimental activities in rural development were conducted in Comilla at relatively small cost to the treasury.
2. An experimental, open-minded approach, involving a great deal of interaction with rural people, was essential to the programs' success.
3. A wide range of subject matter activities, including agriculture, education, roads, women's programs, and health were undertaken because of the interrelations between these activities and the reinforcement of programs that result in the minds of rural citizens.
4. As successful experiments moved to the pilot stage, the target agency for the operation of the wider program was kept in mind and was brought into the planning and operations as soon as possible.
5. The evaluation function was essential to document change, and to aid in reviewing the effectiveness of programs.

The New Type of Agricultural Cooperatives

Beginning with experimental pilot activities in 1959, a new type of village agricultural cooperative was developed in Comilla Thana. By 1971, 301 agricultural cooperatives were registered in the thana with 11,673 members. Loans overdue more than a year among this group were at a 2 percent level. Expansion of this cooperative system into ten other thanas resulted in a total of 2,360 village cooperative societies with a total membership of 68,632 by 1971.

Evaluation of the effects of these cooperatives in Comilla Thana indicate they have had major economic impact. A number of studies show rapid increase in input use, in the planting of high-yielding varieties, and in rice production. Between 1964 and 1969, one comparative study contrasts an estimated 10 percent increase in rice yields in an adjacent thana, where cooperatives have only recently been organized, against a 98 percent increase in rice yield in Comilla Thana. In 1970, in Comilla Thana where per capita incomes were in the $100 range, the central agricultural cooperative federation and its village cooperative societies operated a credit program with an average loan of $53 per member with per member shares and savings equal to $29. This cooperative system was financially stable with steady annual increases in loaning activity. Additional evidence of the promise of the system came from approval in the fall of 1970 for the expansion of these types of cooperatives to all 411 thanas of East Pakistan. Additional impact of the cooperatives in the social and political areas has also been shown.

The following points are of particular importance in considering the development of this type of village cooperative system.

1. The Comilla experience has demonstrated that small farmers in low-income nations can be organized voluntarily into effective village cooperatives. This system, therefore, represents a viable rural institutional system for serving small farmers.
2. This cooperative approach includes: small primary units of up to sixty members based upon preexisting social groups, a cost of credit to farmers approaching 15 percent, and a pos-

sible requirement, particularly in the early stages, of partial monopolies in the supply of new inputs to defray the appreciable costs of serving small farmers.

3. Integral to the system is the self-selection of the leaders of the primary cooperatives coupled with their continuous training in cooperative management and new agricultural technology.
4. The combination within the cooperative of agricultural extension activities and the provision of credit is productive. Through local communication channels, the agricultural knowledge extended through the cooperative passes to all members of the village; hence, the national treasury may appropriately pay some of the costs of extension carried out by the cooperatives.
5. Vital to success of the system is the continuous access of the central cooperative organization to new, high-return, agricultural technology.

Improving Rural Government—The Training and Development Center

Early activity by the academy focused on improving local government performance. The result was the acceptance by the East Pakistan government in 1964 of the thana training and development center concept for the 413 thanas in East Pakistan. The physical facilities for those centers had been completed in most thanas by 1970.

Continuous effort by the academy has been focused on the more difficult task of greatly improving the performance of government officials at the thana level. Major successes were achieved in pilot activities that developed the thana-level Rural Public Works Program and the Thana Irrigation Program. The models developed at Comilla were the basis for province-wide expansion of these programs, recognized nationally and abroad as significant contributions to rural development in Bangladesh. Without the changed concepts of rural government that they embodied and the kind of organization for local development that they demonstrated, these activities would either have been impossible or of much lower productivity. The World Bank in its East Pakistan Action

Program of 1970 supported this rural development model for local administration.

The following points about the approaches and programs of the Comilla Rural Training and Development Center appear important.

1. Rural areas require a training and development center at a central physical site that includes all the agencies needed by rural people. The center should be as close as possible to a heavily frequented market. In connection with the establishment of such a center, care is required that these services of the lowest levels of government be located so that most rural citizens may conveniently conduct their business in a round trip by local transportation during one day.
2. Rural government should focus on activities that affect most rural residents directly and that require joint action. To assure effective action, responsibility for development activities such as roads, water control, schools, and health should be clearly separated from other rural government functions such as law and order and taxation. In the Comilla experience, rural government was not effective in agriculture and other specialized sectors that involved only a portion of the population directly. Responsibility for these specialized development activities should be clear; they appear to require specialized organizations such as the agricultural cooperatives or other special cooperatives.
3. A training center should be an integral part of rural government. All significant institutional and program changes require certain amounts of training for different groups: farmers, women, government officials, and so forth. Also, the experience of having officers from the agriculture department and other agencies take on the new role of teachers of rural citizens has proved to be of considerable value to both groups, particularly in increasing communication and understanding.
4. Of particular value was the regular bringing together in the thana council of representatives of government agencies and valid representatives of rural people for discussions of

plans and action programs. In this way, villagers gained much increased involvement in local government decision-making. Improved program performance resulted, as representatives of government agencies have the technical expertise and control of the allocation of major funds and supplies and rural leaders were able to obtain decisions from communities and mobilize people to participate in development projects.

5. Of fundamental importance in developing successful pilot programs is the early participation of agencies for which the pilot program may become a model. Joint planning and operation of pilot programs with target agencies should be undertaken to as great an extent as possible so that the program, if successful, may more easily become adopted as the agency's own.

Robert D. Stevens served as an adviser to the Academy for Rural Development at Comilla as a member of the Michigan State University Pakistan Project. He received his Ph.D. degree in Agricultural Economics from Cornell University in 1959, and has conducted research in a number of nations in Asia and Latin America. He is currently associate professor of Agricultural Economics at Michigan State University.

NOTES

1. See particularly pages on the Special Cooperative Societies Federation in Pakistan Academy for Rural Development, *A New Rural Cooperative System for Comilla Thana*, 1961, and Annual Reports for the years 1962–1970.

2. Personal communication with Peter Bertocci.

3. Personal communcation with Anwarul Hoque, instructor, Bangladesh Academy for Rural Development.

4. Personal communication with R. R. Faruqee, C.S.P.

BIBLIOGRAPHY

Ahmed, Jahrunessa
    1969. *Women's Education and Home Development Program.* Fourth Annual Report for 1966–1968. Comilla: Pakistan Academy for Rural Development.

Asian Studies Center
    Forthcoming. *Bibliography of Publications Relating to the Pakistan
        Academy for Rural Development in Comilla, 1959–1971.* East
        Lansing: Asian Studies Center, Michigan State University.
Bari, Fazlul
    1969.   "A Comparative Yield Trial with Different IRRI Selections."
            Comilla: Pakistan Academy for Rural Development. Mimeo-
            graphed.
Bertocci, Peter
    1970.   Elusive Villages: Social Structures and Community Organiza-
            tion in Rural East Pakistan." Ph.D. dissertation, Michigan
            State University.
Bhuiyan, Ali Asgar
    1968.   *Imams as Teachers.* Comilla: Pakistan Academy for Rural De-
            velopment.
Faidley, LeVern W.
    1975.   "Computer Simulation of the Cooperative Approach to Tractor
            Mechanization in a Developing Country." Ph.D. dissertation,
            Michigan State University.
Government of Pakistan
    1970.   *P. C. I. Form on the Integrated Rural Development Pro-
            gramme.* Islamabad: Planning Commission, Government of
            Pakistan
Hayami, Yujiro, and Ruttan, Vernon W.
    1971.   *Agricultural Development: An International Perspective.* Bal-
            timore: The Johns Hopkins University Press.
Hough, Richard L., and Ness, Gayl D.
    1968.   "The JCRR: A Model for Internationally Induced Develop-
            ment." *International Development Review* 10 (3): 14–17.
Johnston, Bruce F.
    1966.   "Agriculture and Economic Development: The Relevance of
            the Japanese Experience." *Food Research Institute Studies* 6
            (3). Stanford: Food Research Institute, Stanford University.
Kazi, O. H.
    1969.   *Potato Research Project Report.* Comilla: Pakistan Academy
            for Rural Development.
Khan, Akhter Hameed
    1961.   Letter to Chief Secretary of East Pakistan, dated Comilla,
            January 15, 1960, as printed in *A New Rural Cooperative Sys-
            tem for Comilla Thana.* First Annual Report. Comilla: Pakis-
            tan Academy for Rural Development.
    1963a. "The Role of Women in a Country's Development." Transla-

tion of a talk in Bengali, presented on March 5, 1963, at the Pakistan Academy for Rural Development, Comilla, East Pakistan. As quoted from Arthur F. Raper, *Rural Development in Action*. Ithaca: Cornell University Press, 1970.

1963*b*. "The Basic Principles of the Comilla Program." East Lansing: Asian Studies Center, Michigan State University. Mimeographed.

1971. *Tour of Twenty Thanas*. Comilla: Pakistan Academy for Rural Development.

Khan, Akhter Hameed, and Hussain, M. Zakir
1963. *A New Rural Cooperative System for Comilla Thana*. Third Annual Report. Comilla: Pakistan Academy for Rural Development.

Luykx, Nicholas G. M.
1970. "The Comilla Project, East Pakistan." In *Change in Agriculture*, edited by A. H. Bunting, pp. 361–370. London: Gerald Duckworth.

Mannan, M. A.
1968. *The Comilla Pilot Project in Family Planning*. Fifth Progress Report. Comilla: Pakistan Academy for Rural Development.

Mohsen, A. K. M.
1963. *The Comilla Rural Administration Experiment: History and Annual Report 1962–1963*. Comilla: Pakistan Academy for Rural Development.

1969. *Evaluation of the Thana Irrigation Program in East Pakistan 1968–1969*. Comilla: Pakistan Academy for Rural Development.

Muyeed, Abdul
1966. *School Works Program*. Comilla: Pakistan Academy for Rural Development.

1969. "Strategies Involved in a Development System of Planned Social Change in Rural East Pakistan." Ph.D. dissertation, Michigan State University.

Myren, Delbert T., ed.
1970. *Strategies for Increasing Agricultural Production on Small Holdings*. A Report on an International Conference, Puebla, Mexico. Mexico City: International Maize and Wheat Improvement Center.

Nekby, Bengt
1971. *CADU—An Ethiopian Experiment in Developing Peasant Farming*. Stockholm: Prisma Publishers.

Ohkawa, Kazushi; Johnston, Bruce F.; and Kaneda, Hiromitsa

1969. *Agriculture and Economic Growth: Japan's Experience.* Princeton: Princeton University Press.

Pakistan [now Bangladesh] Academy for Rural Development, Comilla.

1963a *An Evaluation of the Rural Public Works Program, East Pakistan, 1962–1963.*

1963b *The Comilla Pilot Project in Irrigation and Rural Electrification.* (Rev. ed., 1966).

1963c *The Comilla Rural Administration Experiment—History and Annual Report 1962–1963.* Subsequent annual reports for 1964, 1966, 1967, 1968, and 1969.

1965 *An Evaluation of the Rural Public Works Program, East Pakistan, 1963–1964.*

1968 *The Comilla Rural Administration Experiment—Annual Report for 1967.*

The following two entries present reports published in succeeding years under one title. Publication information presented in the first entry of each title are pertinent except where otherwise noted.

A New Rural Cooperative System for Comilla Thana. Comilla: Pakistan Academy for Village Development, Pakistan Academy for Rural Development.

1961. *First Annual Report for 1960.*

1962. *Second Annual Report for 1961–1962.*

1963. *Third Annual Report for 1962–1963.*

1965. *Fourth Annual Report for 1963–1964.*

1966. *Fifth Annual Report for 1964–1965.*

1967. *Sixth Annual Report for 1965–1966.*

1968. *Seventh Annual Report for 1966–1967.*

1969. *Eighth Annual Report for 1967–1968.*

1970. *Ninth Annual Report for 1968–1969.*

Annual Report. Comilla: Pakistan Academy for Village Development, Pakistan Academy for Rural Development.

1960. "First Annual Report." Mimeographed.

1961. "Second Annual Report for June 1960–May 1961." Mimeographed.

1962. "Third Annual Report for June 1961–May 1962." Mimeographed.

1963. *Fourth Annual Report for June 1962–May 1963.* (First report with name of Pakistan Academy for Rural Development.)

1964. *Fifth Annual Report for June 1963–May 1964.*

1965. *Sixth Annual Report for June 1964–May 1965.*

1966. *Seventh Annual Report for June 1965–May 1966.*

1967. *Eighth Annual Report for June 1966–May 1967.*
1969. *Ninth Annual Report for 1967–1968.*
1970. *Tenth Annual Report for July 1968–June 1969.*

Rahim, S. A.
1961. *Voluntary Group Adoption of Power Pump Irrigation in Five East Pakistan Villages.* Pakistan Academy for Rural Development. Technical Publication No. 12. Comilla: Pakistan Academy for Rural Development.
1963. *Diffusion and Adoption of Agricultural Practices.* 2nd ed. Comilla: Pakistan Academy for Rural Development.
1965. *Communication and Personal Influence in an East Pakistan Village.* Comilla: Pakistan Academy for Rural Development.
1968. *Collective Adoption of Innovations by Village Cooperatives in Pakistan.* East Lansing: Department of Communication, Michigan State University.

Rahman, Mahmoodur
1964. *Irrigation in Two Comilla Villages.* Comilla: Academy for Rural Development.
1967. *Cost and Return Study: A Study of Irrigated Crops in Comilla Villages.* Comilla: Academy for Rural Development.

Raper, Arthur F.
1970. *Rural Development in Action.* Ithaca: Cornell University Press.

Schultz, T. W.
1964. *Transforming Traditional Agriculture.* New Haven: Yale University Press.

Schuman, Howard
1967. *Economic Development and Individual Change: A Social-Psychological Study of the Comilla Experiment in Pakistan.* Center for International Affairs, Occasional Paper No. 15. Cambridge, Mass.: Center for International Affairs, Harvard University.

Shen, T. H.
1970. *The Sino-American Joint Commission of Rural Reconstruction.* Ithaca: Cornell University Press.

Skrubbeltrang, F.
1953. *Agricultural Development and Rural Reform in Denmark.* Agricultural Studies No. 22. Rome: Food and Agriculture Organization of the United Nations.

Stevens, Robert D.
1967a. *Institutional Change and Agricultural Development: Some Evidence from Comilla, East Pakistan.* Agricultural Econom-

ics Report No. 64. East Lansing: Department of Agricultural Economics, Michigan State University.

1967*b*. "Notes on Project Costs and Gains to Cooperative Farmers, Comilla Thana, East Pakistan." Unpublished draft.

1972. *Rural Development Programs for Adaptation from Comilla, Bangladesh*. Agricultural Economics Report No. 215. East Lansing: Department of Agricultural Economics, Michigan State University.

Sultan, K. M. ed.

1966. *The Works Program in Comilla Thana: A Case Study 1962– 1966*. Comilla: Pakistan Academy for Rural Development.

Thomas, John W.

1968. "Rural Public Works and East Pakistan's Development." Ph.D. dissertation, Harvard University.

1971*a* "Agricultural Production, Equity and Rural Organization in East Pakistan." Preliminary draft presented to Research Workshop on Rural Development in Pakistan, Asian Studies Center, Michigan State University.

1971*b* "The Rural Public Works Program in East Pakistan." In *Development Policy II: The Pakistan Experience*, edited by W. P. Falcon and G. F. Papenek, pp. 186–236. Cambridge, Mass.: Harvard University Press.

6

Introduction and Use
of Improved Rice Varieties:
Who Benefits?

LeVern Faidley and Merle L. Esmay

Introduction

There is lack of agreement as to who benefits from the improved crop varieties and modern farming practices introduced by the green revolution. This chapter presents an analysis of the effect the green revolution has had on the farmers of Comilla Thana in Bangladesh, where since 1960 an experimental laboratory has been developed for the testing of rural development programs by the Academy for Rural Development. As this rural development concept is to be replicated throughout Bangladesh, this analysis provides some indication of the probable results and benefits throughout the country.

Farm Size and Subsistence Incomes in Comilla Thana

Comilla Thana in 1969 contained 51,560 acres of agricultural land and had a population of approximately 200,000 people, an average density of 2,500 people per square mile. In 1969 there were approximately 31,000 families living in the villages of the thana. About 15 percent of the families were landless and about 70 percent owned less than 2 acres (Table 1). The mean landholding per rural family was 1.46 acres. In almost all cases, landholdings consisted of fragmented, widely scattered plots, ranging in size from 0.10 acres to 0.40 acres with a negligible number of plots larger than 1 acre.

Muyeed's data on income levels of the families living in the agricultural villages, as appraised by the families themselves, show that 44 percent of the families considered themselves as living at

TABLE 1. Landholdings of Agricultural Families

Landholdings	% of Families
no cultivable land	15
0.01 – 0.8 acres	26
0.81 – 2.0 acres	28
2.01 – 4.0 acres	18
4.01 – 6.0 acres	8
over 6.0 acres	5

SOURCE: Muyeed (1969).

less than a subsistence level of income, while 27 percent considered themselves at a subsistence level (Table 2). Table 1 indicated that 41 percent of the people had less than 0.80 acres or were
landless, while 28 percent of the people had from 0.8 to 2.0 acres.
If it is assumed that there is a correspondence between landholding
size and income levels, then the landless and those families with
less than 0.80 acres (41 percent) probably had incomes below the
subsistence level, while those with 0.81 to 2.0 acres (28 percent)
would appear to have had incomes approximately at the subsistence level. Families with more than 2.0 acres would then make up
the majority of persons with incomes above the subsistence level.

Membership in Comilla Cooperatives

The Academy for Rural Development introduced the cooperative scheme into Comilla Thana in 1960. Primary cooperative

TABLE 2. Income Levels of Agricultural Families

Income Levels	% of Families
Income below subsistence level	44
Income at subsistence level	27
Income above subsistence level	22
Income at higher level	7

SOURCE: Muyeed (1969).

societies were formed in the agricultural villages and a central cooperative was established to provide the primary cooperatives with (1) banking and supervised credit; (2) agricultural extension and training; (3) agricultural inputs, including mechanical power; (4) water development, irrigation, and rural electrification; and (5) processing and marketing facilities.

Rapid growth of the primary cooperative societies resulted in members owning 51 percent of all land in the thana in 1969 (Table 3).

Over 37 percent of the families in the thana belonged to cooperatives in 1969. Although no direct evidence is available to indicate a causal relationship, accelerated cooperative growth took place in the three years from 1967 to 1969, at the time improved rice varieties were being adopted.

The largest single category of cooperative members (43 percent) were farmers with landholdings from one to two acres (Table 4). Of farmers with this size of landholding, 68 percent belonged to cooperatives. Most cooperative members owned the medium and larger landholdings in the area. Families with more than one acre

TABLE 3. Growth of Cooperative Membership and Land Ownership in Comilla Thana

Item	1964/65	1965/66	1966/67	1967/68	1968/69
Number of agricultural coops	152	158	225	251	301
Number of coop members	4,910	5,161	8,462	11,518	11,673
Percent of families who are coop members	15.7	16.5	27	36.7	37.3
Land owned by coop members (acres)	10,100	11,700	19,150	26,050	26,410
Percent of total land owned by coop members	19.6	22.7	37.2	50.5	51.2

SOURCE: Pakistan Academy for Rural Development (1970).

TABLE 4. Distribution of Total Population and Cooperative Membership by Farm Size

Farm Size in Acres	% of Total Rural Population	% of Cooperative Members	% of Rural Population Who Are Coop Members
nil	15.3	2	5
.01–1	30.5	12	15
1.01–2	24.2	43	68
2.01–3	14.4	18	47
3.01–5	10.6	16	56
over 5	5.0	8	60

SOURCE: Akhter (1969).

made up 86 percent of the cooperative membership while only 55 percent of the total rural population owned one acre or more. The landless and near landless (those with less than one acre) made up over 45 percent of the total population; however, they represented only 14 percent of the cooperative membership.

There are several reasons that may explain why the landless and near landless families did not belong to the cooperatives. First, Comilla cooperative societies required that members make regular cash and in-kind savings deposits, which many families with low incomes would find difficult to do. Second, the loan policy of the cooperative generally excluded persons with less than one acre from taking its loans, and thus, the small landholders and low-income families could not easily benefit from cooperative membership. Fortunately, as is shown later, this did not prevent some of these persons from benefiting from the agricultural transformation that has taken place in Comilla Thana.

Irrigation—A Strategy for Agricultural Development

Under conditions of traditional agriculture and unpredictable weather, the high uncertainty involved in growing crops during both the aus and the aman seasons has often meant that investments made in these crops were lost. The academy therefore judged that the greatest return from investment could be realized during the dry winter season when the loss due to weather would be minimal. However, crops grown during this season required irrigation. Since winter irrigation was very limited in the thana before 1960 because manual irrigation methods were primarily employed, a mechanized irrigation scheme was proposed. This scheme involved using low-lift water pumps from perennial water sources and deep tubewells to tap the groundwater sources.

Since 1965, mechanized irrigation has expanded greatly and replaced much of the manual irrigation (Table 5).

The irrigation program was administered through the Central Cooperative Association, which was responsible for the installation and maintenance of the tubewells and pumps. The wells and pumps were only located in villages where there were cooperatives and then only when these cooperatives made a request and paid a rental fee in advance. This rental fee was a flat rate per pump or tubewell and was independent of the acreage irrigated. The village cooperatives were responsible for digging and maintaining channels for the distribution of the irrigation water, as well as for setting

TABLE 5. Winter Crop Coverage (in acres) under Different Irrigation Methods

Irrigation Method	1965	1966	1967	1968	1969
Tubewell	1018	1127	2412	3891	6201
Power Pump	129	170	727	1227	2324
Total Mechanized	1147	1297	3139	5118	8525
Manual [a]	6024	5493	3967	2186	1430
Natural [b]	1290	870	874	1324	853
Total Traditional	7314	6363	4841	3510	2283

SOURCE: Pakistan Academy for Rural Development (1965–1970).

[a] Manual irrigation refers to water moved by hand without the aid of any mechanical devices.
[b] Natural irrigation refers to low-lying areas where sufficient standing water is retained to grow a crop without irrigation.

up a procedure for sharing the irrigation water among the people who were to use it. Although the pumps were rented to the village cooperative societies, use of the water was not limited to cooperative members. Often persons who were not members, but who had land within the area that could be irrigated, purchased irrigation water from the cooperative societies, usually at a price somewhat higher than that paid by cooperative members. This has permitted persons who were not cooperative members to participate in winter cropping and derive benefits from it.

The Impact of Improved Varieties

With this background information concerning the organization for agricultural development, the effect of the introduction of improved rice varieties will be considered. Since improved rice varieties have, at this writing, mainly been designed for use on irrigated land during the dry winter season, this discussion is limited to the introduction of improved varieties during this season. First, the effect of cooperative membership on the adoption and yield of improved varieties and the use of recommended practices will be discussed, followed by analysis of the effect of farm size on the growing of improved varieties.

Rate of Adoption

Improved rice varieties for the winter cropping season were first introduced for general use by farmers in Comilla Thana in 1965. Cooperative members were the first to adopt improved varieties of rice and their rate of adoption was rapid, from 7 percent to 98 percent in only five years (Table 6). However, the rate of adoption by persons who were not cooperative members was even more

TABLE 6. Rate (%) of Adoption of Improved Varieties

	1966	1967	1969	1970
Coop Members	7	31	87	98
Nonmembers	—	1	66	98

SOURCE: Pakistan Academy for Rural Development (1965–1970).

remarkable—increasing from 1 percent to 98 percent in only four years. The lag in adoption by persons not in the cooperative can probably be attributed to the assumed high risk of growing improved varieties during their initial introduction. However, once a third of the cooperative members demonstrated that the varieties could be successfully grown, and that there were large economic benefits to be derived from them, adoption by almost everyone quickly followed. Until 1970 only three types of new varieties were grown: IR-8, Pajam, and Taipei-177. In 1970, however, the East Pakistan Rice Research Institute made available several additional improved varieties, which were used by some of the cooperative members. The nonmembers, however, chose to grow only the three original improved varieties.

Yield

Yields from improved varieties were two to three times larger than for nonimproved varieties each year. There was also a steady annual increase in yields for the improved varieties. The cooperative members were continually able to obtain higher yields for both improved and nonimproved rice varieties. It is important to note, however, that although the yield for improved varieties was continually larger for cooperative members than nonmembers, the

TABLE 7. Yield of Improved and Nonimproved Rice
(in maunds)

	1966	1967	1969	1970
Improved rice:				
Coop members	35.09	43.49	44.02	48.14
Nonmembers	——	33.20[a]	40.36	44.76
Nonimproved rice:				
Coop members	16.94	18.00	19.25	16.56[a]
Nonmembers	11.74	15.21	15.74	25.16[a]

SOURCE: Pakistan Academy for Rural Development (1965–1970).
NOTE: 1 maund = 82.29 pounds.
[a] These values were derived from survey data containing less than four observations.

magnitude of the difference between their yields decreased from 24 percent in 1967 to 7 percent in 1970 (Table 7). In 1966 and 1967, with most persons growing nonimproved rice varieties, cooperative members growing these varieties had 30 percent and 16 percent greater yields, respectively, than nonmembers. In 1970, with almost everyone growing improved varieties, cooperative members had only a 7 percent greater yield than nonmembers growing these varieties. Thus, it appears that the improved varieties contributed to an equalization of yields between cooperative members and nonmembers. The effects of cooperative membership on yields, therefore, were actually less with the improved varieties than they were with the nonimproved varieties.

Method of Sowing

The use of improved varieties has brought many changes in almost all farming operations. In 1966, 62 percent of the cooperative members and 40 percent of the noncooperative rice growers broadcast their rice. Twenty-seven percent of the coop members and 58 percent of the nonmembers random transplanted their rice. Only 11 percent of the cooperative members and 1 percent of the nonmembers transplanted their rice in lines, which was the improved planting method. In 1970, 99 percent of both cooperative members and nonmembers used line transplanting. Line transplanting requires about twenty man-days per acre compared to eighteen man-days per acre for random transplanting and two man-days per acre for broadcasting. Thus, the use of improved varieties significantly increased the labor requirement for sowing. Line transplanting is important in growing improved varieties since it makes cultivation and plant protection operations easier.

Weeding

Weeding is the second farming operation that has changed greatly with the introduction of improved varieties. In 1966, 60 percent of the cooperative members and 82 percent of the nonmembers did no weeding in growing the winter crop. In 1970 all of the cooperative members and all but 1 percent of the nonmembers used some type of weeding. Of those weeding in 1970, 70 percent of the cooperative members and 53 percent of the nonmembers used both hand and machine weeding while 29 percent of the cooperative members and 45 percent of the nonmembers used only hand weeding. Machine weeding refers to a small, one-row weeder, which is pushed by hand between the rows of rice in the paddy field. In hand weeding in 1966, both cooperative members and nonmembers weeded the crop an average of 1.25 times. In 1970 they weeded the crop an average of over 2.2 times. Those weeding both by machine and by hand weeded over 3.7 times. This indicates a significant increase in the labor used to produce the improved varieties compared with the indigenous varieties.

Land Preparation and Threshing

The number of times a field is tilled before planting has also increased with the introduction of improved varieties, although this increase is not as significant as the increase in the number of weedings. In 1966 coop members tilled their fields with bullocks for the winter crop an average of 4.07 times, while nonmembers tilled an average of 3.5 times. In 1970 both members and nonmembers tilled an average of slightly over 4.75 times. Since it requires a bullock pair about two days to till one acre each time, the total time required for land preparation per acre has increased from 8.0 to 9.5 days for coop members and from 7.0 days to 9.5 days for noncoop members.

The threshing of improved varieties has also increased labor requirements. In 1967 about 4.5 man-days per acre were needed for nonimproved varieties, while about 9.0 man-days per acre were needed for improved varieties (Hoque 1970).

Use of Fertilizer

Thus far, this discussion has dealt mainly with the change in the use of nonpurchased inputs with the introduction of improved varieties. There also have been major changes in the use of purchased inputs, such as fertilizer and insecticides.

Usually twice as much fertilizer was used to grow improved rice varieties than to grow nonimproved varieties (Table 8). Also, total investments in fertilizer by cooperative members have been

TABLE 8. Value (in rupees) of Fertilizer Used per Acre, 1966–1970

	1966		1967		1969		1970	
	Rs/acre	%	*Rs/acre*	%	*Rs/acre*	%	*Rs/acre*	%
Improved Rice								
Coop Member								
Cow Dung	35.80	43	19.30	24	32.20	24	31.20	29
Commercial	47.40	57	59.89	76	94.04	76	78.61	71
Total	83.20		79.19		126.24		109.81	
Noncoop Member								
Cow Dung			17.05[a]	33	31.40	32	37.80	34
Commercial			34.32[a]	67	68.32	68	73.22	66
Total			51.37[a]		99.72		111.02	
Nonimproved rice:								
Coop Member								
Cow Dung	20.40	50	17.70	37	26.50	35	23.10[a]	43
Commercial	20.87	50	30.32	63	49.27	65	30.23[a]	57
Total	41.27		48.02		75.77		53.33[a]	
Noncoop Member								
Cow Dung	11.70	56	13.00	47	10.45	53	22.20[a]	28
Commercial	9.26	44	14.81	53	9.08	47	56.95[a]	72
Total	20.96		27.81		19.53		79.15[a]	

SOURCE: Pakistan Academy for Rural Development (1965–1970).

NOTE: $1 U.S. = Rs. 4.76.

[a] These values were derived from survey data containing less than four observations.

significantly larger than those by nonmembers when growing improved varieties. Cooperative members used about three-quarters of their total fertilizer investment on commercial fertilizer, while nonmembers used only two-thirds of their total fertilizer investment on commercial fertilizer. Cow dung is usually available from a farmer's own animals at no cash cost, while commercial fertilizers (oil cake, urea, potash, and phosphate) require cash expenditures. Cooperative members thus made both proportionately larger cash investments as well as larger total investments for fertilizer than nonmembers.

Increased diversification has occurred in the types of fertilizer used. For example, in 1966, 7 percent of the coop members and 54 percent of the nonmembers used no fertilizer at all, with only 15 percent of the coop members and 6 percent of the nonmembers using both cow dung and all four of the commercial fertilizers. In 1970 everyone used some type of fertilizer. Seventy-nine percent of the coop members and 74 percent of the nonmembers used all five types of fertilizer.

Use of Insecticides

The use of insecticides has increased significantly since the introduction of improved varieties. In 1966, 53 percent of the coop members and 85 percent of the nonmembers did not have a pest attack and did not apply an insecticide. Of the cooperative members who did have a pest attack, 20 percent sprayed before the attack, 7 percent after the attack, and 17 percent both before and after the attack. Three percent did not spray. In 1970 only 1 percent of the coop members and 2 percent of the nonmembers did not have a pest attack and did not spray. Twenty-five percent of the coop members and 12 percent of the nonmembers sprayed but did not have an attack. Thus, in 1970 only 26 percent of the coop members and 14 percent of the nonmembers were free of a pest attack. Of those who did have an attack, 37 percent of the coop members and 38 percent of the nonmembers sprayed after the attack. Twenty-seven percent of the coop members and 37 percent of the nonmembers sprayed both before and after the attack.

The average number of times the fields were sprayed has also increased. Between 1966 and 1969, the number increased from 1.5 to 2.75 applications per crop for those who sprayed after the attack; it increased from 1.2 to 1.9 applications for those who sprayed before the attack; and it increased from 2.25 to 3.25 applications per crop for those who sprayed both before and after a pest attack.

Farm Size and the Improved Varieties

In examining the relation between farm size and the use of improved varieties, data is available for both cooperative members and nonmembers (Table 9). Ideally, if benefits from growing the new varieties were to be obtained equally by persons from all farm sizes, the distribution of farmers in each size growing winter crops would be the same as the distribution of farm sizes. For example, in 1966, 43 percent of the cooperative members had a farm size of from one to two acres while only 36 percent grew winter crops, instead of 43 percent. Similarly for nonmembers, values under heading 5 would equal that under heading 4 if benefits were equal. It must be emphasized that the estimates of Table 9 are only approximate, but they do give at least some indication of the trends in the use of winter cropping by farmers.

On closer examination of these data it would appear that for cooperative members, farm size had a fairly negligible effect on who is able to grow a crop. Thus, the cooperative was fairly successful in distributing the benefits of winter irrigation among all of its members regardless of farm size. Even the landless and near-landless cooperative members are represented in winter irrigation in about the same proportion as they were represented in the total cooperative membership.

Unfortunately, this is not the case for nonmembers. While over 65 percent of the nonmembers had less than one acre of land or were landless, no more than 31 percent of the nonmembers, who own farms of this size, were able to utilize irrigation water to grow a winter crop in any one year. It is important to note, however, that this percentage was increasing each year. The farmers who seemed to benefit the most were those having from one to five acres in that more than the proportionate share of these farmers were able to grow winter rice crops. Actually, it is the one- to two-acre farmers who seem to have used winter crops in a higher proportion in comparison with their number than farmers in any other category.

Table 10 shows the relation between size of farm and the percentage of farmers' land that is winter cropped. First, the small farmers, both coop members and nonmembers, irrigated a larger proportion of their farmland than larger farmers. The absolute acreage under cultivation, however, increased with increasing farm size. Second, cooperative members had a much larger proportion of their farmland under winter irrigation than nonmembers. Also, cooperative members with small landholdings of less than one acre

TABLE 9. Distribution by Farm Size of the Number of Farmers Growing Winter Crops

(1) Farm size (acres)	Cooperative Members					Nonmembers				
	(2) % Coop members with given farm size	(3) Of members growing winter crop, % with given farm size				(4) % nonmembers with given farm size	(5) Of nonmembers growing winter crop, % with given farm size			
		1966	1967	1969	1970		1966	1967	1969	1970
nil	2	—	—	3	2	24	—	2	7	4
0–1	12	22	11	11	18	41	16	23	22	27
1–2	43	36	33	41	32	13	41	42	32	22
2–3	18	19	29	11	11	12	30	20	15	26
3–5	16	19	18	24	19	7	13	10	24	15
over 5	8	3	8	8	18	3	3	2	2	5

SOURCE: Pakistan Academy for Rural Development (1965–1970).

NOTE: All columns do not total 100 percent because individual percentages were rounded off.

TABLE 10. Percent of Land Owned
by the Farmer That Is Winter Cropped

Farm Size (acres)	Coop Member				Nonmember			
	1966	1967	1969	1970	1966	1967	1969	1970
0–1	80	60	195[a]	208[a]	—	—	58	77
1–2	53	50	77	79	—	—	53	55
2–3	46	56	75	66	—	—	23	59
3–4	25	65	66	70	—	—	38	23
4–5	—	22	51	47	—	9	25	66
Over 5	—	48	60	56	—	—	—	25
Average	44	53	68	67	—	9	42	53

SOURCE: Pakistan Academy for Rural Development (1965–1970).

[a] Numbers larger than 100 result from these farmers renting land in addition to the land they owned.

had a definite advantage over nonmembers with this same landholding in their ability to rent land and thus increase their cultivated acreages.

In only one year (1970) was there a significant relationship between farm size and yield (Table 11). Even then, it was the farmers with one to four acres whose yields seemed to be lower than the others. It is evident from this table that the small landholder with less than one acre could effectively compete in the production of improved varieties with those with larger landholdings. Although evidence is inconclusive, it does appear that larger landholders, those with over four acres did, on the average, have somewhat higher yields than persons with smaller landholdings. However, this does not appear to be cause for concern since persons with all sizes of landholdings adopted the improved varieties at about the same rate. Thus, farmers of no single landholding size derived benefits from the improved varieties at the exclusion of the others.

Conclusions

1. Cooperative members come mainly from farms larger than one acre.

TABLE 11. Average Yield of Improved Varieties for Different Farm Sizes (in maunds per acre)

Farm Size (acres)	Coop Member				Nonmember			
	1966	1967	1969	1970	1966	1967	1969	1970
nil	—	—	44.62[a]	59.00[a]	—	—	50.57	45.16
0–1	39.14[a]	32.41[a]	39.92	48.40	—	—	34.63	41.23
1–2	25.85[a]	48.72	43.06	45.42	—	—	37.27	43.90
2–3	44.13[a]	34.43	45.28	43.61	—	—	46.92	45.61
3–4	31.48[a]	56.19	45.06	45.72	—	—	42.09	39.51
4–5	—	31.75[a]	49.37	52.51	—	33.20[a]	49.67[a]	54.70
over 5	—	34.93	45.30	53.58	—	—	—	50.66
Level of Significance	.79	.255	.563	.01			.172	.059

SOURCE: Pakistan Academy for Rural Development (1965–1970).

NOTE: 1 maund = 82.29 pounds.

[a] These values were derived from survey data containing less than four observations.

2. Mechanized methods of lifting water have almost completely replaced manual methods in Comilla Thana.

3. Since the operation of tubewells and pumps is controlled by cooperative members, they are able to derive greater benefits from the irrigation program and thus greater benefits from the improved varieties than nonmembers. The only way in which nonmembers can obtain water from mechanized irrigation is through purchase from the primary cooperatives. Cooperative members have been able to irrigate a larger proportion of their farmland than nonmembers.

4. The rate of adoption of improved rice varieties during the winter-cropping season was very fast, requiring only five years for cooperative members to reach almost complete adoption and four years for nonmembers. The faster rate for nonmembers can be attributed to the achievements demonstrated by cooperative members.

5. Use of improved rice was limited to three varieties through

1969. In 1970, however, additional improved varieties were introduced and used by cooperative members.

6. Yields for improved varieties were from two to three times larger than those of local varieties.

7. Cooperative members have continually obtained higher yields and invested more in the factors of production than nonmembers. The yield differences between cooperative members and nonmembers, however, have been less with improved varieties than they were with nonimproved varieties. Thus, the improved varieties have tended to lessen the unequal distribution of benefits of winter irrigation between cooperative members and nonmembers.

8. Introduction of improved varieties has led to an increase in the use of both traditional and nontraditional production inputs for both cooperative members and nonmembers.

9. Farmers appeared to adopt improved varieties at about the same rate, regardless of farm size. Cooperative members, however, adopted before nonmembers.

10. Nonmembers with less than 1.0 acre and the landless are the only groups who have consistently been represented in winter irrigation in a smaller proportion than they are in the total population.

11. Small farmers appear to be able to grow improved varieties as successfully as large farmers.

LeVern Faidley received his Ph.D. in Agricultural Engineering in 1974 from Michigan State University. He conducted research on the mechanization of rice cultivation in Bangladesh from 1969 to 1970.

Merle L. Esmay is professor of Agricultural Engineering at Michigan State University. He received his Ph.D. in Agricultural Engineering from Iowa State University in 1951. He has conducted research and been an adviser on many international development missions since 1962.

Research for this paper was done with the cooperation and assistance of the Bangladesh Academy for Rural Development and financed by a grant from the Midwest Universities Consortium for International Activities.

BIBLIOGRAPHY

Akhter, Farkunda
  1969. *Characteristics of the Members of Comilla Cooperatives*. Survey and Research Bulletin No. 10. Comilla: Pakistan Academy for Rural Development.
Hoque, Anwarul
  1970. "Cost and Returns from Winter Crops." Unpublished Manuscript. Comilla: Pakistan Academy for Rural Development.
Muyeed, Abdul
  1969. "Strategies Involved in a Development System of Planned Social Change in Rural East Pakistan." Ph.D. dissertation, Michigan State University.
Pakistan Academy for Rural Development
  1967. *Eighth Annual Report for June 1966–May 1967*. Comilla: Pakistan Academy for Rural Development.
  1970. *Tenth Annual Report for July 1968–June 1969*. Comilla: Pakistan Academy for Rural Development.
  1965–1970. *Winter Crop Cutting Surveys, Comilla Kotwali Thana*. Comilla: Pakistan Academy for Rural Development.

7

Experience with Low-Cost Tubewell Irrigation

Khondaker Azharul Haq

Before the introduction of mechanized irrigation, agriculture in Bangladesh had been perennially dependent on the monsoon and subservient to its vagaries. Both the monsoon crops, aus and aman, have always been subject to damage by drought and flooding, the extent of the harm done depending on the duration and intensity of the wet and dry periods. It was realized that the problem of drought, at least, could be solved by the artificial application of water, even if there were few measures that could be taken in the near future to control flooding.

Because it was felt that the rapidly needed gains in agricultural production might best be made during the winter (boro) season, normally the period of lowest production during the year, in 1959 the Academy for Rural Development at Comilla initiated pilot projects to provide farmers with irrigation facilities for winter cropping. These projects gradually expanded, utilizing variously and with different rates of success, gravity flow systems, low-lift pumps, and "low-cost" tubewells. By 1970, tubewell irrigation accounted for the overwhelming majority of Comilla Thana's irrigated acreage. So successful was this mode of irrigation that in 1968 the government of East Pakistan agreed to start a province-wide Thana Irrigation Program, based on the Comilla model of organization of irrigation. This step was regarded as a most important one toward increasing agricultural production. This chapter analyzes various problems related to the installation, repair, and maintenance of tubewells, discusses the types of economic benefits derived from their use, and summarizes recommendations for the improvement of tubewell performance and efficiency.

In contrast to the monsoon season, which usually extends from the middle of May to the middle of September and receives most of the 80-inch yearly rainfall, the period from October to May is quite dry with very little precipitation. This dry season has the maximum sunshine, with average maximum and minimum temperatures of 90°F and 57°F, and is considered most favorable for crop production. But very few crops can be grown without irrigation, and thus the most productive period of the year has remained largely unutilized. As a first step toward supplying water, power pumps were introduced in the cooperatives of the Comilla Kotwali Thana, situated on both sides of the Gumti River. In 1971, eight cooperative groups irrigated 274 acres with power pumps (PARD 1961:49). This irrigated area produced 6,000 maunds (494,000 lbs.) of paddy. The yield was 22 maunds per acre (1,810 lbs. per acre) as compared to 14 to 16 maunds per acre for the monsoon rice crops. By 1964, the area under irrigation and the total winter paddy production had increased more than three times. At a larger stage, introduction of dwarf "miracle" rice varieties, which could be favorably grown during the dry season with a yield more than three times that of local varieties, generated a tremendous additional demand for irrigation among the cooperative farmers of the thana.

Experience with Hand-Dug Tubewell Irrigation

Surface water resources of the thana were not sufficient, however, to meet the ever-increasing demand for water. The Gumti is the only river in the thana with some potential for surface water development, but its flow is as low as 300–400 cubic feet per second during the driest periods. It was estimated that with almost full utilization of surface water, only 7 percent of the 51,000 acres of the thana's cultivable land can be supplied with water from surface sources. Although the low-lift pump power in the thana provided great stimulation to production and income in the villages where they were used, the major limitations to their use were water shortages and organizational problems. In 1962, after three years of experience with low-lift pumps, it was concluded that surface water resources in Comilla Kotwali Thana were insufficient for wide-spread irrigation. The only alternative was the installation of tubewells to supplement surface water. To meet the needs of the entire thana, a comprehensive tubewell irrigation plan was developed. The first experimental 6″-diameter wells were installed in

1963, and the experience gained during these first years contributed to the rapid expansion of mechanized irrigation (PARD 1966). With the introduction of new crops and rice varieties and the diversification of the cropping patterns in Comilla Thana, the utilization of irrigation has increased greatly (Table 1 and Figure 1).

Tubewells have irrigated larger areas than surface-water pumps of the same capacity. Average irrigation coverage of about fifty acres per well was achieved by 1966/67. Both the tubewells and surface pumps had rated output capacities of 2 cubic feet per second (cusec).

A general complaint about the Comilla tubewells is that the area irrigated per cusec is low. This is based on the assumption that the discharge from the well is 2 cubic feet per second. Although theoretically correct, in practice there are complications. First, the maximum efficiency of a pump coupled with a diesel engine is 70 percent compared to 90 percent when coupled with an electric motor. Other technical factors such as aquifer characteristics, the design of the well screen, well development procedure, and the quality of well construction and installation also affect the yield.

TABLE 1. Irrigation and the Use of Pumps and Tubewells in Comilla Kotwali Thana

	1964/65	*1965/66*	*1966/67*	*1967/68*	*1968/69*
No. of Pumps Used	3	4	17	37	67
No. of Tubewells Used	34	25	46	91	126
Area Irrigated by Low-lift Pumps (acres)	128.75	178.28	726.49	1292.02	2323.14
Area Irrigated by Tubewells (acres)	1006.08	1127.25	2350.43	3891.54	6204.08
Total Area Irrigated (acres)	1134.83	1305.53	3076.92	5183.56	8527.22
Acres Irrigated per Low-lift Pump	42.92	44.57	42.73	34.92	34.67
Acres Irrigated per Tubewell	29.59	45.05	51.09	42.75	49.23

SOURCE: PARD 1970*b*.

The average measured discharge from the wells is 1.2 to 1.3 cusecs; thus, each cusec irrigates between 35 and 40 acres. With more effort and research, the output of the Comilla 2-cusec tubewells can be increased to 1.7 cusecs. This will increase the area irrigated and reduce the per acre cost of irrigation.

One dimension of the situation is that the demand for tubewells accelerated at such a pace that it was not possible to satisfy all demands with the limited number of drilling rigs. Due to

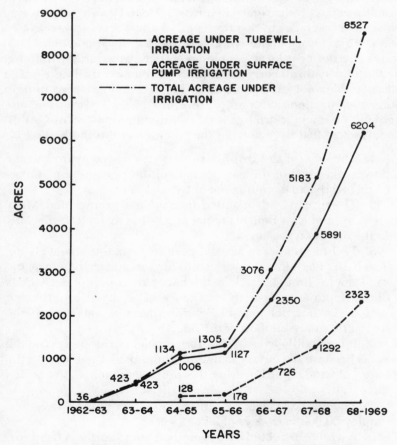

Figure 1. Acreage under Irrigation in Comilla Kotwali Thana

this, and because of a lack of additional technically qualified
people, it was not possible to significantly improve the yield from
the wells already dug. However, the average area covered per well
has increased greatly from eighteen acres in 1963 to forty-nine
acres in 1969 (PARD 1970*b*:61).

A look at the process of hand digging tubewells will clarify
some of these technical issues. Tubewells in Comilla are installed
by the manually operated cable-tool method. The only criticism has
been that it is a very slow method, taking from six to eight weeks to
install a well with an average depth of 300 feet. However, there may
be some advantages to this time period since it is utilized in two
ways. First, local people work with the technical crew and subsequently the best local people are hired. After further training,
they are placed in charge of drilling with a new drilling rig. If a
vacancy does not exist in Comilla Project, they are sent to help
other organizations. Second, during this period, discussions are
held with farmers to arrange for water distribution and use. Additional factors that have favored the adoption of this method are:

1. The cost of the drilling rig is very low compared to the
power rig. Most of the components of the rig can be manufactured locally, an encouragement to local industries.

2. The rig can be dismantled and manually transported. Many
areas in rural East Bengal are not accessible by roads, especially
in the monsoon season.

3. Technicians are in a better position to analyze the well log.
The bailer has a function similar to the soil auger; therefore, the
soil samples brought back by the bailer are true representatives
of the depth as well as the sequence of occurrence in the soil
profile. This is not possible with either the water jet of the
hydraulic rotary method of drilling.

4. It is possible to have a uniform gravel envelope around the
wells because the outer casing runs throughout the length of the
bore hole and, after lowering the well components, it is pulled
out.

5. The method is labor intensive, and ten rigs, on an average,
employ 60,000 man-days of labor a year.

6. A well constructed by this method is less costly. A hand-dug
well having a depth of 250 feet costs Rs. 27,000, as compared to

the Rs. 49,000 cost of the water jet method. One basic idea behind the hand digging of wells was that the next generation of wells could thus be installed by the respective cooperative societies in the Comilla cooperative system.

The expected life of a hand-dug well is ten years. When their useful life is over, components of the well can easily be pulled out of the ground and most of the well components can be reused. Only about Rs. 10,000 is required for reinstallation of such a well. The Comilla cooperatives have reached the stage in which the village societies are psychologically prepared to seriously consider paying for the investment required for reinstallation.

The discharge of a well normally decreases every year. This decrease in yield is primarily due to incrustation of the well-screen, although there are some instances of aquifer depletion. The aquifer in the Comilla area is composed mostly of fine to medium sand. Though some of this finer sand is removed in the well-development process, some does make its way through the gravels and sticks to the outside of the well screen. Chemicals from the groundwater tend to cement this material. Over a period of time it thus forms an impermeable layer, preventing water from entering the well. This situation can be improved by research on the "redevelopment" of old wells through chemical treatment and by using compressed air and surge-blocks. If preventive maintenance is carried out at regular intervals, well life can be extended beyond the expected ten years.

Another potential of these wells is their use as drainage wells to remove excess water from fields during the monsoon season. The well tops are situated, on an average, ten feet below the ground surface. Water flowing into the wells is absorbed by the aquifer. Experiments in other parts of the world have shown that by this process, 1.5 to 2.0 cusecs can be absorbed by an aquifer, depending on local geologic and hydrologic conditions. If this is possible in Bangladesh, a new chapter in monsoon agriculture will open.

Repair and Maintenance Issues

The greatest problem faced so far has been the adequate repair and maintenance of the wells. The standard of maintenance on the well, its components, and the prime-mover is much below desired levels, and in most cases maintenance costs are excessive. Yearly repair and maintenance of the engine and pump alone costs about 25 percent of the purchase price, as compared to the 5 to 7 percent estimated by the manufacturers. The following factors have contributed to make this problem chronic.

1. When this project was started in Comilla, there was practically no available skill and experience in East Pakistan in this particular field of engineering. Therefore, the staff learned through the process of trial and error.

2. No systematic procedure was followed in the daily, periodic, and preventive maintenance of the engine and pump until 1970. No maintenance was done on the wells.

3. Spare parts were not readily available as most of the engines were imported. The parts neither arrived in time nor met the demand. The need for available parts was filled by locally made imitations. These were of poor quality, but as expensive as imported parts. In some cases, an engine overhauled with imitated parts at a cost of Rs. 1200 lasted only a few days.

4. Diversification of engines has added to the existing problems. At least five makes of engines from many nations are installed on existing wells.

Types of Economic Benefits

Three types of economic benefits have resulted from using tubewells: (1) major increase in winter dry season cropped acreage, (2) benefits in higher yields for the spring and fall crops, due to supplemental irrigation at the beginning and end of the rainy season, and (3) an incentive to shift to higher-yielding varieties, brought on by the availability of winter irrigation.

The area under winter crops increased rapidly with the introduction of mechanized irrigation (Table 1 and Figure 1). In the year 1968/69, the area covered reached a total of 8,527 acres, constituting about 25 percent of the total cultivable land of the thana. Seventy-five percent of this area was covered by tubewells and 25 percent by low-lift pumps. Further increase in winter crop area will depend entirely on tubewell irrigation, since the meager surface water resources have been utilized.

Though these wells are primarily constructed for irrigating the winter crops, their use in supplementing natural precipitation in the aus and aman seasons adds benefits. Both aus and aman crops are subject to drought. In aus it occurs mostly during the early stage, and in aman during the flowering and seed formation stage. Water shortage during the latter period may result in total or partial crop failure. There has been (as of this writing) no detailed study, but it has been estimated that the yields of both aus and aman crops can be increased by 15 to 20 percent with irrigation at the required period. The yield of boro (winter) paddy showed an increasing trend also, from 21 maunds per acre in 1965 to 40 maunds in 1969 (Safiullah 1969:8).

With the introduction of new varieties and diversification of cropping patterns, the ratio between acreage under improved varieties and total acreage has increased (Table 2). For example, in 1967/68, of 5,184 acres of irrigated land, 1,027 acres were planted

TABLE 2. Irrigation of Different Crops
and Rice Varieties, Comilla Kotwali Thana (acres)

CROPS	1967/68			1968/69		
	Tubewell	Pump	Total	Tubewell	Pump	Total
IR-8	1361.09	578.24	1939.33	3123.48	1180.00	4303.48
Taipei-177	1726.92	261.41	1988.33	1878.00	311.00	2189.00
Pajam	—	—	—	390.00	59.00	449.00
China-I	—	—	—	40.00	—	40.00
Local Boro	264.49	94.22	358.71	335.50	386.00	721.50
Broadcast Shaitta	343.19	324.80	667.99	106.60	325.24	431.84
Potato	153.58	4.08	157.66	311.50	44.00	355.50
Watermelon	20.53	3.31	23.84	18.00	18.90	36.90
Vegetable	21.80	25.96	47.76	—	—	—

SOURCE: PARD 1970*b*.

with local varieties (Local Boro and Shaitta). In the following year, total irrigated acreage had increased to about 8,527 while the acreage under local varieties had increased to only 1,153. During this two-year period, the percentage of acreage under local varieties to total irrigated acreage had declined from about 20 percent to about 14 percent.

Summary and Conclusions

The installation of tubewells for winter cropping has increased income and employment in Comilla Thana. The net return for irrigated crops has amounted to as much as Rs. 1000 per acre for some farmers who invested Rs. 300 per acre. Winter cropping provides employment for a considerable part of the agricultural labor force, who would otherwise be unemployed.

Though the tubewell irrigation program in Comilla was quite a success, there are some areas in which improvements can be made:

1. Every tubewell is constructed with the same specification of well-screen and pumping set. Since the composition of the aquifer varies from place to place and since all wells do not yield the same amount of water, the capital cost per cusec yield of the well becomes quite high for low-yielding wells. To avoid this, after conducting pumping tests, the wells should be supplied with engines and pumps of the requisite horsepower.

2. High repair and maintenance costs should be reduced. This can be achieved by continuously training operators and mechanics, and by carrying out periodic and preventive maintenance as recommended by the engine and pump manufacturers.

3. Well development is not carried out currently on the Comilla wells. As a result, yield and the life span of each well is reduced. For better efficiency and performance, proper testing and development should be carried out.

4. Greater attention to the water distribution system is required for increased efficiency. Before installing a well, the area commanded should be surveyed in order to have a proper layout of the water distribution system. Some land leveling should be done if necessary to maintain the proper slope, eliminating unnecessary ponding of water observed in some channels.

5. More wells should be supplied with electricity to reduce

fixed and operating costs and to permit increased hours of operation and coverage.

6. An intensive study of the groundwater resources of the thana should be carried out to determine the potential groundwater reserves.

7. Greater efforts should be made to convince the cooperatives to purchase wells, considering the huge benefits they derive from them. In this way, the capital of the central cooperative may be released for other uses.

8. Efforts should be made to manufacture diesel engines locally. The complicated high-speed diesel engines should be replaced by relatively simple low-speed diesel engines.

9. Chemical analysis of the groundwater is not now being done, but it is an extremely important means of determining the type of incrustation that blocks well-screens. If this information were available, it would be possible to apply the correct chemical in the well maintenance and redevelopment process.

10. The locally manufactured well-screens provide a favorable surface for the seating of incrusting material and bacteria. The quality of these screens should be improved to eliminate this unfavorable characteristic.

Khondaker Azharul Haq is principal scientific officer, Bangladesh Rice Research Institute, Joydevpur, Bangladesh. He was previously the director of the Irrigation and Mechanical Cultivation Section, Kotwali Thana Central Cooperative Association, Comilla, Bangladesh. He received a B.Sc. in Agricultural Engineering from the Pakistan Agricultural University at Lyallpur and an M.Sc. in Agricultural Engineering from the University of Hawaii.

BIBLIOGRAPHY

Hoque, Anwarul
    1970. "Cost and Returns from Winter Crops." Unpublished Manuscript. Comilla: Pakistan Academy for Rural Development.
Pakistan Academy for Rural Development (PARD)
    1961. *A New Rural Cooperative System for Comilla Thana. First Annual Report for 1960.* Comilla: Pakistan Academy for Village Development.

1964.   *The Comilla Pilot Project in Irrigation and Rural Electrifica-tion*. Comilla: Pakistan Academy for Rural Development.
1966.   *Winter Crop Cutting Survey. Comilla Kotwali Thana, 1965–1966*. Comilla: Pakistan Academy for Rural Development.
1970*a*. *A New Rural Cooperative System for Comilla Thana. Ninth Annual Report for 1968–1969*. Comilla: Pakistan Academy for Rural Development.
1970*b*. *Pakistan Academy for Rural Development—Tenth Annual Report for July 1968–June 1969*. Comilla: Pakistan Academy for Rural Development.

Safiullah, M.
1969.   *Boro Crop Survey in Comilla Kotwali Thana*. Comilla: Pakistan Academy for Rural Development.

8
Social Organization
and Agricultural Development
in Bangladesh

Peter J. Bertocci

Introduction

This paper examines what little is known about rural social
organization in Bangladesh, with special reference to the new nation's experience with agricultural development efforts under
Pakistan rule. It is a baseline study, since the events subsequent to
March 1971, leading to the eventual independence of Bangladesh,
constitute a watershed and a cutoff point in the history of East
Bengal's agricultural development. The relationship between social organization and rural development as it has evolved in the past
will be analyzed with emphasis on problem areas and the implications for possible strategies for future agricultural growth.

The subject matter is organized into three related albeit
somewhat disparate parts. The first examines briefly the ecological
base of rural social organization in East Bengal, and attempts some
tentative, hypothetical generalizations regarding the parts of the
province about which most is known. The second describes the
role rural social groupings have played in the organization of past
developmental efforts and the part they might play in the future.
The third section continues in this comparative vein by centering
attention on the known results of efforts to implement the green
revolution in East Pakistan prior to 1971, and their implications for
future diffusion of the new varieties in varied parts of the new
nation. A broad and hopefully provocative sweep is made rather
than a pinpoint analysis of detail since, because the development
scene in Bangladesh is still fluid, it seems most fruitful to focus on
the general import of past lessons as a guide in making plans for the
future.

The Ecological Base

It is a truism to say that the whole of East Bengal is characterized by a low-lying deltaic plain and a monsoon climate to which
exceedingly dense populations have historically adapted via the
medium of a preindustrial technology. But agriculture in the province is influenced by regional and microregional differences in soil
type, rainfall, and other hydrological conditions that result in corresponding variations in the types, quantity, and quality of crops
grown (see, e.g., Rashid 1967:260–286). It follows that form and
variation in rural social organization throughout the province ought
similarly to occur in a manner related to settlement patterns and
population densities as they are alternately conditioned in each
type of agricultural environment.

The major distinctions between East Bengal's agriculture and
rural social organization are generally related to the delta's major
ecological zones: the moribund, mature, and active delta areas, as
well as those parts of the province that are marginal to the current
courses of the great river systems (for a detailed discussion see
Nicholas 1962; with reference to East Bengal, Bertocci 1970*a*). But
unfortunately there is to date no universally accepted schematiza-
tion of East Bengal's agricultural zones. Even more sadly, we possess even less knowledge of regional variations in rural social
organization; in this respect, Bangladesh is one of South Asia's
least-studied culture areas.

Nonetheless, from sources of aggregate demographic data and
general descriptions of settlement patterns, we are able to
hypothesize tentatively regarding the outlines of regional differences. Such a hypothetical attempt is made in Table 1.

The most obvious differences among the various regions of
Bangladesh are in their respective population densities, at least as
best as these can be known from 1961 census data. Although the
province contains population agglomerations that stagger the im-
aginations of demographers, the observed regional variations in
population concentration, which correspond broadly with the deltaic ecological zones, figure importantly in differences in social
organization. Population densities affect settlement patterns. Thus,
at the microregional level in particular, the degee to which densities affect tendencies toward nucleation or dispersal in settlement

TABLE 1. Population Densities and Settlement Patterns in East Bengal's Regions, 1961

Region/Delta Area/Division	Pop. Density per Sq. Mi. of Cultivated Area[a]	Predominant Pattern of Settlement[b]
"North Bengal" (northwest region)/Marginal; moribund/ Rajshahi	1,080	Generally dispersed, but an observed tendency to form "line villages" along roads; more nucleation than elsewhere
"South Bengal" (southwest and south central regions) /Moribund in north; mature; active in South/Khulna	1,230	Generally dispersed, to the extreme in South Barisal; some "line villages" along embankments and roads
"Central Bengal" (and north central districts) /Marginal in north; active elsewhere/ Dacca	1,570	Generally dispersed throughout; high mound building seen in parts of Mymensingh
Northeast and southeast districts/Active except in Sylhet, parts of Chittagong/Chittagong[c]	2,000	Generally dispersed, absence of nucleation; low population in Sylhet, which is in a marginal zone
All-Bangladesh population density	1,350	

[a] Adapted from Rashid 1967, Table 96.
[b] Summarized from Ahmad 1956.
[c] Chittagong Hill Tracts excluded.

patterns has implications for the character of integration and social solidarity of peasant communities in different parts of the province. This will be evident, for example, in the discussion about the most heavily populated southeastern districts of East Bengal. Secondly, however, population densities and their variations affect the degree of land pressure in different parts of the province and, thus, the size of holdings; the latter is crucially relevant to understanding the economic class and social power structures of peasant communities in diverse areas. The discussion of rural class differences on a regional basis, relevant to the diffusion of the green revolution as noted below, will make this reasonably clear. Thus, in an otherwise remarkably similar rural scene observable everywhere in East Bengal, population densities, in addition to local topographical and climatological nuances, require crucial distinction in social analysis.

But the Bengal Delta is, nonetheless, notable for its relative homogeneity in overall appearance. Everywhere in East Bengal the abiding impression is one of an amorphous countryside, whose seemingly shapeless character allows the casual observer no easy guide to the differentiation of one village community from another. It is this very homogeneity which, in the absence of detailed field studies for most of the province, tempts one toward the tentative extrapolation of possible uniformities in structure and organization on the basis of existing, admittedly minimal, data.

Organization and Development in the Southeastern Districts: Evidence from Comilla

As earlier noted, East Bengal is one of the most understudied parts of South Asia, at least by sociologists and anthropologists. What we do possess in the way of detailed field studies of rural communities comes largely from Comilla District (Bertocci 1970*a*, 1970*b*; Glasse 1965; Qadir 1960; Zaidi 1970). In addition to published research available in Owen (1962) and Islam (1974), some unpublished material on Dacca District can be found. Smith's "culture-at-a-distance" report (1946) on an area in Sylhet District is the only other easily available account of another part of the province.

In this section is a brief review of the major features of rural social organization in the former Comilla District, particularly in Comilla, and the development efforts of the Comilla academy and its allied institutions. Some hypotheses as to the generalizability of these findings for the rest of East Pakistan are also offered.

Community organization in Comilla Thana displays the following general features:

1. As elsewhere in the province, the area has a great density of population—about 2,000 persons per square mile of cultivated area. Its people live in scattered settlements and the nucleation of dwelling in any marked degree is absent.

2. There are several important referents for the term *gram* or "village"—the *mauza* (revenue unit) and the "census village" among them—but the term also implies "natural" social groupings of family homesteads (*bari*). These are commonly referred to as "local villages" and as such designate socially defined communities. In Comilla Thana the socially defined village is surprisingly small considering the great size of the area's population. According to what may be calculated from the Comilla Academy for Rural Development Research Section's *Coordinated List of Villages for Comilla Kotwali Thana* (1963), there were at that time some 463 "local villages" in the thana. These communities averaged about 340 persons in population size, living in an average of between eight and ten homesteads. The mean area occupied by such groupings, including cultivation land, was approximately 135 acres.

3. The smallness of "local villages" seems to be determined by the fact that they consist in the main of clusters of peasant homesteads lying in relative proximity to one another. Although kinship plays a role in uniting these entities, the daily contact over time resultant from this geographical proximity seems to be the dominant factor in uniting member homesteads and lineages.

4. Political and social leadership in "local villages" centers on the economically dominant lineages and their most prominent members. These dominant lineages tend to organize what exists in the way of collective activities, be these religious or secular, and most commonly certain of their members are the *sardar*s or *matabbar*s ("village leaders") who exercise political leadership. But a great degree of centralization in village affairs is lacking; indeed, its opposite is more nearly the rule.

5. Territorially and demographically small in size, the Comilla

"local village" is capable of localized identifications, which in some contexts are quite strong. Even where the "local village" encompasses a greater than average population and area, such as, for example, that studied by Ellickson (1972) with over 1,000 inhabitants and an area of around 600 acres, neighborhood (*para*) organization is quite strong as a centrifugal force. And in the small "local villages" more typical of the thana, where rivalry has long been a feature of the relations between resident dominant lineages, one may describe the community as "vertically segmented," the allegiants to one or the other lineage—or its *sardar/matabbar* or other factional leader—constituting which is called in the local dialect his *reyai*, literally, his "group of proteges."

6. But this "intensive" character of village and intravillage organization at one level is counterbalanced at another by the fact of "extensiveness" in political organization, on the one hand, and in individual and group relations on the other hand. Thus, for example, each of the *sardar*s in any given village is likely to be a member of a multivillage "council of elders"—known as *samaj*—whose main function has historically been the settling of disputes in any of the villages under its "jurisdiction." This multivillage political institution supercedes the "local village" in public affairs and in so doing involves individual villagers in a formal institutional structure that counteracts the more inward-oriented tendencies of the villager's immediate smaller community.[1] Ninety percent of villagers' kinship ties in the villages I have studied were extended outside their *gram*s in a gradually expanding pattern throughout the thana (107 square miles) and beyond its borders. People as often as not attended mosques and other religious meetings outside their local villages and their economic dealings—moneylending and labor exchange, for example—often took them far afield. In general, then, the "extensive" character of both group and individual activities beyond the immediate "village level" seems to be a dominant feature of the thana's social organization, contrasting with another salient characteristic, that of localized "intensiveness" at the "village" and intravillage levels of interaction.

The degree to which this general pattern of "intensive" versus "extensive" group organization prevails elsewhere in East Bengal cannot be fully known, given the paucity of field studies. Certainly the work of Glasse (1965) from the Matlab Bazar area of northeastern Comilla District suggests that Comilla Thana is not wholly unique in this regard. Smith (1946:592) discusses a part of Sylhet District in which a "seven-village unit which functions as an economic and social entity" seems representative of that area, although the data she presents suggest differences in detail from that found in Comilla Thana. Indeed, given the broad homogeneity of the Bengal Delta, particularly that of its most populous districts, one is tempted to think this overall pattern of organization, despite local differences in specific form, is markedly similar. Existing studies ought to provide hypotheses for further research throughout the province.

If it is true that large parts of the East Bengali countryside consist organizationally of small groupings that overlap territorially and structurally into larger ones, what strategy, then, is relevant for the social organization of rural development? How should local, indigenous social forms mesh with organizations evolved by government to produce growth and innovation in agriculture? We do have evidence of the results of past attempts to organize development, and in examining these we can at least partially evaluate success or failure with reference to the way they were linked to traditional rural organization.

The union level of developmental organization has, of course, been one of the administrative tools in this respect in the recent past. Under Ayub Khan's Basic Democracies, the union council, composed of a number of representatives from various electoral wards, was the lowest tier of administration. It was also, through its supposed linkage to governmental nation-building departments, the local-level primary unit of focus for development efforts (for a brief description see Ziring 1966 and Rahman 1962:10–15). But the union, while doubtless important as a political unit whose antecedents go back for a century, is not coterminous with indigenous social groupings. Indeed, in drawing up its overall external boundaries, as well as its internal electoral wards, inevitably little reference was, or probably could be, made to the "local village." Thus, the "rice-roots" level of local government lumped many "natural" groupings together, on the one hand, and on the other served in many instances to cross-section them representationally.

While the imposition of this administrative institution over existing social groupings was no doubt unavoidable, it may well be that such an arrangement brought in its train some inherent, if perhaps unforeseen, difficulties in organizing development efforts. Unfortunately, few studies examine in detail the role of the union council in fusing rural administration with development efforts, the major exceptions being the good, if conflicting, assessments made respectively by Thomas (1968) and Sobhan (1968) on the Rural Public Works Program. Otherwise, the evidence for the early years of Basic Democracies is at best mixed regarding judgments on the union's effectiveness as an organizational tool for rural development (see Rahman 1962:68–72 and 1963:37–41).

The one case that indicated the union was seriously tried in agricultural development efforts is that of the USAID-sponsored "Program Building" project in Mymensingh District. In essence, the Program Building procedure was five-fold. It consisted (1) of the establishment of training schools for the district's agricultural workers who (2) would join with local people in union-level surveys to determine the exact nature of local agricultural problems; (3) of a union agricultural committee, composed of farmers plus agricultural officers and (4) of additional subcommittees whose respective charges were related to various specific aspects of agricultural development; and (5) of annual repeats of the original survey, made to assess the degree and rate of progress in development (Stevens 1967:19–23).

While noting that some initial short-run success was made in organizing farmers at the union level for development, Stevens suggests that in the longer run several limitations became apparent. First, there was the danger of co-optation of development efforts, and hence results, as all activities were channeled through the more prosperous farmers through the union council. Indeed, it has been widely observed that in East Pakistan under Ayub Khan the union councils were in many cases the domains of the "surplus farmers." This seemed to be the case in the union that encompassed the villages I studied in 1966–1967, and Sobhan (1968:73–100) utilizes survey data to arrive at an adamant generalization for the former province as a whole in this respect. Given the widespread attacks on Basic Democrats in 1969 and the end of the "Ayub Khan era," one is tempted to accept the truth of rural economic elite dominance of local councils. Thus, while a laudable attempt, Program Building as an effort to organize development at the union level of political administration seemed likely to founder on the rocks of the rural class system of East Bengal in that it risked concentrating the benefits of development in the hands of the wealthier farmers, thus enhancing the distrust of the poorer peasants who in the main were more numerous. Moreover, the inability of the Program Building approach to cope with the perennial problem of rural credit (Stevens 1967:24) is perhaps indicative of this difficulty posed by the rural class structure.

The question of inequality of access to, and benefits from, developmental efforts organized at the union level was compounded by the fact that, compared to local village groupings in which most farmers feel immediately at home, the union, as an arbitrary agglomeration of these smaller units, contained elements of an inherent organizational unwieldiness. It was no doubt a positive aim of the Program Building approach to "break down the village walls of cliquishness," as Ben Ferguson, the project's mentor, put it (as quoted in Stevens 1967:20). But offsetting this goal was the likelihood that the approach reached local, intensively organized village groupings only indirectly at best and this through the medium of a territorially extensive class system. Thus, its long-run effectiveness seems likely to have been seriously hindered (see the discussion by Stevens 1967:24ff.).

This analysis and judgment as to the outcome of the one known attempt to organize development at the union level suggests real shortcomings with the union council as the territorial basis of local level administration, and in newly independent Bangladesh it may not so remain. But whatever the initiating unit will be for rural development at the local level in East Bengal, the shortcomings of operating with agglomerations of local villages, given the character of indigenous social organization outlined above, ought to be considered.

The Comilla experiment is instructive as an alternative approach. It is not necessary to recapitulate the main features of the Comilla program here, as Stevens' paper in this volume refers to it in ample detail and the interested reader may further consult the definitive summary provided by Raper (1970). However, the manner in which the "Comilla model of development" fits into the thana's traditional social organization and its relationship to the latter should be emphasized as an underlying (and unsung) factor in the project's relative success.

The Comilla cooperative project has from its inception taken the "primary village community" as its grass-roots organizational focus. Indeed, it seems fair to say that most development activities in Comilla Kotwali Thana have in effect bypassed the union level of political and administrative organization, with the single important exception of the Rural Public Works Program. Most cooperative societies in Comilla Thana would appear to be coterminous with the area's many "local villages." And where in the larger-sized villages cooperative societies are formed, it is common for such communities to have more than one cooperative, each of these established in parts of the village where neighborhood loyalties, as against those felt toward the larger collectivity, are strong. In a word, Comilla cooperatives tend to overlap with the project area's "natural" social groupings.

But the problems of excessive localism this fact might engender are offset by the direct linkage of the cooperative societies to the Central Cooperative Association, which provides supervisory, banking, credit, and training functions. Thus, the Central Cooperative Association, in effect, coordinates development activities by linking activities geared to rural uplift to one "central place" at the thana level of the old administrative system.[2] At the same time, the association, by reaching directly into the socially "intensive" local villages and their subunit, serves to unite the otherwise "amorphous" Comilla countryside's myriad social groupings into a territorially broad-based developmental scheme.

In this respect, the Comilla experiment can be seen as an attempt to pour new wine into old bottles. It focuses on traditional social groupings in the project area, but aims at bringing into being new social roles and new leadership groups consonant with "modernization" in agriculture as well as other spheres of rural life. It has the strategic advantage of building on indigenous forms of rural social organization, working with groupings familiar to the peasant, and does not attempt to create wholly new (and uncomfortable) entities. It brings development to the demographically over-whelmed and socially fragmented countryside, which the union councils, functioning above the "village level," have not been able to do.

This does not mean, however, that the Comilla "system" has been unencumbered with the problems of differences in wealth and power, which troubled the Program Building approach. The manifestations of these kinds of difficulties at Comilla will be discussed in some detail below, but suffice it to say here that attempting to pour new wine into old bottles has obvious disadvantages. Efforts to reorient the old order to the new tasks and roles required by rural development find their first resistances in the structure of the old order itself. Opposition to the cooperative experiment, grafted as it has been onto the traditional community structure, came precisely from those who perceived they might lose in the new change (traditional village leaders, religious influentials, and moneylenders who gained most from the indigenous system of rural credit.) But once early opposition was overcome in many cooperative societies and the advantages of cooperation, tied to access to irrigation facilities and new seed varieties, became widely perceived (see chapter 6), the danger has arisen that the benefits of development might here also be co-opted by the traditionally dominant elements in the "local villages." The advantage in the Comilla system of rural development organization in combating this tendancy has been the fact that supervision at the thana level—reaching down into the rice-roots communities individually—has helped control the undermining of the cooperative system.

The basic problem discussed here has been, however, that of finding appropriate organizational techniques for diffusing the innovations associated with agricultural development to the myriad overlapping communities that proliferate in the East Bengali countryside. The Comilla model of development has aimed at reaching local people in the social groupings where they are most "at home," while at the same time centralizing a coordinated and complex diffusion of new ideas and technology at a higher level of administration. To the extent that the social organization of Comilla Thana represents much of what is found elsewhere in Bangladesh—a likelihood that can only be substantiated by further research—thana-level centralization of development efforts directed at local communities is possibly the most fruitful strategy for the future.

The Extensions of the "Local Village": Their Relevance for Development

Above, and in more detail elsewhere (Bertocci 1970*a*, and 1970*b*), I have tried to show the way in which small, "intensive" village groupings and their subunits in Comilla Thana merge "extensively" into larger groupings across the countryside. One key nexus of rural social groupings, which provides further organizing focus to the "local village" and *samaj* groupings, is the local market area. In Comilla Thana, much of the social, as well as economic, life of local villagers takes place in and around small, nearby *hat*s or rural markets, which number well over twenty in the rural areas of the thana.[3] These markets constitute "central places" for the villages that surround them and it is possible to estimate that each currently active market in rural Comilla Thana (comprising approximately 100 square miles) covers a "hinterland" of between three to five square miles. In the village area I studied, there was a local market that served as an economic and social "central place" for some fifteen to twenty *mauza*s and "local villages," as well as three *samaj* groupings surrounding it. Its ten permanent shops were locally owned and/or rented and nearly all the sellers and buyers who frequented its biweekly meetings were from the same fifteen to twenty *mauza*s. As it happened in this instance, the union council headquarters for the area were located in the market, as was a primary school. The market was a recreational area for many villagers and it was the place for religious meetings of an ad hoc sort that attracted large numbers of the faithful. The market's total hinterland was approximately four square miles in area and encompassed a population of some 6,000 people. In addition to the informal ties and social contacts implied by the above description, 40 percent of some 441 marriage ties I was able to record, covering three generations, crisscrossed the market area (see also Islam 1974:78–79). Thus, in addition to the formal "intensive" and "extensive" social groupings that give shape to the Comilla countryside, the market area provides a "central place" around which many crucial rural activities are focused.

There is, moreover, empirical evidence that the Comilla Thana area is not unique in this regard. The *Bengal District Gazetteers* for 1910 (Allen:1912) lists 343 *hats* and larger markets for the district as a whole, which in 1901 covered 2,777 square miles and had a population of nearly 3 million living in 8,695 *mauzas* and no doubt many more "local villages." Thus, at that time each market in Dacca District covered an average area of about nine square miles and served an average population of perhaps 8,600 located in some twenty-five *mauzas*. Patel (1963) reports for Rajshahi District in North Bengal the existence of 408 rural markets and from data on that district's area and population in 1961 one can calculate a standard marketing area of about nine square miles and a population of nearly 7,000. The average distance between markets in Rajshahi is between five and ten miles, but often smaller distances prevail. Thus, evidence from two other districts suggests that a common pattern of market area focus to rural people's activities may be found in further research, besides that which seems to prevail in Comilla Thana alone.

It is possible, then, that throughout Bangladesh the rural marketing community provides the mechanism for "integrating myriad peasant communities into [a] single social system. . .," an observation Skinner makes in his study of marketing and social structure in rural China (1964:3). Skinner further points out that Communist attempts to modernize rural China had to come to terms with the existence of these natural social units (1965:382–399). First the cooperatives, then ultimately the communes themselves, had to be scaled to the size of these traditional units of organization. "By the winter of 1960–61, Communist planners and cadremen alike had gained new respect for the enduring significance of natural social systems, and were seeking ways to use traditional solidarities for their own organizational ends" (Skinner 1965:396).

What organizational ends in rural development might the market area in Bangladesh serve in the future? Clearly, given the inadequacies of the union as a supravillage developmental unit, the same would apply to market areas in most respects, despite the latter's seemingly more tightly knit social fabric. But one area in which the social ties of the market area might serve developmental goals is that of land consolidation. It is well known that East Bengal exhibits a classically minifundist profile in land tenure, individual farms split up into many small plots. Should it prove necessary, for example, to consolidate landholdings as a prerequisite for increased agricultural productivity, the market area might constitute an appropriate and socially acceptable unit within which to agglomerate small, fragmented holdings. The individual holdings of most farmers most often contain plot fragments lying outside the boundaries of their "local villages," either in neighboring *samaj* villages or in the market area at large. Thus a multivillage, *samaj*, or market-area unit might be adopted as the consolidation unit for a moderate scheme falling short of nationalization and communization of land. (Even should the latter occur, the market area as a likely unit might well be considered, if the Chinese experience is at all relevant here.) Given the fact that social organizational units in rural Bangladesh overlap in increasingly wider circles—this to an extent not readily found in other peasant societies—awareness of their territorially extensive character ought to guide both research and strategy for development in the future.

Rural Class Structure and the Green Revolution

New, high-yielding varieties of rice adaptable to the winter growing season have been in use in East Pakistan since 1966. The beginnings of tubewell and other irrigation schemes also date from about this period and therefore the introduction of the new varieties, in particular IR-8, complemented efforts to utilize the potential of the dry and normally minimally productive boro or winter season. Varieties capable of sustaining high yields during the monsoon period, when the aus (summer) and aman (autumn) seasonal cropping takes place, have only been widely tested in 1970. This experimentation, primarily with IR-20 during the aman season, aims at finding a variety of the new rice that will be productive under East Bengal's particular monsoon agricultural conditions. Despite these hopeful beginnings, the spread of irrigation and the diffusion of new crop varieties in the former East Pakistan generally lagged behind that achieved in West Pakistan.

The paper by Faidley and Esmay in this volume (chapter 6)

summarizes some of the recent results of the green revolution in Comilla Thana, where, under the aegis of the cooperative program, concentrated efforts to induce widespread adoption of the new varieties have taken place. Their findings allow several important observations. Firstly, Faidley and Esmay have usefully shown once again that smallness of holdings is not necessarily an impediment to either the adoption of or benefit from mechanized irrigation and the new rice varieties. There appears to be growing agreement on this point and the study under discussion drives one more nail into the coffin of the rationale behind the "elite farmer strategy" for the diffusion of the green revolution, which has assumed a higher degree of entrepreneurship among large farmers and that the economies of scale possible on larger farms are necessary for a quick growth in overall production. Secondly, however, the study also points out the need for a well-developed institutional structure, which, at least at the outset, controls the diffusion of the new technology, especially assuming the provision of credit and inputs at reasonable prices. In this case, that institutional structure has been the Comilla cooperative system.

One is tempted to draw a third conclusion from these findings. Given the appropriate institutional structure, many of the initial problems, not merely of adoption but also of distribution of benefits, of the new technology are perhaps more easily avoidable under conditions of comparatively egalitarian land tenure. It is well known that in East Bengal the average size of holdings is around three acres. The Hindu landlord exodus in 1947, followed by the East Bengal State Acquisition and Tenancy Act of 1950, allowed lands formerly concentrated in large scale zamindari holdings to devolve in large measure to the tillers (see Ahmed and Timmons 1971 for a discussion of land reforms in the former East Pakistan). From the fact that great concentration of holdings is absent in East Bengal's land relations, one is tempted to hope that the major social and political impediments to fairly equal distribution of the green revolution's benefits will be minimized. (For a discussion of the opposite kind of situation, see chapters 13, 15, 17.)

Certainly the fact that in Comilla thana land is widely distributed among holders, albeit in exceedingly small farm sizes, is related to the success of the project thus far in disseminating the new varieties and technology fairly widely.[4] In this respect, Comilla is generally representative of tenurial conditions present in the most populous southeastern and central districts of East Bengal. Thus, the spread of the Comilla program to these areas, as has now been decided upon by the Bangladesh government, ought to achieve similar results, assuming the same levels of institutionalization of the cooperative program.

Land tenure conditions by themselves, however, obviously do not guarantee success, either at Comilla or elsewhere. The Comilla cooperative system, built laboriously over ten years of effort, has provided by example one mode of institutional organization that is so crucial to the process of diffusion. The Comilla system furnishes rural credit, it centralizes the diffusion of irrigation techniques and the new seed varieties and supervises the activities necessary to the spread of the green revolution in the thana. Adoption of the same kind of strategy in other areas of Bangladesh appears now to have been chosen as the handmaiden to the spread of the new technology. At the same time, however, the Comilla system has been no more successful than many other developmental schemes in solving the problem of the landless. Faidley and Esmay (chapter 6) note that a goodly proportion of the land poor and landless seem unable to benefit from joining cooperative societies organized along Comilla lines. One wonders, indeed, if at Comilla the gap between the one- and two-acre farmers will, if not increase, come to be stabilized over time, in a way which the rural proletariat comprised of 15 percent of the thana's farm population will remain such.

Moreover, there is a continuing problem related to the dynamics of landownership and land transfer in the thana. Smallness of holdings does not prevent the emergence of a rural class system based, at least in part, on possession or control of land. I have tried to show elsewhere (Bertocci 1972) that difference in class, status, and power in Comilla villages are largely correlated with variation in farm size, according to whether one is a "surplus," "subsistence," or land poor or landless farmer.

The rural class stratification of Comilla Thana is admittedly embryonic in that it is in large measure incomparable with the more elaborate and "closed" class and caste systems found elsewhere on the subcontinent. Possession of better than the mean amount of farmland has allowed, both historically and presently, the relatively more prosperous "surplus" farmers to emerge as dominant figures in their local villages. The "dominant lineages" can be said to be part of this rural class, for under the conditions of "traditional" agriculture in a monsoon environment, possession of more than the average amount of land usually has meant the production of sufficient grain surplus as to allow investment of the latter in economically and politically profitable activities. Crucial to this process is the lending out of land, grain, or money made possible by the possession or control of better-than-average holdings. In particular, given the absence in the thana of large-scale outright tenancy in the form of land rent and sharecropping, the usufructuary mortgage has been an important means of land transfer to the surplus farmers (see A. A. Khan 1968 for a discussion of rural credit in Comilla Thana). But at the same time, since land pressure is so great, it is difficult for a surplus farm family to retain possession of land gained. This also relates in part to a system of partible inheritance, which mitigates against joint ownership of family land and thus weakens the ability of a family to prevent loss of its holdings over time. The result is, as some have calculated, a three-generational rise and fall of surplus farm families. And the local status and power systems generally correlate with this pattern of dynamics. Thus, rural social stratification in Comilla Thana—and one may hypothetically posit the same for the most populous other districts on ecological grounds—appears flexible and fluid in its "circulation of elites" over time and space.

The dynamics of social stratification in Comilla villages is thus related to land pressure and competition for landownership, fueled in turn by the scarcity of rural credit. The Comilla cooperative system has in particular aimed at replacing the indigenous system of moneylending through provision of credit to farmers at lower rates than the traditional system of agricultural finance with all its risks has allowed. And the cooperative project has registered success over time in its efforts. But it is appropriate to wonder whether the historically endemic competition for land still constitutes a threat to egalitarian distribution of benefits of the new technology thus far observed in the thana's cooperatives. It seems that the demonstrated advantages of the new varieties have reinforced already high land values. Faidley and Esmay observe that farmers with even the smallest holdings have begun, with presumably the advantage of cooperative credit, to seek expansion of their holdings by renting land. It also appears likely that farmers holding land in mortgage will be even more reluctant than under the traditional system to seek repayment of loans.[5] Finally, it also may be that those farmers who in the past have rented out their land or given it to sharecroppers now will be increasingly reluctant to do so as higher profits from augmented yields make it more worthwhile to keep one's land and if necessary to work it with hired labor. Underlying these concerns is the fact that in an area with population densities of 2,000 and more per square mile, there is limited land available and the new varieties plus irrigation have made land all the more valuable. We may see at Comilla a sharpening of conflict over land possession, which may have as an added long-term result certain tendencies toward social polarization. The latter is already a distinct possibility between cooperative members and nonmembers. It remains to be seen whether within individual cooperative societies themselves this occurs between the smaller and larger landholders.

Regional Variations in Land Tenure and the Strategy of Diffusion

The diffusion of the new technology in Comilla Thana has, thus far at least, resulted in the drastic maldistribution of benefits reported for other areas where the green revolution has been in progress. And East Bengal's most populous southeastern and central districts might well have the same experience, at least in the short run, given a Comilla-like institutional strategy of diffusion, for these districts display tenurial conditions similar to those of Comilla Thana.

But regional variations in land control and social structure, those related to differences in ecology, do exist despite the widespread existence of small holdings and the lack of large-scale ownership throughout the province. The *Agricultural Census of Pakistan* (Government of Pakistan 1960), Table 3, allows the calculation that 51 percent of all farms in Bangladesh even today consist of holdings ranging from zero to 2.4 acres in size. These collectively amount to only 16 percent of the total cultivated area, however. If one includes farms of up to 4.9 acres in size, it may be said that in 1960 some 77 percent of the farms occupied 43 percent of the total cultivated area. Thus, land ownership in Bangladesh, while small scale and comparatively egalitarian, is by no means absolutely so.

Tables 2 and 3 in this chapter allow a brief glimpse into regional variations in land tenure for 1960. They compare gross areas, the divisions, which, as suggested in Table 1, broadly correspond to the different ecological zones of the Bengal Delta. In particular, the comparison between "North Bengal" or Rajshahi Division with the rest of the province is rather striking. Table 2 compares the land-ownership data of each division as percentage categories of the whole province. Its major finding is that tenancy, particularly sharecropping, is considerably higher in North Bengal than in the rest of the province. In 1960, North Bengal contained 51 percent of all the fully tenant (no ownership) farms in Bangladesh. Forty-four percent of the province's sharecroppers were in Rajshahi Division, which accounted for 37 percent of the total sharecropped area.

Table 3 presents comparative data for 1960 on land tenure in each division. Again, the same kinds of variation in landownership and tenancy are observable. In general, the size of holdings for all farms shifts from larger to smaller as one goes from northwest to southeast. The number of owner farms correspondingly varies from 51 percent in the northwest to 74 percent in the southeast. Sharecropping and other forms of tenancy are again shown to be higher in North Bengal and it can be assumed that these figures underestimate the overall as well as the comparative situations even for 1960. There is no reason to believe, in the absence of more recent data, that these tenurial conditions have changed from this general direction of subprovincial variance.

It may be argued that these differences, in a part of the world where the average farm size is little more than three acres, do not mean much and that they pale in significance beside the great concentrations of ownership in the Punjab, for example. But the smallness of farm size is no barrier to inegalitarian land relations. Indeed, Mukherjee's recently republished economic study of six

TABLE 2. Regional Differences in Land Tenure, 1960–1961

Division	% of Rural Population[a]	% of Owner Farms[b]	% of Owner-cum-Tenant Farms[b]	% of Tenant Farms[b]	% of Sharecropped Cultivated Area[c]	% of Share-croppers[d]	% of Landless Laborers[d]	% of Rice Production[e]
Rajshahi	24	21	30	51	37	44	23	22
Khulna	20	19	21	15	27	19	23	23
Dacca	30	28	32	24	24	18	30	29
Chittagong (excluding Hill Tracts)	26	32	17	10	12	19	24	26
TOTALS	100	100	100	100	100	100	100	100

[a] Government of Pakistan 1961, part 2, Table 2.
[b] Government of Pakistan 1960, Table 5.
[c] Government of Pakistan 1960, Table 9.
[d] Government of Pakistan 1961, part 5, Table 51.
[e] Government of Pakistan 1962, chapter 3, Table 1.

TABLE 3. Land Tenure Differences by Division, 1960–1961

Division	Owner Farms[a] (%)	Owner-cum-Tenant Farms[a] (%)	Tenant Farms[a] (%)	Share-croppers[b] (%)	Mean Farm Size per Cultivated Area[c]		
					Owner Farms	Owner-cum-Tenant Farms	Tenant Farms
Rajshahi	51	46	3	7	3.7	4.2	2.6
Khulna	59	40	1	4	2.9	4.9	2.8
Dacca	58	41	1	2	2.3	3.2	1.6
Chittagong (excluding Hill Tracts)	74	25	1	2	2.0	2.9	1.8
AVERAGE	61	38	2	4	2.7	3.8	2.2

a Government of Pakistan 1960, Table 2.
b Government of Pakistan 1961, part 5, Table 51.
c Government of Pakistan 1960, Table 2.

Bogra District villages in the North Bengal region shows this area to
have displayed marked disparities in land ownership in 1946,
which situation probably still obtains in goodly measure (Mukherjee 1971). Moreover, Nicholas' (1962) comparison between different ecological zones in deltaic West Bengal (India) shows the contrast in social structures and land relations reported to be considerable. The absolute dominance of the small landlord over his tenants
in the moribund delta of West Bengal varies only in quantity of
power when measured by the standard of the big landlord of West
Punjab or Sind; qualitatively, one doubts from the tenant's point of
view that there is much difference. There is, moreover, reason to
believe that this applies to the same region of East Bengal as well.

What implications, then, does this variation in land tenure in
Bangladesh's regions have for a long-run strategy for the green
revolution? Several are obvious.

1. Unless concerted efforts are made in North Bengal to assure
diffusion of the new technology to the tenants and sharecroppers,
the tendencies already apparent in areas of inegalitarian landownership elsewhere are likely to reproduce themselves. This is all
the more possible given the weakness of East Pakistan's land laws
regarding tenancy, which the new state will inherit. Ahmed and
Timmons note:

> It is, in fact, a glaring defect of the present [East Bengal State
> Acquisition and Tenancy Act of 1950]. . . that the bargadars
> [sharecroppers] are for all practical purposes considered as
> the equivalent of landless laborers and therefore can be
> ejected at will. (1971:58)

At the present time, the main season during which the new varieties have been successful is the (boro) winter season. But in
1968, as one representative recent year, Rajshahi and Khulna divisions respectively produced only 6 and 4 percent of that year's total
provincial boro crop, at which time only 7 percent of Rajshahi's and
4 percent of Khulna's cropped area was under boro cultivation
(Government of Pakistan 1969). This suggests that as tubewell irrigation spreads to the northwest land will increase in value, and it is
entirely possible that eviction of tenants will take place. It is, of
course, also possible that landlords in North Bengal and its south-

ern neighboring districts may find it equally profitable to continue utilizing tenant services as before, particularly in the absence of mechanization. But this will depend upon the relative factor costs of sharecropper versus wage labor (as provided by the landless), and if the latter proves less expensive under conditions of excess labor supply, the likelihood of large-scale tenant eviction seems more imminent. This would affect a large number of farmers, for, as Table 3 indicates, 37 percent of all farms in Bangladesh are of the owner-cum-tenant variety and this figure rises to nearly 50 percent in North Benga. Thus, many farms are dependent on some form of tenancy for their total cultivated acreage. Massive evictions would, then, not merely affect those who are tenants outright, but also the much larger number of "partial" tenants so prevalent throughout the province and thus bring on considerable social and economic polarization.

2. If, however, sharecroppers and tenants are not evicted, they still may not equally benefit from the green revolution, despite the fact that the Comilla experience shows relative neutrality to scale in the short run. As Ashraf (1971) has shown for West Pakistan, payment of rent in cash or kind takes profits from increased yields away from those who must rely on others for their cultivation land. Although they may benefit in some measure from improved varieties, their overall condition may well remain unchanged. As a pessimist might put it, their poverty merely moves to another level. The usual mode of payment for sharecroppers is in kind to the amount of half the crop. At the time of Partition, a widespread peasant movement in East Bengal called for *"tin bhag"* or "three division," that is, two-thirds of the crop to the cultivator, the rest to the landlord. One wonders whether or not the green revolution might not, at least in North Bengal, usher in a replay of the Tebhaga Movement of 1946.

Thus, all regions of the province reflect the dependence in varying degrees of farmers on rented and sharecropped land. When considering the "subsistence" farmer, this fact ought to be remembered, for, as Ahmed and Timmons (1971) suggest, the land laws of East Pakistan did not really protect the rights of either the renter or the sharecropper. Moreover, the "legislation placed great powers in the hands of revenue [and other] officials, thus increasing the charges of petty tyranny." Neither the land laws nor the actual practices of revenue and court officials in the former East Pakistan protected the rights of either owner or tenant in full measure, as anyone acquainted with Bengali peasant litigations knows. And in the continuing struggle over land possession, possibly enhanced by the demonstrated profitability of mechanized irrigation and the new rice varieties, little stands in the way, under current conditions, of polarization if those who have traditionally rented out land decide to evict their tenants.

As of this writing, Bangladesh has undertaken to develop as rapidly and effectively in agricultural production as it can—and rightly so. This brief summary has attempted to describe the social organization of the countryside, with which the new government must now deal in the effort to achieve increased agricultural production. There are, as to be expected, weaknesses and pitfalls awaiting the developers who now confront the old order; but, with skillful research and planning, the countryside may reveal concrete advantages as well.

NOTES

1. The two small villages I studied in 1966–1967 were part of a *samaj* grouping that covered eight *mauzas*, an area of over one square mile (640 acres), and encompassed a total population of about 1,800. At that time the *samaj* consisted of fourteen *sardars*, each representing intravillage groupings known as *reyai* (Bertocci 1970a:20).

2. One might, of course, argue that the centralization functions now carried out at the thana level in Comilla could equally be done in each union. However, the costs involved in setting up all the features of the thana training center in each union would be in all likelihood prohibitive. They are, as the thana-level experience at Comilla shows, unnecessary as well.

3. I am grateful to Dr. Nicolaas Luykx, director of the Food Institute of the East-West Center, Honolulu, and a former Michigan State University Adviser at Comilla, for providing me with a list of Comilla Thana markets from his own research notes. He lists some thirty-nine markets, both rural and urban, in the thana, not all of which were currently active at the time of his research.

4. The average size of holding in Comilla Thana is about 1.5 acres. Nearly 70 percent of all landholding families have two acres or less and

over 80 percent of them report their incomes as being at the subsistence level only or below it. See chapter 6, Tables 1 and 2.

5. In his discussion of the traditional system of rural credit in Comilla Thana, A. A. Khan notes:

Since the agriculturalist lenders enjoy the annual output of [the] land as interest [on] their money, they do not bother about the realization of debt. They rather like to continue [sic] their possession [of] such mortgaged land by not realizing debt. (1968:25)

How much less inclined will mortgage holders be to relinquish control over valuable land under the new productivity conditions of the green revolution?

BIBLIOGRAPHY

Ahmad, Nafis
  1956. "The Pattern of Rural Settlement in East Pakistan." *Geographical Review* 46:388–398.
Ahmed, Iftikhar, and Timmons, John F.
  1956. "Current Land Reforms in East Pakistan." *Land Economics* 47:55–64.
Allen, B. D.
  1912. *Bengal District Gazetteers: Dacca*. Allahabad: Pioneer Press.
Ashraf, Muhammed
  1971. "Micro Level Causes of Income Disparity in Rural Punjab." Paper presented at the Workshop on Rural Development in Pakistan, Michigan State University.
Bertocci, Peter J.
  1970a. "Elusive Villages: Social Structure and Community Organization in Rural East Pakistan." Ph.D. dissertation, Michigan State University.
  1970b. "Patterns of Social Organization in Rural East Bengal." In *Bengal East and West*, edited by Alexander Lipski, pp. 107–137. East Lansing: Asian Studies Center, Michigan State University.
  1972. "Community Structure and Social Rank in Two Villages in Bangladesh." *Contributions to Indian Sociology* (n.s.) 6:28–52.
Ellickson, Jean
  1972. "A Believer among Believers: The Religious Beliefs, Practices and Meanings in a Village in Bangladesh." Ph.D. dissertation, Michigan State University.

Glasse, Robert
  1965. "La Société Musulmane dans le Pakistan Rural de l'Est."
        Études Rurales 1966:188–205.
Government of Pakistan
  1962. *Agricultural Census of Pakistan 1960.* Vol. 2. East Pakistan.
        Agricultural Census Organization. Ministry of Food and Ag-
        riculture.
  1962. "Production of Crops by Provinces, Divisions and Districts,
        1947–48 to 1961–62." *Land and Crop Statistics of Pakistan.*
        Chap. 3. Fact Series No. 3. Department of Agricultural
        Economics and Statistics.
  1964. *Population Census of Pakistan 1961.* Vol. 2. East Pakistan.
        Ministry of Home and Kashmir Affairs. Division of Home Af-
        fairs. Karachi: Manager of Publications.
  1961. *Yearbook of Agricultural Statistics, 1968.* Fact Series No. 7.
        Ministry of Agriculture and Works. Food and Agriculture Di-
        vision.
Islam, A. K. M. Aminul
  1974. *A Bangladesh Village: Conflict and Cohesion.* Cambridge,
        Mass.: Schenkman Publishing Co.
Khan, Akhter Hameed.
  1970. *Tour of Twenty Thanas.* Comilla: Pakistan Academy for Rural
        Development.
Khan, Ali Akhtar
  1968. *Rural Credit in Gazipur Village.* Comilla: Pakistan Academy
        for Rural Development.
Mukherjee, Ramkrishna
  1971. *Six Villages of Bengal.* Bombay: Popular Prakashan.
Nicholas, Ralph W.
  1962. "Villages of the Bengal Delta." Ph.D. dissertation, University
        of Chicago.
Owen, John E., ed.
  1962. *Sociology in East Pakistan.* Dacca: Asiatic Society of Pakistan.
Patel, Ahmed M.
  1963. "The Rural Markets of Rajshahi District." *Oriental Geog-
        rapher* 7:140–151.
Qadir, S. A.
  1960. *Village Dhaniswar: Three Generations of Man-Land Adjust-
        ment in an East Pakistan Village.* Comilla: Pakistan Academy
        for Rural Development.

Rahman, A. T. R.
    1962. *Basic Democracies at the Grass Roots: A Study of Three Union Councils of Kotwali Thana, Comilla*. Comilla: Pakistan Academy for Rural Development.
    1963. *An Analysis of the Working of Basic Democracy Institutions in East Pakistan*. Comilla: Pakistan Academy for Rural Development.

Raper, Arthur
    1970. *Rural Development in Action: The Comprehensive Experiment at Comilla, East Pakistan*. Ithaca: Cornell University Press.

Rashid, Haroun Er
    1967. *East Pakistan: A Systematic Regional Geography and Its Development Planning Aspects*. 2nd ed. Lahore: Sh. Ghulam Ali and Sons.

Research Section
    1963. Coordinated List of Villages for Comilla Kotwali Thana. Comilla: Pakistan Academy for Rural Development. Mimeographed.

Skinner, G. William
    1964. "Marketing and Social Structure in Rural China, Part I." *Journal of Asian Studies* 24:3–43.
    1965. "Marketing and Social Structure in Rural China, Part III." *Journal of Asian Studies* 24:363–399.

Smith Marion W.
    1946. "Village Notes from Bengal." *American Anthropologist* 48:574–592.

Sobhan, Rahman
    1968. *Basic Democracies, Works Programme and Rural Development in East Pakistan*. Dacca: Bureau of Economic Research, University of Dacca.

Stevens, Robert D.
    1967. *Institutional Change and Agricultural Development: Some Evidence from Comilla, East Pakistan*. East Lansing: Department of Agricultural Economics, Michigan State University.

Thomas, John W.
    1968. "Rural Public Works and East Pakistan's Development." Mimeographed. Cambridge, Mass.: Development Advisory Service, Harvard University.

Zaidi, S. M. Hafeez
    1970.   *The Village Culture in Transition: A Study of East Pakistan
             Rural Society*. Honolulu: East-West Center Press.
Ziring, Lawrence
    1966.   "The Administration of Basic Democracies." In *Administra-
             tive Problems in Pakistan*, edited by Guthrie S. Birkhead, pp.
             31–62. Syracuse: Syracuse University Press.

PART II
RURAL
DEVELOPMENT IN
PAKISTAN

9

Themes in Economic Growth and Social Change in Rural Pakistan: An Introduction

Robert D. Stevens

Rural development in the late sixties in Pakistan (formerly West Pakistan)[1] has been hailed as an outstanding example of effective government planning combined with vibrant private entrepreneurship. Contrary to the expectations of many at the time of Independence in 1947, Pakistan had apparently achieved an economic breakthrough, ending the vicious cycle of centuries-old stagnation and poverty. But, ironically, as international recognition of these accomplishments grew, civil disturbances occurred in 1969 that not only brought down the government that had been heralded as the initiator of the nation's economic growth, but also led to the traumatic crises of civil war, division, and new political leaders who veered sharply away from previous policies.

These economic and social developments raise questions in a nation still largely rural. For example, a major puzzle is, To what extent were the developments in the economic and political areas independent of each other or, What were the significant social and economic interrelationships influencing the outcome? In order to shed light on these and many other questions, the chapters that follow provide detail of significant social and economic developments in rural areas of Pakistan. They also offer alternative theses about the amount of social and economic change that has occurred and analyses of the effects of these types of changes on political change.

Pakistan covers an area of 310,000 square miles. This nation of an estimated 62 million persons in 1971 is composed of four major language and cultural groups in distinct geographic regions: the large irrigated plains of the Punjab containing more than half the population; the mountainous regions of the North-West Frontier Province where the Pushto-speaking people reside; the flat, partly irrigated desert of the Sind; and mountainous, sparsely populated Baluchistan. In terms of both area and value, wheat is by far the most dominant crop in the nation. Rice, sugarcane, and cotton are other major crops. Except for the rain-fed northern highlands and mountainous areas, the production of a large proportion of the major crops is dependent upon the vast irrigation systems of the Indus river basin, which water three-quarters of the cultivated area.

In the following pages, a brief background to the political and economic development of Pakistan is offered to place the individual chapters in perspective. In a subsequent section, themes and controversies that emerge in the contributions of the several authors are highlighted. On some issues, there is general consensus among writers with different disciplinary backgrounds; while on other topics sharply divergent views are held, based to some extent on alternative hypotheses about the nature of the economic and social change occurring in Pakistan.

Brief Background on Political and Economic Development

In the light of economic and political development theory, Pakistan over the last two decades presents a disappointment to some and a paradox to others. It was once thought that success in economic development—that is, growth in national income—was the key to social and political progress and stability. No better example of the validity of this belief, at least in the eyes of some observers, was to be found than in the Pakistan of the mid-sixties in the heyday of the Ayub Khan era. The Pakistan of that period seemed to provide living proof that, given the "right" policies, economic development with "stability" was possible for an exceedingly poor country. As Gustav Papanek put it in his summary of the achievements of the former Pakistan that contained both east and west wings, the country had confounded the prophets of gloom.

By the middle 1960s the rate of economic growth was more than double the rate of population growth; investment was approaching a healthy 20 percent, and savings exceeded 10 percent of domestic resources. Prices were stable, foreign exchange earnings were increasing at 7.5 percent a year, and foreign resources were being used with increasing effectiveness. Pakistan was widely regarded as one of the half dozen countries in the world with the greatest promise of steady development. In the face of its pitiful resource and capital endowment at independence, and in comparison with other countries, Pakistan's performance was outstanding. (Papanek 1967:2)

The Pakistan of that period achieved an annual rate of economic growth of 6.2 percent between 1959 and 1965, as against 2.6 percent throughout the 1950s.

Industrial development was the star performer of the Pakistani economy from 1950 onward with five-year average rates of growth of between 12 and 34 percent in West Pakistan.[2] Agriculture, the "sick child" of the 1950s with an annual 1.8 percent growth rate,[3] was regenerated with remarkable vitality after 1959. In West Pakistan, the growth rate from 1961 to 1971 reached 5.6 percent annually (Gill 1973:38), an extraordinary performance. There can be no denying Pakistan's economic achievements, at least by conventional measures.

During this period of economic florescence, there was frequent applause by some Western observers for Pakistan's "political stability." To them, Ayub Khan, hailed by some as the "DeGaulle of Asia," had erected a system of political management that was succeeding in maximizing economic growth while containing those elements in the country's political structure that threatened continually to disrupt the "progress" toward a strong and viable nation-state. Other analysts, however, noted underlying, and increasingly active, sources of instability in Pakistan. A rereading of their writings of the mid-sixties reveals a chronicle of the successive challenges to Ayub's political system (see, for example, Ahmad 1967:150–182; Sayeed 1967a, 1967b, 1968; Sobhan 1968). Regional disparities in the benefits of growth were creating increasing discontent. Disquiet was evident in urban areas, where perceived relative deprivation was producing an inchoate, but mountingly effective resistance. Finally, the country's intelligentsia, inspired by the vision of political modernity, displayed growing restiveness in the grip of the autocratic presidential system.

Thus, while for some the Ayub Khan era was proof of the close interrelationship between political stability and economic growth, for others the evidence was more mixed. While few denied Pakistan's impressive growth rates, attention was drawn by the cautious pessimists to what can in retrospect perhaps be perceived as the "gathering storm."

The failure in 1969 of Ayub Khan's political system disappointed those to whom it had promised much in the way of vindication of traditional theories of national development. At best, it seemed a paradox that despite economic success, political stability could not be registered. Some see Ayub's fall as evidence that a paternalistic leader, surrounded by a traditionalistic elite, is not capable of mobilizing a disparate national population to the task of achieving national unity (see, for example, Ziring 1970). For others, Pakistan's experience provides sad evidence of the difficulty inherent in the attempts of a highly pluralistic political culture to realize the value consensus upon which political development must be based (Wheeler 1970). And, in contrast to these views, left-oriented analysts have, not surprisingly, seen the events of 1968 and 1969 as the natural outcome of capitalist development— concentration of wealth, the polarization of social classes, the growth of class consciousness, and the beginning stages of revolution, which may eventually envelop the whole of the subcontinent (see, for example, Ali 1970). Whatever grains of truth may be found in these analyses, it will probably be some time before we are able to assess fully the Ayub Khan period in Pakistan and the meaning of Ayub's fall. But these recent attempts to do so have at least one virtue that will inform future efforts. They raise serious questions about the thesis that economic growth alone is sufficient for national well-being. Pakistan's recent history teaches us that economic growth and political stability are not necessarily natural correlates.

The sweeping success in West Pakistan's fall elections of 1970 of Zulfikar Ali Bhutto's Peoples' Party, which was based on a reformist platform, was in part a political expression of some of the recurring themes in the following chapters. For example, Bhutto's announcement in March 1972 of a land reform to involve over one million acres was a political expression of concern with the great inequality in income. The crisis and abrupt change in politics in Pakistan may be signs of a crisis of social and economic development policy that result from a certain line of development. While neither inevitable nor necessarily unique, the experience may well hold important lessons for students of economic and social change.

Major Themes and Controversies in Rural Development

Five major themes and controversies stand out in the following chapters on rural economic growth and social change in Pakistan: (1) agricultural stagnation and growth, including explanations of growth and identification of the beneficiaries of growth; (2) the regional effects of agricultural growth; (3) the nature of the changing relationships in the political and social sphere associated with economic and technical changes in rural areas; (4) impending crises and possible outcomes in rural development; and (5) implications for the role of government and political institutions in the solution of rural problems. Each of these themes is now considered in turn.

Dimensions of agricultural stagnation and growth in particular areas of Pakistan are woven into parts of most chapters, but the four chapters by Raulet, Gotsch (chapter 17), Burki, and Rochin focus most directly on these issues. In chapter 10, Raulet examines major factors shaping the rural economy in the colonial period of present-day Pakistan. He points to the stagnation of agriculture in the unstable conditions of the subcontinent during the eighteenth century. In the following century, agricultural expansion occurred because of colonial actions that greatly strengthened law and order and also improved transportation. Of particular importance were the fifty years of major canal irrigation projects that began in the 1880s. Thus, at Independence, Pakistan inherited one of the largest gravity irrigation systems in the world. In spite of this, as a result of the slowing down in the expansion of irrigated areas in the 1930s, per capita crop output appears to have begun to decline in the two decades prior to Independence. This trend continued after Independence. In the 1950s, agriculture in Pakistan grew at less than 2 percent per annum. Coupled with a population growth estimated at 2.3 percent per annum, food production per capita continued its gradual decline, and food imports had to be increased.

Gotsch, in chapter 17, provides details of the extraordinarily rapid agricultural growth of the 1960s, in which crop production is estimated to have increased at a rate approaching 6 percent annually. Burki (chapter 15) adds depth to our understanding of these developments in the early 1960s by pointing out that these increases were due primarily to greatly increased use of tubewell water and fertilizer. The high-yielding wheat and rice varieties did not become widely available in Pakistan until 1967. There is a general consensus in the chapters that follow about the outline presented here of agricultural stagnation and subsequent growth.

The authors focus the greater part of their writing on explanations of the dramatic acceleration in agricultural production in the 1960s. Parts of the analysis in Gotsch's two chapters provide details of such direct causes as the greater availability of agricultural inputs, including seed, fertilizer, and water. Using a linear programming model, Gotsch demonstrates that on a typical 12.5-acre farm using tubewell water and advanced rice, maize, and wheat technology the index of cropping intensity could profitably increase from 110 to 152 with an associated 85-percent increase in net revenue (chapter 13). Rochin also shows the impact of the new inputs on production in the rain-fed district of Hazara where the dwarf wheats have doubled yields per acre (chapter 14). As little had been known about the performance of the new dwarf varieties in nonirrigated farming areas this research result is of particular interest.

A more general interdisciplinary explanation for the stagnation of agriculture in the 1950s and its acceleration in the 1960s was sought by Burki. While granting the increased input flows in the latter decade, he pursues the thesis that government decision-making had a major influence on agricultural growth and asks the underlying questions as to why decisions in Pakistan's political economy were made that first caused agricultural stagnation and then acceleration. More specifically, why were the flows of agricultural inputs accelerated in the 1960s? Burki advances two hypotheses: (1) that the interests of the politically dominant landed aristocracy in the 1950s resulted in little attention to increased agricultural productivity; and (2) that the rise of the new middle-class capitalist farmers in the 1960s, resulting at least partly from the Ayub Khan land reforms of 1958, influenced government policy and the civil service to shift to activities that supported increased productivity in agriculture.

The authors are in substantial agreement that the major beneficiaries of the green revolution in Pakistan have been the medium (50 to 100 acres) and large farmers. However, during this revolutionary change, a large proportion of farmers in all size categories appear to have obtained some absolute increase in production through the widespread adoption of the high-yielding rice and wheat seeds as shown in the details of Rochin's study and Gotsch's chapter 13. In this chapter, Gotsch also indicates the special conditions under which the relative position of small farmers might improve. However, in spite of the widespread adoption of the new varieties, rural income disparities have increased considerably. Thus, the outstanding achievement of rapid growth in agricultural production has brought with it unanticipated consequences for social and political structures in rural areas, an issue elaborated on by a number of the authors.

Although the second major theme of increasing regional income disparities during the 1960s may appear on hindsight to be obvious, the one-unit government in West Pakistan until the late 1960s and the dominance of Punjab Province in the economy tended to obscure regional problems. The extent of increased regional disparities is documented by Alavi (chapter 16) and Gotsch (chapter 13) and commented on by Hasan (chapter 12). The data show strong relative gains by the Punjab generally and by particular districts in the Punjab.

More diverse views show forth on the third major theme—the changing relationships between rural Pakistan's political and social structures and economic and technological changes. The authors address themselves to various parts of these relationships using different professional tools. Perpsective is provided by Raulet's historical approach in which he points to major factors shaping the rural economy during the two centuries of the colonial period. The significant changes include much improved rural security, greatly increased transportation, and immense expansion of irrigated areas. This history illustrates the now classic Schultzian model of expansion of agriculture under virtually stagnant technology (Schultz 1964). During these decades, the social system, in spite of such internal changes as the expulsion of the rural moneylender, appears to have maintained mechanisms, such as tenancy and credit, for extracting most of the additional income from peasant farmers. Hence farmers' levels of living in 1947 appear not to have been much higher than a century earlier.

The premise that representative local government is a precondition to genuine rural development is employed by Ahmad (chapter 11). His research thus focuses sharply on the development of rural self-government in Pakistan as he traces the limited colonial effort toward local self-government and examines the reasons for the continuing weakness of local democracy after two decades of independence. In particular, he finds an inherent contradiction in charging the civil service bureaucracy with the task of encouraging local democracy, for this in turn would reduce the power of the bureaucracy. This contradiction, he suggests, has caused rural local government to remain an adjunct of central administration. Perhaps the most critical factors considered by Ahmad for the development of local self-government are those that show the weakness of democratic values in rural society in Pakistan. In conclusion Ahmad asks whether the civil service can change its role in Pakistan so as to limit its actions in order to assure the free operation of local government. If not, he sees the bureaucracy continuing the strategy of struggling against elected representatives to retain power in rural areas.

Burki, from experience within the Civil Service of Pakistan, takes the view that the rural bureaucracy is sufficiently responsive to changes in the rural power structure, and, in particular, that it is not wed to any one group such as the landed aristocracy. Thus, he judges it will align itself with new political groups as they emerge in rural areas, such as the new middle class farmers. However we evaluate these different conclusions about the role of the civil bureaucracy past and future, there is little doubt that the actions of this group will greatly influence future events in rural areas whether in an evolutionary manner or toward more violent changes.

The fourth major theme, on future trends in rural development in Pakistan, arose from evidence of increasing tension in rural areas. One way of posing the question is to ask: To what extent will changes in rural social and political structures be required by continued rapid growth in agriculture associated with further widening of income disparities? Gotsch and Burki, who address themselves most directly to this question, come to different conclusions, the former more pessimistic. Gotsch foresees the new class of progressive larger farmers with increasing political influence pressuring for continued high agricultural price supports and low taxes while opposing increased public control over water resources and mechanization. The result of this package of policies will be to increase income disparities and further exacerbate rising rural unemployment. Gotsch is not optimistic that in the near future Pakistani society will easily develop the reformist instruments necessary to cope with these contradictions. In contrast, Burki sees evidence from the rise of the middle-class farmer, helped by the Basic Democracies electoral process and the associated political adjustments, that the social system is sufficiently elastic to accommodate to changing conditions. He, however, does foresee increased rates of political conflict with the emergence of new political groups and changes in economic and social structures.

The fifth major theme relates to the implications of these analyses for the role of government and political institutions in Pakistan. On this theme, the professionally disparate scholars in this volume seem in general accord. In all cases, a strong government role appears to be assumed or to be required, implicitly in the case of Burki, more specifically by other authors. Gotsch and Hasan point to the particular economic roles required of government, such as adjusting domestic agricultural product and input prices so as to be more in line with international prices. Both emphasize the need to increase taxes on agriculture, especially in view of the windfall gains from the new seeds obtained by larger farmers. A related needed policy change involves the reduction of subsidies on agricultural inputs, including particularly mechanical inputs, fertilizer, and pesticides. While documenting the increased regional income disparities resulting from the green revolution in Pakistan, a phenomenon observed worldwide, Hasan, Gotsch, and Alavi particularly ask government to undertake actions that will modify or compensate for this trend.

With respect to the role of government in support of the small farmer, four policy thrusts stand out in these analyses. First, Rochin has shown how the success of the new wheats among *barani* farmers has encouraged these farmers to expect government to provide more income-increasing technology. Second, Hasan and Gotsch mention the possibility that small farmers might obtain more land through land redistribution. Lack of emphasis on this possibility was probably due to pessimism at the time of writing about the political realities of such a reform being carried out or having significant impact. Third, the ominous problem of immense rural unemployment is discussed by Hasan and is stressed by Gotsch. Hasan calls for specific government policies that would influence the rate and kinds of technological change in agriculture so as to prevent rapid decreases in agricultural employment. The final policy thrust relates to the bureaucracy's role in aiding self-government among the predominantly small-farmer populations of rural areas. Ahmad advises that the withdrawal of the bureaucracy from rural politics would greatly aid self-government, while Gotsch, following similar thinking, calls more specifically for the development of farmer-dominated grass-roots organizations.

In the 1960s, Pakistan commenced an immense rural agricultural transformation that will continue throughout this century. The impact of economic and technical changes on rural society has hardly begun. Effective, farseeing technical and social science research could have a major productive impact on Pakistan by helping to guide the nation more smoothly through the pressures and contradictions of rapid social, technical, and economic changes in rural areas. The costs of inappropriate and bad policies can be great, especially for the poorer half of the population.

NOTES

The author appreciates Peter Bertocci's aid in developing parts of this chapter.

1. Throughout this volume the designation Pakistan, unless otherwise indicated, is used to identify the area of land formerly called West Pakistan in the larger Pakistan of the years 1947–1971.

2. For additional data, see Papanek (1967:20, 318).

3. Derived from Papanek (1967:317).

BIBLIOGRAPHY

Ahmad, Kamruddin
  1967. *The Social History of East Pakistan*. Dacca: Mrs. Raushan Ara
    Ahmed.
Ali, Tariq
  1970. *Pakistan: Military Rule or People's Power*. London: Jonathan
    Cape
Gill, Amjad H.
  1973. *Pakistan's Agricultural Development and Trade*. Washington,
    D. C.: Economic Research Service, ERS-Foreign 347, U.S.
    Department of Agriculture.
Papanek, Gustav F.
  1967. *Pakistan's Development: Social Goals and Private Incentives*.
    Cambridge, Mass.: Harvard University Press.
Sayeed, Khalid bin
  1967a. *The Political System of Pakistan*. London: Oxford University
    Press.
  1967b. "The Capabilities of Pakistan's Political System." *Asian Survey* 7:102–110.
  1968. "Pakistan: New Challenges to the Political System." *Asian
    Survey* 8:97–104.
Schultz, Theodore W.
  1964. *Transforming Traditional Agriculture*. New Haven: Yale
    University Press.
Sobhan, Rahman
  1968. *Basic Democracies, Works Programme and Rural Development in East Pakistan*. Dacca: Bureau of Economics, Dacca
    University.
Stevens, Robert D.
  1972. *Rural Development Programs for Adaptation from Comilla,
    Bangladesh*. East Lansing: Department of Agricultural
    Economics, AER No. 215, Michigan State University.
Wheeler, Richard S.
  1970. *The Politics of Pakistan: A Constitutional Quest*. Ithaca: Cornell University Press.
Ziring, Lawrence
  1970. *The Ayub Khan Era: Politics in Pakistan, 1958–1969*. Syracuse: Syracuse University Press.

10

The Historical Context
of Pakistan's Rural Economy

Harry M. Raulet

Over the years, beginning well back in the nineteenth century, there has been an interest in accounting for the impact of British rule on the South Asian agrarian economy, and in explaining the backwardness of agriculture in the subcontinent. Much of the discussion is polemical, and there is disagreement on many points; nevertheless, there is considerable convergence in viewpoint, even between some of the earlier writers and the more recent. This chapter explores briefly, in the light of the more or less classic Indian experience, some of the major factors shaping the rural economy of the Pakistan region before Independence: the expansion of irrigation, tenancy, moneylending, and agricultural debt. This analysis is confined almost entirely to the Punjab.

The Early Impact of British Rule

It is assumed that the Moguls and the rulers of successor political entities, such as the Sikhs, held to a major policy aim of maximizing revenue from the agricultural surplus of cultivators. A principal means of accomplishing this in any given area was to take measures to increase the total number of cultivators, a feasible approach in view of the relative abundance of cultivable land at the time. Some writers estimate that yields were considerably higher in Mogul times than in the recent past, because marginal land was seldom used, and because with abundant pasturage, a much larger amount of animal manure was used for fertilizer (Raychaudhuri 1969: 82–83; Habib 1963:53–57). Presumably there was relatively little concern with increasing productivity. The main objective of the rulers was to maintain sociopolitical conditions favorable to stable or increasing numbers of cultivators, and to realize the treasury's share of the surplus, in competition with other claimants: revenue officials, assignees, zamindars, and the cultivators themselves, along with village menial clients of the latter. It has been held generally that land was not a commodity to be bought and sold on the market and that the system focused instead on the rights of various claimants to the product.

British rule is credited with having provided law and order and stable conditions for agriculture, particularly in contrast to the tumultuous political and military atmosphere that prevailed after the breakdown of the Mogul empire. In some areas law and order and political stability came only after a long period of economic decay, to which the British East India Company and its officials made a considerable contribution. Under the British, during the nineteenth century, an elaborate new legal basis for landownership was erected involving more or less absolute proprietorship, along with a system of revenue assessment and collection that was based partly on native precedent.

By the time the British Raj was several decades old in the Indus Plains region to the northwest of the Sutlej River, procedures for dealing with periodic famine conditions had evolved, and with the construction of roads and railways and swift interregional movement of food supplies, effective measures for meliorating the loss of human life associated with severe famines were at hand. At the same time, the improved transportation served distant domestic and export markets for agricultural products, and fostered regional specialization in crops.

Under the systems of land tenure introduced by the British, variable as they were, proprietors generally had the right to sell or mortgage holdings, and the new judicial system facilitated the recovery of money debts and protected the rights of mortgage holders. Proprietors often sought loans to pay the government revenue assessments or arrears in their assessments, or fell into debt when, after having sold their crops at the low price prevailing at harvest time, they borrowed to buy them back six months later at high prices. The market value of land tended to increase rapidly, beginning at least by the 1860s, and the alienation of land to mortgage holders became common. A factor in this process was the increase in population, slow until 1921 and increasingly rapid thereafter. Given the system of partible inheritance of land under customary law, and, perhaps even more important, the failure of employment opportunities outside of the agricultural sector to keep pace with the growth of population, there was increasing competition for available land (Thorner and Thorner 1962:77; Gadgil 1959:155). This exerted an upward pressure on the price of land and encouraged the entry of land into mortgage transactions. At the same time, there arose the general practice of proprietors, "original," or those who acquired land through mortgage or sale, giving their holdings over to tenants for cultivation, sometimes for cash rents, always for a major share of the product of the land.

There is some disagreement on the net effects of British rule on agriculture. Some writers have stated that the nineteenth century was a period of growth in the sense of expanded per capita output (Morris 1969:8; Neale 1962:141–148). If such growth occurred, it probably was not of great magnitude. Increased income to cultivators is said to have resulted in part from the shift from grains to high-value commercial crops during the second half of the nineteenth century (Raychaudhuri 1969:91). In the famine decades of the 1870s and 1890s there was a tendency to shift back to subsistence crops along with a decline in the double-cropped area (Gadgil 1959:89). Blyn, in a study covering the period 1891–1947, found that in all India the per capita production of all crops expanded slightly faster than population until around 1921/22; after 1922 growth in output fell behind population growth (Blyn 1966:247). In the last decades of British rule (particularly in the Punjab) contributions to increased yields may have come from improved seeds (Blyn 1966:200–202). On the other hand, the decreased availability of animal manures for fertilizer and the reduced size and increasing fragmentation of holdings are thought to have been dampening influences on yield (Blyn 1966:195–197, 211–212). There was little change in agricultural equipment, and on the whole, the level of technology did not advance throughout the whole period.

The evidence seems to favor those who claim that the new socioeconomic order was decidedly unfavorable to progress in agriculture. The decisive feature is the nexus of relations between the cultivators and the new rural elites, the landlords and the moneylenders, by means of which the agricultural surplus was distributed. The Thorners have stated:

In retrospect, the net effect of British rule was to change dras-

tically the social fabric of Indian agriculture, but to leave virtually unaffected the basic process of production and the level
of technology. The upper strata of this new agrarian society
benefited handsomely. The position of cultivators deteriorated. Capital needed for the development of agriculture was
siphoned off, and the level of total output tended toward stagnation. (1962:11)

In summary, British rule provided law and order and stable
political conditions for agriculture in place of the instability characteristic of the eighteenth century in India. A new legal framework,
involving absolute proprietorship of land, superceded the native
system of land control and provided a new basis for credit and sales
transactions. The market for agricultural products expanded, and,
ultimately, as the transportation and communications networks
grew and administration became more refined, famines were
brought under control. Population began to increase, and in the
absence of sufficient expansion of alternative employment, the agricultural sector became increasingly crowded, the price of land
increased, wages remained near subsistence level, and tenancy
became prevalent.

The perspective provided by the foregoing analysis is misleading in at least one respect. It conveys an impression of abrupt dis-
continuity in rural social structure from precolonial to late colonial
times, as one-sided as would be an account that depicted rural
society persisting unchanged to the present. Moreover, one might
suspect that if the new order was unfavorable to the genuine development of the rural economy, it might have failed also to provide
conditions favorable to the emergence of qualitatively new rural
institutions. As Geertz has suggested in his analysis of "posttradi-
tional" rural society in Java, behind the appearance of institutional
innovation there may lurk a reality of traditional structure (Geertz
1963:90).

Irrigation Development and Economic Growth in the Punjab

The human geography of the Indus Plains today, particularly
that portion that now constitutes the heartland of Pakistan, is

closely tied in with the development of modern irrigation works. Before the construction of these projects, rainfall agriculture was practiced in the submontane districts and irrigation agriculture was supported by means of inundation canals along the rivers, but the *doab*s (or areas between the rivers) were sparsely inhabited, as were most of the desert areas to the east and west of the Indus. Without the modern irrigation system, Michel estimates that the population of Pakistan today would be hardly more than 20 million (Michel 1967:12). The irrigation system and the great canal colonization projects shaped the distribution of the modern transportation network, the location of large towns and cities, and the distribution of major ethnic and religious communities as we know them today. It also was due primarily to the irrigation and canal colony projects that the Punjab shifted from a position as one of the most economically backward provinces in the last century to that of the most progressive in the early twentieth century.

The first perennial scheme, the Upper Bari Doab Canal, is said to have been planned primarily to provide employment to Sikh army veterans (Michel 1967:61). The wave of projects begun in the 1880s was designed to bring irrigation to sparsely inhabited crown lands. It was expected that these colonization projects would increase the amount of revenue and provide a surplus of grain for famine-prone areas, while at the same time they would relieve population pressure in the congested areas of Gurdaspur, Amritsar, Jullundhur, and Hoshiarpur districts (Paustian 1930:68–69; Michel 1967:75–76).

The later canal colonies, with initial conditions unusually favorable to agricultural growth, became the site of an agrarian prosperity perhaps unparalleled in South Asia at the time. The Lyallpur colony, opened in 1893 in the lower Chenab colony area, is a prime example of this development. Land had been distributed to colonists in grants of one or more perennially irrigated squares (approximately twenty-five acres), and 70 percent of the cultivated area was estimated to have been in owners' holdings of twenty-five acres or more in 1925 (Calbert 1925:14). Allotments were made mostly to "peasant" grantees (as distinguished from "yeoman" and "capitalist" grantees), who were selected from among the cultivating castes of Central Punjab and who were regarded as among the most skilled in the province. With an agricultural college at Lyallpur and with special grants throughout the colonies for experiments in agricultural development, the environment for technical innovations seemed favorable. In the 1920s agricultural prices were at record levels, cultivators' incomes were high, and optimism was rather general. It was in reference to Lyallpur and similar canal colonies that Malcolm Darling speculated on the possibility of a "new agricultural civilization" emerging in the Punjab (Darling 1947:36).

These canal colony projects resulted in a more equal distribution of population throughout the Punjab. In 1921, the density of population in the above-named districts ranged from 401 to 583 per square mile and was approximately the same as it had been in 1881. On the other hand, the growth of population in the western Indus Plains caused some anxiety about the economic future. In Multan, population density increased over the same period from 94 to 150 per square mile; in Shahpur the increase was from 86 to 161; in Montgomery, from 78 to 154; and in Lyallpur District from 12 to 301 per square mile (Paustian 1930:82).

During the early part of this period the total cultivated area expanded faster than did the population, but beginning about 1920 the process reversed, and the average size of holdings shrank throughout the Punjab, and in the canal colonies as well, where natural increase was augmenting population growth. By 1926/27, the average size of cultivators' holdings in the canal colonies was only 9.8 acres (Paustian 1930:101). At this time, the large Sutlej Valley project, intended to irrigate 5 million acres, was yet to be completed, and in the neighboring Sind Province, irrigation potential had not yet been fully exploited, so there was no immediate crisis. But in retrospect, the significance of the trend was clear; it was noted in the 1920s and 1930s by observers such as Malcolm Darling.

Increasing Rural Tenancy

Views on the problems posed by tenancy in the Punjab have been varied. Although the cultivation of land by tenants has been common since at least the 1880s, the Punjabi agricultural scene has retained the image of an area dominated by peasant proprietors. The Jats are by far the largest caste group in the province, and, under Sikh rule, they gained control over a large proportion of the cultivated tracts (van den Dungen 1968:75). Unlike the Rajput zamindars, whose control over many tracts was broken during the Sikh times, the Jats were by tradition cultivators, personally engaging in agricultural work. Tenancy in its modern sense apparently did not exist in pre-British times. *Biradaris* (lineages) would sometimes invite members of other castes to cultivate in their tract and share the burden of heavy revenue assessments imposed by Sikhs or other rulers. And, of course, zamindari groups claimed a share of the product or revenue. When the British made the early revenue settlements, they usually conferred proprietorship on the *biradaris* that cultivated and claimed traditional rights in the land. Consequently, in the initial years of British rule the Punjab was relatively free of proprietors having superior claims over the actual cultivators, and occupancy tenants were less characteristic than in the provinces to the east. However, in 1880/81 the proportion of total cultivated area cultivated by tenants is given as 34.7 percent, it rose to 46.0 percent in 1890/91, 54.0 percent in 1903/04, and was well over 50.0 percent in 1925 (Imperial Gazetteer of India 1908:307; Calvert 1925:9).[1] The tenant category was not clear-cut in the Punjab as a large proportion of those renting in land were themselves owners, and there was generally no sharp caste distinction between tenants and owners (Calvert 1928:11).

Before the turn of the century, holdings of 100 acres had been given to the "yeoman" category of colonists, and two or three times that much to "capitalist" grantees, in the hope that they would have a catalytic effect in improving the agriculture of the colony (Paustian 1930:69–70; Darling 1947:117–122). The new peasant grantee, however, proved to be inclined toward absentee landlordism rather than progressive farming, and the practice of making such grants discontinued. By the mid-1920s the majority of cultivators owned less than 7.5 acres (Darling 1947:7), and the persistence of the tenancy patterns was taken for granted. It was hoped that some of the productivity-dampening effects of tenant farming might be meliorated when the larger landowners learned to make improvements on the land let out on *batai* (on shares), and even that more of the large landowners might try to realize the somewhat higher profits available from direct cultivation of their land (Stewart 1926:1–2, 1927).

The New Class of Agricultural Moneylenders

By the 1920s, the moneylenders as well as the larger landholders were more and more often from the cultivating castes. In the nineteenth century the primary source of credit was the village *sahukar* (professional moneylender), of Bania, Khatri, or Arora caste. By the turn of the century there was considerable alarm over the level of rural debt, the transfer of land to nonagriculturalists through mortgage, and the share of the provinces' wealth appropriated by the moneylenders. A series of legal measures, beginning with the Punjab Land Alienation Act of 1900, were taken to prevent the transfer of land from cultivators and to strengthen them against the moneylenders in other ways. Apparently the *sahukar* remained strong through the period of World War I (Darling 1947:175), but after this his monopolist position in supplying credit was broken, and the agriculturalist moneylender appeared on the scene. With funds accumulated through soldiering, as traders, or as emigrants to Australia, cultivators, particularly Jats, entered the moneylending market on a large scale, and throughout the prosperous 1920s the agriculturalist moneylenders increased their numbers and operations, while, it is reported, the *sahukar*s actually began to leave the villages (Darling 1947:192). By 1930, one-half of the total agricultural debt, 70 crores, was owed to the agriculturalist moneylenders who held almost all of the usufructuary mortgages (Darling 1947:197; see also van den Dungen 1968 on the subject of Jat moneylenders). Darling comments that:

> It has been shown that only the small minority [of agriculturists], probably not more than 26%, are free of debt. Allowing for those who borrow as well as lend, the probability is that the 70 crores are held by at most 30 per cent of the agriculturists of the province. If so, the inference is that while the bulk of the peasantry have been steadily getting more involved, a favored few have been growing increasingly prosperous.(1947:214)

The moneylender, in spite of his negative image, is commonly regarded as having provided a necessary service to the credit-hungry peasant economy. Legislation designed to curtail the *sahukar* did not abolish moneylending, but gave a competitive edge to the agriculturist moneylender. The latter had other advantages as well. The Jat, particularly when he had financial strength, occupied a more secure position in the power structure of the community, both in relation to members of his own *biradari* and to clients of other castes. He was normally more difficult to intimidate than the *sahukar*, and could more easily recover debts and acquire mortgaged land.

The economic heterogeneity of the localized *biradari* may have, in itself, contributed to the increasing level of indebtedness. Although the *biradari* has remained an important grouping in the villages to the present, it became very heterogeneous as far as the economic condition of members' households was concerned. The membership of a Jat *biradari* within a given village might range from poor households, dependent entirely upon cultivating small, rented-in parcels of land, to households with income from large landholdings, moneylending, and other business interests. During the post-World War I period of prosperity, the cost of marriage increased considerably throughout most of the Punjab (Darling 1947:54). The less affluent members of a respectable *biradari* were under pressure to meet the high standards of expenditure for ceremonies set by the more affluent members in order to maintain *izzat* (social position) or merely to succeed in arranging a marriage. For this purpose, money would be borrowed, and, increasingly, the source of credit was the agriculturalist moneylender.[2]

Evidently the agriculturalist moneylender was no more inclined to channel his wealth into the improvement of agriculture than was the *sahukar*. In the absence of a favorable economic environment, such as might have been created by a radically new agricultural technology, there was little incentive to invest in agriculture. From an economic point of view, where alternatives for land-poor agricultural households were lacking, land could be given to tenants at a cost to the renter not greater than that of employing agricultural laborers. In this way the moneylender who had accumulated land could save the costs and inconvenience of farm management, including overseeing laborers.

The agriculturalist moneylender combined his new role as village banker with that of broker, or intermediary, between the village and the outside, a role which had traditionally been played by prominent members of the dominant agricultural castes. In the early colonial period, as land entered the market, and as law courts and official records became basic to decisions in land cases, ability to cope with officials and outsiders became crucial to gaining position or maintaining it in the local community. In the early 1900s, the Punjab gained a reputation as a highly litigious province, and disputes between important villagers frequently became factional fights in which followers, or clients, were lined up as witnesses. Villagers who lacked political skill or who were less successful in mobilizing the resources for upward mobility were in need of the services of a patron to protect them and represent them in dealing with officials or powerful local men. The broker, by obliging peasants with protection and representation, established a following that was useful to him in any contest for power. The relationship between the broker-patron and his followers was, however, an ambiguous one. His role was not only to protect the interests of his followers, but also required that he sometimes assist the police and other officials in their dealings in the community, and his usefulness depended upon his ability to manipulate villagers. He also used his influence both locally and with the outside to better his own economic changes in various ways: as middleman in a milk business or in garden produce, in mobilizing scarce agricultural labor, and, as we have seen, in lending money (see Raulet and Uppal 1970). The activities of the broker-patron, both in the economic sphere and in the use of power, tended more to reinforce the economic marginality of most of his followers rather than to lead them toward economic progress.

Increasing Agricultural Debt

In revised portions of Malcolm Darling's book *The Punjab Peasant in Prosperity and Debt* (1947), which were written in the early 1930s, the optimistic views he expressed earlier about the Punjab are less in evidence. By this time a precipitous drop in agricultural prices had reduced the annual value of the agricultural product of the province by almost 50 percent, and the long period of prosperity had ended. But of more significance was the observation that increased indebtedness of cultivators had in the past decade gone hand in hand with prosperity. Lyallpur District, where the colonists began unencumbered by debt, showed signs of becoming the most indebted district in the province (Darling 1947:211). In "insecure" districts, where water supply was uncertain and holdings small, the debt position of the majority of cultivators was unfavorable even in times of high prices, in accordance with classic patterns. But the evidence that the most advantaged canal colony districts were equally part of this system dampened any hopes that the province might be shifting toward a more advanced form of agriculture under British leadership.

For the entire Punjab, the agricultural debt in 1929 was estimated at 135 crores; the debt's multiple of land revenue was 25.5 percent higher than in any other province. The debt had grown by 56.0 percent from an estimated 90 crores in 1921; in the previous two decades it had grown by only 40.0 percent (Darling 1947:16–18). Lyallpur and similar canal colony districts such as Montgomery and Shahpur were still, in 1924, considerably less indebted than the rest of the province, but their debt was increasing rapidly and, in the six years ending in 1930, the mortgage debt in Lyallpur had increased by 141 lakhs (Darling 1947:211, 224). The growth in indebtedness of cultivators proved especially burdensome, as it was for farmers in other countries, when the slump in agricultural prices occurred.

But the main problem was that the debts had been incurred largely for "unproductive" expenditures. Part of the debt was incurred to meet immediate necessities of household consumption or to deal with reverses such as loss of draft animals (Darling 1947:19). A large part of the debt, labeled in surveys as "unproductive" or "personal," and usually more than 50 percent of the total, represented borrowing for the purpose of meeting wedding, litigation, and other similar expenses, and especially for the servicing of accumulated debts. The pattern evidently did not differ much among the canal colonies (see Board of Economic Enquiry, 1932:100; 1963:72–73). Assuming an average interest rate of 12 to 13 percent payments for debt accounted for an enormous share, some 17 to 18 percent of the total agricultural product of the province in 1929 (Darling 1947:191).

The small landholder (less than ten acres) inevitably found it difficult to keep out of debt even in a period of rising farm prices, unless he displayed unusual energy, enlarged his holding by renting in land, or had a secondary occupation. As marketable surplus was small, output was subject to periodic fluctuations, and there was the need to replace draft animals and meet family consumption requirements; the small holder was more likely to enter the market as a buyer than as a seller (Darling 1947:247–248). The indebtedness of the larger holders and canal colonists was more difficult to explain in purely economic terms, and was often attributed to their "improvidence," their spendthrift habits, lack of managerial skill and business knowledge. I have already suggested how an analysis of rural society could help provide a more systematic explanation for this phenomenon.

If, as the Thorners, Gadgil, and others have suggested, the colonial rural socioeconomic system siphoned off potential capital, it seems to have worked with impressive flexibility and efficiency. When terms of trade were favorable to agriculture and the value of output increased, and in prosperous districts with high output, the debt mechanism seemed to work automatically to maintain the poverty of the peasants.

Summary and Conclusions

As in other parts of India, British rule in the Punjab in the nineteenth century provided law and order and relative political stability. With the construction of a modern transportation network came an expansion of the market and increased commercialization of agriculture as well as population growth. At the same time the new legal system helped create the conditions for widespread tenancy, mortgaging of land, and rural indebtedness. Initially, the settling of the canal colonies relieved population pressure and increased crop output, and up until around 1920 cultivated area expanded more rapidly than population in the province as a whole. However, after 1920 this process was reversed and the average size of agricultural holdings began to shrink. Moreover, rural indebtedness had become a serious problem in the canal colonies, as elsewhere in the province. After the turn of the century, prosperous agriculturalists began to replace the professional moneylenders as the major source of rural credit. But members of this new class of moneylenders, who tended also to be landlords and village politicians, were no more inclined than their predecessors to channel money into agricultural development. By the end of the decade of the 1920s, payments for debt accounted for an enormous share of the total agricultural production of the province. Indebtedness seems to have grown most rapidly in prosperous districts and during periods of favorable terms of trade to agriculture; as mechanisms for siphoning off potential capital, the colonial rural social system and the credit system worked with remarkable flexibility and efficiency. Beginning two decades before Independence, the per capita all-crop output of greater Punjab began to decline, and there was increasing evidence that the rural economy of the province was subject to limitations similar to the rest of India.

The administration was aware of the problems associated with rural indebtedness and was concerned about it. Their principal weapon against the moneylender, the cooperative society, proved to be insufficient to the task. For one thing, cooperative societies were organized in accordance with the principle of unlimited liability. When prices fell, members with assets were pressed to pay the debts of others and the cooperative movement tended to lose favor (Michel 1967:401). Lack of flexibility, compared with private moneylenders, and the ability of the more prosperous and powerful agriculturalists to dominate available funds, are also reasons for the limited impact of the cooperative movement (Mellor et al 1968:65). "Cancellation" of debts accompanying the exodus of Sikhs and Hindus at the time of Partition did more than previous efforts to relieve the burden of debt in the Pakistan part of the Punjab (Michel 1967:400).

It is true that even in the canal colonies, the measures of the colonial administration cannot be characterized as single-minded support for progressive agriculture. In these areas, concessions were made to the demands of various government departments, and allotments were made for such purposes as raising horses and camels for the military and for supplying cantonments with dairy products. "Capitalist" grantees were given allotments in the colonies not only in an attempt to infuse a "progressive spirit" but also to strengthen the "landed gentry" as a counterweight against the rising nationalism of urban, educated classes (Darling 1947:118). Thus in many cases, long-term economic purposes played a smaller part than immediate administrative and political aims of the raj.

Perhaps a major handicap to the sustained growth of agriculture was the lack of sufficient growth in the nonagricultural sector of the economy. Compared with the rest of India, the Punjab was well endowed with occupational alternatives to agricultural employment, but in the seventy years prior to Independence, the population of this province increased by about 65 percent compared with only 50 percent for India as a whole. Population growth of this magnitude, in an economy in which nonagricultural sectors were not growing rapidly, and given the rural institutions I have described, could only reinforce the stagnation of agriculture. Today, Pakistan, particularly the areas that were embraced by the canal colony experiment, is relatively well-situated in agricultural and water resources to take advantage of new technologies and other forces now favorable to agricultural growth. In part this is due to the legacy of the progressive episodes of the past. But a legacy of the cumulative effects of tenancy and agricultural debt may pose major obstacles to strategies for economic development.

Harry M. Raulet, Jr., is professor of Anthropology at Michigan State University. He received a Ph.D. in Anthropology from Columbia University in 1959 and an M.S. from the School of Public Health, Harvard University, in 1961. From 1961 to 1964 he was director of Social Studies, Medical Social Research Project, Lahore, West Pakistan, while a faculty member of the Department of Social Relations, Johns Hopkins University.

NOTES

1. The price of land rose sharply from Rs. 10 per acre in 1869/70 to Rs. 77 in 1900/01, and Rs. 275 in 1919/20 (Paustian 1930:105).

2. An extended discussion of the economics of the peasant household is offered by Wolf (1966). He maintains that since the peasant household is a family unit as well as an economic undertaking, its decisions about production take into account not only economic factors such as market conditions, but also, at the same time, family and kinship needs. Ceremonial expenditures play a part in linking household members into a network of social

relations in the community, and the provisioning of the household must allow for a "ceremonial fund" as well as for a "subsistence fund." This is a different perspective from that of many observers of the rural scene who tended to regard ceremonial expenditures as primarily a sign of improvidence.

BIBLIOGRAPHY

Blyn, George
  1966. *Agricultural Trends in India 1891–1947: Output, Availability and Productivity*. Philadelphia: University of Pennsylvania Press.
Board of Economic Inquiry, Punjab
  1932. Publication No. 27. "An Economic Survey of Kala Gaddi Thamman, a Village in the Lyallpur District," by Randhir Singh. Lahore, Punjab, India.
  1963. Publication No. 129. "An Economic Survey of Abbaspur (Chak No. 2/10-L)," by Niaz Mohammat Kham. Lahore, Punjab, West Pakistan.
Calvert, H.
  1925. *The Size and Distribution of Agricultural Holdings in the Punjab*. Rural Section Publication 4. Lahore, Punjab, India: Board of Economic Inquiry.
  1928. *The Size and Distribution of Cultivators' Holdings in the Punjab*. Rural Section Publication 11. Lahore, Punjab, India: Board of Economic Inquiry.
Darling, Malcolm L.
  1947. *The Punjab Peasant in Prosperity and Debt*. London: Oxford University Press.
Eglar, Zekiye
  1960. *A Punjabi Village in Pakistan*. New York: Columbia University Press.
Gadgil, D. R.
  1959. *The Industrial Evaluation of India in Recent Times*. London: Oxford University Press.
Geertz, Clifford
  1963. *Agricultural Involution*. Berkeley: University of California Press.
Habib, Irfan
  1963. *The Agrarian System of Mughal India*. Bombay: Asia Publishing House.

Imperial Gazetteer of India
    1908. *Imperial Gazetteer of India*. London: Trübner & Co.
Mellor, John W.; Weaver, Thomas F.; Lele, Uma J.; and Simon, Sheldon R.
    1968. *Developing Rural India*. Ithaca: Cornell University Press.
Michel, Aloys A.
    1967. *The Indus Rivers: A Study of the Effects of Partition*. New Haven: Yale University Press.
Morris, Morris D.
    1969. "Towards a Reinterpretation of Nineteenth Century Indian Economic History." In *Indian Economy in the Nineteenth Century: A Symposium*, edited by Morris D. Morris et al. Delhi: Hindustan Publishing Corporation.
Neale, Walter C.
    1962. *Economic Change in Rural India: Land Tenure and Reform in Uttar Pradesh 1800–1955*. New Haven: Yale University Press.
Paustian, Paul
    1930. *Canal Irrigation in the Punjab*. New York: Columbia University Press.
Raulet, H. M., and Uppal, J. S.
    1970. "The Social Dynamics of Economic Development in Rural Punjab." *Asian Survey* 10:336–347.
Raychaudhuri, T.
    1969. "A Re-interpretation of Nineteenth Century Indian Economic History?" In *Indian Economy in the Nineteenth Century: A Symposium*, edited by Morris D. Morris et al. Delhi: Hindustan Publishing Corporation.
Stewart, H. R.
    1926. *Some Aspects of Batai Cultivation in the Lyallpur District of the Punjab*. Rural Section Publication 12. Lahore, Punjab, India: Board of Economic Inquiry.
    1927. *Accounts of Different Systems of Farming in the Canal Colonies of the Punjab*. Rural Section Publication 15. Lahore, Punjab, India: Board of Economic Inquiry.
Thorner, Daniel, and Thorner, Alice
    1962. *Land and Labour in India*. Bombay: Asia Publishing House.
van den Dungen, P. H. M.
    1968. "Changes in Status and Occupation in 19th Century Punjab." In *Soundings in Modern South Asian History*, edited by D. A. Low. London: Weidenfeld and Nicolson.
Wolf, Eric R.
    1966. *Peasants*. Foundations of Modern Anthropology Series. Englewood Cliffs, N. J.: Prentice-Hall.

11

Rural Self-Government in Pakistan: An Experiment in Political Development through Bureaucracy

Muneer Ahmad

Outline of the History of Local Self-Government

One aspect of rural development is political development: the introduction and sustenance of institutions of participatory democracy. Sometimes it is sought as an end in itself and sometimes as a means to economic growth and social change. In most cases, democratic institutions do not already exist nor do they emerge spontaneously from traditional political cultures. They need to be deliberately created. A significant part of this process is the socialization of rural communities in democratic political behavior. In this sense, political development requires the full-time and devoted tutelage of sympathetic institution builders. In Pakistan, as in many other developing countries, this role has fallen on the professional public servant. The Pakistani experiment with this model of political development has revealed inherent contradictions and has shown how the inbuilt tendencies of bureaucracy operate to frustrate a major purpose it is supposed to serve, the development of participatory democracy.

The Limited Colonial Effort toward Self-Government

A modern framework for rural self-government was introduced in the subcontinent in the last quarter of the nineteenth century. It was a deliberate cross-cultural transplantation. Its author, Viceroy Ripon, had stated the objective to be political education, not administrative efficiency (Tinker 1968:44). However, the implementation of the reform was entrusted to the provincial governments composed almost exclusively of civil servants. Contrary to his wishes they severely circumscribed the democratic features of Ripon's model for local councils (Tinker 1968:46ff.) by retaining inhibiting control over the councils' initiative. For example, the councils were not wholly elective. When elections were held the franchise was so restricted that the electorate was minute. Further limitations on democracy were the provisions that the offices of presiding officer, chief executive, and controlling authority of the local councils were all reserved for the members of the civil service. These unfortunate decisions left such a far-reaching impact on rural government that eighty years later when an independent country under indigenous rulers set in motion a resolute drive to revitalize local government, this same authoritarian model was replicated with little change.

On the eve of Independence this circumscribed model of rural self-government was operating in practically all the districts of two major provinces of Pakistan, the Punjab, and the Sind while some headway had been made in the North-West Frontier Province (NWFP) (Figure 1). The significant exceptions were the province of Baluchistan, all the princely states, and the tribal areas. These areas were still considered to be too politically unripe to receive "advanced" institutions. Of the three "progressive" provinces, the Punjab possessed by far the strongest traditions of rural local government. Not only was this province the first to follow the lead of Lord Ripon's resolution in establishing rural self-governing institutions at the district level, it was also the only province that had established the grass-roots local government units known as panchayats. However, even in this province over 75 percent of the villages legally eligible for the panchayat form of local government were without it.

Local Self-Government in the Post-Independence Period

A surge of democratic spirit in the wake of the successful independence movement led to increased representativeness in local government in Pakistan. Universal adult franchise was introduced in place of the extremely restricted colonial franchise. The councils of the district governments were made fully elective and were empowered to elect their own chairmen from among themselves (Riz-

Figure 1. Map of Pakistan Showing the Dates of Promulgation of Comprehensive Legislation for Rural Local Government in the Four Provinces.

vil 1966:57). Plans were prepared to extend panchayat-style local government to more villages in the Punjab and in other provinces. In addition, the relatively advanced Punjabi laws on local government were extended to Bahawalpur and the North-West Frontier Province (West Pakistan Yearbook 1956:113, 116). The gains symbolized by most of these predominantly legal reforms were, however, undone by the failure of the government to follow them up with positive action. The situation in the North-West Frontier Province was particularly discouraging in this respect, for by 1951/52 all the district local governments in this province had been suspended (West Pakistan Yearbook 1956:113, 116; Rizvi 1966:57).

Another impulse of self-government activity was witnessed shortly after the integration of West Pakistan into one unit in 1955. At this time the Punjabi law on panchayats was extended by ordinance to the whole of Pakistan (West Pakistan Yearbook 1958:135). Plans were prepared to make the local government laws uniform throughout Pakistan and an election commission was appointed in order to prepare ground for holding elections to local bodies. At the same time a Local Government College and a journal on local government were started (West Pakistan Yearbook 1956:116). Subsequent government action, however, was very much in the opposite direction. For example, twenty-four out of thirty-four district governments stood superseded in 1957 (Masud-ul-Hasan 1966:67).

A further complication for the development of local self-government was involved with the operation of the new Village Agricultural and Industrial Development Program (V-AID). For rural development, the government created a network of new institutions under V-AID while at the same time it withdrew many functions the local governments were already performing. The ad hoc councils created under V-AID, however, failed to mobilize the villagers because they lacked roots in the people. The already existing councils of rural local government could not be utilized for this purpose because short-sighted government policy had starved them of initiative and a meaningful economic development role. Masud-ul-Hasan noted that there was a good deal of hostility between the V-AID-created organizations and the already existing local bodies with the result that "on the one hand the *Panchayats* languished, and on the other the V-AID failed to take root" (Masud-ul-Hasan 1966:76). Thus it appears that the uncertain thesis that the economic development of rural communities could be separated from their political development had been assumed by government.

The second decade of independence saw the emergence of Basic Democracies institutions. The singular distinction of the Basic Democracies thrust was the explicit and formal recognition of the positive role of local government in national development. Accordingly, uniform institutions of local government, both at the district and grass-roots level, were established for the first time in every part of Pakistan. The scheme also explicitly recognized these institutions as instruments of both political education and economic development.

This scheme, however, repeated the folly of placing local governments under the tight control of bureaucrats. Following in the footsteps of their imperial predecessors, the Pakistani bureaucrats again hedged in the independence of local councils by remaining as presiding officers, chief executives, and as the controlling authorities. At the district level the franchise was restricted by introducing indirect elections. In the first phase of Basic Democracies, the district councils were not wholly elective as the civil service retained the right to nominate a sizable portion of the membership in the councils.

This brief historical account of local government in Pakistan shows that succeeding governments have felt obliged to establish some kind of local government institution in order to mobilize rural communities. All sought to achieve this goal under the leadership of professional public servants. It is significant that none of these attempts has succeeded in producing viable local governments.

After two decades of uninterrupted political independence, rural self-government in Pakistan is in a weak state of health. Rural self-government has not become an instrument that would limit bureaucratic discretionary power, nor has it become a check on centralizing forces. It also has failed to perform a primary role of providing second- and third-rank democratic leadership in rural areas.

In contrast, the authoritarian institutions, particularly the bureaucracy, have prospered. This occurred not infrequently with corresponding loss to the decentralizing and participatory institutions. Far from being a substitute or a partner, rural local governments remained adjuncts to central administration.

Reasons for the Weakness of Local Democracy

Focus is now placed on explanations for the slow development of rural self-government. Three major sets of factors are explored: the continued dominance of the civil bureaucracy, the nature of the impact of public officials on rural people, and the weakness of the socioeconomic base for the building of democratic values.

The Continued Dominance of the Civil Bureaucracy

In analyzing the reasons for the weakness of local self-government, a beginning observation of major importance is the continuity from colonial times of the civil bureaucracy's dominance in administration, particularly at the district level. Appearing in the days of ascending colonialism the district administration—identified with arbitrary and authoritarian government—has survived such cataclysmic changes as the Independence (1947), and the subsequent experiments with parliamentary (1956–1958), presidential (1962–1969), and unitary (1955–1970) constitutional frameworks. Regardless of its formal shape at a given time, government in Pakistan has continued to be authoritarian and centralizing. The district administration, therefore, has continued to be authoritarian in form and substance, lending the same color to whatever type of local government was attempted. In effect the civil bureaucracy was willing only to associate the people with the administration on its own terms. Thus the nearest district administration has come to democratic administration is to a kind of paternalism. The central feature of this paternalistic administrative structure is that it creates the illusion of popular participation in administration, yet gives the ordinary citizens no control over the governing elite. Government officials do not jeopardize their jobs, nor are they criticized if they do not act to the benefit of citizens.[1]

Higher bureaucracy's conceptualization of local government is ambivalent. Local government is simultaneously a desirable goal and a convenient instrument for the realization of administrative tasks. As a goal it is visualized as an ultimate substitute for the already existing administration through the transfer of the functions of planning, management, and administration of local affairs to elected officials (Memorandum 1969:22, 26). As an instrument of administration, local government is viewed as an extended arm of the administration for the fulfillment of economic and administrative tasks defined by the bureaucracy within the allocation of resources determined by the administration. The driving force for local government has often been not so much the love of democracy as the desire to achieve economic and other physical targets.

This ambivalent attitude toward local government gives rise to the problem of displacement of goals. In his anxiety to achieve physical targets (such as the number of miles of road built during a fiscal year), the public official tends to overlook or sacrifice political development. The dilemma of the low-ranking official, working in a face-to-face relationship with the villager, is even greater. On the one hand, his role as extension agent demands the promotion of general social, political, and economic development—a nonphysical goal not easily measurable. On the other hand, his role as a career public servant requires the rapid achievement of physical targets. As his superiors often heavily weigh his performance on the basis of physical targets, his efforts toward those ends are understandable (Ansari 1962:59). The role of the public official acquires critical significance in the evolution of local government in this context, for in the transitional phase between no rural self-government and full-fledged rural self-government, a peculiar relationship is required between the appointed and the elected officials that would ensure physical achievements but at the same time permit a change in decision-making authority from the appointed to the elected official.

In the present period after Independence, the policy of the government and the attitude of the higher civil servants directly managing the local government institutions betray a lack of appreciation of the need for special efforts to promote political development. One indicator of this indifferent attitude toward the growth of self-governing institutions is the failure of succeeding governments to organize regular elections for the local councils. A sample survey of eleven district councils in West Pakistan revealed that elections to most of these bodies were not held at the prescribed interval of years. In extreme cases the average interval between two elections ranged as high as twenty-two, twenty-one, and sixteen years (Table 1) (Ahmad 1967). By denying the people the opportunity to elect new councils, the administration prevented them from learning the attitudes and habits of a democratic process. Also, by allowing the councillors to stay in office beyond their normal tenure, the government encouraged undemocratic practices inside the councils and apathy and cynicism among the people.

A second indicator of lack of appreciation of the special requirements for fostering local self-government is indicated by the

TABLE 1. Average Years between Elections in Sample District Councils

District Council	Years between Elections
Mardan, NWFP [a]	21.0
D. I. Khan, NWFP	22.0
Rawalpindi, Punjab	10.0
Jhang, Punjab	9.5
Sialkot, Punjab	7.0
Multan, Punjab	11.5
R. Y. Khan, Punjab	16.0
Larkana, Sind	6.5
Sanghar, Sind	5.0

SOURCE: Ahmad 1967.

NOTE: No comparable data were available for Baluchistan as district-level, local self-government had been introduced for the first time in 1959.

[a] NWFP is North-West Frontier Province.

actions taken by officials in the Basic Democracies. Under the Basic Democracies scheme these officials acted as the chief executives and presiding officers of the local councils. They tended to treat the local government little better than any another government department. In keeping with their bureaucratic training, they expected the conduct of local politics to be neat and tidy. At the slightest pretext they would send the entire elected council home—an act described in legal terminology as "supersession"[2] —and replace it with a bureaucrat.

Under the Basic Democracies scheme, the office of the chairman of the local councils above the first level of government was assigned to a public official. The filling of this position, the incumbent of which could play a fatal role in the promotion or retardation of local government, was treated as a matter of ordinary routine.

A third indicator of indifferent attitudes on the part of the civil service toward local government is the fact that little consideration was given to the aptitude of a civil servant for institution-building or to his suitability to a particular cultural area (Ahmad 1967). The lack of continuity in the office of the district chief executive is well known. Between 1958 and 1963, the average length of stay for a deputy commissioner in a district was a little over twenty months (Minhajuddin 1964:39). This factor, along with others, contributed to the shallowness of the attempt to develop local government among the people.

In conclusion, there is something inherently contradictory in expecting the public official to build the institutions of local self-government when they are intended, in due course, to take over a great deal of his authority. The actual roles taken by government servants entrusted with rural local government leaves an observer with little optimism. The whole administrative structure, especially the higher bureaucracy, tends to neglect political development as a desirable goal in its competition with other goals.

The Impact of Public Officials on Rural People

The inadequacy of the public official as a tutor of people for local self-government in Pakistan is most conspicious at the lowest level. Most government departments that have crucial roles in rural local governments (Agriculture, Cooperatives, Health, Education, and Animal Husbandry) have no permanent official at the village level (Tehmasap 1964:77). A second and more serious shortcoming is that the lower officials, working for the most part in the field, fail to operate as extension agents. As members of the traditional bureaucracy and as successors to a colonial administration, these civil servants were not trained for development and institution-building roles. Whereas rural development requires some kind of personal involvement, their outstanding characteristics have been impersonality and unimaginative adherence to rules and procedures.

In a close examination of the contacts between the villagers and public officials in three villages in the Punjab, Zuhra Waheed found that government departments directly responsible for rural development did not have sustained contact with the villagers. In addition she observed that whenever contact was established it was predominantly through privileged local influentials. Thirdly, she found that the elected Basic Democrat was not able to improve substantially the contacts between the villagers and the officials.

With the exception of the Department of Agriculture, the departments that had the most frequent contact with the villagers were predominantly regulatory in function. The descending order among departments of frequency of contact was Revenue, Agriculture, Irrigation, and Police. The departments with relatively limited contact, contrary to their expected roles, were: Cooperatives, Animal Husbandry, Health, and Basic Democracies (Waheed 1964:13–15, 54). The Departments in the second category are mainly welfare-oriented (described in Pakistan as "nation-building"). This pattern of contact leaves a negative image of government in the villagers' minds.

The Waheed study also found that high proportions of respondents described the attitude of the officials toward people as "bad" or "very bad." These proportions were the highest for the Irrigation, Police, and Revenue departments (Table 2). The attitude of the officials from the nation-building departments was described as "good" or "very good" (Waheed 1964:60). In view of these reactions, government could probably have improved its image by further increasing the contacts by personnel of nation-building departments.

TABLE 2. Villagers' Opinions about Attitudes of Officials from Different Departments (Percent)

Department	Good or Very Good	Average	Bad or Very Bad	No Response
Agriculture	65	20	9	6
Animal Husbandry	58	20	17	5
Basic Democracies	55	25	15	5
Cooperatives	55	18	6	21
Education	55	13	23	9
Health	44	26	28	3
Irrigation	14	31	51	4
Police	20	28	50	3
Revenue	33	21	41	5

SOURCE: Waheed 1964:60. The sample included 150 respondents.

The limited government-people contact was restricted further to the propertied and the influential. During their visits to the villages, 48 percent of the officials "met the people" at the residence of the local gentry (the union council chairman and the *numberdar*) (Table 3). Only 45 percent of the officials chose the neutral ground of the office of the union council as the meeting ground. Similarly, in 53 percent of the cases, contact was sought with the local propertied and influential persons (such as the union council members, the council's chairman, the *numberdar*, and the *patwari*).[3] Thus the majority of the less-privileged classes were deprived of goods and services supplied by government. Ironically, the failure of the goods and services to reach their intended destination, the whole village population, was not a consequence of public policy but the result of the idiosyncracies of the mediating public officials.

Some had expected that the introduction of an institutional arrangement like the Basic Democracies would have improved the relations between public officials and villagers. Evidence, however, falsifies this expectation. In the Waheed survey 46 percent of the responding villagers felt that the Basic Democrats had not helped establish closer contact between themselves and officials (Waheed 1964:59). In a study by Chaudhri only 34.7 percent of the respondents who were Basic Democrats, the chairman and ordinary villagers, felt that the Basic Democrats have been able to introduce a change in the attitudes of officials of the nation-building departments (Chaudhri 1967:8–9). When asked to comment on

TABLE 3. Meeting Place Chosen by Officials
for Contact with Villagers

Meeting Place	Times Chosen (%)
Union Council Office	45
Chairman's House	41
Numberdar's House	7
School	4
Model Farm	3
TOTAL	100

SOURCE: Waheed 1964:64.

whether the Basic Democrats had helped improve understanding between government departments and the people, only 45.0 percent of these same respondents agreed (Chaudhri 1967:12–13). When asked to suggest measures for improving the role of the chairmen of the union councils, 43 percent demanded "less interference by officials (Chaudhri 1967:33). The percentages of villagers who thought the Basic Democrats had heightened political consciousness or had encouraged local leadership were higher (Table 4).

Weakness of Democratic Values in Rural Society

The most serious obstacle in the way of the development of local government, however, remains the weakness of the socioeconomic base as the foundation of democratic values in rural Pakistan. Left to itself Pakistani village society tends to sustain an authoritarian or paternalistic political system. The introduction of institutions of democracy, therefore, has to be fostered deliberately from the outside. In this situation the nonegalitarian social system

TABLE 4. Extent to Which Basic Democrats Fulfilled Aspirations of Villagers

Aspirations	Not at All (%)	To Some Extent (%)	To Great Extent (%)	No Response (%)
Encouragement of Local Leadership	4.7	44.1	51.3	—
Inculcation of Self-help	2.8	38.1	58.8	0.3
Change in Attitudes of Nation-building Departments	4.7	60.6	34.7	—
Meeting Needs of People at Local Level	4.1	42.5	53.4	—
Creation of Political Consciousness	7.2	15.9	76.9	—

SOURCE: Chaudhri 1967:8–9.

of the rural society tends to overwhelm nascent democratic institutions and often bends them to suit its antidemocratic needs. Public officials who are supposed to foster democracy are likely to give in to the pressures of the feudal society of the village with the result that the process of democratization by government becomes self-defeating.

The interaction of democratic institutions from outside the nondemocratic economic structure and value system of rural society yields unanticipated and dysfunctional consequences. Two such negative consequences have attracted the attention of students of democracy. One is the accentuation of factional strife as a consequence of the introduction of elections in a traditional society. The other is the misuse of the office of public representative by its incumbents.

According to one analysis in Pakistan, one faction finds satisfaction in the humiliation, economic loss, and suffering of another. In this scale of values, extinction of the enemy is most important (Slocum et al. 1959:30). According to another report, a major characteristic of a Pakistani faction is that a member feels obliged to support a fellow member in a quarrel regardless of whether the disputant is right or wrong (USGPO 1965:169). The factional attitude is obviously destructive of cooperative effort in elected councils. Factions also view political dissent as treachery and a political opponent as the enemy (see, for example, Inayatullah 1964:269–270). During electoral contests, therefore, appeals are made to factional loyalties and not to the merits of the issues. Electoral defeat is viewed as humiliating. The winners usually fail to show magnanimity to the vanquished, and the losers are hesitant to cooperate with the winners in good grace.[4]

A study of the backgrounds of the elected members of the district councils of Pakistan revealed that, in 96 percent of the cases, the councillor or a near relative of his was simultaneously a member of the grass-roots local council also. In 45.3 percent of the cases, the members were second-generation councillors (Ahmad 1967). This situation may be interpreted to indicate the excessive hold of family or *biradari* (kinship) in the rural society of Pakistan. It appears that the rural people look upon political office as an end in itself. The occupation of the political office in a particular area by the rival *biradari* or faction, or by a social inferior, is regarded as a serious affront to the prestige of a given faction.

Dominant social values of rural society emphasize nondemocratic attitudes. For example, they stress differences of status, emphasize obedience as opposed to individual freedom, and underline excessive loyalty to family (USGPO 1965:169–171). In such a milieu the public representative or the elected official also tends to behave in an authoritarian manner and acts more like the agent of his family or *biradari* than as an "efficient catalyst" for social change for the whole community.[5]

One interpretation is that the ordinary villager needs to be saved not only from the "indulgent" bureaucrat but also from the rapacious local politician. If, therefore, the ordinary villager distrusts the elected official as much as he does the appointed official it is understandable. As far as he is concerned both are not amenable to popular influence. The common voter possesses no mechanism to compel accountability to him on the part of the councillor during the period between elections. Given sporadic (rigged) elections and the continuation of councillors in office many years beyond their original tenure, the elected official can afford to be as indifferent to the needs of the people as is his brother bureaucrat.

It is significant that many of the reform measures suggested under the section on local self-government in the Election Manifesto of the Pakistan Peoples' Party (1970) seem to be safeguards against the unreliability of the representative after the election. The manifesto underlines "the maximum *direct* participation *of all citizens* in all local self-government bodies" as the essence of reform. It stipulates that a majority of the inhabitants and not only the elected members be consulted on important local questions. It makes it obligatory for local bodies to render accounts of their actions to people in half-yearly public meetings. It also makes the mandate of members revocable at any time by the electors.

The response the professional public servant sometimes makes to this situation is unhelpful to the growth of rural self-government. Upon seeing these negative consequences of the early steps in the introduction of democratic institutions, he attempts to take the ordinary villager under his protection—by placing the local government under his guardianship. He justifies his control over the local politician with the argument that by doing so he protects the interests of the ordinary man. Thus, over the short term, he may afford relief from petty injustices to rural people, but in the long run the impact of his conduct on political development is damaging. In this response, contrary to the norms of democracy, the bureaucrat cultivates in the villager the habit of dependence upon bureaucracy as well as an attitude in the local politician of accountability to the bureaucrat instead of to the villagers. Unchecked democracy, he is inclined to argue, would lead to domination by the wealthy. The conclusion is that the fate of local government should be made or unmade by the people and not by the public official.

The cultivation of democratic institutions requires that the local councillor learn to be accountable to the people. This will happen if he is exposed to control from below and not from above. If the public official is really interested in safeguarding the interests of the villager, he should institutionalize control from below. To do this he needs to ensure that frequent and fair elections take place. The elections should be direct and based on universal adult franchise. The civil bureaucrat would do democracy a great service if he were to content himself with the role of impartial umpire.[6]

Conclusion

All parties interested in the fate of local democracy seem to agree that viable representative local governments are a precondition to genuine rural development. These institutions help identify the local leadership and through them local needs, aspirations, and resources. The most outstanding contribution expected of local governments is the release of the initiative now locked in the rural communities. Once generated, the popular initiative has the potential to counter bureaucratic red tape as well as to make the process of economic growth self-generating.

This analysis has explored the roles and outcomes of the public bureaucrat's activities in the experiments directed toward establishing rural self-government in Pakistan and has highlighted some major inherent contradictions of these roles. The professional public servant will continue to have a significant role to play in local democratic development and these inherent contradictions may be overcome. Effective use of bureaucratic power to this end will not be accomplished by spoon-feeding local governments but by eliminating economic and bureaucratic barriers to their free and unfettered operation.

Muneer Ahmad received his doctorate at Munster University (West Germany) in 1965. He is currently working as an assistant professor in the Department of Administrative Science, Punjab University, Lahore, Pakistan. He was Visiting Research Fellow at the Southern Asian Institute, Columbia University, from 1971 through 1972.

NOTES

This chapter previously appeared in slightly different form in the *Journal of Rural Development and Administration* 10 (July-September 1973):53–73. The permission to reprint granted by the Pakistan Academy of Rural Development is gratefully acknowledged.

1. Compare Almond and Verba: " . . . the problem of assessing the degree of democracy in a nation becomes one of measuring the degree to which ordinary citizens control those who make the significant decisions for a society—in most cases, governmental elites" (1965:136).

2. Basic Democracies Order, 1959, Article 78 in Mahmood (1964:485).

3. See Waheed (1964:64), and also Tehmasap (1964:83) who says, for example, "Some of the Nation Building Departments continue to look after the interests of the big landlords and influential people in the area. The needs of petty farmers are ignored."

4. Inayatullah and Shafi (1963:120) illustrate graphically the disruptive role of factional politics in cooperative work in the case study of a Pakistani village. The "work committee" formed by the extension workers for the purpose of digging an irrigation channel through the village required, to begin with, an equal representation of the village's two major factions. No chairman of the committee was elected in order to avoid "imbalance of power." The leader of one faction avoided the committee for quite some time on the grounds that its meetings were held at a place where he was not prepared to go. The leaders of the other faction demanded the expulsion of the former.

A curious device to counteract the factional division disrupting local government was adopted in Andhra Pradesh in India by offering monetary reward to a panchayat if it would elect all its members unanimously (Seshadri 1964:214).

5. "The members, with their close involvement in village life, are not sufficiently different from their fellows to be efficient catalysts. . . . Before

the elected officials' influence can be utilized to accelerate village development they need to be 'reeducated' " (Cambridge University Asian Expedition 1962:59).

6. Developing the same theme, Narain suggests that the administrative elites should be prepared to practice a self-denying regimen in regard to power (Narain 1966:564–578).

BIBLIOGRAPHY

Ahmad, Muneer
   1967. "From District Boards to District Councils: A Study of District Level Local Government in West Pakistan." Survey conducted for the Government of Pakistan in 1966–1967. Unpublished.
Almond, Gabriel A., and Verba, Sidney
   1965. *The Civic Culture, Political Attitudes and Democracy in Five Nations*. Boston: Little, Brown & Co.
Ansari, M. A. Salam
   1962. *Village Workers and Rural Development*. Peshawar: West Pakistan Academy for Village Development.
Cambridge University Asian Expedition
   1962. *The Budhopur Report: A Study of the Forces of Tradition and Change in a Punjabi Village in the Gujranwala District, West Pakistan*. Lahore: Social Sciences Research Centre, University of the Punjab.
Chaudhri, Haider Ali
   1967. *Union Councils: A Study of Sahiwal and Lyallpur Districts*. Karachi: Planning and Evaluation Unit, Basic Democracies Wing, Ministry of Information and Broadcasting, Government of Pakistan.
Government of West Pakistan
   n.d. *West Pakistan Yearbook 1956*. Lahore: Public Relations Department, Government of West Pakistan.
   n.d. *West Pakistan Yearbook 1958*. Lahore: Public Relations Department, Government of West Pakistan.
Inayatullah
   1964. *Basic Democracies, Development and District Administration*. Peshawar: Pakistan Academy for Rural Development.
Inayatullah, and Shafi, Q. M.
   1963. *Dynamics of Development in a Pakistani Village*. Peshawar: Pakistan Academy for Rural Development.
Mahmood, Afzal
   1964. *Basic Democracies*. Lahore: All-Pakistan Legal Decision.

Masud-ul-Hasan
  1966. "Local Bodies in West Pakistan 1947–1966." *Pakistan Quarterly* 14:65–73.
Memorandum
  1969. Submitted to the Services Reorganization Committee by the Civil Service of Pakistan Association. Rawalpindi: Ferozsons Ltd.
Minhajuddin
  1964. "Some Aspects of District Administration." In *District Administration in West Pakistan, Its Problems and Challenges*, edited by Inayatullah, pp. 27–43. Peshawar: Pakistan Academy for Rural Development.
Narain, I.
  1966. "Administrative Challenge to Panchayati Raj." *Indian Journal of Public Administration* 12 (3): 564–578.
Rizvi, Shahid Ali
  1966. "Local Bodies in Pakistan." *Pakistan Quarterly* 14: 50–57.
Seshadri, K.
  1964. "The Principle of Unanimity in Panchayat Elections in the State of Andhra Pradesh, India." *Journal of Local Administration Overseas* 3 (4): 214–220.
Slocum, W. L.; Akhtar, Jamila; Sahi, Abrar Fatima.
  1959. *Village Life in Lahore District: A Study of Selected Sociological Aspects*. Lahore: Social Sciences Research Centre, University of the Punjab.
Tehmasap, Anwar
  1964. "Structure and Functions of Nation Building Departments." In *District Administration in West Pakistan, Its Problems and Challenges*, edited by Inayatullah, pp. 75–86. Peshawar: Pakistan Academy for Rural Development.
Tinker, Hugh
  1968. *The Foundations of Local Self-Government in India, Pakistan and Burma*. New York: Praeger.
U. S. Government Printing Office (USGPO)
  1965. *Area Handbook for Pakistan*. Washington, D. C.: U.S. Government Printing Office.
Waheed, Zuhra
  1964. "Contacts between Villagers and Public Officials in Three Villages of Lyallpur Tehsil." Mimeographed. Lahore: Pakistan Administrative Staff College.

12

Agricultural Growth and Planning in the 1960s

Parvez Hasan

Introduction

During the decade of the 1960s, agricultural output in Pakistan (formerly West Pakistan) grew at an average rate of over 4.5 percent per annum (crop production rising by 5.4 percent per annum), in sharp contrast to the agricultural growth rate of 1.3 percent per annum during the 1950s. The impressive increases in production of all major crops—wheat, rice, cotton, and sugarcane—have reflected in varying degrees the impact of new and improved inputs, notably fertilizers, tubewells, and miracle seeds. While it is true that the agricultural revolution in Pakistan already was underway in the first half of the 1960s, it was the second half of the decade that was especially dramatic. During the period from 1965 to 1970, wheat and rice output increased by nearly 75 percent; fertilizer use increased nearly fivefold;[1] the number of private tubewells doubled; and the new seeds covered nearly 75 percent of the irrigated areas under wheat and rice. The following study centers upon the policy and planning framework for agriculture as it evolved and affected the spread of the green revolution.

Government policies should not be seen as having played a central role in agricultural growth. Support and subsidy policies no doubt had a major part in helping the growth of agriculture in Pakistan, but whether or not they were a catalytic agent is difficult to say. Land reform also set the stage for agricultural progress, but the answers to what actually motivated the agricultural entrepreneurs and radically transformed their attitudes may lie beyond economics. Given the fact that responsiveness to change already existed at the beginning of the Third Plan period (July 1965), the policies affecting the rate of subsidy and availability of key inputs, support prices of major agricultural commodities, and the organization of research and extension exerted a powerful influence on agricultural production. These policies were, however, hardly perfect, and this chapter will highlight the mistakes as well as the successes in an analysis organized under five headings: Irrigation and Tubewell Development, Fertilizer, Price Support Policies, Areas Needing More Agricultural Policy Analysis, and Income Distribution in Agricultural Development.

Irrigation and Tubewell Development

Pakistan has one of the finest irrigation systems in the world; 31 million of the 40 million cultivated areas are irrigated. The development of water resources, therefore, has occupied a central place in agricultural planning. It was fortunate that basic general planning of water and power resources was taken up early through the establishment of the West Pakistan Water and Power Development Authority (WAPDA) in 1958. The concern with problems of salinity led to intensive studies of the quality and extent of groundwater resources. These studies were partly responsible for the major discovery in the early 1960s of the possibility of tapping the groundwater both to supplement irrigation and to lower the water table in the sweet water areas. The commissioning of the first public Salinity Control and Reclamation Project (SCARP I) coincided with a spontaneous growth of private tubewells, which were a key factor in agricultural growth in the Second Plan period (1960–1965). The Third Plan (1965–1970) showed a great awareness of the role of accelerated groundwater development in agricultural development, and started with an ambitious program of 10,000 public tubewells. In fact, however, only 3,500 public tubewells could be energized during the Third Plan period and the bulk of the increase in net water availability once again was provided by private tubewells.

In planning for the big spurt in public tubewells, the government and the World Bank Group Study headed by Dr. Pieter Lieftinck underestimated the organizational and financial constraints on the program, and exaggerated the relative benefits of public tubewells, particularly over the short and medium run (Lieftinck et al. 1968). The financial stringency actually experienced during the Third Plan could not have been entirely foreseen, but even if the money had been available, WAPDA could not have implemented the program. The bottleneck in implementation was particularly serious in the final stage of electrification of the tubewells. The experience has shown also that the gestation period of the public tubewells project was greatly underestimated at the planning stage, partly because of administrative problems in handing over the completed wells to an operating agency (either the Irrigation Department or the SCARP Authority). In many cases even the watercourses were found to be unready for utilization. This meant that the economic returns originally calculated were overestimated. Similarly, in formulating the public tubewells project, the issue of continuing subsidy on the sale of water was not really faced. Even in the successful SCARP I area, the new water rate (double the standard water rate) barely covers the maintenance expenses of tubewells and, thus, the entire capital cost will have to be written off. The introduction of this special water rate has encountered (and can be expected to encounter in other SCARP areas) serious political difficulties, even though the availability of water per acre, agricultural yields, and land values all have increased sharply.

While the problems involved in undertaking a large public tubewells effort were minimized, the potential of private tubewells development was not fully appreciated. A major constraint on private tubewells development was the availability of electric connections, and WAPDA, by virtue of its monopoly position in power and vested interest in public tubewells, did not wish to orient its power distribution program toward agricultural consumers. However, the food self-sufficiency program adopted by the government of West Pakistan in February 1967 gave high priority to private tubewells development and laid down for WAPDA the target of 5,000 electric connections per annum for private tubewells (Government of West Pakistan 1967). This, combined with measures to limit public tubewell projects in areas of private tubewell concentration and development promise, led to a remarkable growth in the number of private tubewells. The Third Plan target of 40,000 additional wells was exceeded (Government of Pakistan 1970).

It is interesting to note, however, that the rapid electrification of private tubewells was essentially a "second-best" solution. During the Second Plan (1960–1965), most of the private tubewells installed were powered by diesel fuel because of the limited availability of electric connections. Even though the rate of return on diesel tubewells was quite high, it was considerably lower than that on electric tubewells. The difference was due mainly to a heavy indirect tax on diesel fuel and a subsidy on the sale of electricity to agricultural consumers. Studies by the Planning Board showed that private tubewells based on diesel were better investments from a national viewpoint than were electric ones, adjusting for these distortions and applying appropriate shadow prices. However, electric tubewells were still encouraged because maximization of the number of private tubewells, with their flexibility and short gestation periods, was considered desirable. Also, additional public investment in power for private tubewells appeared to have a higher payoff than the equivalent investment in public tubewells, especially over the time horizon (1967–1970) with which the food self-sufficiency program was concerned. The ideal policy course would have been to remove the heavy excise duty on diesel fuel or to give a corresponding subsidy for the operation of diesel tubewells. But both these alternatives were found to be impractical for administrative reasons.

Fertilizer

Increased fertilizer use combined with new seeds made a greater impact than did increased availability of water on agricultural output during the Third Plan. Surprisingly, only one new fertilizer plant came into operation in Pakistan during this period, and a large part of the increased domestic demand had to be met through imports. This imposed a serious though necessary drain on foreign exchange. The preoccupation with water development in the early 1960s may have led to a relative neglect of fertilizer-production planning. There are some very real difficulties in projecting fertilizer use trends. On the one hand, given the relationship of input and output prices, the rate of acceptance of new technology cannot easily be predicted. On the other, it is even more difficult to try to relate the changes in financial return resulting from fertilizer use to changes in demand for it. In Pakistan, returns of 5:1 or 4:1 on fertilized crops have not been uncommon, particularly for wheat. What would happen if the returns drop, either from a lowering of the support price or a raising of fertilizer prices through a reduction in subsidy, to a range of 2.5:1 or 2:1? What should be the risk premium? What is a reasonable rate of return in agriculture? Answers to these questions are crucial if ad hoc decisions on agricultural policy are to be avoided.

Price Support Policies

The government's decision to fix the support price of wheat at Rs.17/-per maund in 1967 was essentially such an ad hoc decision. The rates of returns of practices adopted under the new technology were determined by the support price, not vice versa. It was not realized that a support price of Rs.15/- per maund instead of Rs.17/- would have had only a marginal effect on the rate of return (say 3.5:1 instead of 4:1) and consequently might have had little influence on the spread of technology. On the other hand, the burden on government finances of a high procurement price was considerable since wheat release prices could not be adjusted upward in the interest of the urban consumer. On the total procurement of around 1 million tons, the government "loss" can be estimated at around Rs.50 million (U.S. $10 million). Providing these windfall gains to essentially prosperous farmers was totally unjustified socially, particularly because the mobilization of a part of the additional income in the form of agricultural taxation proved very difficult.

The basic idea of a support price for wheat, however, was quite sound. It had the effect of stabilizing the grain market at a critical time. Throughout the first half of the sixties, domestic trading in wheat was thin; barely one-tenth (or about 400,000 tons) of the wheat production was marketed at the *mandi* town level. With the bumper crop of 1968, the marketable surplus of wheat jumped to 1.2 million tons, a threefold increase. Of the total marketable surplus, over two-thirds was purchased by the government. It is very doubtful whether commercial operations could have handled the increased harvest without a serious fall in prices and disruption of the market. The additional credit needs were quite large, totalling nearly $100 million alone, and probably the banking system would not have shown sufficient flexibility and speed in entering this new field if the government had not intervened. A floor support price for wheat may remain necessary for an indefinite period because of the extreme seasonal character of production. But it should be possible for the private sector to handle increased wheat trading, provided the present subsidy on the wheat release price to consumers can be eliminated.

The government record in supporting rice prices and state trading in rice has been considerably less satisfactory. Even though the procurement and production of superior varieties of rice increased sharply from 1967 to 1969, showing a very favorable response to upward adjustment in prices, the Trading Corporation of Pakistan, which had the monoply of rice sales abroad, did not show enough flexibility with regard to prices to dispose of a growing volume. At the end of 1969, *basmati* rice stocks with the Pakistan government exceeded a year's average export volume. Hesitation about incurring a loss in rupees may have been a factor in not reducing export prices. The fact that the exchange rate was patently overvalued and that real value of foreign exchange was much greater than indicated by the conversion at the official rate probably were not taken into account. The failure to adjust the exchange rate also hampered the growth in cotton production, at least until 1970 when raw cotton exports were also given a 10 percent bonus. Yet another example of distortion in agriculture caused by trade and exchange policies was the heavy protection given sugar, which resulted in a misallocation of resources and in high sugar prices to the consumer. Indeed, some calculations showed that in international prices the returns on fertilized sugarcane were actually negative.

Areas Needing More Research

The shortcomings of agricultural policy in Pakistan, in what was otherwise a period of record achievement, point to the considerable need for the application of agricultural economic research and the growing need for a large number of trained agricultural economists. The exciting period of agricultural development in

Pakistan is far from over. In the overall context of uncertain balance of payments prospects and a tight domestic resource situation, the need for extending productivity gains in agriculture has become paramount. Provided realistic exchange and trade policies are followed, there is considerable scope for the expansion of agricultural exports; overcoming the market constraint will become increasingly important. One should be willing, however, to put up with a deterioration in the commodity terms of trade for agriculture if income and factor terms of trade improve.

To improve the bases upon which the major decisions relating to agricultural policy are made, there is an urgent need to extend our knowledge in the areas of changing technology, of production functions for various crops, of the economic returns of various inputs and combinations of inputs, and of the elasticity of the supply of total agricultural output in terms of a package of incentives. The most interesting problems in Pakistani agricultural planning may not relate to the optimal allocation of existing resources with the given technology but to the need for improving research and extension capabilities in the context of changing technological relationships.

Dr. Norman Borlaug, his associates, and the Ford Foundation deserve a lot of credit for coordinated research and extension programs for wheat and rice. But, basically, both agricultural research and extension remain neglected. Professional positions and prospects do not attract talented people; priorities of research and extension are not linked closely with the overall policy objectives. There is need for a massive mobilization of talent and funds for agricultural research, including research in agricultural economics. The Indus Basin Consultants Study, on which the Lieftinck group based its report, cost nearly $7 million. At present, even 1 percent of this amount is not being spent annually for a systematic updating and improvement of this comprehensive intersectoral study of water, power, and agriculture. This is a great pity, particularly because the key assumptions of the study about the desirable rate of groundwater development in the public sector, the potential of private tubewell development, and the rate of growth of fertilizer use and the resulting yields have turned out to be unrealistic.

Income Distribution in Agricultural Development

In their preoccupation with raising output levels, policy makers relegated the distributive aspects of their policies to the background. There is little doubt that 10 percent of the farmers in Pakistan, owning twenty-five acres or more and accounting for 43 percent of the farmed area, spearheaded the agricultural change and were its main beneficiaries. Consequently, the income disparities within agriculture certainly have widened. Greater social justice in agriculture is likely to be a major issue of the 1970s.

Four distinct aspects of the social justice or distribution problem in agriculture are important. The first relates to the more vigorous use of agricultural taxation to mobilize a part of the increased income in agriculture. Much of the criticism of government policies in this regard is not well founded. It is true that agricultural incomes are exempt from the normal income tax and that collections from the agricultural income tax (a multiple of the land revenue) are negligible. However, according to estimates, if the normal income tax, with all its exemptions, were extended to the agricultural sector, the realization would not be much more than Rs.100 million annually. The basic problem is that the rate of taxation of middle incomes in Pakistan is extremely low, though the budget proposals of M. M. Ahmad would definitely increase these effective rates (Ahmad 1971). Unless the average rates of taxation on incomes of around Rs.15,000 to Rs.20,000 per annum rise to 10 to 15 percent, taxing agricultural incomes would not yield positive results.

The other important area of agricultural taxation is the water rate, which has been raised several times during the last decade. During the last three years, two successive increases of 20 percent were made. Nevertheless, there remains a large element of subsidy in the sale of water, but upward adjustments can be made only gradually.

The issue of agricultural taxation must also be viewed in relation to the large expenditure of Rs.100 million or more on fertilizer subsidy. Since the use of fertilizer seems to be well established, it would be more desirable to reduce that subsidy rather than impose additional taxation. The problem, however, becomes complicated because of the likely adjustment in the exchange rate, which would raise sharply the prices of imported fertilizer and thus make the removal of the subsidy difficult. An offset for this, of course, would be provided by a more favorable exchange rate for agricultural exports. The interrelationship between various aspects of government policy should be stressed, as well as the inadequate knowledge about relationships between agricultural supply functions on the one hand and output and input prices on the other.

A second distribution issue in agriculture relates to the sharp disparities in regional development. Almost all the gains in production have been in the irrigated areas; the rainfed areas have suffered definite declines in per capita production. Part of the solution would be to improve the technology for rainfed areas. It is doubtful, however, that agricultural investments in the rainfed areas would return the kind of payoff the irrigated areas have enjoyed. Choices between subsidization of agriculture in these areas or the shifting of population out of them are extremely difficult.

The third issue of social justice, creation of employment opportunities, is also closely related. Indirect subsidies on agricultural machinery have had an adverse effect on the growth of employment in rural areas and have encouraged the displacement of labor from land. Some adjustments have been made by imposing an import duty and sales tax on farm machinery imports. The increased cost of foreign exchange would further tend to restore balance between use of capital and labor.

The biggest single challenge in agriculture is to improve the living standard of landless laborers and the small farmer who has less than five acres. These people account for 45 percent of the farm population. Since these small farmers account for only 10 percent of the total farm area, quite obviously the rate of growth of total output is not greatly dependent upon them. To improve the average size of holding for this group, a major land redistribution would perhaps be necessary. Even if only 10 percent of the land area becomes available for redistribution as a result of further land reform, the farmers with fewer than five acres could double their holdings. New technology is fairly divisible and, therefore, the lot of the small farmers may not be altogether hopeless. However, some cooperative form of organization would be necessary to give them access to inputs, particularly of tubewell water and fertilizer.

Parvez Hasan received his Ph.D. in 1961 from Yale University. He was chief economist and additional secretary, Planning Department, Government of West Pakistan from 1965 to 1970. Currently he is at the International Bank for Reconstruction and Development, Washington, D. C.

NOTE

1. The level of fertilizer use, however, is still rather low, being less than 12 kg. of nutrients per irrigated cropped acre in 1969/70.

BIBLIOGRAPHY

Ahmad, M. M.
    1971. "Central Budget for 1971–72." Karachi: *Dawn*. June 27.
Government of Pakistan
    1970. *Preliminary Evaluation of the Third Five-Year Plan (1965–70).*
        Islamabad: Planning Commission, Government of Pakistan.
Government of West Pakistan
    1967. *Food Self-Sufficiency Programme.* Lahore: Planning and Development Department, Government of West Pakistan.
Lieftinck, Pieter; Sadove, A. Robert; and Creyke, Thomas C.
    1968. *Water and Power Resources of West Pakistan: A Study in Sector Planning.* Baltimore: Johns Hopkins University Press.

13

Relationships between Technology, Prices, and Income Distribution in Pakistan's Agriculture: Some Observations on the Green Revolution

Carl H. Gotsch

Introduction

"Progress" has been defined as a process in which one set of problems is exchanged for another. Though the observation may be shopworn, it appears to be the most apt description of the profound economic, social, and political changes currently taking place in a number of the less-developed countries of the world associated with the green revolution.[1] The story of these radical increases in agricultural output has been widely told: how research work on cereals, initially under Rockefeller Foundation auspices in Mexico and subsequently under a joint Ford Foundation-Rockefeller Foundation venture in the Philippines, produced new genetic materials capable of utilizing much higher fertilizer dosages; how these varieties were spread, again largely through the work of private foundations but complemented by U.S. technical assistance, to a large number of countries throughout the world; and how the "miracle seeds," coupled in many areas with water development, have resulted in an entirely different attitude toward the potential contribution of the agricultural sector in a number of less-developed countries.[2] Although the first wave of enthusiasm regarding the extent to which these activities provide an answer to the problem of feeding or employing the world's poor is now beginning to wear off, there seems to be little doubt that these efforts constitute some of the most far-reaching technical assistance programs ever undertaken.[3]

But the problems associated with the radical changes in the

underlying production structure have not been long in showing themselves. Wharton, for example, writes:

> It will be no easy task to achieve the potential increased production offered by the new technology, particularly when it involves millions upon millions of diverse farms and farmers scattered over the countryside. If the increased production is in fact obtained, this will automatically produce a whole new set of second-generation problems which must be faced if development is to be sustained and accelerated. Therefore, two considerations need to be borne in mind. First, there is reason to believe that the further spread of new varieties will not be as fast as early successes might suggest. Second, new problems arising out of the spread of the new technology, whatever its speed, need to be foreseen and acted upon now. The probable developments in each case have the greatest significance for economic growth and for the conduct of international relations. (Wharton 1969)

The following study seeks to provide more quantitative evidence on certain of the latter issues—particularly those dealing with the relationship between prices, technical change, and selected dimensions of the income distribution question. The vehicle for the investigation is a case study of a district in the Pakistan Punjab, an area that, in addition to having a rather large body of base data for agriculture, has experienced a green revolution of unparalleled swiftness.

There are no general census materials that provide a basis for ascertaining the impact of the new technology on the relative incomes of various social classes in the rural areas of Pakistan. Consequently, the best that can be done is to build up quantitative estimates of its likely effects by first examining its effects on individual farms and then applying the results to a distribution of land by farm size. The first question is discussed here in the context of a set of farm management models that seek to determine what happens to the allocation of resources when the input-output coefficients in agriculture have changed significantly from their traditional values. These results are then applied to a farm size distribution taken from Sahiwal District, the area in which the data for the model were collected. A brief epilogue deals with the likely political fallout of the calculated changes in the structure of incomes, with conclusions and recommendations following.

Technology, Prices, and the Optimal Allocation of Resources

Supply Responses of a Representative Farm in the Punjab

The microanalysis of various types of representative farms has been carried out within a linear programming framework. The basic model has been presented elsewhere and has been supplemented for this paper with several crop activities (wheat, rice, and maize), whose input-output coefficients are assumed to reflect the new high-yielding cereal varieties (Gotsch 1968). Data for the advanced technologies were drawn largely from the agronomic research carried out by the Department of Agriculture of the government of West Pakistan. At some points, these results were modified by discussions with agricultural experts assigned to the technical assistance programs of the Ford Foundation and the U.S. Agency for International Development.[4]

A number of solutions to the "basic" model are presented in Table 1. The assumptions are that this 12.5-acre farm represents a typical small holding in the Central Punjab, that it is owned and operated by a cultivator and his family, that the source of power is a single pair of bullocks, and that the available surface-water supply is proportional to the land owned under a typical irrigation distributary. In addition to these fixed assets, it is assumed there are two types of resource-augmenting activities. The farmer may hire additional labor in peak seasons at the prevailing wage rate and he owns a one-sixth share in a tubewell, which he uses to pump supplementary water.

Several interesting conclusions about the effect of the new technology emerge from these solutions. First, the increase in net revenue under "advanced" conditions is substantial.[5] A comparison of columns 1 and 8 in Table 1 suggests that under the assumptions indicated above, profit-maximizing farmers could improve their net revenues approximately 85 percent by introducing the new methods. Several factors are responsible. Due to better irrigation facilities, there was a sizable "acreage effect." On a farm assumed to contain 12.5 acres available for cultivation, the cropped acreage increased from 13.8 acres to 17.7 acres, or about 35 percent. A second contribution results from the "yield effect" of the new varieties. Farm demonstration plots suggested that wheat yields could be expected to increase by 60 percent, rice by 100 percent, and maize by 90 percent; these estimates were incorporated into the "advanced" activities of the model. Lastly, for most technologies, there were substantial "cropping-pattern effects." This reallocation of land resources between crops was again due primarily to the flexibility of the supplementary water originating from the tubewell. Note, for example, that with the exception of maize in column 9, the "without tubewell" cropping patterns are quite similar.

The interaction of these factors in the model is significant. If the two changes from traditional to advanced technology (tubewells and high-yielding varieties) are taken independently, they yield an increase in net revenue of 35 and 25 percent respectively. The sum of their individual increases (60 percent), however, is well below the 85-percent increase produced when both are introduced simultaneously. This interaction is not due to physical complementarities of which agronomists speak, but results rather from the opportunity to increase the acreage under the profitable high-yielding varieties (HYV) when a flexible supply of supplemental irrigation water is available.

The effect of variations in output prices on farm production under different technological assumptions is also of interest. For example, the use of tubewells tends not only to shift the predicted supply curve of wheat to the right but also increases its elasticity (Figure 1). This is particularly evident in comparing the *with* and *without* tubewell case under traditional technology.

The results also show that use of supplementary water decreases the comparative advantage of wheat with respect to cotton (the two compete for land during the overlap of the summer and winter seasons), and shifts the wheat supply curve to the left. In addition, this possibility of altering the seasonal distribution pattern of water has made for greater sensitivity to the wheat-cotton price ratio. The result is that the two curves shown for traditional

TABLE 1. Optimal Cropping Patterns on a 12.5-Acre Farm in the Mixed Farming Area of the Central Punjab

	Traditional Technology		Advanced Wheat Technology		Advanced Rice Technology		Advanced Wheat and Rice Technology		Advanced Wheat Rice, Maize Technology	
	(1) Without Tubewell	(2) With Tubewell	(3) Without Tubewell	(4) With Tubewell	(5) Without Tubewell	(6) With Tubewell	(7) Without Tubewell	(8) With Tubewell	(9) Without Tubewell	(10) With Tubewell
NET REVENUE (rupees)	2337	3180	2552	3577	2415	3231	2652	3678	2963	4320
Crops (acres)										
Coarse Rice	.28		1.08		.87	1.70	1.16	3.45		
Summer Fodder (required)	.67	.67	.60	.67	.64	.67	.60	.67	.60	.67
Summer Fodder (optional)	.67	.67	.60	.67	.64	.67	.60	.67	.60	.67
Cotton	2.42	6.86	2.45	2.25	1.52	5.97	2.22	.10	.10	.10
Summer Vegetables	.10	.10	.10	.10	.10	.10	.10	.10	.10	.10

Wheat	4.74	1.69	5.57	6.26	5.87	1.69	5.51	7.00	5.12	6.75
Gram									1.62	1.80
Oilseeds	2.89		1.97		2.06		1.88		.23	
Winter Fodder (required)	.80	.89	.80	.89	.80	.89	.80	.89	.80	.89
Winter Fodder (optional)		.89		.85		.85		.65		.89
Maize					.80				2.75	4.45
Sugarcane	.60	1.00	1.00	1.00		1.00	.14	1.00	1.00	1.00
Winter Vegetables		.20		.20		.20		.20		.20
Fruit		.30		.30		.30		.30		.30
TOTAL CROPPED ACREAGE	13.77	14.57	13.16	14.49	14.10	15.34	13.15	16.23	13.82	19.02
CROPPING INTENSITY (%)(Index)	110	117	105	116	113	123	105	130	110	152

NOTE: The following maximum constraints are operative in the model: optional summer fodder—200 maunds; optional winter fodder—400 maunds; sugarcane—1 acre; summer vegetables—1 acre; winter vegetables—.20 acres; fruit—.30 acres. Cropping intensity is defined as cropped acreage/cultivated acreage. Complete double cropping would produce a cropping intensity of 200 percent. Sugarcane and fruit are counted twice.

wheat varieties cross (Figure 1). The same mechanism produces
the crossing of the curves depicting the impact of additional water
supplies with high-yielding varieties. Its effect is less visible, however, because the profitability of the new varieties ensures that a
major part of the winter acreage in irrigated areas will be planted to
wheat *regardless* of the availability of supplementary water.

Regional Differences in Resource Allocation Changes

From the foregoing description of the impact of high-yielding
varieties and tubewells on agriculture in the Central Punjab, it is
clear that a number of changes in the cropping pattern can be anticipated as new agricultural technology becomes available. Not all
areas in Pakistan have this versatility, and a rather different picture
of the effect of the green revolution emerges from an examination of
technological change in the provinces of Sind and the North-West
Frontier.

The Sind (areas V through IX in Figure 2) comprises a number

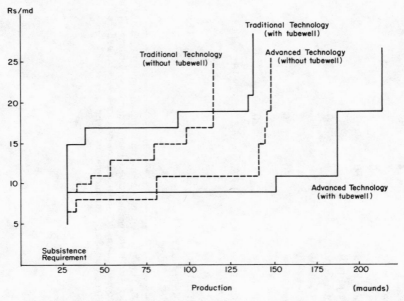

Figure 1. Supply Curves for Wheat on a Representative Punjab Farm.

of different canal systems. Those designated as "non-perennial" supply water only during the summer months when the rivers run full from the monsoons and snow melts in the north. Most of these areas, except for land near the river and the larger canals, are underlain with saline groundwater. This combination of (1) surface water concentrated in the kharif (spring-planted) season and (2) an inability to store water underground severely limits the cropping options that farmers have.

Indeed, until additional fall (rabi) water becomes available from Tarbela Dam, the traditional rice-fallow-rice or rice-*dubari*-rice[6] rotation is virtually the only alternative. The residual rice moisture, which is currently used to grow a crop of vetch or chickpeas in the rabi season, is insufficient for a crop of Maxipak wheat.

Even in the perennial canal areas, much change in land allocation is unlikely as a result of the seed-fertilizer revolution. Yields from the existing wheat and rice areas have increased significantly. But as long as the areas are constrained in their cropping intensities

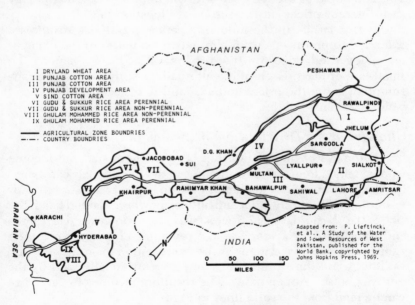

Figure 2. Agricultural Zones of the Indus Basin in Pakistan.

by the availability of canal water, the land trade-offs that figure so prominently in altering the supply curves for crops grown with tubewells (Figure 1) will not be operative.

The predicament of the dryland areas of the North-West Frontier Province (area I) is similar to that of the rice tracts of the Sind. Rainfall is virtually the sole determinant of the cropping pattern and the advent of the new varieties of wheat initially appeared unlikely to produce significant alterations in land use patterns. Fortunately, several recent studies suggest that, in a sizable portion of the area, earlier pessimism can be somewhat modified regarding the ability of high-yielding varieties to increase production and cropping intensity under rainfed conditions (Rochin 1971*a*). However, the general conclusion that the supply curve of wheat in the rainfed area is likely to be highly inelastic remains valid (Gotsch and Falcon 1970; Quereshi 1963).

Technology, Prices, and the Distribution of Incomes

The previous section dealt with the impact of new technology and different prices on the resource allocation decisions of representative farms. In the following paragraphs, these results are extended to produce several alternative estimates of the effect of technology and prices on the distribution of income among the small-farmer class. Each of the alternatives corresponds to an assumption about the prices and availability of seed, fertilizer, and water to various holding sizes.

Changes in the Distribution of Income in the Punjab

Estimates of the relationship between farm size and income were obtained from the programming model by parametrically varying the land, surface water, and tubewell capacity constraints. For example, while family labor and bullock power remained fixed, the size of the "basic" farm (12.5 acres) was varied downward to 5 acres and upward to 25 acres. The net revenues obtained were then reduced by such fixed items as the depreciation of equipment and buildings and the various taxes and cesses normally paid by the cultivators (see Appendix A). The resulting incomes by farm size can be read from the solid lines in Figure 3.

Where advanced technology is available to all, small farmers benefit relatively more than do their larger neighbors, as they are able to obtain higher yields through more intense application of the other constrained resources. For example, on the five-acre farm, income increases from Rs.350 to Rs.1250 or approximately 250 percent; on the twenty-five-acre farm, the increase is from Rs.3750 to Rs.5875 or 57 percent.

A more general impression of the effects of technology can be gained by comparing the income distributions of the "traditional" and "advanced" solutions. Lorenz curves show that incomes under traditional technology tend to be less equitably distributed than land (Figure 4 and Appendix B). The reason for such a result is not difficult to find. Examination of the programming model indicates that under traditional technology, *net revenue*, including only operating costs, increases in proportion to the increases in land and

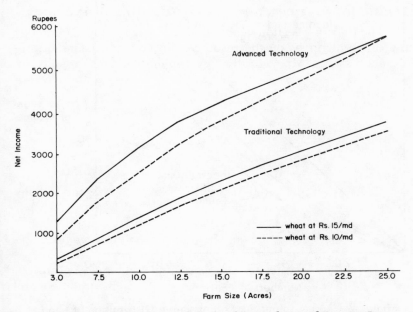

Figure 3. The Effect of Advanced Technology and Size of Farm on Income, Representative Punjab Farm, Pakistan.

its associated surface water over almost the entire five- to twenty-five-acre range. The "dual" of the model indicates that constraints on bullocks and family labor are not binding and thus are not the basis for diminishing returns to land. This Lorenz curve describing net revenue by farm size under traditional technology would be virtually identical with the Lorenz curve of the distribution of land.

Subtraction of appropriate fixed costs from the net revenue of each holding, however, generates a Lorenz curve of income that lies below the curve representing the distribution of land.

The effect of fixed costs also is evident on the distribution of income under advanced technology. However, due to the sig-

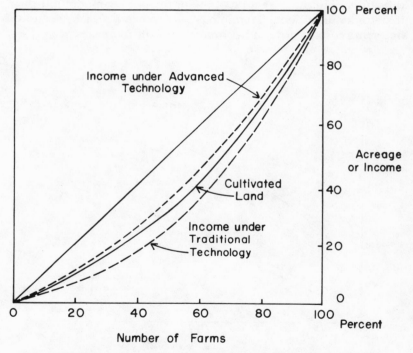

Figure 4. Comparison of the Lorenz Curve Distribution of Land and Income under Both Advanced and Traditional Technologies, Sahiwal District, Pakistan.

nificant increases in intensity resulting from increased water supplies and the increased labor requirements associated with the high-yielding varieties, bullock and human labor constraints quickly become binding as farm size increases. As a result, the disproportionate impact of fixed costs on the small farm is offset by a comparative advantage in high-value, labor-intensive activities.

The results shown in Figure 4 flow directly from production theory. They are extremely important, for they illustrate virtually the only condition short of land redistribution in which the distributive effect of the green revolution can lead to greater income equality. The assumptions are strong: that all new inputs are divisible, either intrinsically or through a competitive market for hired services; and that everyone has equal access to the institutional services that dispense the knowledge and credit required for their use.

Recent research suggests these assumptions are, at least in part, correct. Work by several authors, summarized by Rochin (1971*b*), indicates there is little difference among different farm-size groups regarding the percentage of cultivators now using improved seeds. The same is true of fertilizer, although here there is some difference between large and small farmers in the *level* of use. It seems that despite the general lack of concern regarding small farmers that traditionally has been associated with various government agencies, the simplicity, divisibility, and profitability of seeds and fertilizers have been such that the diffusion process has penetrated to groups of all sizes.

There is, however, one aspect of the research that is crucial and provides considerable cause for concern. In a recent survey (Naseem 1971), little difference was found between farm sizes in the diffusion of the seed-fertilizer package, but the same was not true for access to supplementary water. This is to be expected since the tubewell is a "lumpy" input whose spatial immobility imposes rather severe limitations on the emergence of a competitive market for water.

Imposing constraints on the availability of supplementary water to the small farmers making up the lower portion of the holding-size frequency curve would undoubtedly produce a Lorenz curve of income distribution below that associated with traditional technology, that is, small farmers would be better off in absolute terms but substantially less well off than their larger neighbors in relative terms.

Thus far the analysis has dealt almost exclusively with the distributive effects of the highly divisible technology associated with the seed-fertilizer revolution. Of interest also are the distributive effects of alternative prices under conditions of changing technology. What would the impact be, for example, of permitting wheat prices to fall to approximately world market levels? The dotted lines in Figure 5 show the results of parametrically varying the land and water constraints in the model under an assumption that wheat prices have been decreased by one-third. (Farm income includes fixed costs as in the previous exercise.)

Lorenz curves were also calculated from the income estimated by size of farm class (Appendix B) and compared with those obtained when wheat was set at its prevailing domestic market value (Figure 5).

In the case of both technologies, the decline in the price of wheat has altered the distribution of income in favor of the larger farmers. The familiar fixed cost or "lumpy input" phenomenon— here represented in large part by the family and the bullocks associated with traditional agriculture—again provides the mechanism by which this increase in the inequality of relative income distribution occurs. Both large and small farmers would suffer a decline in income under the circumstances postulated. However, for those whose income was already small, a further decline would only accentuate the disproportionate impact of fixed costs. The smaller the income relative to a constant fixed cost, the more disparate the income distribution among groups.

A reduction in the price of wheat would also tend to produce greater *inequality* among the different size groups under the assumption that advanced rather than traditional technology is being used (Appendix B). An examination of the cropping patterns associated with various farm sizes quickly reveals why this is so. As farm size increases, the additional flexibility associated with *advanced* technology, especially supplementary water, causes the wheat activities to exit from the model long before they do under *traditional* conditions. Consequently, the downward change in

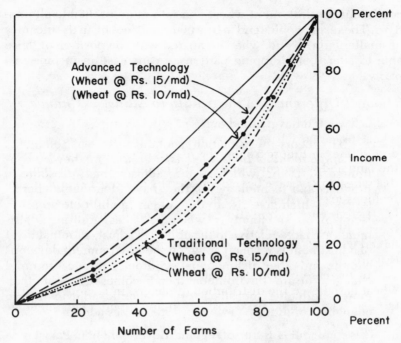

Figure 5. The Distributive Effects of Alternative Wheat Prices.

wheat prices have little effect on the larger farmers with farm sizes above 12.5 acres, for they have no wheat in the cropping pattern. Small farmers, who do not feel the pressure of power constraints to the same degree, do not seek to reduce their wheat acreage. The result is a relatively greater decline in incomes when the wheat price falls and an increase in income disparity.

The most significant distributive effects of a fall in wheat prices, however, would again be associated with a situation in which the smaller farmers do not have access to the new technology. In this situation the inelasticity of supply, particularly among those without supplementary water, means that falling prices will produce significant declines in income. On the other hand, those whose farming operations have attained a high degree of flexibility through the use of modern inputs can be expected, under the same conditions, to shift out of wheat and into more profitable alternatives. The result would tend to be a marginal decline in the incomes of smaller farmers and, when compared with the position of those able to alter their cropping patterns, an increase in income disparity.

Regional Differences in the Ability to Adjust to Change

As Tweeten has pointed out:

> The theory [of stagnation] contains three basic elements *that apply to individuals, regions or groups*: (a) they are confronted by factors which require adjustments in resources, products and technology, (b) they have identifiable characteristics which give rise to differences in ability to adjust to factors in (a), and finally (c) when the forces requiring adjustments are large relative to the ability to adjust, a liminal level of adjustment is reached at which the environment develops anomie and other disfunctional syndromes inimical to rapid change. The area environment then becomes less rather than more conducive to satisfactory economic adjustments to changing conditions. (Tweeten 1968, italics added)

This comment is as true of regional development in Pakistan as anywhere else. Whether one is talking about the "flexibility" of an area or an individual farmer, the lack of alternatives in the face of changing conditions is the essence of increasing disparity.

The characteristics that are perhaps most relevant in identifying the likely course of regional growth in agriculture have to do with the distinction between (1) areas in which only the yield effects of new technology are available, and (2) areas in which changes in both yields and cropping-pattern effects can be anticipated.

An example of the first case is much of the dryland wheat area in the northern portion of the Indus Basin (area I in Figure 2). As Rochin's recent work has shown, there is now reason to believe that, at least in the higher rainfall areas (30–50 inches), some benefits can be expected from the seed-fertilizer technology (Rochin 1971a). His field survey, based on a sample of farmers, shows that average yields of nineteen maunds per acre were obtained in Hazara District using modern technology. This was an average increase of 103 percent over the control group. Lawrence also reports significant yield increases associated with tractor-power cultural practices (deep-plowing and fallow) similar to those practices in the dryland areas of the United States (Lawrence 1970).

As a consequent of these findings, the extreme pessimism of earlier years is giving way to a somewhat more optimistic view that yield increases in some parts of the dryland areas will be sufficient to make discernible improvements in the welfare of farm families living there.

An even more optimistic picture for future progress is presented by another traditionally backward area of Pakistan: the southern portions in the province of Sind (areas V, VI, and VII in Figure 2). As indicated elsewhere, the new rice varieties have shown themselves to be unusually adapted to the dry, sunny climate of the area. Although there again appears to be little possibility of crop diversification, farm incomes can be expected to improve significantly through the yield effects alone. The latest report of the rice research stations at Kala Shah Kaku and Dokri indicates, for example, that yields of sixty maunds of rice are now commonplace (Abbasi 1968). Severe institutional and marketing constraints continue to exist, but these are problems that, unlike the basic climatic, soil, and water constraints, can in time be solved.

The real beneficiaries of the fruits of technical change, however, are farmers in the more versatile areas of the Central Punjab (areas II and III in Figure 2). Not only are they able to take advantage of the increased productivity associated with the seed-fertilizer revolution, the water distribution is such that they can respond in cropping-pattern terms to the increase in comparative advantage of the new varieties of rice and wheat. Again, if the evidence of more-developed agricultures is any guide, this basic flexibility (here demonstrated by the ability to take the ultimate advantage of new technology) will prove to be the central fact in maintaining the dominance of this area in Pakistani agriculture in the long run.

Thus far, comments on the effects of modernization on regional incomes have focused on the impact of the new technology itself. No attention has been given to the indirect effects produced by the impact of increased output on the prices of such widely grown commodities as wheat and rice. Given the recent gluts on the world cereal markets, it is probably unrealistic to assume that the government will want to maintain current price relatives in the face of significantly increased domestic supplies. The most reasonable assumption would be that some type of downward adjustment will take place in those cereal prices that are most seriously distorted, at least over the medium and long run.

Not surprisingly, the vulnerability of various areas to price changes is closely linked to their ability to adopt new technology. As in the case of technology alone, flexibility or range of choice is the key. The dryland areas, constrained by the rigidity of the environment from adopting new technology, face exactly the same set of constraining factors as far as price response is concerned. Indeed, the cropping-pattern effect, described earlier as an acreage response to the changes in comparative net revenues, is the same phenomenon regardless of whether the alteration in net revenues results from a change in the market price of the output or a change in its unit cost. One would therefore expect the severest effect on incomes of declining wheat prices to occur in these areas that have highly inelastic supply curves for wheat. A major caveat is that this only applies to the marketed surplus. As nearly every farmer sells something, to that extent he is vulnerable. At best, sharp declines in wheat prices will make it more difficult to raise living standards above the subsistance level in these areas.

Incomes in the rice areas of the Sind also are affected almost proportionately by declines in the price of rice. Although the supply curve has shifted out, it remains quite inelastic.

Again in the Central Punjab the ability either to profit from or to minimize the adverse consequences of various price policies is obviously greatest. The reader will by now recognize that the source of *both* the ability to respond to prices *and* the ability to adopt the new technology have their origin in the availability and seasonal flexibility of the irrigation water supply.

Technology, Prices, and Political Influence

As any student of public policy is aware, government programs are deeply embedded in the political processes of a country. The decisions surrounding policies regarding agricultural prices and technology in Pakistan are no exception. Indeed, there is much about the makeup of that society that permits some fairly convincing analogies to be drawn between the experience of developed countries—particularly the southern portion of the United States—and the likely course of agricultural transformation in the Indus Basin.

The previous section's discussion of the economics of the distributive effect of technology took a very narrow, static view. Even in terms of its focus on farmers with less than twenty-five acres, the dynamics of the distributive effects have not been examined fully. This is perhaps the key group in the process since it comprises the majority of the cultivators.

An additional dimension is the considerable casual evidence that, among the larger farmers (50–100 acres), substantial amounts of the high returns from new seed-water-fertilizer combinations are being used to modernize further their already progressive enterprises. Thus, the compound effects of growth among this group are well underway.[7]

At the same time economic change is taking place, however, a political process is also underway. As subsequent paragraphs will argue, the wealth of this new class of progressive larger farmers, partly derived from their use of technology but equally supported by a distorted set of commodity prices, is reflected in their increasing political influence. This is a matter of fundamental importance, for the history of agricultural policy in virtually every society underscores the fact that this group of better-educated, more progressive farmers, owning most of the factors of production but containing a minority of the people, will, if permitted, attempt to speak for all of agriculture on matters of technology and prices. Based on the U.S. experience, the following pressures from this commercial sector can be anticipated:

(1) The larger farmers will be strongly opposed to any reduction in the government's current support of output prices. An example of their waxing power was the recent reestablishment of the wheat support price in the face of the almost unanimous opposition of economists in the provincial and central planning agencies.

(2) The larger farmers will be against any program of selective mechanization. There is already considerable literature on the premature mechanization of agriculture in Pakistan, particularly since the equipment is being imported at a subsidized exchange rate and is being provided under special credit arrangements.[8] Several authors have argued this subsidy should be eliminated, and obviously such proposals should be supported. But there is some question as to whether this will greatly retard the rapidity with which the larger landowners will modernize their operations (Bose and Clark 1969; Johnston and Cownie 1969). First, tractors are likely to be produced soon in Pakistan. It is exceedingly difficult to see how planners or concerned administrators will be able to resist the pressure of an alliance between the industrialists (foreign and private) and the larger farmers for such plants. Second, even if tractors and equipment were imported at the economy's current shadow price of capital, private costs and benefits would still diverge from their social values. So long as groundwater supplies are not under public control, the 150 percent cropping intensity figure for Pakistan cannot be regarded as an effective constraint. With appropriate equipment and enough tubewell capacity, there is every reason to believe that in the near future, efficient operators will be able to doublecrop fully the land they operate. Such an intensive use of land, only feasible if modern equipment is available, provides private rates of return that make agriculture one of the most profitable enterprises in the economy.

(3) The larger farmer will resist public control of the water-bearing aquifer. Currently, the water table is within the reach of the centrifugal pumps that even the slightly above-average-size farmer can install on his tubewell. In the long run, however, the water table can be expected to drop below the reach of the pumps currently in use, to depths that require modern turbine pumps. The latter are expensive and necessitate a capital outlay many times that of centrifugal pumps. Obviously, as the water table continues to fall, only those having access to capital for pumps that can tap the deeper layers of the aquifer will be able to continue to expand their operations.

(4) Lastly, the increasingly powerful political position of the new agricultural class will make difficult the institutional reforms

needed to capture—in a progressive fashion—some of the overall increase in agricultural productivity for development purposes. Pakistan's current mobilization of domestic resources as a percentage of GNP is extremely low, even by developing country standards. With a deteriorating foreign aid picture, it must rely more heavily on internally generated resources. Yet the Fourth Plan gives no evidence of a willingness to deal with these hard issues; in particular, nothing of significance is proposed for appropriating the windfall gains of farmers referred to earlier. If anything, the introduction of the necessary institutional reforms seems as distant now as it was a decade ago.[9]

The preceding description of the forces on the stage in Pakistan paints a not unfamiliar picture to students of U.S. agricultural policy. Indeed, some foreign agriculturalists are actually pleased by the prospects outlined above, since, in the short run at least, it will undeniably lead to a continuation of the high rate of agricultural growth. To others, however, the prospect of modernizing agriculture "U.S. style" is distinctly unappealing. This is particularly true when one adds to the previously indicated components of change a 3 percent rate of population growth. As Johnston and Cownie show, the employment problems that arise, even with optimistic increases in nonagricultural employment and reasonable projections of migration, are staggering (Johnston and Cownie 1969).

Conclusions and Recommendations

It is clear the green revolution has set in motion a process that will entail significant shifts in the allocation of Pakistan's agricultural output. It seems equally obvious that these same forces, working through both the economic and political structure of the society, can be expected to exacerbate an already high degree of income disparity. Given this diagnosis, what sort of technical recommendations could be made that would tend to promote efficiency and to make possible a more humane type of structural change than that which has prevailed in most developed societies?

(1) First, there is a need on efficiency grounds to bring domestic relative prices in line with world market relatives. This is true of cereals; it is even more important in the case of sugarcane. Finding

the correct absolute levels, however, will be no easy task. The terms of trade between agricultural products and nonagricultural products are badly distorted. Hence, without considering a radical alteration of the overall foreign exchange policy (e.g., revaluation), simply lowering prices to the absolute level of world prices would be inappropriate. The least disruptive (but also perhaps least effective) tactic would be to approach world relatives from both above and below. This would require downward adjustments for sugarcane, maize, and wheat, and upward adjustments for rice and cotton.

(2) The institutional assumptions that underlay the analysis of income distribution by farm size were optimistic indeed. There is little evidence that the current institutional structure is capable of insuring that *all* farmers have access to those inputs that are, by their nature, infinitely divisible. Moreover, the experience of other countries suggests that efforts to provide such a guarantee through governmental bureaucracies is prohibitively expensive. Eliminating the possibility of a "top-down" strategy leaves no alternative but to accept the political risks of promoting various forms of grassroots, farmer-dominated organizations. Whether they be in the form of cooperatives or communes, small farmers and the landless have no weapon against the system but organization.

(3) Pakistan must take seriously the problem of regional imbalance. No one program or policy will suffice; what is required is an approach that permits some people to stay on the farm by expanding their holding size, others to be educated for migration to areas of demand as industrial and agricultural labor. Where possible, efforts at decentralization of industrial activity into growth centers close to the affected regions would have a high payoff.

Such efforts at mitigating the growth of regional disparity are, of course, standard recommendations, and some observers have cautioned that they may be too expensive in terms of national growth for a country at Pakistan's level of development. The appropriate effort is indeed a matter for calculation. However, the evidence from developed countries is that the downward spiral of poverty that is so prominent a feature of backward regions is difficult to reverse.

(4) The proposals recently made regarding the need to capture some of the windfall gains of technological change must be implemented. Even casual arithmetic shows that the *income* terms of

trade have turned in agriculture's favor during recent years. Rather than capturing some of the surplus associated with the green revolution for the provision of nonagricultural employment, the government has permitted it to remain in the hands of agriculture.

(5) Lastly, what is needed most is a national policy toward technological change. By investigating further the effects of the economics of mechanization, for example, it should be possible to define more carefully the magnitudes of such parameters as wage rates, interest rates, excise taxes, and subsidies that would create an environment for structural transformation in agriculture consistent with the ability of the nonagricultural sectors to absorb surplus rural labor. Once these have been ascertained, the government should not hesitate to implement a program that might result in significant deviations from that dictated by the unregulated market.

The above technical recommendations are largely the product of direct economic analysis. If they are to have real credibility, however, they should also be accompanied by a description of the political and social mechanisms by which they are to be implemented. This means, above all else, a description of the nature of the class interests that dominate the various aspects of Pakistan's economic policy, an identification of the extent and potential evolution of the political consciousness of these groups, and proposals for alliances that would move in the right direction.

Such an analysis is beyond the scope of this paper; however, I would suggest that one can be anything but optimistic about the ability of Pakistan's society to develop instruments capable of coping with the country's growing income inequality.

Carl H. Gotsch received his Ph.D. from Harvard University in 1966. He was a member of the Harvard Advisory Group in Pakistan from 1964 to 1966. He is a lecturer in the Department of Economics and Adviser with the Development Advisory Service of Harvard University; he is currently on leave and working with the Ford Foundation, Beirut, Lebanon. He continues research on rural development in Pakistan.

NOTES

This paper is a summary and extension of work carried out under AID/ NESA Contract 403. I am grateful to Walter P. Falcon both for collaboration on the original work and for comments on the specific contents of this paper. I am, of course, responsible for any errors that remain.

1. The term "green revolution" is taken to include the complex of factors that has led to rapid growth in the agricultural sector: tubewells, seeds, fertilizer, insecticides, etc. It explicitly does not consider the impact of tractor mechanization, for, as yet, the latter has had no widespread effect.

2. A sample of the more recent writings might include: Barker (1970), Brown (1970), Falcon (1970), Hardin (1969), Johnston and Cownie (1969), and Kaneda (1969).

3. In describing the green revolution in India, Mort Grossman points out that the increased productivity is thus far confined to a limited number of crops in a limited number of areas. The case for a cautious interpretation of the implications of recent events in India is given empirical backing in Minhas (1970).

4. Much of this information is contained in the Annual Reports published by the Government of Pakistan. See, for example, Munshi et al. (1969).

5. Net revenue is defined as gross revenue minus variable or out-of-pocket costs incurred during the crop year.

6. *Dubari* is the general name given to winter crops sown in the residual moisture of the rice fields.

7. In another chapter of this volume, Burki argues that the political influence of this class was the catalyst to the economic transformation described above. Whatever the direction of causality, there is no disagreement regarding the broadening of the political base of agricultural interests since the middle 1960s. See also Burki (1971).

8. An excellent discussion and summary of this whole argument is to be found in R. S. Bose's unpublished paper dissenting from the conclusions of the government committee set up to investigate the farm mechanization problem. The latter report (Government of Pakistan 1970) does a disservice to those in Pakistan committed to rational policies for structural change in agriculture. See also Kaneda (1969).

9. For a general argument linking policies that promote income disparity with the difficulty of creating institutions that can mobilize resources for saving in the public sector, see Bird (1968).

BIBLIOGRAPHY

Abbasi, Rasul; Shafi, M.; Khan, S.; Mueller, K.
    1968.   *Annual Progress Report on Accelerated Rise Research Program, 1967*. Lahore: Agriculture Department, Government of West Pakistan.
Barker, Randolph
    1970.   "Green Revolution." *Current Affairs Bulletin*. Vol. 45, January 26.

Bird, Richard
    1968. "Income Redistribution, Economic Growth and Tax Policy."
        In *Proceedings of the Sixty-first Annual Conference on Taxa-
        tion*, edited by Stanley J. Bowers, pp. 146–152. Columbus,
        Ohio: National Tax Association.
Bose, Swadesh R., and Clark, Edwin H., III
    1969. "Some Basic Considerations on Agricultural Mechanization
        in West Pakistan." *Pakistan Development Review* 9, (3):
        273–308.
Brown, Lester
    1970. *Seeds of Change*. New York: Praeger.
Burki, Shahid Javed
    1971. "Interest Groups and Agricultural Development." Unpub-
        lished. Cambridge, Mass.: Center for International Affairs,
        Harvard University.
Falcon, Walter P.
    1970. "The Green Revolution: Generations of Problems." *American
        Journal of Farm Economics* 52 (December): 698–710.
Gotsch, Carl H.
    1968. "A Programming Approach to Some Agricultural Policy Prob-
        lems in West Pakistan." *Pakistan Development Review* 8
        (2):192–225.
Gotsch, Carl, and Falcon, Walter
    1970. "Supply Response of Individual Agricultural Commodities by
        Region: The Historical Experience." Chapter 4.1 in "Agricul-
        tural Price Policy and the Development of West Pakistan."
        Vol. 1, Final Report. Mimeographed. Cambridge, Mass.: Har-
        vard Development Advisory Service, Harvard University.
Government of Pakistan
    1970. *Farm Mechanization in West Pakistan*. Report of the Farm
        Mechanization Committee, Ministry of Agriculture and
        Works, Government of Pakistan. March.
Hardin, Lowell
    1969. "Later-Generation Agricultural Development Problems." In
        Agricultural Development, pp. 44–49. New York: Rockefeller
        Foundation.
International Bank for Reconstruction and Development
    1969. *Water and Power Resources of West Pakistan: A Study in Sec-
        tor Planning*. Comprehensive Report. Baltimore: Johns Hop-
        kins University Press.
Johnston, Bruce F., and Cownie, John
    1969. "The Seed-Fertilizer Revolution and Labor Force Absorp-
        tion." *American Economic Review* 59 (September): 569–582.

Kaneda, Hiromitsu
  1969.   "Economic Implications of the 'Green Revolution' and the Strategy of Agricultural Development in West Pakistan." *The Pakistan Development Review* 9, (2): 111–143.
Lawrence, Roger
  1970.   "Some Economic Aspects of Farm Mechanization in Pakistan." Mimeographed. Rawalpindi: Ford Foundation.
Minhas, B. S.
  1970.   "Rural Poverty, Land Distribution and Development Strategy: Facts and Policy." Mimeographed. Washington, D. C.: Economic Development Institute, International Bank for Reconstruction and Development.
Munshi, Z. A.; Hassan, M. M.; Hassan, S. F.; Bajwa, M. A.; Qureshi, S. A.; Morales, I. N.
  1969.   *Fourth Annual Technical Report: Accelerated Wheat Improvement Program 1968–69*. Lahore: Agriculture Department, Government of West Pakistan.
Naseem, Muhammad
  1971.   "Small Farmers in the Structural Transformation of West Pakistan Agriculture." Ph.D. dissertation, University of California (Davis).
Quereshi, Sarfraz Khan
  1963.   "Rainfall, Acreage and Wheat Production in West Pakistan: A Statistical Analysis." *Pakistan Development Review* 3 (Winter): 566–593.
Rochin, Refugio
  1971a. "Dwarf Wheat Adoption by Barani Smallholders of Hazra District: Technological Change in Action." Mimeographed. Islamabad, West Pakistan: Ford Foundation.
  1971b. "The Impact of Dwarf Wheats on Farmers with Small Holdings in West Pakistan: Excerpts from Recent Studies." Mimeographed. Islamabad, West Pakistan: Ford Foundation.
Singh, Inderjit; Day, Richard H.; and Johl, S. S.
  1968.   *Field Crop Technology in the Punjab, India*. Madison: Social Systems Research Institute, University of Wisconsin.
Tweeten, Luther G.
  1968.   "Rural Poverty: Incidence, Causes and Cures." Mimeographed. Stillwater: Oklahoma State University.
Wharton, Clifton R., Jr.
  1969.   "The Green Revolution: Cornucopia or Pandora's Box?" *Foreign Affairs* 47 (April):464–476.

APPENDIX A. Calculation of Farm Income
at Domestic Prices

Farm Size (acres)	Gross Revenue (Rs.)	Fixed Costs (Rs.)					Net Income (Rs.)
		Bullocks[a]	Equipment[b]	Buildings	Tube-well[c]	Total	
Traditional Technology							
5.0	836	250	136	100	—	486	350
7.5	1361	250	136	100	—	486	875
10.0	1864	250	136	100	—	486	1378
12.5	2337	250	136	100	—	486	1851
15.0	2787	250	136	100	—	486	2301
17.5	3180	250	136	100	—	486	2694
20.0	3543	250	136	100	—	486	3057
22.5	3900	250	136	100	—	486	3414
25.0	4240	250	136	100	—	486	3754
Advanced Technology							
5.0	1784	250	136	100	62	548	1236
7.5	2939	250	136	100	94	580	2359
10.0	3757	250	136	100	125	611	3146
12.5	4442	250	136	100	156	642	3800
15.0	4943	250	136	100	187	673	4270
17.5	5319	250	136	100	219	705	4614
20.0	5770	250	136	100	250	736	5034
22.5	6250	250	136	100	281	767	5483
25.0	6675	250	136	100	312	798	5877

[a] One pair of bullocks is assumed to cost Rs. 2000 and have a working lifetime of eight years.
[b] Equipment list and life taken from Singh, Day, and Johl 1968.
[c] Tubewell assumed to cost Rs. 10,000 and have a lifespan of ten years.

APPENDIX B. Effect of Advanced Technology and Alternative Wheat Prices on Distribution of Income among Different-Size Farms

Farm Size (acres)	Number of Units (thousands)	%	Income Traditional Technology Rs. 15/maund Total Rs. (millions)	%	Rs. 10/maund Total Rs. (millions)	%	Advanced Technology Rs. 15/maund Total Rs. (millions)	%	Rs. 10/maund Total Rs. (millions)	%
6.25	104	26.9 (26.9)	62.4	10.0 (10.0)	52.0	9.4 (9.4)	187.2	14.7 (14.7)	135.2	12.5 (12.5)
8.75	85	22.0 (48.9)	93.5	15.0 (25.0)	80.8	14.6 (24.0)	233.7	18.3 (33.0)	178.5	16.5 (29.0)
11.25	57	14.7 (63.6)	91.2	14.7 (39.7)	79.8	14.5 (38.5)	199.5	15.6 (48.6)	163.9	15.2 (44.2)
13.75	45	11.6 (75.2)	94.5	15.2 (54.9)	83.2	15.1 (53.6)	182.2	14.3 (62.9)	159.8	14.8 (59.0)
16.25	35	9.0 (84.2)	87.5	14.1 (69.0)	78.8	14.3 (67.9)	156.6	12.3 (75.2)	141.8	13.1 (72.1)
18.00	27	7.0 (91.2)	78.3	12.6 (81.6)	70.2	12.7 (80.6)	131.6	10.3 (85.5)	122.8	11.4 (83.5)
21.25	20	5.2 (96.4)	64.0	10.3 (91.9)	59.5	10.8 (91.4)	105.0	8.2 (93.7)	101.0	9.3 (92.8)
23.75	14	3.6 (100.0)	50.4	8.1 (100.0)	46.9	8.5 (99.9)	79.1	6.2 (99.9)	77.7	7.2 (100.0)
TOTAL			621.8		551.2		1274.9		1080.7	

NOTE: Numbers in parentheses are cumulative percentages.

14

The Adoption and Effects of High-Yielding Wheats on Unirrigated Subsistence Holdings in Pakistan

Refugio I. Rochin

Introduction

Dwarf wheats are high-yielding varieties, which were developed in Mexico and introduced into and multiplied in West Pakistan. Their diffusion and widespread adoption on irrigated land in the past five years have been instrumental in attaining food grain self-sufficiency in Pakistan.

Contributing to this remarkable achievement has been a 25-percent increase in wheat acreage and a 35-percent increase in yields, resulting in a record high national average in 1969/70 of 12.9 maunds per acre. Governmental season and crop reports show the following changes in Pakistan wheat acreage and yields in recent years (Table 1). Of the wheat acreage, 70 percent is irrigated and 30 percent is *barani*, or rainfed.[1]

On irrigated land, the average wheat yields have increased by as much as 70 percent in recent years. Official records show no such change in yields of wheat grown under *barani* conditions. Little is known about the impact of the new wheat varieties in these less favorably endowed areas of Pakistan, where water supplies are uncertain and where farmers are subject to much more risk in experimenting with yield-changing innovations. Only a modest effort has been given to research on wheat production on *barani* land and to study of the socioeconomic characteristics of *barani* farming. Aside from Sturt's study (1965), little is known about *barani* farmers' methods of cultivation, standard of living, and willingness to

TABLE 1. Wheat Acreage and Yields
in West Pakistan, 1964–1970

Year	Acreage (in thousands)	*Yields in Maunds per Acre*		
		All Wheat	Irrigated Wheat	*Barani* Wheat
1964/65	13,140	9.4	11.3	5.7
1965/66	12,738	8.2	10.1	4.2
1966/67	13,205	8.8	10.9	3.9
1967/68	14,785	11.6	13.9	6.2
1968/69	15,221	11.6	14.1	4.5
1969/70	15,089	12.9	17.2	4.4

SOURCE: Government of Pakistan 1964/65–1969/70.

accept innovations. Available research often takes a negative view of the *barani* farmers who live in the northern regions of Pakistan. They are thought to be resistant to change and to maintain irrational farm management methods (Sharif 1965).

The degree to which *barani* smallholders adopt dwarf wheats is of considerable concern to policy makers. One view is that the new varieties will provide widespread benefits in many agricultural areas, including the *barani* regions. An alternative view, explored by Gotsch in the preceding chapter, suggests that *barani* areas are likely to benefit little from the new, high-yielding cereal varieties and their complementary inputs. Should this be true, alternative rural development policies may be required for these areas.

A study of the adoption of dwarf wheats by *barani* farmers presents an opportunity to examine the general process of the diffusion of a message, in this case, the idea that dwarf wheats are more productive. Diffusion is carried out through communication steps that usually involve four elements: a source, communication channels, the receiver or adapter, and the impact of the innovation.

Specifically, this study was undertaken to determine (a) to what extent the dwarf wheats were being adapted by *barani* farmers; (b) the nature of the diffusion process that influenced these farmers; and (c) to gauge the impact of the dwarf varieties on a *barani* area.

Survey Locations and Sample Characteristics

General Characteristics of Hazara District

Field surveys for this study were conducted in Hazara District of the North-West Frontier Province. The district is characterized by rough and mountainous terrain. Even though it comprises a total area of 4 million acres, only about 600,000 acres are cultivated annually. Of the cultivated acreage, 85 percent is exclusively *barani*.

Approximately 30 percent of the district's cropped area is sown with wheat during the winter (rabi) season. *Barani* wheat covers 88 percent of the district's 200,000 wheat acres. About 45 percent of the cropped area is sown with maize during the summer (kharif) season in Hazara and 88 percent of its 290 thousand maize acres are rainfed.

Hazara's agricultural sector, which holds 95 percent of the district's population, faces two interrelated problems of constant urgency: intense population pressure and poverty. In 1961, approximately 1.38 million people lived there. Since it has been difficult to increase productivity and cultivable area in Hazara, increases in population have made it difficult to raise per capita incomes. Those living in Hazara are generally poor. According to the 1960 agriculture census, 77 percent of the 270,000 farms are less than five acres in size; barely 2 percent are larger than twenty-five acres. Almost all farmers own their land, live on hillsides, and farm multiterraced plots. Subsistence crop production of maize and wheat is their main agricultural pursuit.[2] Rough topographic conditions have made it difficult for tractor mechanization and irrigation schemes to penetrate the district.

The Study Site: Lora and Oghi Villages

The sample of respondents was chosen from villages in Oghi and Lora thanas (counties),[3] which are relatively large geographic areas representative of most of Hazara District. The two thana areas are one hundred miles apart and hold a number of interesting contrasts and similarities. Oghi has rich forested land and Lora is practically deforested and subject to extensive erosion and soil deterioration. Both grow primarily wheat in winter and maize in summer.

Annual rainfall for the last ten years has averaged around 45 inches in Oghi and 52 inches in Lora, with a variation of plus or minus 5 inches in any given year for each area. Both areas experience heaviest precipitation during the months from July to September and February to April. However, the former monsoon period is also the hottest, with temperatures soaring to 100°F during the day, resulting in a high rate of evapotranspiration that nearly matches the rate of precipitation. The rainfall is extremely erratic however, falling in unpredictable, explosive torrents. One field may receive the brunt of a thundershower and a neighboring field may continue to suffer from drought. Many *barani* farmers still adhere to the practice of leaving land fallow each growing season to "give the land rest and rebuild its power."

Data for the study were collected during two field surveys in 1970, which coincided with the postharvest periods for wheat and maize: June and November, respectively. The method of data collection involved approaching and interviewing farmers who were in the field or on the trail in the vicinity of villages, which were chosen at random by the interviewing team.

The first survey has 143 usable interviews with *barani* smallholders. In the second survey, 98 farmers were interviewed. Due to the particular sampling technique used, 15 farmers were interviewed twice, and on a few occasions, smallholders could not answer questions well. Thus, the size of sample for certain questions changes in the following analysis.

Salient Characteristics of Barani *Smallholders*

Approximately 96 percent of the sample of respondents cultivate less than 15 acres; 87 percent cultivate less than 10, 64 less than 5, and 34 percent of all the respondents cultivate less than 2.5 acres. About 82 percent of the respondents own their land, 4 percent both own and rent land, and the rest are tenants. However, tenants usually did not pay rent since ownership of their land is in dispute under land reform legislation. The average size of cultivated area is thus about 5 acres; *barani* land comprises 97 percent of this cultivated acreage and is used primarily for wheat and maize. What little land is irrigated is sown with rice during the summer season.

Nearly all the farmers struggle with small and widely separated plots of land passed on by Muslim inheritance practices. Since each plot averages around one-quarter of an acre in size, farmers cultivate on the average fifteen separate plots that are terraced. Government efforts to consolidate holdings so far have been futile (Rizvi et al. 1965).

Most families live in homes made of rock covered with hand-molded mud. The average family has a few fruit and/or nut trees around the home, a buffalo and/or goat to provide its dairy foods, some chickens, and a pair of bullocks for plowing. Some homes have a private well for drinking water or a nearby well shared by village neighbors; none of the homes in the villages have indoor plumbing.

Village homes are without electricity; the kerosene lamp is now replacing the candle. Wood and fuel oil are used for heating and cooking. Due to the cost and scarcity of both, however, cow dung mixed with straw is more frequently burned. Latrines are nonexistent. Few homes are located near an all-weather road. Most are nestled against protective mountainsides. Provisions have to be carried by hand or sometimes by donkey rented for a small carrying fee.

The extended families average between ten and eleven people, about two to three per cropped acre. Most extended families have relatives employed outside the village area. Some husbands work in Karachi city, a thousand miles away, and keep their wives and children on the farm.

The heads of households interviewed in the survey averaged forty-seven years of age. Although 45 percent said they were literate, they appear to read with considerable difficulty. More and more of the younger males are sent to primary schools, mostly in anticipation of their leaving the farms by the time they reach twenty years of age.

The typical family's total income is about $235 a year.[4] About $150 is the value of the farm-produced crops—wheat, maize, a little rice, with their straw and hay cut from the surrounding hills. Another $25 is earned by the farmer at other jobs in the village. The rest of the income, $60, comes from relatives employed away from the village who send money orders or cash to the family on the farm.

Little of the grain produced by these farmers reaches the market. If a farmer sells any, it is only when debts fall due or when cash is needed to cover costs of medicine or wedding ceremonies. The poorest families consume practically nothing besides the grain they produce.

Overall, the *barani* smallholders of Hazara District do not appear to be likely candidates to adopt innovations. They simply cannot afford to risk losses in crop production. Yet with limited agricultural advances and a rapid growth in population, Hazarans will continue to add to the mainstream of people joining urban concentrations, a prospect the country can ill afford.

Sources of Dwarf Wheats in Hazara

Dwarf wheats were brought into Hazara District by the field staff of the Regional Department of Agriculture, by the Agricultural Development Corporation (ADC), and by some farmers.[5]

The first shipment of 400 maunds (enough seed for about 400 acres) was distributed to different areas of the district in 1966/67 for use on irrigated land and was sown by the field extension staff on a number of controlled and carefully selected "demonstration plots."

Hazara has three *tehsils* (administrative units): Abbottabad, Mansehra, and Haripur. Twelve maunds of the first shipment were distributed in Mansehra (where Oghi is situated), twenty maunds in Abbottabad (where Lora is situated), and the rest in Haripur (the area with most of Hazara's irrigated farmland). At that time, each bag of dwarf wheat cost the government Rs. 54 per maund, compared to Rs. 20 per maund for the best desi (traditional) varieties.

In 1967/68, 9,000 maunds of dwarf wheat were commercially available to the farmers through the ADC. The price per maund dropped to Rs. 36, but this price was still far above the price of desi varieties.

By 1968/69, dwarf wheat seed reached a significant number of the farmers' fields. The ADC sold a smaller amount (5,500 maunds) than the year before and at a lower price of Rs. 22 per maund.

In 1969/70, the year of this survey, most seed was obtained by trading from farmer to farmer and relatively little was sold by the ADC.

Time Patterns in the Diffusion of Dwarf Wheat and Fertilizer

The Adoption of Chemical Fertilizer and Dwarf Wheats

The Lora and Oghi areas showed a rapid rate of diffusion of new dwarf wheats, particularly Mexipak-65,[6] and chemical fertilizer. The number of respondents who used dwarf wheats and chemical fertilizer for the first time each year since 1966/67 is shown in Table 2. During the first year, fewer than 1 percent of the sampled *barani* smallholders were using dwarf wheats; a slightly larger fraction of farmers used chemical fertilizer. By 1969/70, the majority of *barani* smallholders had already tried dwarf wheats *and* fertilizer.

TABLE 2. Dwarf Wheat and Chemical Fertilizer Use by Farmers in Lora and Oghi Thanas, 1966/67–1970/71

Growing Period	Dwarf Wheat (n-226)			Chemical Fertilizer (n-95)		
	No. of First-time Users	Cumulative Number	Cumulative Percentage of Number	No. of First-time Users	Cumulative Number	Cumulative Percentage of Number
1966/67	2	2	0.83	3	3	3.16
1967/68	28	30	13.26	5	8	8.42
1968/69	45	75	33.17	20	28	29.47
1969/70	75	150	66.35	30	58	61.05
1970/71[a]	50	200	88.47	11	69	72.63

SOURCE: Rochin 1971.

[a] Based on respondents' anticipated use.

Overall, these findings clearly indicate that *barani* smallholders are responsive to innovations and will make rapid adjustments in resource allocation when new profitable varieties of seed and fertilizer become available.

Dwarf Wheat Acreage

In 1966/67, three-fourths of an acre was sown with dwarf wheat by two farmers in the sample (Table 3). In following years other farmers went through a period of experimentation and acquaintance with the variety. Few, if any, sowed 100 percent of their wheat area with the new variety during the first two years. Between the 1968/69 and 1969/70 growing periods, more farmers with smaller holdings began to use dwarf wheats. But due to the increasing proportion of smaller farms among these new users, this did not sharply increase the percentage of total wheat area in dwarf wheats.

The survey results also indicate that dwarf wheat growers were sowing more land during rabi (the winter season) and were leaving less land fallow. In other words, they were increasing multiple cropping.

TABLE 3. Area and Percentage of Farm Wheat Area Sown to Dwarf Wheat on Respondents' Farms, Lora and Oghi Thanas, 1966/67–1970/71

Growing Period	Average Number of Kanals/Farm [a]	Percentage of Total Farm Wheat Area
1966/67[b]	3.0	30.00
1967/68	6.2	34.02
1968/69	11.0	65.04
1969/70	11.3	65.90
1970/71[c]	13.8	72.10

SOURCE: Rochin 1971.

[a] Includes only farms adopting. One *kanal* equals one-eighth of an acre; it is made up of twenty *merla*s, the smallest land unit measured by revenue collectors.

[b] Unreliable figures for comparative purposes due to small number of respondents.

[c] Anticipated area, based on respondents' plans.

Only one farmer in the sample tried dwarf wheats and subsequently rejected them. The stated reason for this rejection was
the "bad taste and quality" of the unleavened bread (chapati) made
from the new wheat. He had a variety with a red grain, which is
considered inferior to white grain. However, the same farmer said
he saw some white-grain types (Mexipak-65) in the village and
would attempt to acquire enough seed to sow his entire wheat
acreage with it.

In the total group of respondents, only two farmers said they
had never heard of Mexipak at the time of the interview. They
represent less than 2 percent of the sample.

Methods of Diffusion

Communication is defined as the process by which messages
are transferred through channels from a source to a receiver.[7] In this
study, the message is an idea that dwarf wheats give higher yields
than do desi varieties.

There are a number of communication channels through
which messages can be conveyed, including interpersonal and
mass media. Both types function in different ways and their effectiveness also differs according to the way they are used.[8] A third
type of communication channel, the demonstration-plot channel,
has been grouped with the interpersonal channels in the following
discussion.

Both interpersonal and mass media channels were important
in creating awareness of dwarf varieties among the sample of respondents (Table 4).

Mass Media Channels

Mass media channels refer to radio, television, films, news-
papers, magazines, and the like, anything with a capacity to reach
large audiences quickly over great distances. Agricultural programs are broadcast daily over the radio in Pakistan. Many are
coordinated by the Bureau of Agricultural Information as part of an
education extension component. In addition, the bureau publishes
a monthly calendar of radio programs for their respective areas.

TABLE 4. Channels of Communication That First
Informed Respondents of Dwarf Wheats

Channels	Number First Informed by	Percentage of Total Respondents
Mass Media	34	23.78
Magazine (Urdu)	1	0.70
Radio	33	23.08
Interpersonal	107	74.82
Localite [a]	51	35.66
Cosmopolite [b]	32	22.38
Demonstration Plots	34	16.78
Not Aware of Mexipak	2	1.40
TOTAL	143	100.00

SOURCE: Rochin 1971.

[a] Fellow villagers.
[b] Persons from outside the village.

Radio programs are presently beamed from Lahore, Rawalpindi, and Peshawar. The first two stations broadcast in Urdu/Punjabi and the third in Pushto.

Sixty respondents interviewed in Lora said they frequently heard either the Lahore or Rawalpindi agricultural programs. The same number of Oghi said they listened to the Peshawar station. Upon further questioning, however, only one-half in both locales—30 each in Lora and Oghi—could give the approximate time of the program to which they claimed to have listened. This type of response could indicate that there is an element of status involved in listening to the radio and that more farmers are apt to say that they listened than actually did. On the other hand, radio programming times do change during the year, a measure calculated to broadcast the agricultural program just after sunset, a time when most farmers are eating dinner. For future questioning on the

impact of radio program offerings upon farmers, it would be important to know which stations are broadcasting and at what hours in
order to cross-check respondents' answers.

Radio was found to be the mass media channel most often
mentioned by smallholders as their source of information on dwarf
wheat performance and availability. Further questioning pointed
out that 56 respondents out of 143 (39 percent) owned radios. Ten
farmers (7 percent) who did not own radios stated that they first
learned of dwarf wheats over this medium.

Altogether, only one smallholder in the sample learned of
Mexipak from the written media: a magazine written in Urdu. No
other type of mass media was mentioned by the respondents as a
first source of information on the new wheat varieties.

Interpersonal Channels

The survey showed that essentially three types of interpersonal channels informed the *barani* smallholder of dwarf wheat
yields:

Interpersonal localite comprising individuals who are members of the social system of the receiver, for example, his
neighbors, village shopkeepers, and so forth.

Interpersonal cosmopolite comprising those who have their
origins outside the receiver's immediate social system, for example, agricultural extension personnel and distributors of farm
supplies. Both Lora and Oghi have offices of the Department of
Agriculture, each headed by an agricultural assistant, usually a
man in his thirties with a bachelor's degree in agriculture from
Peshawar University. Each agricultural assistant, in turn, supervises three or four field assistants. These men, usually in their
late twenties, generally have matriculated in second- or third-
year division and have completed a one-year certificate course in
the Agricultural Training Institute in Peshawar. "A Field Assistant is expected to be the Government's principal contact with
farmers in the area of one or two Unions, which means 10–20
villages, or 10–25,000 people" (Davy 1967:4).

Demonstration plots comprising visual field displays of agricultural innovations, which stimulate discussion among far-

mers. Both Lora and Oghi areas had the same number of demonstration plots installed on farmers' fields by the field assistants; six plots in each area in 1967/68 and five plots in the following two years. For 1970/71, the number was reduced to one each. Their locations were all near the market centers of Lora and Oghi.

The interpersonal localite channels had the largest impact on the farmers. Exchanges between *barani* smallholders were the highest carriers of the dwarf wheat message. The dwarf wheat demonstration plots, when placed next to desi plots, strikingly illustrated the differences between the two,[9] and thus were also effective transmitters of the high-yield message.

It should be noted that field assistants were very instrumental in diffusing dwarf wheat varieties. Besides personally informing farmers of dwarf wheat potential, they were responsible for the installation of many of the demonstration plots on farmers' fields, which, in turn, were catalysts in dwarf wheat diffusion.

Thus, both mass media and interpersonal communication channels appear to be important in introducing innovations to *barani* smallholders of Pakistan. Strengthening the effectiveness of both types of channels is a means of keeping smallholders informed of innovations as they become available.

Reasons for Adoption

Yield appears to be the single most important reason behind dwarf wheat adoption, although farmers mentioned a few other important characteristics as follows:

(1) Dwarf wheats fit the cropping pattern of the farmer more easily and mature earlier than do desi wheats. In particular, dwarf wheats can be planted up to one month later.

(2) Dwarf wheats do not require changes from current practices and farmers can experiment with their culture. Many tasks are still done in the same way for both desi and dwarf wheats, including ground preparation, broadcast sowing, weeding, harvesting, and winnowing. Dwarf wheats are also neutral to scale, so any size farm can use them.

(3) Some respondents like the bearded features of dwarf wheats, which gave some protection against birds.

(4) Other respondents stated that they like the taste of the white variety (Mexipak-65).

One complaint was that dwarf wheat gave less fodder. However, *barani* smallholders were willing to sacrifice fodder for a higher grain yield.[10]

The most important reason for adopting comparative yields is that each year dwarf wheats outyielded desi wheats by a consistently wide margin (Table 5).[11] In 1967/68 both temperature and rainfall were within the range conducive to good yields with the dwarf wheats.

In subsequent years, dwarf wheats were grown on more and more acreage, which apparently included a mix of factors resulting in reduced yields: poorer lands under dwarfs, poorer farm managers growing the new varieties, less ideal weather, and less fertilizer per acre on dwarfs. Yet, in all periods, dwarf wheats continued to yield more than desi wheats.

TABLE 5. Yields of Desi and Dwarf Wheat on *Barani* Land, Hazara District, 1967/68–1969/70

Year	Dwarf Wheat		Desi Wheat	
	Number of Growers	*Yield/ Acre (mds)* [a]	*Number of Growers*	*Yield/ Acre (mds)* [a]
1967/68	26	23.92	17	9.08
1968/69	60	17.52	28	10.24
1969/70	98	15.12	62	8.48
THREE YEAR AVE. 1967/68–1969/70	61	18.85	36	9.27

SOURCE: Rochin 1971.

[a] One maund equals 82.29 pounds.

It was clearly evident to the respondents that dwarf yields are greater than desi yields. Respondents also claimed there is less risk and more certainty in sowing dwarfs; they at least "got their seed back." On the other hand, farmers said that many times because of the low fodder yield they had had to feed their desi wheat as fodder to the animals and they "got no seed back."

The Impact of Dwarf Wheat

Major Direct Effects

The degree to which *barani* smallholders have benefited from dwarf wheats has been of concern to policy makers (Government of Pakistan 1970:262). Thus, the analysis now focuses on an assessment of the effects of the new wheats in Hazara District. The technological change embodied in the dwarf wheats, together with the accompanying change in complementary inputs, has had a number of significant direct effects on the economy of Lora and Oghi. Three are discussed below.

(1) *Greater Cropping Intensity.*[12] Respondents in Lora and Oghi are moving toward increased multiple cropping. Most of that move has been made possible by the introduction of dwarf wheats, which mature earlier than desi varieties. The 1969/70 average cropping intensity index for Lora was 141 and for Oghi 103. By calculating the average acreage respondents say they will sow during the 1970/71 rabi period and by making the safe assumption that respondents will sow the same amount of maize during the following summers, Lora's cropping intensity will increase to 148, Oghi's to 110. This significant change is expected to occur in one year's time.

(2) *Increased Output.* Barani smallholders are not only expanding planted acreage but they are getting higher yields, as noted above. For every given acre of land sown with dwarf wheats, farmers are harvesting at least 70 percent more than before (Table 5). As less money is needed to purchase food grains, more money is available. Some who save "enough" will be able to add further cost-saving innovations (or conversely, yield-increasing innovations) to their farm operations.

All who adopted dwarf varieties have realized comparatively greater output per acre than those who did not use the new varieties. However, among those adopting dwarf wheats there is wide variability in production practices. Some use fertilizers, others do not; some get exceptional yields and others less so, and so forth.

(3) *Increased Employment*. Technological change in the form of new high-yielding varieties is labor using in Lora and Oghi. Analysis of the additional man-hours employed with dwarf wheats as compared to desi wheat for each stage from field preparation through storage shows that overall labor requirements have increased by about 50 percent (Table 6). In essence, there are notable economies with increased output, which mean the average cost per maund of processed dwarf wheat is less.

Wider Effects

The adoption of dwarf wheats in Hazara District appears to have important wider and longer-term effects. They are as follows:

(1) *Increased awareness of changes that could affect agricultural production*. During the many visits to Lora and Oghi, farmers frequently asked where they could acquire new varieties of seed. Many could name some of the varieties they heard about on

TABLE 6. Labor Use in Dwarf- and Desi-Wheat Production, 143 Farmers, 1969/70 Lora and Oghi Thanas (man-hours per acre)

	Field Preparation and Sowing	Harvesting	Clara[a] and Threshing	Winnowing and Storage	Total
1. Dwarf	96.8	74.4	40.8	40.0	252.0
2. Desi	62.4	52.0	28.0	26.4	168.8
3. Added Labor (2 from 1)	34.4	22.4	12.8	13.6	83.2

[a]Clara is a threshing floor prepared by driving bullock teams in circles on a particular spot in the field until the ground is packed hard.

the radio. They were also acutely aware that changes can be made in their maize production as well, a crop that had been relatively untouched in *barani* areas by technological advances. They also knew of government policy changes that affect complementary inputs. A recent announcement by the Ministry of Finance of a tax on fertilizer brought loud outcries from the people of Lora and Oghi.

(2) *Increased demands on extension workers. Barani* smallholders wanted to know what local-level extension workers do and how they can be instructive in understanding the new technology. They also put some pressure on field assistants, fertilizer distributors, and others from the Department of Agriculture and the Agriculture Development Corporation to keep up with new information about improved seeds, types and rates of fertilizer application, pesticides, sowing periods, and so forth.

(3) *Shift to cash payments for services.* Those using dwarf wheats who got good yields preferred paying cash rather than a proportion of their crop for the services of *moeens* (cobblers, blacksmiths, tailors, potters, etc.).[13] Movement is away from barter arrangements toward a cash economy. The effect of this move will be to create cash saving and more investment opportunities for those who are able to participate in the larger money economy.

Summary

A very high proportion of *barani* smallholders adopted high-yielding varieties of wheat in a remarkably short time. Significant in diffusing the new technology were certain types of interpersonal and mass media communication channels, which informed the farmers that dwarf wheats were higher yielding. Interpersonal contacts between villagers created the most awareness. Demonstration plots on farmers' fields made it possible for the potential adopters to see the striking differences between desi and dwarf yields. Of the mass media, radio was most important in Hazara.

Technical and economic factors had considerable influence on farmers and their adoption of dwarf wheats: (1) yields were consistently better with dwarfs; (2) the technology was relatively simple to understand and use; and (3) no major changes were required in the cropping pattern.

The primary effects at the farm level of the technological change brought with dwarf wheats were: (1) to increase cropping intensity; (2) to increase output; and (3) to increase employment. Wider effects are becoming evident through increased social interaction between farmers and extension people and a greater move toward a money economy.

In sum, *barani* smallholders were highly responsive to significantly "better" innovations, which are neutral to scale. They were equally responsive and reachable by mass media and interpersonal channels of communication.[14]

Refugio I. Rochin received his Ph.D. in Agricultural Economics from Michigan State University in 1971. He was a training associate in Agricultural Economics with the Ford Foundation, Pakistan, from 1969 to 1971, and is currently assistant professor of Economics, University of California (Davis).

NOTES

A preliminary version of this paper was published in the form of Rochin (1972). The permission to reprint granted by The Agricultural Development Council, Inc., is gratefully acknowledged. The analysis is based on Rochin (1971).

1. *Barani*, literally translated from Urdu, means 'depending on rainfall'.

2. A village study conducted in Hazara during 1955 pointed out that maize was the main subsistence crop and that wheat was "not so commonly consumed by the villagers." In more recent years, though, wheat has become as important as maize in terms of production and consumption (Matlub 1958).

3. "Thana" means 'police station' in Urdu. Such police stations are located in the larger cities, which serve as main marketing centers. Each thana has a certain jurisdiction over a number of villages known to the villagers and, in turn, each villager can identify himself with "his thana."

4. Estimated on the basis of the international exchange rate of ten rupees per U.S. dollar.

5. General historical coverage of dwarf wheat diffusion and adoption in West Pakistan is found in Eckert (1970:12–36).

6. Mexipak is only one of the commonly used dwarf varieties, but the name is applied to all dwarf varieties by Hazara's farmers.

7. A review of the more recent literature on the process of diffusion is given by Rogers and Shoemaker (1970).

8. Comparisons are discussed in Rogers and Svenning (1969:125).

9. Dwarf wheat with fertilizer gives a dark bluish-green appearance; desi wheat is light green. Moreover, desi varieties stand taller, have thin stems, and sway freely with the wind, while the high-tillering dwarf wheat is short and sturdy against the wind. In addition, Mexipak, which is the most commonly used dwarf, has beards whereas most desi varieties are beardless and hence more likely to be consumed by birds.

10. There is some debate on this point. The usual comparison is 1.5 maunds of fodder for every maund of grain of desi wheat (1.5:1) versus 1 maund of fodder for every maund of grain of dwarf wheat (1:1). From this we estimate whether the amount of fodder is more or less by the amount of grain produced. Judging from the farmers' complaints of lack of fodder, perhaps a more realistic comparison would be 2:1 for desi and 1:1 for dwarf. This, however, is subject to actual measurement on *barani* land.

11. All farmers in the sample know the size of their cultivated acreage and measure grain that has been sun dried on the threshing floor with a *wodi* (a wooden or metal measuring bowl). Each farmer knows how much wheat, maize, and rice weigh in his own *wodi* in terms of seers. In addition to counting the number of *wodi*s of each harvested crop, *barani* smallholders seem capable of recalling production for at least three years. Customarily, they discuss production over the *Hukka* (smoking pipe) in casual gatherings. Thus, the data appear to be reliable. One seer equals 2.057 lbs. or 1/40 of a maund. One maund equals 82.29 lbs. One *wodi* holds approximately 5½ seers of wheat grain.

A few words should be said also about the apparent discrepancy between the survey findings that wheat yields have increased in the Hazara District and Table 1, which shows declining wheat yields in *barani* areas. Hazara receives relatively higher rainfall (conducive to good yield with dwarf wheats) than the vast *barani* areas of the Indus Plains, which sow more acreage to *barani* wheat. As yet, the latter *barani* areas have not been studied as intensively as has Hazara to determine the impact of the new varieties of wheat. There is also the problem that government statistics lag in reporting major changes in the agricultural sector of the Indus Plains. See Falcon (1961:3–9).

12. Cropping Intensity = $100 \times \dfrac{\text{Net area sown } + \text{ Area sown more than once}}{\text{Net area sown}}$

13. It should be noted that almost all labor employed in wheat produc-

tion is family labor; few are hired for the task. Unfortunately, no data were collected on the amount paid by tenants to landlords, thus depriving us of an analysis of whether or not tenants are paying proportionately more or less of their output.

14. More recent research that comes to similar conclusions about the participation of small farmers in the green revolution is contained in Rice (1973). This report includes many of the research results obtained by Max K. Lowdermilk in "Diffusion of Dwarf Wheat Production Technology in Pakistan's Punjab," Ph.D. dissertation, Cornell University, 1972, and by Mohammed Naseem in "Small Farmers and Agricultural Transformation in Pakistan's Punjab," Ph.D. dissertation, University of California (Davis) 1971.

BIBLIOGRAPHY

Davy, Dorvey F.
> 1967. "Improving the Training of Field Assistants in the Agricultural Training Institutes of West Pakistan." Mimeographed. Islamabad, West Pakistan: Ford Foundation.

Eckert, Jerry B.
> 1970. "The Impact of Dwarf Wheats on Resource Productivity in West Pakistan's Punjab." Ph.D. dissertation, Michigan State University.

Falcon, Walter
> 1961. "Reliability of Punjab Agricultural Data." In *Acreage, Production and Prices of Major Agricultural Crops of West Pakistan (Punjab): 1931–59*, edited by Abdur Rab, pp. 3–9. Karachi: The Institute of Development Economics.

Government of Pakistan
> 1964/65–1969/70. "Season and Crop Reports." Karachi and Rawalpindi: Department of Agriculture, Government of Pakistan. Mimeographed.
> 1970. *The Fourth Five Year Plan, 1970–75*. Rawalpindi: Planning Commission, Government of Pakistan.

Matlub, Hussain
> 1958. *A Socio-Economic Survey of Village Baffa in Hazara District of the Peshawar Division*. Peshawar: Board of Economic Enquiry, Peshawar University, North West Frontier Province.

Rice, E. B., (ed.)
> 1973. *Small Farmer Credit: HYV in Pakistan*. AID Spring Review of Small Farmer Credit, vol. 14, No. SR 114.

Rizvi, S. M. Z., et al.
    1965. *Consolidation of Holdings: A Study of the Process of Consolidation of Agricultural Holdings in Selected Villages in Peshawar District*. Peshawar: Pakistan Academy for Rural Development.
Rochin, Refugio I.
    1971. "A Micro-Economic Analysis of Smallholder Response to High-Yielding Varieties of Wheat in West Pakistan." Ph.D. dissertation, Michigan State University.
    1972. "The Spread of Innovation." In *Teaching Forum*. Singapore: Agricultural Development Council.
Rogers, Everett M., and Shoemaker, F. Floyd
    1970. *Communication of Innovations: A Cross Cultural Approach*. New York: Free Press of Glencoe.
Rogers, Everett M., and Svenning, Lynne
    1969. *Modernization among Peasants: The Impact of Communication*. New York: Holt, Rinehart and Winston.
Sharif, C. M.
    1965. *Farmers' Attitudes toward Self-Help*. Peshawar: Pakistan Academy for Rural Development.
Sturt, Daniel W.
    1965. "Producer Response to Technological Change in West Pakistan." *Journal of Farm Economics* 47:625–633.

15

The Development
of Pakistan's Agriculture:
An Interdisciplinary Explanation

Shahid Javed Burki

Introduction

The purpose of this paper is to reach beyond neoclassical economics into other disciplines to provide an explanation for the behavior of West Pakistan's agricultural sector.[1] This interdisciplinary exercise was undertaken to increase our understanding of the complex factors responsible for taking the agricultural sector over a tortuous, and sometimes perilous, course. Economists' traditional tools of analysis cannot adequately explain various important developments in the Pakistani countryside. They cannot by themselves identify the factors responsible for the stagnation of agriculture in the first decade after Independence and the great recovery in the second decade. They cannot isolate the factors that were responsible for inaugurating Pakistan's agricultural revolution some years before the extensive use of the new miracle seeds. And they cannot single out the factors responsible for the distribution and redistribution of factors of production between the agricultural and nonagricultural sectors.

The agricultural sector has been studied intensively by economists; its progress over the years can be viewed through traditional economic prisms. Pakistan's progress has been studied in the framework of a dual economy where, as W.H. Nicholls has correctly pointed out, the process of industrialization is looked upon as the dual of the "Law of the Declining Relative Importance of Agriculture" (Nicholls 1954:146–147). Thus the contribution made by agriculture to the gross provincial product of West Pakistan declined from 49.8 percent in 1948/49 to 41.5 percent in

1968/69, while the contribution of large-scale manufacturing increased from 1.5 percent to 15.4 percent.[2] The process was not a smooth one, as the agricultural sector stagnated in the 1949–1959 decade and prospered in the next (Table 1). In the first decade the rate of growth of crop production per annum was officially estimated to be 2.3 percent, while in the second decade it increased to 5.4 percent. Public investment in agriculture declined from 2.5 percent of the total national investment in 1949/50 to 2.2 percent in 1959/60. However, in the same period, the private sector's investment in agriculture increased from 2.9 percent of the total to 3.5 percent. Per capita income in the agricultural sector declined from Rs. 214 in 1949/50 to Rs. 197 in 1959/60. These figures bring out

TABLE 1. Performance of West Pakistan's
Agricultural Sector

	1949/50	*1959/60*	*1968/69*
Share in Gross Provincial Product (percent)	52	49	41
Per Capita Income in the Agricultural Sector (Rs.)	214	197	278
Total Agricultural Output per Capita (Rs.)	187	171	195
Public Sector Investment in Agriculture as a Proportion of Total Investment (percent)	2.5	2.2	4.8
Private Sector Investment in Agriculture as a Proportion of Total Investment (percent)	2.9	3.5	—
Total Food Grains Production per Capita (Kg.)	188	151	202
Per Annum Rate of Growth of Crop Production (percent)	2.3		5.4

SOURCES: Papanek 1967:317 and Government of Pakistan 1970.

clearly the tremendous differences in the performance of the agricultural sector in the two decades following the emergence of Pakistan as an independent country.

In order to provide an explanation for the performance of West Pakistan's agriculture, a number of economists have provided a set of closely related hypotheses. Following Schultz, these hypotheses are based on an interpretation of traditional agriculture. Traditional agriculture is viewed as in a state of equilibrium in which "the state of the arts remains constant, the state of preference and motives for holding and acquiring sources of income remains constant, and both of these states remain constant long enough for marginal preferences and motives for acquiring agricultural factors as sources of income to arrive at an equilibrium with the marginal productivity of these sources viewed as an investment in permanent income streams and with net savings approaching zero." (Schultz 1964:30). What these three critical conditions of equilibrium in effect imply is agricultural stagnation. This is a picture of an economic man making an efficient use of the sources of production available to him.

This hypothesis points to two important conclusions: (1) That the farmer in a poor country is primitive because of the primitiveness of his environment. There is an element of optimism in this assumption—optimism that takes us to the second conclusion. (2) That agriculture in a poor country can be pulled out of stagnation by changing the state of the arts. The arts are "always embodied in particular factors and, therefore, in order to introduce new technology, it is necessary to employ a set of factors of production that differs from the set formerly employed (Schultz 1964:30). Traditional agriculture can therefore be transformed by supplying to the farmer improved factors of production—"the conditioning factors" (Johnston 1964:92)—at prices that would make their adoption possible by the risk-averting but profit-maximizing farmer. This hypothesis is the basis of a number of explanations that have been provided for the performance of Pakistan's agricultural sector during the sixties.

However, Pakistan's agricultural sector began to lift itself out of a state of stagnation a few years before Schultz produced his work. In fact the regime of Ayub Khan instituted most of the important reforms aimed at the agricultural sector in the early 1960s at a time when a number of economists and social scientists were taking a pessimistic view of poor agrarian economies. For instance, the economists Grunwald (1961) and Khatkhate (1962) and sociologists such as Kusum Nair (1961) appeared to believe that farmers do not respond to economic incentives. Students of Pakistan's agricultural sector assert that the regime of Ayub Khan stumbled accidentally on the idea of inducing change in the agricultural sector by altering the qualitative and quantitative combinations of the factors of production.

The bulk of the evidence in support of this explanation comes from the important work of Ghulam Mohammad, a Pakistani economist who did an intensive survey of factor availability to producers in West Pakistan's agricultural sector. In his field surveys Mohammad concentrated on the availability of irrigation water and its impact on cropping patterns. According to him, "one of the most significant phenomena in agricultural development in Pakistan has been the installation of private tubewells by the farmers of West Pakistan at an exceedingly fast rate during the second plan period" (Mohammad 1970:49). One factor that led to this very important development was the provision of electricity to the rural areas of West Pakistan at a highly subsidized rate (Mohammad 1970:92). However, the subsidy to the rural consumer never was provided specifically for the purpose of promoting the development of tubewells. In fact the village electrification program followed by the government was aimed at lighting up the villages rather than providing power for tubewells. Some other researchers extended the argument to cover a wider spectrum of incentives. For instance, Gustav Papanek, in his study of Pakistan's economic development, argued that the speed-up in tubewell drilling in the early 1960s "seems to have been the result of higher and more stable prices for cash crops and wheat, improved supplies of imported equipment, more widespread electric connections, drilling facilities and credit, and the gradual spread of technical knowledge and information (Papanek 1967:179).

Once Ghulam Mohammad had provided evidence that some of the important developments in agriculture could be attributed to government programs that were designed to achieve totally different objectives, it became easier to formulate a hypothesis for explaining the behavior of the Pakistani farmer. Before outlining that hypothesis, let us briefly consider the wheat policy changes introduced by the military regime.

Among the measures adopted by Ayub Khan was a price policy that turned the terms of trade in favor of the agricultural sector. Before Ayub Khan's coup d'etat of 1958, there existed a cumbersome system of bureaucratic controls on agriculture. Many of these controls, such as the restrictive zoning of surplus areas and the compulsory sale of surplus food grains to the government at less than market prices, had been introduced as war-time measures by the British government in the 1940s. In April 1960 the military regime, despite many dire predictions, abolished direct controls on wheat movement and wheat prices in West Pakistan. Under the new system, the administration guaranteed farmers a minimum price of Rs. 13.50 per maund (82.3 pounds) of wheat. Sales to the government were voluntary, and the Food Department entered usual market channels only when prices dipped below the statutory minimum (Stern and Falcon 1970:39). The net result of these changes was an increase in the price the farmers could expect to get for their surplus wheat.

With this background, focus is now placed on explanations of agricultural growth based on neoclassical economics. This is followed by an attempt to provide a broader interdisciplinary explanation of the causes of agricultural growth in Pakistan in the 1960s.

Economic Explanations of Pakistan's Agricultural Growth

Falcon's research on Pakistan has provided a number of insights on farmer response to changes in price in a near-subsistence economy. The results suggest "that it is possible to shift the composition of agricultural output by changing the relative prices within agriculture. They also emphasize that, unless there is a thoroughgoing reform in the services and facilities made available to farmers (e.g., transportation, credit, fertilizer, technical knowledge, etc.), higher prices alone can have little effect on increasing yield per acre. On the other hand, the average evidence suggests that farmers of the area will respond to economic incentives if given the opportunity to do so" (Falcon 1964:590).

Based on this picture of responsiveness to incentives, Falcon and Gotsch developed an elaborate explanatory-cum-predictive model of the performance of agriculture in both East and West Pakistan. In this model the nearly 5 percent per annum rate of growth in West Pakistan's crop production during the Second Plan (1960–1965) was explained in terms of increased inputs. More than half of the increased output was accounted for by greater availability of water for irrigation, nearly one-third by other improved inputs, such as seeds, chemical fertilizer, and insecticides, and the remaining one-sixth to improved farming practices and increase in labor productivity (Table 2). Accordingly, they considered the agricultural policy aspects of Pakistan's Second Plan to be a bright spot in the government's economic development program. These policy changes, which were designed to stimulate output by providing incentives for the use of improved inputs, proved to be a tremendous success (Falcon and Gotsch 1968:312).

Some of these conclusions were counter to actual developments. In particular, considering the significance attached to the general incentives to agricultural development, a geographically diffused pattern of growth should be expected. This was by no

TABLE 2. Sources of Increased Crop Output, West Pakistan

	Percent per year
Private Tubewells	1.4
Public Tubewells	0.6
Surface Water	0.7
Fertilizer	1.0
Plant Protection	0.4
Seeds	0.2
Improved Practices, Labor, Intensity, etc.	0.6
TOTAL GROWTH	4.9

SOURCE: Falcon and Gotsch 1968.

means the case. Recognizing this factor, Gotsch in a later paper calculated the growth in the value of major crops for sixteen districts of the Punjab. The growth rate in crop production in the period 1960–1965 in these districts ranged between –2.4 percent for Jhelum to 9.6 percent for the district of Lyallpur (Table 3). It was clear from this exercise "that what has been hailed rather widely as 'agricultural growth in West Pakistan' is really a rather remarkable rate of growth in a relatively few districts. For example, Lyallpur, Multan, and Montgomery, 3 out of 16 districts in the Punjab, averaged an increase of approximately 8.9 percent per annum for the period 1959–60 to 1964–65" (Gotsch 1968:190).

Appreciating the fact that changes in general economic incentives were weak in accounting for the uneven growth of West Pakistan's agriculture, Gotsch undertook further analysis based upon a model used by B. A. Minhas and A. Vardayanathan (1964). This model identifies four elements as contributing to the value of crop output—the acreage effect, the yield effect, the effect of the changes in cropping pattern, and the effect of the interaction between changes in yields and changes in the cropping pattern. Based on the results obtained from this model, Gotsch grouped the districts in which the bulk of the increase in output could be explained in terms of the changes in yield and the districts in which the growth was due to both changes in yield and increases in acreage devoted to the cultivation of crops. The remaining districts were lumped together as having stagnated (Table 3).

Let us turn to a more formal farmer behavior model in order to consider some of the sophistications that have been added. In the naïve model, acreage response is directly related to price. However, the work of S. Mushtaq Hussain has shown that in the case of cash crops, the farmer response to price, as reflected by the elasticity of acreage, is higher than that for food crops (Hussain 1968, 1969). He also discovered that the price elasticity of area varies over crops, regions, and time periods, and that they decline for cash crops.

Additionally, Azizur Rahman Khan and A. H. M. Nuruddin Chowdhury (1970:275) found that the amount of surplus food grains marketed by the West Pakistani farmers was directly related to their total output. This means that as "output of food increases

TABLE 3. Growth in Crop Output
in the 16 Districts of the Pakistan Punjab, 1960–1965

Districts	Annual Growth Rate (percent)	Acreage Effect	Yield Effect	Cropping Pattern	Inter-action (percent)[a]	Major Crops Involved (in Order of Importance)
Group I. Stagnating Districts						
Jehlum	-2.4					
Gujrat	2.2					
Sialkot	-1.2					
Rawalpindi	1.0					
Campbellpur	-2.2					
Mianwali	3.2					
Sargodha	2.6					
Group II. Growth Due Primarily to Yield Effects						
Lyallpur	9.6	9.0	71.5	10.0	9.5	Sugarcane, Wheat
Montgomery	8.4	15.7	61.3	16.3	6.2	Cotton, Wheat
Multan	8.2	23.8	6.8	6.8	4.2	Cotton, Wheat
Group III. Growth Due Primarily to Acreage and Cropping-Pattern Effects						
Lahore	4.9	48.5	34.8	9.1	7.6	Wheat, Rice
Sheikhupura	7.9	47.2	44.4	7.0	1.4	Rice, Wheat
Guhrawala	6.2	47.0	45.9	5.1	2.0	Rice, Wheat
Jhang	8.1	39.1	51.3	6.9	2.7	Sugarcane, Wheat

SOURCE: Gotsch 1968:190.

[a]The sum of the four effects, acreage, yield, cropping pattern, and interaction equals 100 percent.

the consumption of food will probably rise, but the incremental consumption of food will probably rise, but the incremental consumption ration is likely to be less than one. Thus, the marketable surplus is likely to increase as a result of an increase in the output of food crops."

Although none of the works cited above deal with the developments in Pakistan's agricultural sector during the first post-Independence decade, they contain clues that can be used to formulate some kind of an explanation for stagnation in the fifties. The emphasis on prices as a major determinant of acreage devoted to producing a particular crop provides an explanation for the fall in per capita production of food grains at a time when the government was deliberately keeping down the price of wheat and rice. The farmer, therefore, produced food grains either for his own consumption or because his land was not good for another crop. While the gross output of food grains remained more or less unchanged in the rainfed areas, it actually declined in the irrigated areas where the farmer could switch to cash crops. Since the principal determinant of marketable surplus is the gross output of food crops, the quantity of food grains marketed stagnated in this period.

In conclusion, public policy plays an important role in all the economic models that we discussed. Public policy has received accolades for the good performance of Pakistan's agricultural sector during the 1960s. Once we recognize this common element in the hypotheses advanced by economists to explain the development of the agricultural sector, we also become aware of one very major shortcoming shared by them. This pertains to the dynamics of decision-making in Pakistan's political economy. Two questions must be asked in any analysis in which policy plays an important role. First, why is a certain decision made by the policymakers; second, What happens after a certain policy has been formulated? In the economic explanations of the growth of West Pakistan's agricultural sector, the first question has received no attention whatsoever. Economists generally have addressed themselves to answering the second question. In what follows I shall attempt to fill this analytical gap. This means crossing disciplinary boundaries, from economics into the political and social sciences.

Class Structure Changes Accelerate
Agricultural Growth in the 1960s

The History of the Landed Aristocracy

To develop the analysis along general social science lines, we have to go back 150 years, into the history of British India, to the time when India's new conqueror transformed herself from a commercial exploiter to a founder and guardian[3] of a new kind of economic and political order in the subcontinent. The introduction of a new system of land administration, known to students of Indian affairs as "settlements," was the starting point of a long process of rural change. These settlements formed "the basis of a political and economic system in which the foreigner, the landlord, and the moneylender took the economic surplus away from the peasantry" (Moore 1966:344). In subsequent developments, the Land Alienation Act of 1901 removed the moneylender from the areas that now constitute Pakistan and the Indian Independence Act of 1947 removed the foreigner from the subcontinent. The political organization that moved in to fill the vacuum left by the departure of the British had been dominated all along by the landed aristocracy. The Muslim League was founded in 1906 by a group of large landlords. In the 1940s, even after Mohammad Ali Jinnah had turned the league into a mass organization, the landed aristocracy accounted for 163 of the 503 members of the party's central council (Sayeed 1966:207). However, Jinnah succeeded in diluting the power wielded by the landlords within the Muslim League organization. As the president of the league, he concentrated a great deal of political power in his hands and by recruiting a large number of urban professonals (lawyers, teachers, doctors, etc.), he was able to create a social group that could effectively challenge the landed aristocracy. Since Muslims living in the Hindu minority areas were more urbanized (Hazelhurst 1966:11–15), the bulk of the challenge to the power of the landlords came from the areas that went to India after the partition of the subcontinent. In spite of the fact that a very large number of Muslim urban professionals migrated to Pakistan, they were not able to create political constituencies for themselves in the new country. When Jinnah died in 1948 he left the leadership of the Muslim League to Liaquat Ali Khan, who was the scion of a landed family. Thus, a year after the emergence of Pakistan as an independent state, the landed aristocracy found itself not only in full control of the economic surplus generated by the peasantry, but also in charge of the country's political apparatus.

Why is it, then, that the agricultural sector of West Pakistan began to stagnate at a time when the big landlords dominated? In order to answer this question we have to disaggregate rural society into a number of strata and then construct different welfare functions for each of the strata.

At the apex of rural society was the landed aristocracy. This class had been created by the British in the image of their own squirearchy. By the time the British reached the Punjab they had no doubt abandoned the principles of political administration that had led them to introduce the Permanent Settlement in Bengal. However, the Mahalwari system adopted by them for the Punjab also resulted in the creation of a class of zamindars. The system provided sufficient incentive for the zamindar to remain on the land. In return for economic rewards and official patronage, the zamindars functioned as agents of the state in their villages. They collected the government revenue from their fellow villagers and in return received *panchotra*, or 5 percent of the total amount due to the government. Moreover, their sons and relations were easily absorbed into government service. Therefore, under the British Raj, the power and prestige of the big landlords expanded rapidly. By virtue of what Lasswell and Kaplan (1960:57–58) have called the process of value agglutination, the landlords were able to add to their holdings of land.

By removing the Hindu moneylenders, the Land Alienation Act of 1901 lent a further helping hand. Peasants now had to turn to their landlords for their cash requirements and often found that the land mortgaged by them could not be redeemed. According to J. D. Anderson, a British civil servant who was in charge of the settlement operations in a southwestern district of the Punjab, "The big Mohammadan landlords speak of the act as their economic salvation, and probably it has to some extent protected them from the result of their extravagance and made it easier to swallow up their neighbors" (1929:9).

Some of West Pakistan's landed aristocracy owes its existence to the help rendered somewhat more directly by the British Raj. In the first quarter of the present century, the government, with the help of a vast irrigation program, converted large tracts of wasteland in the Punjab and Sind into rich agricultural land. While designing the layout of the canals and settling agriculturalists on the new land, the administration was not unmindful of the loyalty that some of the chieftains had shown toward their rulers. Within a couple of decades the government's program of land development placed vast productive resources in the hands of a score of families, particularly in the southern districts of the Punjab and the central districts of the Sind.[4]

The Increasing Power of the Landed Aristocracy in the 1950s

In the 1950s, following the Land Reforms Commission, the landed aristocracy were defined as landlords who owned more than 500 acres. In the Punjab in 1949, the landed aristocracy consisted of 1,000 persons who together owned 10.3 percent of the agricultural land in the province (Table 4). In the North-West Frontier Province the members of this class owned 12.5 percent of the total cultivated area. It was in the Sind that this stratum of the rural society possessed the greatest economic, social, and political

TABLE 4. Area Owned, including Uncultivated Area, by Size of Holdings in the Former Punjab, 1949

Size of Holdings	Acres		No. of Owners	
	(Thousands)	*(Percent)*	*(Thousands)*	*(Percent)*
Less than 10 acres	7,092	31.8	1,809	78.7
10 to 99 acres	10,428	46.7	476	20.7
100 to 499 acres	2,502	11.2	12	0.5
500 acres and above	2,295	10.3	1	0.1
TOTAL	22,317	100.0	2,298	100.0

SOURCE: Government of West Pakistan 1959.

power. In that province, the landed aristocracy possessed 30 percent of the total occupied land (Government of West Pakistan 1959:13). It is therefore understandable why W. H. Morris-Jones felt that "the key to Pakistan's politics is to be found in a little official publication for restricted circulation by the government of India, entitled *The Landed Families of the Punjab*" (1958:225).

The landed aristocracy made its presence felt when the people went to the polls for the first time after the birth of Pakistan. In the 1951 elections to the legislative assembly of the Punjab, the big landowning families captured 80 percent of the seats. In the Sind elections of 1953, 90 percent of the assembly members were large landowners. The landlord group was also in a majority in the legislature elected by the voters of the North-West Frontier Province (Maniruzzaman 1966:86).

Out of the 902 members of the landed aristocracy who surrendered land under Martial Law Regulation No. 64 (Government of Pakistan 1964:33), 108 or 12 percent held ministerial appointments in the central government or the provincial governments of the Punjab, Sind, and North-West Frontier Province. According to the returns filed by these landlords with West Pakistan's Board of Revenue, the total area owned by them amounted to 1.218 million acres, giving an average of 11,280 acres per person. None of them owned less than 850 acres of irrigated land.[5] These statistics can provide some measure of the power wielded by the big landlords in the countryside.

As an average-sized village in the Punjab has 600 acres of cultivable land, landlords who were politically active in the pre-Ayub era were able to control completely at least twenty Punjabi villages. However, a landlord did not have all the land in a village under his control. His land more often than not was scattered over scores (sometimes hundreds) of villages. In each of them, he was the headman, the *lambardar*, the moneylender, the most prominent person. Therefore, the political and economic constituency of the big landlord was not the 11,280 acres that he owned, but the 50 to 100,000 acres of cultivable land in the villages in which he was the paramount power.

In such a situation rationality demanded that landlords should behave not only as economic but also as political and social maximizers. Once the members of the landed aristocracy are regarded not only as economic men, but also as political and social men, the stagnation of West Pakistan's agricultural sector at a time when the big landlords wielded great power no longer seems paradoxical. As an economic man, the landlord had to maximize his returns within the constraints imposed by the availability of resources and the state of the technology. For the big landlord, water, not land, was the real constraint. Therefore, his typical response was "to extend the acreage which he crops each season by reducing the fallow on the land which in the past he left totally unused, rather than to increase the water applied to the acreage he was already cultivating" (Lieftinck et al. 1968:23).

This tendency was reinforced by the behavior of the landlord as a political maximizer. In this capacity, his emphasis was on extensive rather than intensive cultivation. The more land that he could bring under his control, the larger was his constituency and the greater his political power. The big landlord used the political power at his disposal to make available to his class the resource over which the government had the greatest control, that is, irrigation water.

One evidence of this is to be found from an examination of the charges brought by the military regime against a number of politicians who held public office before Ayub Khan took over the administration of the country. The Elective Bodies (Disqualification) Order (EBDO) was issued in August 1959, and was applied to any person who had held any public office or position, including membership of any elective body in the country, and was found guilty of misconduct while holding that office. "The exact number of persons . . . does not seem to have been published. . . . [However], it seems that about 6,000 persons labored under the EBDO disqualification" (Feldman 1967:81). My own investigations reveal that out of 108 members of the landed aristocracy, at least forty-two or 38.9 percent were charged under the EBDO. Of those so charged, thirty-three or 78.6 percent were found to have used their official powers for either "diverting to their lands a higher proportion than allowed by law and custom of the available irrigation water," or "for changing the scope and extent of government-sponsored irrigation schemes in such a way that a higher proportion than that planned originally of new irrigation water was made available for use on their lands."[6]

This near-monopolistic control of a scarce resource for production increased the wealth of the landlords as well as the productivity of the lands owned by them. Therefore, while the agricultural sector stagnated as a whole, the landed aristocracy prospered. Evidence of the difference between the returns obtained by the big landlords and other types of landholders can be obtained from rent data (Table 5). The time series of rents received by landlords of various categories between 1948/49 and 1968/69 is based on records maintained by patwaris in twenty-seven villages in the Punjab. In 1948/49, the landlords who leased out holdings of more than 250 acres received 2 to 21 percent higher rents than smaller landholders.[7] The lowest rent was received for holdings of less than ten acres in size. In the ten-year period between 1948/49 and 1958/59, the rents fetched by the large holdings increased by 39.4 percent, whereas the rents of small holdings (less than twenty-five acres in size) increased between 19.5 and 25.6 percent. The differential between the rents received by the very small and the very large holdings increased considerably, from 21 percent in 1948/49 to 48 percent in 1958/59.

The Effect of the Ayub Khan Land Reforms of 1958

Ayub Khan introduced his land reforms in 1958. While it cannot be said that the reforms resulted in large transfers of land, "the political implications were weighty and, although by no means extinguished as a class, the great landed magnates no longer represented the same vast and sometimes inert agglomeration of power" (Feldman 1967:60). We turn to the rent data for evidence of this decline in the power of the landed aristocracy. The rent series for holdings between 250 and 500 acres stopped increasing after 1959, and in the following ten years fluctuated around a mean of 139. Rents for holdings of less than 10 acres also did not show any appreciable increase after 1959, but fluctuated around a mean of 97. The largest increase in the value of rent after 1959 was registered by the holdings of 25 to 50 acres in size. For these, the rent per acre increased by 33.6 percent in the ten-year period between 1958/59 and 1968/69. For holdings of 50 to 100 acres and 100 to 200 acres in size, the rent per acre increased by 19.3 and 11.3 percent respectively.

TABLE 5. Rents Received by Landlords,
Separated by Size of Holding, in the Punjab, 1948–1969
(rupees per acre)

Year	Size of the Rented Holding (acres)					
	Less than 10	10–25	26–50	51–100	101–250	251–500
1948/49	82	87	91	92	102	104
1949/50	85	92	93	94	104	110
1950/51	85	94	94	96	108	111
1951/52	79	92	95	96	107	108
1952/53	76	93	95	95	105	108
1953/54	94	105	108	121	120	122
1954/55	89	101	110	120	125	128
1955/56	91	107	116	125	130	132
1956/57	88	107	118	130	132	128
1957/58	90	111	122	138	136	137
1958/59	98	117	128	140	142	145
1959/60	96	117	126	140	145	141
1960/61	94	118	135	139	144	139
1961/62	92	118	140	139	142	137
1962/63	97	121	145	142	140	140
1963/64	97	125	148	144	140	141
1964/65	104	128	157	150	142	145
1965/66	92	124	155	146	142	135
1966/67	94	128	160	152	148	132
1967/68	98	130	165	160	151	139
1968/69	102	135	171	167	158	143

SOURCE: Survey by Shahid Javed Burki with the assistance of the deputy commissioners and students of Government College, Lahore. The data are from twenty-seven villages in the Punjab. One village was chosen from Lahore District, two villages from Sahiwal District, and three villages from each of the following districts: Jhang, Gujranwala, Gujrat, Sahiwal, Multan, Dera Ghazi Khan, Lyallput, and Bahawalnager.

These data indicate a new trend, a change in the pattern of development in the agricultural sector. If used as a surrogate for land productivity, these rents show that, except for holdings under

twenty-five acres, increases in output per acre were inversely related to the size of the holding. In other words, in holdings above
twenty-five acres the rate of increase of productivity was the highest for the smallest holdings. These data suggest that during the
Ayub Khan era, a new type of agricultural entrepreneur emerged in
the Pakistani countryside.

We have already noted that the economists' explanation for the
performance of the agricultural sector in the sixties was not totally
satisfactory. One reason was that economists failed to study the
response to the change in technology by different categories of
landowners. Some sociologists, applying the concept developed in
diffusion research, sought to fill this gap. "Diffusion research re-
gards the dissemination of information as the basic sociological
process leading to increased agricultural productivity through the
adoption of innovations. A traditional farmer can become modern,
that is accept change, if he has the necessary knowledge and is
willing to implement new practices. Research into the acceptance
of change, based on such a theory, naturally starts with a study of
how information reaches farmers and what kinds of farmers actively
seek and use it" (Galjart 1971:35). Using this approach, Chaudhari,
Erickson, and Bajwa (1968:97), three sociologists who studied the
process of change in Punjabi villages, found that in two villages in
the district of Sialkot, more than 90 percent of the landlords with
holdings larger than twenty-five acres showed medium or high
levels of adoption of four improved agricultural practices. The innovation capacity of these farmers was considerably greater than
that of the landholders with less than twenty-five acres (Chaudhari
et al. 1968:101).

Chaudhari and his colleagues arrived at a conclusion quite the
opposite of the one reached on the basis of the data of Table 5, for
the simple reason that they used the generalized diffusion model
within the usual sociological framework of traditional and modern
farmers. Like the economists, they also became victims of too much
aggregation. Thus the small farmers, defined as those who owned
less than twenty-five acres, followed the traditional pattern. The
big landlords, or those who owned more than twenty-five acres,
followed the culture pattern of the modern farmer. The latter, being
modern, were not only prepared to adopt agricultural innovations,

but also proved to have changed in many other ways. They made more use of media of communication than did the traditional farmers, participated more often in community affairs, possessed more new equipment, and visited towns more frequently.[8]

By breaking up the ownership of land into six categories, the modern-traditional dichotomy does not work. In fact, as was pointed out above, the direct relationship that Chaudhari et al. discovered between size and innovation reverses itself if we break up "bigness" into four categories.

Diffusion research, like the economists' analysis, casts the farmer in a somewhat passive role. The economists' explanation begins when a qualitative or quantitative change takes place in the availability of inputs. They then go on to study the farmer's response to this change in his environment. Similarly, the sociologists' concern starts when new information becomes available for diffusion and adoption. The question as to why new inputs became available at a certain time is not answered satisfactorily by either. It is the answer to this question that supplies the clue needed to understand the growth of West Pakistan's agricultural sector after the 1958 takeover by the military of the country's administration.

The Rise of the Middle-Class Farmers in the 1960s

The system of Basic Democracies, launched by Ayub Khan in October 1959, was designed to transfer some of the political, social, and economic power wielded by the landed aristocracy to the rural middle class, defined as landholders who own between 50 and 100 acres. With the help of this system the new regime tried to activate politically this group of middle-class landlords who had hitherto taken very little interest in politics. Ayub Khan's approach was based on sound comprehension of the game of political arithmetic—after all the rural middle class was far more numerous than the landed aristocracy and commanded far greater economic resources. The elections of 1959 to the local councils created under the system of Basic Democracies brought a large number of middle landholders into the political arena (Burki 1971:178-179). Once they were there, they exerted their influence on the civil bureaucracy. The civil bureaucracy, in turn, consolidated its position by aligning itself more closely with this new social group (Burki 1969:250–251).

The rural middle class constituted a social stratum different from that of the landed aristocracy—its economic, social, and political goals, and the nature of the constraints facing it, were not the same as those of the big landlords. Thus the middle-class farmer responded to his economic, political, and social environment in a different way. An analysis concerned with understanding the development of the agricultural sector would not be complete without an emphasis on the nature of this response. This new response was possible for two reasons. First, the middle-class farmer, for the first time in the history of West Pakistan, could operate free of the control of the landed aristocracy. Second, the middle-class farmers had access to a large percentage of the cultivated land.

Dimensions of this response were seen in data collected from the survey of twenty-seven villages in the Punjab. Analysis shows that the middle-class farmers increased their crop production most rapidly. A positive and significant correlation was found between the percentage of land in farm ownership sizes of 25 to 50 and 50 to 100 acres and the ratio of growth of crop production (Table 6). Twenty-seven percent of the variance in the rate of growth of crop production is explained by using the percentage of land owned by farmers in the 25 to 50-acre category. By using the percentage of land in the 50 to 100-acre ownership category as the independent variable, the explanatory power of the equation increases from 27 to 59 percent. More than 88 percent of the variance is explained when we introduce the percentage of land owned by the middle-class farmers as the independent variable.

The conclusion we can draw is clear: the middle-class farmers, owning between 50 and 100 acres of land in the Punjab, produced the revolution in West Pakistan's agriculture. They did this first by going in for intensive use of water, and then by quickly adopting the technology made available to them as a result of a breakthrough in the development of high-yielding seed varieties. Thus West Pakistan's agricultural revolution began with water in the early 1960s, more than half a decade before the green revolution—coinciding with the emergence of the rural middle class as a new

TABLE 6. Ratio of Growth in Agricultural Production
in 27 Villages of the Punjab, 1959–1969

Dependent Variable	Constant	Independent Variables	r	Coefficient of Determination
1. ROG =	9.455 (0.642)	− .1122 APOL (.0231)	− 0.70	0.49
2. ROG =	7.257 (0.949)	− 0.0329 BPOL (.0399)	− 0.16	0.03
3. ROG =	2.990 (1.19)	+ .1751 CPOL (.0580)	+ 0.52	0.27
4. ROG =	3.880 (0.477)	+ 0.1359 DPOL (.0225)	+ 0.77	0.59
5. ROG =	6.502 (0.583)	+ .0014 EPOL	+ 0.01	0.00
6. ROG =	0.555 (0.456)	+ 0.1505 CDOL (0.0112)	+ 0.94	0.88

SOURCE: Shahid Javed Burki, Twenty-seven Village Study. See source note to Table 5, this chapter.

ROG = Average per annum rate of growth, 1959–1969.
APOL = Percentage of cultivated area owned by farmers having holdings of 0–10 acres in size.
BPOL = Percentage of area in holdings of 11–25 acres.
CPOL = Percentage of area in holdings of 26–50 acres.
DPOL = Percentage of area in holdings of 51–100 acres.
EPOL = Percentage of area in holdings of 101–500 acres.
CDOL = Percentage of area in holdings of 25–100 acres.

(The figures in parentheses are standard errors.)

powerful and independent factor in the political system introduced by Ayub Khan.

Of particular interest is the fact that the rural middle class, released from the political and social control of the landed aristocracy as a result of the introduction of the system of Basic Democracies, responded with an economic attitude that was close to that of the traditional profit maximizer. The middle-class landlords, unlike the members of the landed aristocracy, had to treat land as a scarce resource. They did not have access to the vast tracts of wasteland that were available for cultivation a decade earlier by the big landlords. Accordingly, they concentrated their attention on expanding their output by increasing land productivity (Gotsch's yield factor in the model outlined above.) This they did by installing tubewells and thereby increasing substantially the supply of irrigation water.

The new regime, mindful of the economic interests of the group it had helped to politically emancipate, was prepared to lend a helping hand. Public policy was geared toward providing this class of landowners with all the inputs they desired at subsidized prices. Tubewell parts were imported at favorable terms of exchange, energy for the tubewells was made available by the state-run Water and Power Development Authority at subsidized rates, and new inputs like fertilizer and insecticides were provided at generous rates of subsidy. According to a study sponsored by the World Bank, the political and economic program of the new regime "was a factor in changing the attitudes of large landowners, and awakening a more active interest in improving the productivity of their lands through increased investments, including tubewells and mechanization of farm operations" (Lieftinck et al. 1968:66). However, the trail was blazed by the middle-sized landowner.

If the middle-class landlord has contributed to agricultural growth to the extent indicated by the above analysis, then it is obvious that he is also its main beneficiary. A good proportion of the increased income from land must have gone to this class of farmer. This is supported by the twenty-seven village survey data, which indicate that of the total land held by the farmers in the 50- and 100-acre range, as much as 19.2 percent was acquired through purchases in the ten-year period between 1959 and 1969. The proportion of land so acquired is far greater for this category of landholder than for any other. Owners of holdings of less than 10 acres and between 10 and 25 acres held respectively 12.2 percent and 6.9 percent less land in 1969 than they did a decade earlier. The big landlords, with holdings of more than 100 acres, also lost 15.7 percent of the land in the same period.

The rise of middle-class farmers has its positive and negative aspects. It was no doubt healthy for the economy that the middle-class landlord emerged as a dominant entrepreneurial influence in the rural sector, prepared and able to make use of the additions to his income in increasing the productive assets at his disposal. In this respect, he displayed a totally different attitude than that exhibited by the landed aristocracy. The latter was a political rather than an economic maximizer in the decade following independence.

The negative aspect of this development was that the middle-class landlord, in his drive to acquire more productive capital, did not hesitate to eliminate those who could not compete with him. Consequently, the rapid strides made by agriculture in several Punjabi districts during the decade of the 1960s caused the displacement of a large number of smaller landholders. It also resulted in the landed aristocracy surrendering to the acquisitive pressure of the middle-class landlord some of their holdings. This paring of their landed possessions helped preempt the political pressure for reducing the size of the maximum holdings permitted under law. While the landed aristocracy were hard on their tenants, the middle-class landlord was hard on his competitors. The small landholders, when deprived of their holdings, often took to urban areas.

Conclusions

From the preceding analysis, it is possible to draw the following three major conclusions. First, the principal determinants of recent change in the agricultural sector of West Pakistan were a new group of middle-class agricultural entrepreneurs who were able to exercise influence over the formulation of public policy. This influence was exercised not only because the policy makers became aware of the potential power of this new group, but also because in a number of cases the policy makers themselves were the members of this class. To a very large extent, the policies favoring the middle-class farmer were formulated because the civil bureaucracy, in charge of the function of policy formulation, saw in this rural group a potentially strong ally. But of equal importance, the very large presence of the members of the rural middle class in the officer corps of the army added strength to the middle-class influence on political and economic affairs.

Second, the Pakistani political and economic system proved elastic enough to accommodate this new middle class. This expansion of the system was described as a revolution by the admirers of the regime of Ayub Khan (Feldman 1967).

Third, it is likely that the new class of agricultural entre-preneurs that Ayub Khan brought into being will also turn itself into a group of political as well as economic maximizers.[9] In doing so the middle-class farmers will be following the model provided by the political culture of the old landed aristocracy. This de-velopment could produce two consequences: it could produce elite conflict when this new group tries to increase power at the com-manding heights of the state apparatus, and it could manipulate what remains of the small-farmer class in a manner consistent with the political style of the landed aristocracy.

We can therefore expect an increased rate of conflict as a result of the emergence of the middle-class farmer. What will this conflict do to the political and economic system? This is a serious question and can be answered in one of two ways. My preference would be to take the line that the system, having adjusted to accommodate conflict before, would do so once again. There is a good possibility that the strain caused by the major change in the agricultural sector will not tear apart the political, social, and economic fabric.

Shahid Javed Burki holds a degree in Economics from Oxford Uni-versity. He is a member of the civil service of Pakistan. His numer-ous government assignments have included: deputy secretary, West Pakistan Department of Basic Democracies; director, West Pakistan Rural Works Program; deputy secretary, West Pakistan Planning and Development Department. He was also a research fellow with the Center for International Affairs, Harvard Univer-sity, 1970–1971. Currently he holds the position of deputy secre-tary, Exports, Ministry of Commerce, Government of Pakistan, Rawalpindi.

NOTES

The hypothesis presented in this paper developed in many discussions that I have had over the past four years with Carl H. Gotsch. I therefore owe him a special debt. I am also grateful to Peter Bertocci and Samuel Popkin for their helpful comments on an earlier draft of this paper. None of them, however, is responsible for the conclusions that I have drawn in this analysis. The twenty-seven village survey, results of which have been used here, was sponsored by the Center for International Affairs, Harvard Uni-versity.

1. For a good discussion of the importance of the interdisciplinary approach in studying developing economies, see Lipton (1970).

2. See Papanek (1967:317) for the data for 1948/49 and Government of Pakistan (1970) for data for 1968/69.

3. Philip Wordruff (1954) in his history of the Indian civil service uses "founders" and "guardians" as subtitles to indicate the nature of the role played by the British in the subcontinent.

4. For an interesting study of the development of irrigation by the British in what is now Pakistan, see Michel (1967).

5. This data was obtained by the author from the Board of Revenue, Government of West Pakistan.

6. These two charges frequently reoccurred in the cases brought by the state under the Elective Bodies (Disqualification) Order of 1959.

7. The data presented in this table include rents received in cash as well as in kind. The value of the rent received was computed from the average price for the year of the commodity given to the landlord by the tenant or the person to whom the land was leased.

8. Some of these authors developed this model in greater detail in a later work (Chaudhari et al. 1970).

9. I am indebted to Peter Bertocci for his contribution to these conclusions: he pointed out that the middle-class farmer could also adopt the model of a political maximizer.

BIBLIOGRAPHY

Anderson, J. D.
  1929. *Final Settlement Report of the Muzaffargarh District, 1920–1925*. Lahore: Government of the Punjab.
Burki, Shahid Javed
  1969. "Twenty Years of the Civil Service of Pakistan." *Asian Survey* 9:250–251.
  1971. "Interest Group Involvement in West Pakistan's Rural Works Program." *Public Policy* 19:178–179.
Chaudhari, Ali Muhammad; Chaudhari, Haider Ali; Raza, Muhammad Rafique; and Rizwani, Abdur Rehman
  1970. *Man, Water and Economy*. Lyallpur: West Pakistan Agricultural University.
Chaudhari, Haider Ali; Erickson, Eugene C.; and Bajwa, Ijaz Ahmad
  1968. "Social Characteristics of Agricultural Innovators in Pakistan." In *Collected Papers of the Pakistan Sociological Association's II, III, and IV Conferences*, edited by Haider Ali Chaudhari, pp. 95–102. Lahore: University of the Punjab.

Falcon, Walter P.
    1964. "Farmer Response to Price in a Subsistence Economy: The
        Case of West Pakistan." *American Economic Review* 54:580–
        591.
Falcon, Walter P., and Gotsch, Carl H.
    1968. "Lessons in Agricultural Development—Pakistan." In
        Development Policy: Theory and Practice, edited by Gustav
        Papanek, pp. 269–318. Cambridge, Mass.: Harvard University
        Press.
Feldman, Herbert
    1967. *Revolution in Pakistan: A Study of the Martial Law Adminis-
        tration.* London: Oxford University Press.
Galjart, Benno
    1961. "Rural Development and Sociological Concept: A Critique."
        Rural Sociology 36:31–41.
Gotsch, Carl H.
    1968. "Regional Agricultural Growth: The Case of West Pakistan."
        Asian Survey 8:188–205.
Government of Pakistan
    1964. *Economic Survey, 1962–1963.* Rawalpindi: Ministry of Fi-
        nance, Government of Pakistan.
    1970. *The Fourth Five Year Plan 1970–1975.* Islamabad, West Paki-
        stan: Planning Commission, Government of Pakistan.
Government of West Pakistan
    1959. *Report of the Land Reforms Commission.* Lahore: Government
        Printing, Government of West Pakistan.
Grunwald, Joseph
    1961. "The Structuralist School on Price Stability and Development."
        In *Latin American Issues*, edited by Albert O. Hirschman. New
        York: Twentieth Century Fund. pp. 95–123.
Hazelhurst, Leighton W.
    1966. *Enterpreneurship and the Merchant Castes in a Punjab City.*
        Durham: Commonwealth Studies Center, Duke University.
Hussain, S. Mushtaq
    1968. "Economic Development of the Agricultural Sector of an Un-
        derdeveloped Country with Special Reference to Pakistan."
        Ph.D. dissertation, University of California.
    1969. *Price Response of Marketable Surplus in a Developing
        Economy: A Theoretical Framework.* Karachi: The Pakistan
        Institute of Development Economics.
Johnston, B. F.
    1964. "The Choice of Measures for Increasing Agricultural Productiv-

ity: A Survey of Possibilities in East Africa." *Tropical Agriculture* 41:91–113.

Khan, Azizur Rahman, and Chowdhury, A. H. M. Nuruddin
1970. "Marketable Surplus Function: A Study of the Behavior of West Pakistan Farmers." In *Empirical Studies on Pakistan Agriculture*, edited by S. Mushtaq Hussain and Mohammad Irshad Khan. Karachi: The Pakistan Institute of Development Economics.

Khatkhate, D. R.
1962. "Some Notes on the Real Effects of Foreign Surplus Disposal in Underdeveloped Areas." *Quarterly Journal of Economics* 79:186–196.

Lasswell, Harold D., Kaplan, Abraham
1950. *Power and Society: A Framework of Political Inquiry*. New Haven: Yale University Press.

Lieftinck, Pieter; Sadove, A. Robert; and Creyke, Thomas C.
1968. *Water and Power Resources of West Pakistan: A Study in Sector Planning*. Baltimore: The Johns Hopkins University Press.

Lipton, Michael
1970. "Interdisciplinary Studies in Less Developed Countries." *The Journal of Development Studies* 7:5–18.

Maniruzzaman, Talukdar
1966. "Group Interests in Pakistan's Politics." *Pacific Review* vol. 39.

Michel, Aloys Arthur
1967. *Indus Rivers: A Study of the Effects of Partition*. New Haven: Yale University Press.

Minhas, B. S., and Vardayanathan, A.
1964. "Analysis of Crop Output Growth by Component Elements: India, 1951–54 to 1958–61." Mimeographed. Delhi.

Mohammad, Ghulam
1970. "Private Tubewell Development and Cropping Patterns in West Pakistan." In *Empirical Studies on Pakistan Agriculture*, edited by S. Mushtaq Hussain and Mohammad Irshad Khan. Karachi: The Pakistan Institute of Development Economics.

Moore, Berrington
1966. *Social Origins of Dictatorship and Democracy*. Boston: Beacon Press.

Morris-Jones, W. H.
1958. "Experience of Independence—India and Pakistan." *Political Quarterly* 29:224–237.

Nair, Kusum
1961. *Blossoms in the Dust*. London: Dunkworth.

Nicholls, W. H.
    1963. "An 'Agricultural Surplus' as a Factor in Economic Development." *Journal of Political Economy* 71:1–29.
Papanek, Gustav
    1967. *Pakistan's Development: Social Goals and Private Incentives.* Cambridge, Mass.: Harvard University Press.
Sayeed, Khalid B.
    1968. *Pakistan: The Formative Phase, 1857–1948.* London: Oxford University Press.
Schultz, T. W.
    1964. *Transforming Traditional Agriculture.* New Haven: Yale University Press.
Stern, Joseph J., and Falcon, Walter P.
    1970. *Growth and Development in Pakistan, 1955–1969.* Cambridge, Mass.: Center for International Affairs, Harvard University.
Wordruff, Philip
    1954. *The Men Who Ruled India: The Guardians.* London: Jonathan Cape.

16

The Rural Elite
and Agricultural
Development in Pakistan

Hamza Alavi

Introduction

An extraordinary air of optimism pervades most discussions of
the green revolution in Pakistan.[1] It is a kind of optimism that
perhaps obscures some fundamental questions that might be raised
about its characteristics, consequences, and alternatives. Scholarly
debate has been focused on explanations for the breakthrough in
application of new agricultural technology and upon the reasons for
the earlier stagnation (see chapter 15), and research has been focused on the incidental difficulties that must be resolved to allow
the green revolution to continue its course.[2] There is, however, a
growing uneasiness about some of the implications of the current
pattern of development (see chapters 13 and 17).

The essentially optimistic view of the green revolution in the
economic sphere is translated into political and social spheres by
Burki in chapter 15. He argues that "middle-class farmers owning
between 50 and 100 acres of land in the Punjab [have] produced the
revolution in West Pakistan's agriculture" and are its main beneficiaries. Furthermore, a new political equation was established
between the political regime in Pakistan and this class, with its
new-found economic power and local influence, which the regime
has "helped to emancipate politically." The rise of the rural middle
class, Burki argues, has eroded the political and economic power of
the "landed aristocracy." My analysis does not support such a conclusion.

Changes in the agrarian economy, referred to as the green
revolution, are the cumulative result of a number of independent
developments, events, and responses of large landholders to the

opportunities that arose. There is no all-embracing scheme that could be described as a "strategy" of agricultural development. However, the term is not altogether inappropriate, in the sense that an underlying logic gave some coherence to the separate and independent decisions of the various authorities and farmers. That logic, it may be argued, was derived from the demands and pressures of the big landholders whose operations are at the heart of the dynamic of agricultural development that was set in motion. For the authorities, it turned out to be a "policy," ex post facto. It was an elite farmer strategy because it rested on the economic power of large landholders who were its principal beneficiaries.

My analysis shows not only a tendency toward increasing disparities of income and wealth between different strata of the rural population, but also a tendency toward widening regional disparities. Such disparities are the outcome of the class basis of the dynamic of agricultural development, in the context that there are structural differences in the agrarian economy in the different regions. However, these differences cannot be explained wholly by reference to ecological imperatives or by suggestions of interregional discrimination. If that were true, a resolution of the problem of regional disparities could not be resolved independently of a shift from the present class basis of agricultural development.

A crucial aspect of the green revolution, little researched as yet, consists of its "secondary effects," which are not apparent if attention is focused exclusively on the agrarian economy. Such effects arise through changes in the patterns of expenditures associated with the changes in incomes. The resultant expansion in demand for manufactured consumer goods and imported commodities has generated inflationary pressures of an unprecedented scale. This has brought about an erosion in the real incomes of those farmers who have not directly benefited from the green revolution, as well as in those of wage and salary earners in the towns. Therefore, although the green revolution has increased the prosperity of some, it has impoverished many.

If such complex secondary effects of the green revolution are taken into account, it is not surprising that, in 1968, when the largest harvests ever had been reaped, the entire countryside erupted with popular discontent on an unprecedented scale. The regional distribution of gains and burdens of the green revolution also has greatly exacerbated interregional tensions. It would be naive to assume that these issues will be readily perceived by the authorities and that a totally new approach will be introduced into the sphere of agrarian development, because the class which has profited most from the present pattern of development holds a powerful position in Pakistan's political system. It would be safer to assume under the political realities that the strains being generated will not disappear. Far from having established a new political equilibrium, the green revolution has generated forces that have been at the center of the successive crises Pakistan has experienced.

The Regional Pattern of the Agrarian Economy

Interregional differences in the structure of Pakistan's agrarian economy originate from ecological differences and consequences of differences in patterns of historical development. However, in past discussions, interregional comparisons have focused almost wholly on natural differences and have tended to obscure the underlying differences in the economic and social structures. The Food and Agriculture Commission, for example, distinguished between the following regions of West Pakistan: Canal Irrigated Plains of West Pakistan, Submontane Regions of West Pakistan, Range Lands of West Pakistan, and Hill Catchment Area of West Pakistan (GOP 1960). This is a simple ecological classification. The commission does not consider other criteria that might be relevant to a further elaboration of the regional pattern, in order to identify issues of public policy. Because such an approach emphasizes "given" natural conditions, the problems of each region appear to be specific to each region. We have no framework in which the problems of the different regions could be interrelated.

A Pakistani geographer, Maryam Elahi, was among the first to pursue systematically the question of regional differences in agricultural productivity (Elahi:1963,1965). She focuses her analysis on physical factors, although at the outset she does recognize that "efficiency of agriculture reflects the influence of varied physical,

economic, social and historical factors." She ranks the regions of
Pakistan in their relative efficiency in agricultural production, taking into account the yield of each crop and the cropping pattern.
The weakness in her analysis seems to lie in the fact that, in ranking
productive efficiency, she allocates an equal weight for every crop
and does not take into account the relative weights of particular
crops in the national economy or in the economy of a particular
region. Her study does bring focus upon the disparities between
regions but it relates them mainly to physical differences.

In another recent study, Gotsch (1968) computed differences
in the rates of growth for the various districts of the Punjab. He
provides valuable insight into various "sources of growth" which
he breaks down into "acreage effects," "yield effects," and "cropping-pattern effects," and he examines the extent to which one or
the other effect has been prominent in the growth of agricultural
production in different regions of the Punjab. He then examines the
factors that have contributed to the predominance of such effects in
the growth of agricultural production in those regions. The critical
variable in his analysis is the provision of water.

An important additional variable that should be considered in
examining the regional impact of the green revolution is farm size.
The structure of the agrarian economy of each region, as determined by the distribution of landownership and farm size, vitally
affects the prospects and problems of development (Alavi 1968).
There are, however, wide variations in the structure of the agrarian
economy within and between Pakistan's provinces. It is convenient for the purposes of this analysis to focus attention on the
province of Punjab and thus limit the range of data we need to
examine.

Furthermore, it has the advantage of showing that explanations
of regional disparity lie primarily in the structure of the agrarian
economy and cannot be explained purely by reference to provincial
political influence. Punjab is the largest and richest of the provinces of Pakistan and politically the most influential. It has 60
percent of the rural population of Pakistan.

Regional differences in the structure of the agrarian economy
are derived from the historical development of the regions, conditioned by their respective physical environments. For the pur-

poses of this analysis, four regions of the Punjab, which have quite distinct characteristics, were specified.

1. the Poor Old Settled Districts of the *barani* (rainfed) region
2. the Rich Old Settled Districts, which have good irrigation as well as good rainfall
3. the Canal Colony Districts
4. the arid and relatively sparsely populated Western Districts of Mianwali, Muzaffargarh, and Dera Ghazi Khan

Recent irrigation projects are changing the characteristics of the Western Districts and will not be treated as separate categories. In the discussion which follows, I have defined the Canal Colony Districts to include Sargodha, Multan, and Bahawalpur divisions, excluding only Mianwali District, which I have classified together with the Rawalpindi Division as constituting the region of the Poor Old Settled Districts. The districts of Lahore Division constitute the region of the Rich Old Settled Districts. I have chosen these somewhat awkward labels for the respective regions to emphasize the historical conditions of their development, which have determined their present state.

The demarcation of the regions owes much to the natural conditions of the regions. To begin with, a primary distinction is established by the alignment of the isoprecipitation lines that differentiate the northern region of the Punjab, consisting of Rawalpindi and Lahore divisions, which receive a sufficiency of rainfall to permit *barani* cultivation. South of that region, until the advent of canal irrigation, the land was by and large an empty waste, peopled mainly in the riverains by seminomadic tribes who practiced a rather perfunctory agriculture on strips of land irrigated by the annual riverain floods. In some parts of this arid region, around wells, there were also a few scattered agricultural settlements.

In the *barani* area, namely Rawalpindi and Lahore divisions, sufficiency of rainfall fostered a settled agricultural population from very early times. Therefore, I have referred to these two regions as the Old Settled Districts. The long history of a settled agriculture in these districts is relevant because, as a consequence, land in these populous districts has been subdivided from generation to generation, and the average size of farms in these two regions is now very small compared to those in the Canal Colony Districts.

The *barani* region (the Old Settled Districts) can be sub-divided into two distinct regions: the Rich Old Settled Districts of Lahore Division, and the Poor Old Settled Districts of Rawalpindi Division. The former region not only has a good rainfall but additional water available from canal or well irrigation. The southern half of that region (Lahore and Sheikhupura districts, as well as much as Gujranwala District) has the benefit of canal irrigation. In the northern half (Sialkot District and parts of Gujranwala District), where topography does not favor the extension of canal irrigation, groundwater supplies are easily accessible and agriculture has been supplemented traditionally by wells operated by Persian wheels and now by tubewells. As a result, the region is highly productive. Rawalpindi Division, on the other hand, with the exception only of a part of Gujrat District, is almost wholly dependent upon rainfall for agriculture. There groundwater is not easily accessible and canal irrigation is limited because of its topography. With the population crowded into small farms, it is a very poor region.

Before the advent of canal irrigation, the dry zone south of the Old Settled Districts, large tracts of land that had little value, was appropriated by big landowners. The introduction of irrigation at the turn of the century transformed the agrarian economy of most of the dry zone. Colonists were brought from all parts of the Punjab and sizable allotments of land were made. The average size of farms in this region is, therefore, relatively large. Too few generations have passed to fragment these large holdings into the extremely small sizes typically found in the Old Settled Districts.

However, one factor has served to introduce a substantial number of small landholders and landless people into the Canal Colonies. Before 1947 a large proportion, although a minority, of the population of the Canal Colony Districts in West Pakistan consisted of Hindus and Sikhs who, at the time of the Partition (of India), were driven out of the country. The "evacuee land" they left behind was allotted provisionally to families of incoming refugees on the basis of one acre per head for evey member of a family. But in 1954, the evacuee land was reallotted among refugees on the basis of claimed holdings in India. This was land reform in reverse. Those who could establish large claims acquired large landholdings; others who could not do so lost what they already had. This great upheaval in landholdings, which included the eviction of those who could not establish a claim, has been ignored by those who have written about agriculture in West Pakistan. But that measure has had a far-reaching effect on the agrarian economy of the Canal Colony Districts. One of its consequences was a large increase in the proportion of the agricultural population that had to look to sharecropping or laboring as a principal means of livelihood.

The size-pattern of farms in the three, principally agrarian regions of the Punjab described above is presented in Table 1. One representative district for each region is presented for purposes of illustration.

TABLE 1. The Size-Pattern of Farms in the Three Principal Agrarian Regions of the Punjab

	Poor Old Settled District: Rawalpindi	Rich Old Settled District: Gujranwala	Canal Colony District: Multan
Size of Farms (%)			
Small Farms (below 5 acres)	74	48	38
Medium Farms (5 to 25 acres)	24	46	51
Large Farms (over 25 acres)	2	6	11
	100	100	100
Size of Cultivated Area (%)			
Small Farms	31	11	7
Medium Farms	58	64	54
Large Farms	11	25	39
	100	100	100
Average Cultivated Farm Area (acres)			
Small Farms	1.3	1.7	1.8
Medium Farms	7.3	10.6	10.7
Large Farms	13.0	32.4	37.2

Source: Government of Pakistan (1963).

Two parameters are of special importance when considering the structural implications of farm size. One is technology, which determines the upper limits of the farm area that can be cultivated with a pair of bullocks and two men. The other is the minimum farm size for family subsistence. Conventionally, 12½ acres is taken by farmers and landowners in Canal Colony Districts to be the maximum that can be cultivated by one pair of bullocks and their complement of human labor. Some place it at 10 acres. The actual figure varies according to the quality of soil, the conditions of agriculture (irrigated or otherwise), the quality of the animals, and so on. The conventional maximum of 12½ acres is significant as a yardstick, since the farmers themselves use it as a basis for judgments. No landlord gives more than about this quantity of land to a tenant who has only one pair of bullocks. If a large tenant family has two pairs of bullocks, he may give them double that area of land, and so forth. Similarly, with regard to self-cultivation, it is rare to find an owner-cultivated farm of more than twenty-five acres that relies on bullock power. Owners of larger holdings have traditionally let out portions of their lands for sharecropping. Tractors, on the other hand, call for much larger farms, and one of the inevitable consequences of their introduction has been the eviction of sharecroppers by landowners in order to resume sufficient land for tractor cultivation. One tractor is estimated to displace a dozen (or more) bullock-drawn plows. The amount of land available for sharecropping depends, therefore, on the degree of concentration of landownership and the method of cultivation employed. In both respects, conditions vary among the regions. In the Old Settled Districts, the amount of land available for sharecropping is limited because farms are small. But the factor inhibits the spread of mechanization. In the Canal Colony Districts there has been much land available for sharecropping, but the large holdings encourage mechanization, which is rapidly diminishing the amount of land available for sharecropping.

The second parameter relevant to the set of problems we are examining is the size of farm required to yield a "surplus" over subsistence needs, that is a farm size that would provide resources for investment and development as well as raise consumption above a minimum. Empirically, there are obvious difficulties in determining the level of subsistence that can be considered a "necessary" or "tolerable" minimum level. Even if a minimum per capita requirement for subsistence is established (arbitrarily), it would be impossible to express it in terms of definite size required for subsistence. Needed size would vary with the number of family members that must be sustained as well as with differences in farm productivity. Nevertheless, a crude "average" figure for an "average" family is not without practical value in dealing with the problem. An International Bank for Reconstruction and Development (World Bank) Survey in 1966 estimated the farm necessary to provide a minimum subsistence for an average family in a canal colony district at five acres. Using five acres as a yardstick, we have some idea of the *order of magnitude* of a subsistence-farm size. A farm substantially above it would be likely to yield a surplus.

Those whose farm holdings are too small for subsistence must look for alternative or supplementary means of livelihood. Because large holdings in the Canal Colony Districts could not be cultivated directly by the big landowners themselves, a substantial amount of land has been given out for sharecropping. The farm economy in the Canal Colony Districts could absorb the available manpower because the number of small holders and landless persons in those districts was comparatively smaller. In the Old Settled Districts, there was a very large number of persons with diminutive holdings and the number of those with large landholdings was relatively smaller. The surplus manpower in these districts had to be absorbed in employment outside the farm economy. Consequently we find two different patterns of employment in the two regions. In the Old Settled Districts of Rawalpindi Division there has been a considerable incentive for emigration to towns or the army. Those who found work outside the villages have generally remitted money to dependents left at home. The deficit farm economy has depended heavily upon funds remitted from outside. In the Canal Colonies, such a symbiotic relationship with outside employment does not exist on a significant scale.

These differences in the economic configuration of the two areas stem from ecological differences and the historical pattern of

their respective development. But these differences are reflected
also in the social and cultural patterns of behavior in the two regions. A most significant difference is in the attitudes toward education and in the actual progress of education in the two regions.
Surprisingly, educational progress is much higher in the Poor Old
Settled Districts of Rawalpindi Division than in the richer regions.
The census data probably even underestimate the greater range of
educated residents of the Old Settled Districts, because many of
them emigrate from the village for outside employment and are
counted as residents of other districts. But their links with their
village homes usually remain close, and economically they play an
important role in sustaining the economy of the village.

TABLE 2. Level of Literacy and
Higher Education in the Punjab
(educated persons as percentage of total population)

Region	Literates with Formal Education		Educated up to Matriculation or Higher	
	Men	Women	Men	Women
Multan Division	14.6	2.6	1.8	0.20
Bahawalpur Division	15.3	2.8	1.9	0.17
Sargodha Division	22.1	4.5	2.8	0.26
Lahore Division	24.6	9.4	4.3	1.00
Rawalpindi Division	33.2	8.3	4.0	0.56
Gujranwala District	25.5	7.7	2.8	0.40
Sialkot District	22.7	7.2	2.8	0.40

SOURCE: Compiled from GOP (1961), Table 3.

The data in Table 2 show the considerable higher level of
education in Rawalpindi Division. The general level of literacy
there is higher than in Lahore Division, despite the fact that the
high figure for the latter includes the concentration of educated
people in the city of Lahore, a major city of Pakistan. For a more

appropriate interregional comparison, data are offered for the two districts of Lahore Division, Gujranwala District and Sialkot District, which exclude Lahore city.

The regional differences in the levels of education may be explained by studying the role education plays in the lives of the rural people. Until recently the principal significance of education in the rural areas was that it was regarded as a passport for employment outside the village—in the government, armed forces, or urban employment. By contrast, in the prosperous Canal Colony Districts, sons were needed to work the farms. Education was not looked upon with favor because it carried the threat of alienation; educated sons were likely to leave their villages and family farms, attracted to jobs in town.

Attitudes toward education have begun to change in recent years in the Canal Colony Districts, especially among the prosperous big farmers. The revolution in mechanical and chemical technology now employed in agriculture is making new demands upon the capabilities of farmers. They are becoming increasingly aware of the value of education in terms of their own situations, namely for better farming and coping with the new technologies. However, the new purpose education must now serve also raises questions about the relationship between education and development. We have found that progress in agricultural technology did not make great strides in the region that had the highest level of education. On the contrary, it was in areas of much lower levels of education (where the economic and ecological conditions were conducive for introduction of new technology) that progress has been the greatest. But the latter has created a new demand for education, and a demand for a new kind of education.[3]

Innovation is a function of economic feasibility and not simply that of education and attitudes toward modernization. The differences in the structure of the agrarian economy of regions of the Punjab, as well as those of other provinces of Pakistan, are reflected in the degree to which they have shared in agricultural prosperity. In the Punjab, the Poor Old Settled Districts, which have high education but a predominance of small farms, progressed least. An index of the uneven distribution of agricultural wealth among the

different regions of the Punjab, and among different provinces of
Pakistan, is provided by data on the regional shares of crop production (Table 3).

Wide disparities in the agricultural prosperity of the various
regions can be seen by comparing the share in the production of the
principal crops with the proportion of the rural population for each
region. The prosperity of the Punjab is in marked contrast to the
poverty of Baluchistan and the North-West Frontier Province
(NWFP). In the poorer regions, more of coarse cereals are produced
relative to wheat and cash crops such as cotton and rice. But the
NWFP's very large share of the production of maize must be
viewed in the light of the fact that total acreage under maize in the
whole of Pakistan was only 3 percent of the cropped area as compared with 33 percent of the cropped area under wheat. Punjab and
Sind together, which have 76 percent of the rural population of
Pakistan, accounted for no less than 91 percent of wheat, the staple
food crop, all of cotton, the principal cash crop, and over 98 percent
of rice. But in the Punjab, there are marked differences among
regions. The production of wheat per capita in the Poor Old Settled
Districts was about the same as that in the Rich Old Settled Districts in 1964/65. But the latter had a substantial lead in the production of other commodities, especially rice. The Canal Colonies
have a dominating lead in the production of wheat and cotton, as
well as in other crops, over the other regions.

In 1964/65 there were already very marked differences in the
agricultural wealth of the different regions of Pakistan. However, as
a consequence of the pattern of subsequent development, these
differences have been accentuated. For example, the relative position of the Poor Old Settled Districts worsened in the period between 1964/65 and 1967/68 (Table 3). The relative positions of
Baluchistan and NWFP have also deteriorated. The position of
Sind improved marginally in the production of wheat; there was
also a change in its cropping pattern since it gained in cotton production but lost ground in rice, a major crop for that province.

Tubewells and the New Technology

The green revolution was the cumulative result of a series of
independent developments. The most important of those is the

TABLE 3. Regional Share of Population and Crop Production in West Pakistan

	Rural Population 1961 (%)	Wheat	Cotton	Rice	Gram	Bajra	Jowar	Maize
		Share of Cropped Area of West Pakistan 1964/65 (%)						
West Pakistan	100.0	33.0	9.3	8.5	7.6	5.9	3.6	3.0
		Share of West Pakistan Production in 1964/65 (%)						
Baluchistan	2.8	1.7	—	0.2	—	0.2	4.5	0.37
NWFP	20.5	7.0	0.1	1.1	7.4	4.6	6.9	51.0
Sind	16.2	12.5	21.0	48.5	17.2	36.0	42.8	1.3
Punjab	60.4	78.6	49.8	49.8	75.0	59.0	45.5	47.3
of which in Punjab								
Poor Old Settled Districts	11.5	11.4	1.4	3.3	24.9	21.6	12.0	10.3
Rich Old Settled Districts	12.8	12.8	3.5	35.2	5.9	8.0	1.3	8.1
Canal Colony Districts	36.2	54.1	73.9	11.4	42.7	29.0	32.0	28.4
		Share of West Pakistan Production in 1967/68 (%)						
Baluchistan		1.6	—	0.2				
NWFP		6.2	0.1	2.5				
Sind		13.6	25.5	45.0				
Punjab		78.7	74.6	52.2				
of which in Punjab								
Poor Old Settled Districts		9.5	1.1	3.3				
Rich Old Settled Districts		12.5	2.9	36.0				
Canal Colony Districts		56.6	70.6	12.9				

SOURCES: Compiled from district-wide data in:1) Government of West Pakistan (n.d.) and 2) Government of West Pakistan 1968 for 1967/68.

NOTE: The regions of the Punjab have been demarcated as follows: Poor Old Settled Districts comprise Rawalpindi Division and Mianwali District; Rich Old Settled Districts comprise Lahore Division; Canal Colony Districts comprise Multan Division, Bahawalpur Division, and Sargodha Division, excluding Mianwali District.

extensive installation of private tubewells, which began in the middle fifties and gathered momentum in the sixties.[4] It is noteworthy that this crucial factor did not find a place in the priorities recommended by the Food and Agriculture Commission in 1960; the well-known "Five Firsts" were provision of better seed, fertilizer, plant protection capabilities, better cultivation techniques, and short- and medium-term credit (GOP1960:64). The commission pointed out that these prescriptions were not new, that the chief problem was to find "a way for their effective implementation." Private tubewell development proved to be the catalyst. By the mid-sixties, the number of private tubewells installed in the country had grown very large and its effects became manifest (Mohammad 1964). In 1965 a noted agricultural economist wrote, "One of the most significant phenomena in agricultural development in Pakistan has been the installation of private tubewells by farmers of West Pakistan at an exceedingly fast rate... [Consequently] West Pakistan is likely to attain a rate of increase in agricultural production which will be unparalleled in the history of agriculture" (Mohammad 1965).

Private tubewells not only made available a greatly increased quantity of water for irrigation but also its timely availability. That made possible substantial increases in the application of chemical fertilizers, which facilitated the introduction of high-yielding dwarf varieties of wheat and rice. An estimate of the contribution of various factors to the increase in agricultural production between 1960 and 1965 was included in the Third Five-Year Plan (GOP1965:462). The estimate shows an overall increase in crop production of 26 percent, which was attributed to various factors (Table 4). This estimate is based on limited data and may not claim precision, but it indicates the probable order of importance of the various factors. Increased availability of water, either through tubewells or canals, was estimated to account for half the total increase in output. Furthermore, the availability of tubewell water was the crucial precondition for increase in other inputs also, because adequate timely watering is needed for profitable increase in application of chemical fertilizer. These two inputs are necessary conditions for profitable cultivation of the high-yielding varieties of seed, which also benefits most from plant protection measures. Private tubewell development would thus appear to be

TABLE 4. Sources of Increased Output during Second Plan Period, 1960–1965

	percent
Groundwater Development	9
Additional Surface Water	4
Fertilizer	5
Plant Protection	4
New Seed	3
Other Factors	1
TOTAL INCREASE IN OUTPUT	26

SOURCE: GOP 1965.

the most important single factor contributing to the green revolution in this period. The importance of tubewells can be seen by a comparison of the water situation in the Poor Old Settled Districts of Rawalpindi Division with other regions. In that region, tubewell development has not gone very far and canal irrigation is absent. In unirrigated areas it is only in the most northern districts, for example, Hazara District, which receive relatively greater and more dependable rainfall, that some progress has been made with new seed and fertilizer, as shown in Rochin's study included in this volume (chapter 14). The relatively meager progress made in these areas, however, is reflected in the data of regional shares of crop production (Table 3).

In the period 1960–1965, private tubewells accounted for no less than 63 percent of the increase in water supply (Table 5).[5] The

TABLE 5. Sources of Irrigation Water in the Indus Plain

Year	Canals	Private Tubewells	Public Tubewells	Persian Wheels	Total
			(million acre feet)		
1960	55	0.3	2.0	1.7	59
1965	58	5.3	2.7	1.7	68
1968		13.0			

SOURCE: Developed by the author from a number of major studies.

pace of installation in the subsequent five-year period was much higher.

A *Report on the Farm Mechanization Survey 1968* estimated that the number of private tubewells in Pakistan increased from 31,600 at the end of 1964 to 75,700 in 1968, or by 2½ times (GOP 1969:67).[6] Its relative importance as a source of irrigation water is increasing.

Tubewell development in Pakistan, however, is highly concentrated in the Rich Old Settled Districts and in the Canal Colony Districts of the Punjab. The Farm Mechanization survey showed that 91 percent of the 75,700 tubewells in Pakistan were located in the Punjab, of which only 3 percent were in the Old Settled Districts of Rawalpindi Division. These latter districts, however, had 10.9 percent of the public tubewells in West Pakistan (GOP 1969:55).

It is sometimes argued that the relatively small number of tubewells in the Poor Old Settled Districts is due to the absence of adequate groundwater supplies. But there is physical evidence of considerable potential for tubewell development in many parts of this region. Relative costs would be greater than in other areas because the water table is lower and the groundwater more difficult to mine. In addition to higher costs, the preponderance of small farms in the area would appear to be a major obstacle to the expansion of private tubewells. Our hypothesis is that the backwardness of the Poor Old Settled Districts cannot, therefore, be attributed wholly to natural factors. It is rooted also in the fragmented structure of its agrarian economy. Under these circumstances, a public tubewell development program might be very successful. But the lack of political influence to effect the allocation of resources for this purpose is another obstacle in the way of development in this region. Evidence supporting this comes from the Basic Democracy Institute at Lala Musa. In 1967/68, the institute had worked out a viable scheme for tubewell development in Kharian Tehsil, which was vetted and approved by experts and given formal approval at the district level. But the scheme never got off the ground because those who were committed to its implementation lacked the necessary "political resources" to influence the powers that be.[7] It is vital for the development of the *barani* region that the potentialities for identifying such possibilities be explored in every part of the region and then pursued with determination.

Outside the Punjab there is very little tubewell development. It is limited to Peshawar Division, which had 2.7 percent of the private tubewells, and Khairpur Division, which had 1.7 percent (GOP 1969:55). The prospects of tubewell development in the NWFP and Sind are partly limited by a shortage of accessible groundwater and a high degree of salinity in the groundwater.

The pattern of concentration of tubewell ownership has not only an interregional aspect, but, within each region, it has also a stratification aspect. There is a high degree of concentration of tubewells on farms over twenty-five acres. For example, a Pakistan Institute of Development Economics (PIDE) survey conducted in 1965 indicates a concentration of tubewells on large farms, as shown in Table 6.

Because private tubewell development is closely related to concentration of land in large farms, the green revolution has tended not only to intensify already large disparities in wealth, but it has also widened disparities between different regions.

The available data show a high concentration of new inputs on large farms, although they are insufficient for detailed and precise judgments.[8] Some benefits have percolated to smaller farmers, at which level there has been extensive tubewell development, insofar as big farmers sell surplus tubewell water to neighbors. The latter, however, are at a considerable disadvantage not only because of the relatively higher cost of water, but also because they cannot always have it at a time of their own choosing. This introduces a factor of uncertainty, which increases their risk and inhibits

TABLE 6. Installation of Private Tubewells, 1963–1965

District	Total Number of Tubewells	Tubewells on Large Farms (above 25 acres)	Percentage of Tubewells on Large Farms
Gujranwala	3,776	3,289	87
Multan	3,076	2,639	86

SOURCE: Pakistan Institute of Development Economics (n.d.).

innovation. Big landowners, very often, are only too eager to buy
the land of poorer neighbors. During a year's stay in Punjabi villages in the course of my research, I came across several landlords
who refused to sell water to their smaller neighbors at critical times
although previously they had sold it regularly. They then pressed
them to sell their land. Diffusion of benefits through purchased
tubewell water is limited and is fraught with uncertainty.

The Rural Elite

There is a high degree of concentration of landownership in
Pakistan, a fact reflected in persistent demands for land reform and
repeated promises of successive governments to introduce land
reform measures. Despite interest in the subject, reliable data are
noticeably absent. Even the Land Reforms Commission for West
Pakistan decided to make do with makeshift data in its published
report, in spite of the rich source of information maintained by the
Revenue Department in the form of detailed records of land rights.
Admitting that "reliable statistics for West Pakistan [were] not available," the commission's 1959 report used 1946/47 data for Sind,
1952/53 data for Bahawalpur, and 1954/55 for Punjab. It was unable
to specify dates for the data on NWFP, Baluchistan, and Khairpur
(Government of West Pakistan 1959, Appendix I). A factor that
modified that picture in later years, especially in Sind and the Punjab, was the reallotment of refugee land in the mid-fifties. The
resettlement had the effect of dispossessing very large numbers of
small landholders and transferring land to large landholders. Ayub
Khan later called it "a perfectly ridiculous formula: it meant that if a
person could produce two witnesses who deposed that he owned
half of India, then the Government of Pakistan would have to accept this!" (Khan 1967:94). Ayub Khan characterized the Refugee
Rehabilitation Policy as creating "a new class of Nawabs." However, Ayub Khan's land reform in 1959 did not succeed in altering
the picture very much. To assess its impact we might compare the
"cultivated land" in West Pakistan (i.e., "net sown area" and "current fallows") with the cultivated land actually surrendered under
the land reform. The total area of "cultivated" land in West Pakistan, as reported by the Land Reforms Commission, was 31 million
acres. The cultivated area surrendered under the land reform was

871,000 or about 2.4 percent of the total (Government of West Pakistan 1959:10, 1969:100). In the light of the high degree of concentration of land, the situation remained, for the most part, unchanged.

We examined the data provided by the 1960 Pakistan Census of Agriculture to estimate the degree of concentration of land ownership in West Pakistan. The data relate to farms as operational units, whether cultivated by owners or by tenants. The census does not provide information about size of holdings by ownership. However, a careful examination of the data allows us to arrive at reasonable estimates, which show the relative magnitudes involved, although they cannot provide precise figures for the various categories of the rural population.

TABLE 7. Proportion of Farms and Farm Area in Size and Tenure Categories, 1960 (in %)

Farm Size	Owner Farms		Owner-cum-Tenant Farms		Tenant Farms		All Farms	
	number	area	number	area	number	area	number	area
Small Farms (under 5 acres)	25.0	4.2	5.7	1.4	19.2	3.7	49.9	9.3
Medium Farms (5 to 25 acres)	13.5	14.6	9.5	10.8	19.8	22.0	42.8	47.4
Large Farms (over 25 acres)	2.8	19.4	2.0	10.0	3.1	13.0	7.9	42.4
TOTAL	41.3	38.2	17.2	22.2	42.1	38.7	100.6	99.1

SOURCE: GOP (1963), Table 5.

The size interval used by the census to classify "small farms," namely those below 5 acres in size, identifies units below the subsistence level in the case of owner-operated farms. One-quarter of all owner-operated holdings were below the subsistence level (Table 7). The corresponding dividing line that defines subsistence level of tenant farms is 10 acres, assuming an equal division of produce between landlords and sharecroppers. The census does not use that size interval. Data for farms between 5 and 7½ acres are available. If we add the number of tenant farms and owner-cum-tenant-operated farms of below 5 acres size to that of farms between 5 and 7½ acres size, we arrive at a figure of 33 percent of all farms that are tenant and owner-cum-tenant farms below subsistence level. That would be an underestimate, since the figure does not include tenant farms between 7½ and 10 acres, which, too, are below subsistence level. The categorization of owner-cum-tenant farms would depend on the relative proportion of owned and tenanted areas, and the middle point between 5 and 10 acres might be appropriate in their case to define subsistence level. We conclude, therefore, that more than 58 percent of all farms in West Pakistan are below subsistence level. The total number of rural *households* below the subsistence line might be greater, not only because many farms are jointly cultivated by more than one household, but also because we must include in that category landless laborers who constituted about 11 percent of the civilian labor force in agriculture in 1961 (GOP 1964:v=28, Statement 6.15).[9]

At the other extreme, 70 percent of the farm area was owned by noncultivating landowners and owner-cultivators of large farms. Nineteen percent of the farm area was accounted for by large farms, which numbered 2.8 percent of all farms. A further 49 percent of the farm area in West Pakistan was tenant operated, of which 88 percent was cultivated by sharecroppers (GOP1963:Table 9). To estimate the number of households who control that land, we might consider data provided by the population census. The 1951 census estimated the number of noncultivating landowners in West Pakistan at less than 4 percent of all "landowners" (GOP1955:110–111, Table 15). The number of households indicated by that figure must be considerably less, since individual households have several persons enumerated by the census in that category. The 1961 population census does not show the number of noncultivating landowners. In view of the substantial reallotment of land that took place in the fifties, we cannot assume their number will have remained unchanged. But in view of the very small number of households indicated by the 1951 figure, it is unlikely that the overall order of magnitude will have changed sufficiently to alter the broad picture, namely, that about 5 percent of all the rural households in Pakistan (including "absentee" landowners) possess about 70 percent of the land.[10]

Although the rural elite *controls* 70 percent of the land, nearly half the total farm area was in the hands of sharecroppers in 1960. That pattern of land use is, however, changing rapidly due to the spread of farm mechanization. Landowners are taking over share-cropped land for mechanized "self-cultivation." Because of the progressive reduction in land available for sharecropping, the desparation of evicted sharecroppers to secure land and the additional demand from smaller landowners for rented land with which to build holdings for economical use of a tractor have resulted in an adverse change in sharecropping rates. Although in 1968 the crop was still being divided equally between landowner and sharecropper, sharing was subject to prior deductions by the landowner on a variety of counts. As a result, the effective rate of sharing had been reduced to about one-third or less for the sharecropper. The deterioration of rates affects sharecroppers of all landowners, not only those directly affected by farm mechanization. For both these reasons, the rural elite, as a result of farm mechanization, appears to be appropriating a progressively larger share of agricultural production.

Feudal and Capitalist Agriculture

We now examine the composition of the rural elite to see if it constitutes a single class or if it is differentiated into separate classes with competing or conflicting interests. The terms "feudal," "semifeudal," or "landed aristocracy" often are used rather loosely to describe an arrangement by which a small class of landowners appropriates one-half or more of the produce grown by sharecroppers. We do not propose to determine whether the term "feudal" is appropriate in this context, but will use that term limiting its connotation to the arrangement stated above. It is argued that the feudal structure is giving away to a "capitalist" structure as a result of self-cultivation of land by middle-class landowners who employ hired labor and invest in modern technology.

In popular usage, the terms "feudal landowners" or "landed aristocracy" connote very large landholdings of several hundred or thousands of acres. Burki has attempted in chapter 15 to give some precision to the term by defining the landed aristocracy thus: "Following the Land Reforms Commission, I define landed aristocracy as landlords who owned holdings of more than 500 acres each." But no reasons for this definition are offered. The Land Reforms Commission did not attempt to *define* the term. The commission merely stated its view that its proposed ceiling on land ownership would "eradicate the feudalistic elements from the existing tenure structure" (Government of West Pakistan 1959:30). The ceiling level was subject to some controversy, even among the members of the commission. A pragmatic decision was reached to place it at 36,000 produce index units, which, it was indicated, would place it at about 500 acres of the best irrigated land and about 1,000 acres of unirrigated land. But the figure was a compromise involving a variety of conflicting considerations. The validity of Burki's definition of landed aristocracy rests on the strength of his analysis. He attempted to demonstrate that the landed aristocracy are political maximizers rather than economic maximizers. In opposition to them he defines a rural middle class, the owners of 50 to 100 acres, who cultivate their land intensively and invest substantially in the new agricultural technology; they are economic maximizers. This class, he argues, has promoted the green revolution and is its main beneficiary.

In considering class formation in rural Pakistan, it would be misleading to make a sharp distinction between feudal landlords and capitalist farmers, because of the complex combination of the two modes of production. Nor in the absence of analytical criteria can we justify isolating a landed aristocracy as families who own hundreds of acres or even by some arbitrary standard such as 500 acres. Distinction between very rich and very poor farmers is not without significance, but, for a scientific analysis, such a prior distinction without specification of the relevant criteria would obscure rather than clarify the issues.

Until mechanized farming was introduced, all landowners who owned more than 20 or 25 acres employed sharecroppers. Owner-cultivators were those who had just enough land that could be cultivated by one or at most two pairs of bullocks and family labor. Conventionally, 12½ acres (half a "square") of land is taken to be the maximum area that can be cultivated by two men and a pair of bullocks. A large family might employ two pairs of bullocks, but rarely more. The feudal mode of production, therefore, is to be found not only on lands of those who own hundreds of acres but also on the lands of large numbers of landowners who own as little as 20 or 25 acres. A landholding of 25 acres might appear small, but it is five times as large as a subsistence holding for an owner-cultivator (estimated to be 5 acres). The 1960 Pakistan Census of Agriculture classifies farms above 25 acres as "large farms." Smaller landowners share with owners of very large tracts not only a privileged position in the rural economy, but also participation in the political power structure. Thus big and small landowners are different segments of a single continuum, on which they are placed according to differences in their wealth and share in political power, without any structural criterion differentiating their interests for setting them apart into separate classes.

Although in recent years there has been a tendency to resume land from tenants for self-cultivation by mechanized methods, mechanization has not created a middle class or capitalist farmers. Rather, it is the big landowners who have made the greatest progress in the direction of farm mechanization (Table 3).

Only part of the total land owned by persons who have tractors is under mechanized cultivation; land not cultivated by them is in the hands of sharecroppers who employ bullocks. However, there is a close interdependence between mechanized cultivation and sharecropping on large landholdings. It is convenient to use the term "mechanized farm sector" here in reference to the total area of land affected by mechanization as contrasted with the area cultivated by tractors.

Owners of holdings of 50 to 100 acres numbered only 27 percent of the landowners in the mechanized farm sector, and they accounted for no more than 10 percent of the cultivated area of landholdings in that sector in 1968. However, they owned 25 percent of the tractors, which suggests that the degree of mechanization, or the proportion of land cultivated by tractors, was greater.

Landlords with holdings above 100 acres owned 86.5 percent

TABLE 8. Classification of Landholdings of Tractor Owners

| | Total Acreage | | Cultivated Area per Holding | | |
Size of Holdings (acres)	Proportion of Total Acres (%)	Size of Average Holding (acres)	Proportion of Total Acres (%)	Average Holding (acres)	Cultivated Area per Tractor (acres)
500 & over	52.3	1,317	43.0	1,231	714
200–499	25.4	342	26.0	334	270
100–199	11.9	156	17.5	155	145
50–99	6.9	81	10.0	82	79
25–49	2.5	43	2.8	44	42
under 25	0.4	—	0.1	—	21

SOURCE: GOP 1969: Tables 3, 4.

of the land in the mechanized farm sector and 55 percent of the tractors. Two conclusions follow from these figures. Firstly, it is probable that middle-class landholders, as defined by Burki, who own 50 to 100 acres, probably cultivate their land more intensively; the relatively higher investment of capital in terms of the tractor/land ratio may be reflected in the case of other inputs also. Insufficient investigation has been made of farm management on different size holdings in Pakistan.[11] It would not, however, be surprising if such studies showed a greater intensity of cultivation and higher productivity on farms in that category. A second conclusion is that the bigger landlords control vastly greater resources. The total amount of land and capital controlled by middle-class landowners is not of such an order that they can be said to dominate the rural economy. Quite the contrary is true.

However, we may question the significance of drawing a distinction between these groups of landowners. We cannot accept the implication that they constitute separate classes, since their interests do not conflict. Their goals on all essential issues of public policy are identical, whether they be questions of prices of agricultural commodities, taxation of agricultural incomes, or provision of facilities and services and subsidized inputs to landowners. Similarly, they share an identical position on issues of class relationships in the rural society vis-à-vis sharecroppers and landless laborers and on questions of public policy and legislation.

There is, however, one significant difference between the effects of farm mechanization on large landholdings and on smaller holdings of less than 100 acres. The capacity of a medium-size tractor of the type in general use in Pakistan is reckoned to be "over 100 acres" (GOP 1967:10; Rafi 1967).[12] Owners of holdings below 100 acres who buy a tractor tend to evict all their tenants (sharecroppers) to resume sufficient land for mechanized farming. Because such landowners account for less than 15 percent of the mechanized farm sector, only a small proportion of sharecroppers are deprived of all their land and evicted. In the case of owners of large holdings, sharecroppers are not evicted from the land when tractors are introduced. Instead, the big landowners take away a proportion of the sharecropped land to resume sufficient land for tractor cultivation. Hence, each of the remaining sharecroppers is left with a reduced holding. Whereas before mechanization an average sharecropper's holding of eight to ten acres was just about enough to provide a bare subsistence, his reduced holding is not sufficient for that purpose. The sharecropper must find alternative ways to supplement his diminished income such as undertaking seasonal labor for the landowner. Because of the growing shortage of sharecropping land, the landowner's bargaining position with his sharecroppers is very strong, and he has a prior claim to the latter's services. The sharecroppers constitute a tied, assured, and cheap source of supplementary labor. Because of increasing labor requirements, the availability of such tied labor is of vital importance, especially for the bigger landowners who cannot find sufficient free labor to meet their large requirements. Although the eviction of sharecroppers of smaller landowners has increased the number of landless laborers, there is a shortage of labor to cope with seasonal peak requirements because of the rise in production.

The fact that big landowners keep a sufficient number of sharecroppers to meet their labor requirements explains what might be a puzzling feature of the data quoted in Table 8. The data show average holdings of 270 acres per tractor in the case of holdings of 200–499 acres, and higher in the larger category of landhold-ings. Land in excess of about 100 to 150 acres (per tractor) on such holdings is cultivated by sharecroppers. The problem of meeting labor requirements inhibits a higher degree of mechanization on very large holdings. It would be a mistake to attribute it purely to attitudinal differences between big and small landowners.

Because of the functional role of sharecropping on large mechanized farms, a question arises about the characterization of such a mode of production. For the bulk of the land affected by mechanizations, namely 86.5 percent, *both* modes of production, the feudal mode of sharecropping and the capitalist mode of mechanized cultivation by hired labor, are intertwined. Because of the labor requirement of the mechanized farming operations, the capitalist component of the enterprise is not self-sufficient and via-ble without the feudal component. The latter, on the other hand, with diminished holdings of the sharecroppers, is not viable with-out the seasonal employment offered by the capitalist component, which enables sharecroppers to stay on their diminished holdings. The feudal and the capitalist relations of production constitute a single, multiplex mode of production, which has its own complex and specific characteristics. It is tempting to describe it as transi-tional, on the assumption that, following the eventual, inevitable mechanization of harvesting and threshing operations, the big landowners' need for a supply of seasonal labor would disappear and they would no longer be held back from introducing more tractors and evicting all their sharecroppers. But one would hesi-tate to use the term transitional. Such a term is less precise than a concept of a multiplex mode of production, and the term transi-tional suggests a process of cumulative and necessary change from the one mode to another. But it is by no means certain that the present course of development will continue on a linear path and result in a fully capitalist farm economy. The consequences of a large-scale eviction of sharecroppers, with no alternative sources of livelihood in rural or urban employment, are incalculable. We can-not, therefore, rule out a critical point when change will cease to be progressive and quantitative and will set in motion a total, qualita-tive transformation.

Rural Bases of Political Power

We might consider Burki's thesis that the political power of a landed aristocracy has been displaced by a rural middle class. This is parallel with the widely believed idea put forward by the Land Reforms Commission in 1959 that its proposals would eradicate feudalistic elements in the agrarian economy, an idea that the system of Basic Democracies, introduced by President Ayub Khan, had displaced the landed aristocracy from a position of political dominance and that it had brought about a shift in the locus of political power into the hands of a rural middle class. This claim was put forward by the Ayub regime for the new political system it introduced. We find, however, that the predominance of the big landowners in the agrarian economy has by no means ended, nor has that occurred in the political arena. What was altered by the system of Basic Democracies, now defunct, was not a shift in the locus of power, but rather a change in the mode of articulation of power at the village level into the national political system. To understand the significance of the change, we examine the way in which power has been articulated between the local and the national levels to determine who wields power in the rural society and how the demands of the rural elite are transmitted to the national political system.

At the village level, economic power is a major factor in the establishment of political leadership positions. Burki's suggestion that "landlords in the pre-Ayub era were able to control at least twenty Punjabi villages" is a reference to the exceptional case rather than the rule. Few villages were (or are) owned by a single family. In the typical village of about 1,200 acres,[13] there are usually a few big landowners (some of whom may own more land in adjoining *mauzas* or villages), plus a large number of small peasant proprietors, as well as members of other classes. Given such a rural population, it would be simplistic to explain political power in the rural society merely by references to exceptional cases of landlords who own whole villages. That would leave unexplained political power in the vast majority of villages. Political power in such mixed villages is typically organized by factions. The faction leader, typically a big landowner, organizes support by a variety of means. Such landowners rely on a core of supporters, namely their economically dependent sharecroppers, who have little option but to follow their master. The core of the faction would probably include their close relatives, who might also be big landlords in the neighborhood having their own economic dependents. The faction leader enters into alliances with fellow landlords, who bring their economic dependents. Economic power, by that token, is the aggregated power of members of a landowning class in close alliance with each other, rather than the power of a single individual or a family. Because economic dependents are tied to landlords in factional politics as they are tied to them in the economic field, political cleavages are not horizontal *along* class lines but vertical *across* class lines. The transformation of the factional mode of politics into class politics is just beginning to manifest itself; instances of it are few so far.

With the power of his core behind him, the faction leader sets out to recruit a following from among other sections of the rural society, principally the independent, small, peasant proprietors. Individually, the latter are weak, but often they are organized under the authority of their *biraderi panchayat* (lineage council) (Alavi 1972). Action leaders enter into alliances with *biraderi's*, for which they use a variety of means of persuasion. A powerful factor is the ability of a faction leader to bestow favors and patronage. For this, the faction leader's relationship with the administration and his access to official favors is of special importance. Another way to secure support is by threat or coercion. Big landowners who have influence at high levels are protectors (*rassagirs*) of small bandits (*goondas*) through whom they operate (Alavi 1971).

Rival local factions are integrated with similar factions in other villages and form larger factions at successively higher levels. Leaders of local factions participate in the dealings of the higher level factions. Individuals and political parties with ambitions in district, provincial, or national politics, seek grass-roots support with the local faction leaders. Participation of faction leaders in party political competition institutionalizes alliances of factions into political parties. Because, structurally, rival factions replicate each other in their class composition, factional conflict is not class conflict. However, because factions are based on the power of the landowning class at all levels of their organization, all factions stand for common goals of social and economic policy that embody the interests of the rural elite. At the level of national policy-making, it is such a leadership that participates in legislative institutions, and the members of the landowning class proliferate in the bureaucratic establishment. This pattern of political alignment is subject to pressures generated by the green revolution because of disaffection of various strata of the rural population whose interests are not articulated through the existing political structure. But such disaffected groups are not the rural middle class, who are well entrenched in the existing factional structure, in alliance with rather than in opposition to big landlords. The disgruntled groups, rather, are the very small, peasant landholders and sharecroppers who are deprived of their livelihood as a result of the green revolution. This is a compressed outline of a complex pattern of organization of political power in the rural areas of Pakistan. But it is essential to grasp this pattern in order to go beyond a simplified picture of the local basis of the political and economic power of big landowners.

Under British colonial rule, articulation of power between the village and the colonial regime was achieved by appointment of locally powerful men to the hereditary office of *lambardar*. Similarly, appointments were made to higher offices such as *zaildar*. The *lambardar* held a crucial position in the system. Formally, his function was to collect land revenue for which he was allowed to retain a commission called *pachotra*. But that was the least important of his functions. He was not a servant of the state, but the holder of a quasi-political office. He represented the village before the administration and the administration before the village. To be effective, it was essential that he be a powerholder in the village. The appointment was, therefore, always from the leading landlord family of the village, or the head of a *biraderi* (lineage) of peasant proprietors where such a *biraderi* was large. By virtue of his role as a mediator between the people of the village and the administration, the *lambardar* was in a position to bestow favors and patronage, which further reinforced his power. Because the power at the village was assimilated into the political system of the colonial regime, through the administration, the *lambardari* system consolidated the power of the administration against political challenge, especially, as posed by national politicians.

With the progressive devolution of power and induction of political leaders into office, following the Government of India Act, 1919, political parties attracted local factional leaders, who established ties with aspiring leaders. With politicians installed in office, a new channel of articulation of power between local and national levels was established. Because the articulation of power was no longer exclusively through administrative channels, a certain tension existed between the political leadership and the administrative hierarchy. The dominance of a bureaucratic-military oligarchy in the Pakistani political system and challenges from political leadership have punctuated the political history of Pakistan with a series of crises.

The main significance of the system of Basic Democracies introduced by President Ayub Khan must be seen in light of the tension between the bureaucratic-military oligarchy and the political leadership. Its effect was to restore the mode of articulation of power that existed under the new colonial regime, namely, through the administration. However, the new system was different in important ways insofar as it did not rely on nominated and hereditary officeholders, the *lambardars*, who did not always hold de facto power locally. Instead, by introducing the elective principle at the local level, a relationship was established with those who demonstrably held local power. In the capacity of chairmen of union councils, the local powerholders were brought into a regular and institutionalized relationship with the administration by their ex-officio membership in the *tehsil* councils, which were presided over by *tehsildars* or subdivisional magistrates. When political parties were reestablished, great political skill was demonstrated by an effective deployment of influence through administrative channels in a manner that rival factions were accommodated and members of one faction were prevented from dislodging all the members of a rival faction. Thus the local powerholders could not be enticed away by opposition politicians, whose strength in the past had depended on their ability to recruit and to hold the allegiance of local factional leaders. One aspect of the struggle for democracy in Pakistan was the disaffection of political leaders who were isolated from the bases of their power. But, by that token, we cannot infer that it was the landed aristocracy that was dislodged from power. That class was represented at every level in the structure of power of the new regime, symbolized best by the nawab of Kalabagh, the powerful governor of Pakistan.

Indirect Effects of the Green Revolution

Finally there is one further aspect of the green revolution that merits attention, for it poses some central issues of policy. That aspect is the indirect consequences that follow from the changes in rural incomes. The gross provincial product from agriculture in West Pakistan almost doubled in the decade of the sixties. But the unequal distribution of the income from agriculture has brought about a manifold increase in the incomes of the rural elite, mainly in the Canal Colony Districts and the Rich Old Settled Districts of the Punjab and in Sind. On the other hand, the incomes of small farmers in these districts and, especially, of farmers in other poorer regions have failed to improve or have not improved in the same measure. The indirect consequences of the green revolution for the latter follow from the impact of the additional purchasing power in the hands of the former on the demand for and the prices of manufactured consumer goods. The main thrust of inflationary pressure derives primarily from the greatly increased incomes of the rural elite, for the weight of agricultural incomes in the total national incomes accounts is very large. In 1967/68 it was 42 percent of the gross provincial product in West Pakistan as compared with incomes from manufacturing, which were only 16 percent of the total.

The great increase in the incomes and consequently the expenditures of the rural elite have tended to make heavy demands on the available flow of domestic manufactured goods and imports. Economists who emphasize adverse changes in terms of trade for agriculture in relation to industry, to suggest a worsening plight of farmers in general, focus narrowly on *price effects* and do not take into account *income effects* in the economy and the implications of changes in income distribution for the different sections of both the rural and urban societies. Despite the adverse changes in the terms of trade, the rural elite enjoy considerably enhanced real incomes, as indeed do the urban entrepreneurs whose profits multiply as a consequence. But other sections of the community, both urban and rural, have suffered as a consequence of the inflation in prices due partly to the changed rural income distribution.

The additional income that has passed into the hands of the rural elite has not only increased the total of consumption expenditure, it has also been accompanied by a structural change in the pattern of the consumption expenditure. The demand for manufactured consumer goods has expanded at a relatively faster rate, and, because of the multiplication of the incomes of those who were already well to do, the overall increase in consumption expenditure has been accompanied by a relatively greater expansion in the demand for luxury goods, particularly those which are imported or which have a high import content. This "Engel's Effect" can be readily observed in West Pakistan villages and is attested to by traders who have prospered in this boom. This change appears to have contributed not only to the inflation of the prices of consumer goods in general, but also, in particular, to the pressure on foreign exchange because of the higher import content of the additional consumption expenditure. Even in the case of investment in the farms, the preference for mechanization has added to greater pressure on foreign exchange resources.

An example of these secondary effects is that the incidence of agricultural taxation and subsidies has served to accentuate disparities between different strata of farmers and different regions. This is because land revenue is levied on the basis of a flat rate per acre and is borne equally by all classes of farmers, whereas the benefits from agricultural subsidies are distributed in proportion to the use of the subsidized inputs. The rich farmers who have prospered most have also had the lion's share of the subsidies. Land revenue rates do vary from district to district. But that variation does not reflect any rational basis for the differentiation; it is only the accidental result of history. The rates originally were established at different times in different districts, on the basis of productivity of the land in the respective areas. The result is little uniformity, and many decades have passed since the current rates were established. Land revenue rates were to be raised slightly in 1962 on an ad hoc basis, and some token changes were made in a few districts.

Intended changes in some other districts were not implemented. The Land revenue rates in the 1960s varied from Rs. 9.13 per acre in Lyallpur District to Rs. 1.04 per acre in Hazara District, inclusive of cesses on land revenue. The overall effect of land revenue on agricultural incomes has been negligible, for it amounted to no more than Rs. 182 million as compared with the gross provincial product from agriculture in West Pakistan in 1968/69 or Rs. 14,797 million, that is, about 1.2 percent. The rural elite has, however, fairly successfully resisted proposals to tax agricultural incomes, to reduce subsidies, or to lower the high support prices for certain agricultural commodities.

To conclude, a small rural elite, less than 5 percent of the rural population of Pakistan, controls an overwhelming proportion of the land. It has profited most from the green revolution. Within the rural elite, the biggest landowners continue to maintain a dominant position in the control of economic resources, as well as of political power. There is little evidence to support a view that there are any essential conflicts of interest or structural differences that might justify categorizing sections of the rural elite into separate classes. As a whole, they have successfully defended their interests by their influence on public policy. The present course of the green revolution, however, appears to have brought about a deterioration in the conditions of life of a majority of the population, and further progress of farm mechanization is creating a situation in which a very large number of the rural population will be faced with the prospects of having no viable means of livelihood. Far from having established a new political equilibrium, the green revolution has set in motion a dynamic that makes the existing position untenable.

Hamza Ali Alavi is a member of the Department of Politics, University of Leeds, England. He was born in Karachi and received his M.A. in Economics from Muslim University, Aligarth, India, in 1944. His activities have included being a principal officer of the State Bank of Pakistan, founding and editing *Pakistan Today* and serving as a research officer at the Institute of Development Studies, University of Sussex, Brighton, England. His writings include numerous professional publications.

NOTES

This paper is part of a study of rural social structure and economic development in Pakistan undertaken by the author at the Institute of Development Studies at the University of Sussex, under a grant from the United Kingdom S.S.R.C.

1. Sir Arthur Gaitskell, in a foreword to Nulty (1972), writes: "This . . . would certainly appear to be one of the greatest agricultural advances in history, and it has been argued that West Pakistan would thereby be a prototype for other countries to follow." He was referring to discussions of the green revolution and the strategy of agricultural development in West Pakistan (Kaneda, 1969).

2. Kaneda (1969:112) writes: "The opportunities created by the 'Green Revolution' present some challenging economic issues besides the mechanization question. A rapid increase in agricultural output and the consequent increase in the marketable surplus of agricultural products are expected to overwhelm the processing, warehousing, distribution and marketing systems that exist today. . . .Now that agriculture has experienced a rapid increase in productivity it must face an increasingly difficult problem of expanding effective demand to match the growth of supply."

3. These remarks are based on personal observations during a year (1968) spent in Punjabi villages for research fieldwork.

4. The initial impetus came from the implementation of the "Rasul Tubewell Scheme," which was originally suggested by W. H. Nicholson in 1927. It was not until 1954 that implementation of the scheme got under way. Firms that were engaged in the installation of the tubewells, and acquired equipment and expertise for the task, promoted the subsequent development by persuading landowners to install tubewells. For details of the Rasul Tubewell Scheme, see Michel (1967).

5. Data taken from Bose (1969). He quotes data from the Water and Power Development Authority (1964) and International Bank for Reconstruction and Development (n.d.). The output of tubewells in 1968 was estimated by the author to be 2½ times that in 1965.

6. The number of private tubewells increased by 45,090 between the end of 1964 and the time of the survey in 1968, reaching a total of 75,720.

7. A dossier about the scheme was examined by the author during a visit to the institute in 1968.

8. A senior official of the Pakistan Planning Commission, for example, expressed such a view (Aziz 1970).

9. The figure has been adjusted for the fact that, unlike the 1951 census, the 1961 census classifies women under the category of "Unpaid Family Help."

10. This conclusion is based on the assumption that virtually all land

operated by tenants belongs either to noncultivating landowners or to owner-cultivators who operate farms of more than twenty-five acres.

11. The Ministry of Agriculture, Government of Pakistan, issues a regular series of studies entitled Farm Management Studies for various districts. But those studies are of little value for the purpose that we have indicated here.

12. Because farmers, in practice, tend to undertake fewer operations than those on which the above calculations are based and also because they tend to employ tillers instead of plows, the medium-size tractors are often used to cultivate as much as 150 cropped acres.

13. Burki greatly underestimates the size of villages in the Punjab, which he places at 600 acres. Typically villages are two or three times that size. We find that the average *farm area* per village in certain districts for which data are readily available is as follows: Sargodha District, 2,100 acres; Shekhupura District, 1,000 acres. In addition to the farm area, the village area would include other categories of land for which we do not have the data. In the densely populated Old Settled Districts, the average farm area is a little less. The biggest landholdings, of the kind that Burki has discussed, are, however, to be found in the Canal Colony Districts such as Sargodha, Multan, and Jhang. (Source: GOP 1963 for farm area, and GOP [n.d.] for the number of villages in the respective districts).

BIBLIOGRAPHY

Alavi, Hamza
> 1968. "The Structure of the Agrarian Economy of West Pakistan and Development Strategy." *Pakistan Administrative Staff College Quarterly*: 57–76.
> 1971. "Politics of Dependence—A Village in West Punjab." *South Asian Review* (2): 111–128.
> 1972. "Kinship in West Punjab Villages." *Contributions to Indian Sociology* 6 (n.s.): 1–27.

Aziz, Sartij
> 1970. "Problems and Prospects of the Green Revolution." *Pakistan Economist*, vol. 9.

Bose, S. R.
> 1969. "East-West Contrast in Pakistan's Agricultural Development." Paper presented at the International Economic Association Conference on Economic Development in South Asia at Kandy, Ceylon. Mimeographed.

Elahi, Maryam K.
> 1963. "Agricultural Land Use in West Pakistan." *Pakistan Geographical Review* 18: 25–67.

1965. "Efficiency of Agriculture in West Pakistan." *Pakistan Geographical Review* 20: 77–116.

Gaitskell, Sir Arthur
1972. Foreword to *The Green Revolution in West Pakistan*, by Leslie Nulty. New York: Praeger Publishers.

Gotsch, Carl
1968. "Regional Agricultural Growth—The Case of Pakistan." *Asian Survey* 8: 188–205.

Government of Pakistan (GOP)
n.d.   "District Census Reports."
1955. *Census of Pakistan 1951*. Vol. 1. Karachi: Civil and Military Press.
1960. *Report of the Food and Agriculture Commission*. Karachi: Ministry of Food and Agriculture, Government of Pakistan.
1961. "Census Bulletin No. 4." Population Census of Pakistan, Pakistan Office of Census Commissioner. Karachi: Educational Press of Pakistan.
1963. *Census of Agriculture 1960*. Vol. 2. West Pakistan. Parts 2 and 3 published in 1964. Karachi: Agricultural Census Organization, Government of Pakistan.
1964. *The Census of Pakistan—Population, 1961*. Vol. 1. Pakistan Office of Census Commissioner. Karachi: Educational Press of Pakistan.
1965. *The Third Five Year Plan 1965–70*. Karachi: Planning Commission, Government of Pakistan.
1967. *Report on the Tractor Survey in West Pakistan 1967*. Karachi: Planning Commission.
1968. *20 Years of Pakistan in Statistics 1947–67*. Karachi: Central Statistical Office, Government of Pakistan.
1969. *A Report on the Farm Mechanization Survey 1968*. Lahore: Agricultural Census Organization, Government of Pakistan.

Government of West Pakistan
n.d.   *Yearbook of Agricultural Statistics for 1964/65*. Lahore.
1959. *Report of the Land Reforms Commission for West Pakistan*. Lahore.
1968. *Year Book of Agricultural Statistics for 1967/68*. Lahore.
1969. *Land Reforms in West Pakistan*. Vol. 3. Lahore.

International Bank for Reconstruction and Development
n.d.   "Program for the Development of Irrigation and Agriculture in West Pakistan." Vol. 5, annex 7, "Water Supply and Distribution." Washington, D.C.: International Land Development Consultants.

Kaneda, Hiromitsu
  1969. "Economic Implications of the 'Green Revolution' and the Strategy of Agricultural Development in West Pakistan." *The Pakistan Development Review* 9: 111–143.
Khan, M. Ayub
  1967. *Friends Not Masters*. London: Oxford University Press.
Michel, Aloys A.
  1967. *Indus Rivers: A Study of the Effects of Partition*. New Haven: Yale University Press.
Mohammad, Ghulam
  1964. "Some Strategic Problems in Agricultural Development in Pakistan." *Pakistan Development Review* 4: 223–260.
  1965. "Private Tubewell Development and Cropping Patterns in West Pakistan." *Pakistan Development Review* 5: 1–53.
Nulty, Leslie
  1972. *The Green Revolution in West Pakistan*. New York: Praeger Publishers.
Pakistan Institute of Development Economics
  n.d. "Statistical Series of Private Tubewell Development in West Pakistan."
Rafi, M.
  1967. "What are the Basic Farm Machinery Requirements of West Pakistan Farms." In *Report of the First Farm Machinery Conference and Exhibition*. Lahore: Government of West Pakistan.
Water and Power Development Authority (WAPDA)
  1964. "Program for Water and Power Development in West Pakistan through 1975." Lahore: Harza Engineering Company.

17

The Green Revolution
and Future Developments
of Pakistan's Agriculture

Carl H. Gotsch

Introduction

Growth in Pakistan's agricultural sector continues to be a bright spot in an otherwise confused and uncertain development picture. Despite considerable fluctuation— understandable in a decade that has witnessed war, unprecedented drought, and in recent years a high degree of political instability—increases in the gross value of the major crops have continued to be on or around the trend rate for the last decade, about 6 percent per annum. Also, judging from the increased acreage under fodder, the past rate of increase in livestock products of 3.5 to 4.0 per annum is being maintained.[1] This latter point is significant both for what it says about the aggregate growth rate in the agricultural sector, as livestock products make up about one-third of the total value added in agriculture, and for what it implies about the improvement in the nutritional value of West Pakistani diets.

Statistics on the use of modern inputs are also impressive. The rate of annual growth in fertilizer offtake has slowed as one would expect, but the incremental sales have continued to be above fifty thousand tons per year. Although for various reasons, the public tubewell program has lagged, the number of private tubewells in operation far exceeds all but the most optimistic projections made in the mid-sixties.[2] By mid-1971 high-yielding varieties of wheat were being used on nearly 90 percent of the land sown to wheat, and it is anticipated that within the next several years the entire rice acreage will also be under varieties with significantly improved genetic potential. Even pesticides—an input that is more difficult and complicated to use—are being applied each year to a significantly larger portion of the land under crops.

Despite the evidence that a naïve projection of the momentum generated during the past few years is the best forecast for the immediate future, there is a growing uneasiness among knowledgeable people about the long-run implications of the growth process that is so obviously underway.[3] The sources of concern are several. First, there is the question of the ability to sustain the demand for increased agricultural output, especially for wheat and rice. This has not been the immediate problem that projections based on the experience of the harvest of 1967/68 suggested it might be. In addition to less favorable weather conditions, the offtake during the past several years has increased somewhat above expectations largely as a result of the continuing food deficit in the east wing. Moreover, the substantial increase in 1971 in the price of cotton—which competes for land with both wheat and rice—can be expected to hold down the acreage committed to these two crops. Nevertheless, the current situation should probably be viewed as a breathing spell.

Secondly, concern over the distributive effects of growth in the agricultural sector is becoming more widespread. The evidence regarding regional disparity is mixed when measured at the provincial level (Table 1). District data indicate that regional aggregates do not really tell the tale, as other data indicate that variation in growth rates is much greater within provinces than between. For example, the dryland areas of the Punjab continue to fall further behind the central or mixed-farming areas. Likewise, the newly colonized areas of the Sind are barely managing to sustain a subsistence economy, let alone keep up with the rapidly increasing incomes in the Khaiput and Rohri areas.[4]

Even more disturbing are the implications of technical change for the social and economic structure of rural society. For example, there have been widespread reports of tenant evictions as medium and large farmers sought to resume their lands for personal cultivation. In part, this is a result of the profitability of a combination of

TABLE 1. Growth in the Production of Crops, by Region, 1960–1970

	Annual Growth Rate (%)		Regional Percentage of Total Crop Value	
	1960–65	1965–70	1964–65	1969–70
Baluchistan	6.2	8.9	0.8	0.9
NWFP	3.9	1.9	8.3	6.5
Punjab	6.2	8.8	69.8	70.4
Sind	4.9	7.7	21.1	22.2
TOTAL			100.0	100.0

SOURCE: Government of Pakistan 1972.
NOTES: Figures are based on the gross value of major crops.
NWFP is North West Frontier Province.

high-yielding grain varieties, water, mechanization, and good farm management. Without question, however, it also reflects a response to the growing militancy of the tenant class.

As for the small owners, recent research suggests that, for the most part, they have participated in only the simplest manifestations of the green revolution. For example, most farmers, regardless of size, now use improved seeds and at least some nitrogen fertilizer. Many, however, do not know what the optimal input combinations are, or do not have access to the resources to take full advantage of input complementarity. Perhaps of greatest importance for small farmers is the lack of a really widespread, competitive market for supplementary water. The majority of the small farmers also have little knowledge or access to the next round of improvements, such as mixed fertilizers and the plant protection measures that have shown themselves to be so profitable when applied to cotton, oilseeds, corn, and rice. It does not take long for productivity differentials to be capitalized into perceived differences in land purchase or rental values—differences that can form the basis for land agglomeration even before the introduction of equipment possessing significant economies of scale.

The following pages explain at greater length the issues raised above. The first part will be concerned with adding greater detail and interpretation to the previously cited growth statistics. In particular, recent performance will be contrasted with that described in an earlier paper by Falcon and Gotsch (1969). In the second section, I shall develop a conceptual framework to speculate about the future. Considering the present uncertainty regarding the direction of the political processes in the country, this is not an inappropriate characterization of the analysis, for while one may have some confidence in statements about the future where international demand based on comparative advantage is concerned, the distributive aspects of growth are intimately linked with the outcome of current political struggles and therefore scenarios involving structural change are highly dependent on them.

The Green Revolution in Pakistan

The scope of this paper does not permit an exhaustive examination of the recent performance of the agricultural sector in Pakistan. My observations are therefore selective and confined to those elements of the present scene that appear to have the greatest relevance for future developments.

Sources of Growth

The data on the growth of crop production in the last decade show that calculations can be quite sensitive to the periods and end points chosen, especially for small samples. It is well to examine these matters carefully. Details of the provincial and commodity rates of growth are given in the Appendix.

First, it would be quite inappropriate to date the green revolution in West Pakistan from the mid-sixties and attempt to measure its impact from that time on (Figure 1). It is clear that the two drought years 1965/66 and 1966/67 are significantly below the trend for the decade; indeed, the radical increase in output in 1967/68 (particularly of wheat) would perhaps be better seen as a year of recovery than as a year of revolution. However, if one were to compare, say, 1959/60 with 1964/65 and the latter year with 1969/70, one would conclude that a significant break in the data had occurred that could properly be pointed to as a fundamental discon-

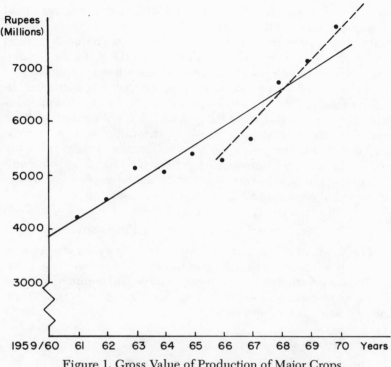

Figure 1. Gross Value of Production of Major Crops.

tinuity in the growth picture. As will be discussed later, there may be grounds for such a view, but it does not emerge from any simple before and after comparison of the figures on the value of aggregate output.

Secondly, it is instructive to examine the crop composition of the increase in output, which has not been proportional over the last decade (Figure 2). In the early and middle sixties, for example, the leading edge of growth appears to have been sugarcane. The average index of increased output for cane in 1964/65–1965/66 stood at 154 (1959/60 = 100); while, for the same period, rice stood at 148, wheat at 116, cotton at 140, and all other crops at 112. Then came the year of Mexipak (1967/68) when both the acreage and the

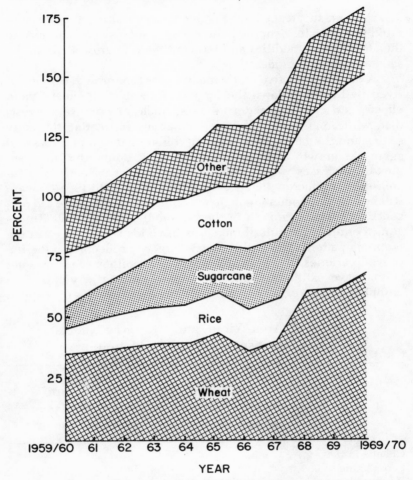

Figure 2. Index of Gross Value of Production of Major Crops
in West Pakistan (1959/60 Prices).

yield of wheat jumped radically. The index of wheat production in
that year rose to 170, largely at the expense of sugarcane. In the
most recent past, increases in wheat output have slowed somewhat,

and rice and sugarcane have regained their position as crops with rapid growth rates. Cotton alone has remained somewhat outside the affected commodities and has continued to grow at about the same rate in all periods.

A third perspective on the nature of recent growth can be derived by breaking down the increase into acreage effects, yield effects, and cropping-pattern effects. Such an exercise suggests that, while one may have little confidence in treating the early sixties and the late sixties as being differentiable on the basis of aggregate growth statistics, there is little doubt that different growth processes were at work (Table 2). For example, the increases in production that occurred from 1959/60 to 1964/65 were still heavily dependent upon increases in cropped acreage (35 percent). In contrast, growth in the period 1964/65 to 1969/70 was almost entirely a result of increases in yields and changes in the cropping pattern. The yield effect is largely a reflection of the improved varieties of wheat and rice, since neither sugarcane nor cotton have exhibited significant improvements in yields. The cropping-pattern effect is interesting because it shows once again

TABLE 2. Area, Yield, and Cropping Effects of Increases in Crop Production

	Change 1960 to 1965		Change 1965 to 1970	
	Rs. (000)	%	Rs. (000)	%
Change in the Gross Value of Production	1,319	100	2,363	100
Area Effect	459	35	157	7
Yield Effect	705	53	1,753	74
Cropping Effect	108	8	465	20
Interaction	47	4	−12	−1

NOTE: Another example of this "budget" approach can be found in Falcon and Gotsch (1969).

that West Pakistani farmers were quick to make shifts in their enterprise combinations when the potential for higher returns to their farming activities showed itself.

Growth and Distribution

The distributive aspects of growth, as expected, are much more difficult to assess than the magnitude of the increase in inputs and production. However, by taking as a point of reference the size distribution of land and relating various aspects of the new technology to holding size, a good deal of evidence exists that supports the intuitive conclusion that income disparity is increasing. This is not to deny, of course, that nearly everyone engaged in agriculture is currently absolutely better off, with the probable exception of evicted tenants. The absence of severe price effects from increased output has meant that greater production has been accompanied by increased revenues to producers. Moreover, though there is as yet only meager evidence to support the argument, the increases in labor demand that have resulted from tubewell-related increases in cropping intensity and from seed/fertilizer related increases in yield are surely greater than the increase in supplies resulting from the still rather limited effects of tractorization. Thus the welfare of full- or part-time farm laborers has probably also improved in an absolute sense.

It is the *relative* position of a number of groups in the agricultural sector that has declined. Though in the short run this may seem to be a minor matter, in the long run it is important, for relative incomes provide much of the momentum for the sectoral transformation of society.

The experience of developed and less-developed countries alike is that decisions to migrate and sell out are based on a comparison of opportunities. People leave an occupation or an area not because they have been unable to improve their circumstances at all, but because they have not improved relative to their expectations of the possibilities that are apparent elsewhere. Indeed, such mobility is an asset and is desirable in a society, *provided* that the social costs are not too high. Major costs include providing the necessary additions to the services in the cities and the social and political costs of crowding together of large numbers of people newly alienated from the land. Given the likely growth of industrial investment and jobs in the large cities of West Pakistan, it seems unlikely that these costs can easily be mitigated, a point to which I shall return in the final section.

The increasing disparity in incomes has both regional and class dimensions. The regional dimension is highlighted by district data, which indicate that some areas, notably those with relatively assured water supplies, have been growing more rapidly than others. This comes as no surprise as farm management studies throughout South and Southeast Asia show clearly that the green revolution, with its accent on high levels of plant nutrients, has been successful primarily where moisture levels are also high relative to plant requirements. This does not, of course, necessarily imply irrigation. As Rochin's chapter on Hazara District shows, when the dwarf wheats are introduced into a dryland area whose mean rainfall is 30 to 40 inches with good seasonal distribution, significant yield improvements can be obtained. But these are somewhat unusual conditions for the *barani* lands of Pakistan. Much of the dryland wheat acreage that could potentially be put under improved varieties cannot be expected to respond as dramatically because moisture conditions are poorer.

A similar picture is presented by another traditionally backward area of Pakistan, the Sind. The new rice varieties have shown themselves to be unusually adapted to the dry, sunny climate of the area. Although there appears little possibility of crop diversification as in the North-West Frontier Province, farm incomes can be expected to improve significantly in areas where soil salinity is not too great and ample water supplies exist. Not all parts of the Sind are suitably endowed. In the southernmost parts, particularly in the canal commands under the Ghulam Mohammad Barrage, the quality of the soil and water is such that cultivators are lucky to maintain themselves and their animals from one year to the next.

The real beneficiaries of the fruits of technical change have been the farmers located in the areas of the Central Punjab underlain by usable groundwater. Not only have they been able to take advantage of the increased productivity associated with the seed-fertilizer revolution, but access to supplementary irrigation water via tubewells has made it possible to alter cropping patterns in the direction of higher-valued crops.

It would be worth pursuing the implications of the observed regional growth patterns for the overall development process. However, at this point I would merely note that many of the districts that have shown the slowest growth, that is, made least use of the green revolution technology, are also those in which average holding sizes are small. In terms of country-wide Lorenz curves, therefore, it means that a large number of small farmers will be weighed in with traditional incomes simply on the basis of their regional location.

The second major dimension of the increasing disparity of incomes involves the apportionment of income between various classes of farmers. A number of empirical studies done during the past several years make it possible to offer at least some tentative conclusions about the impact of technology to date on different classes of farmers.[5]

1. There is little or no difference in the percentage of farmers in different size categories with respect to the adoption of improved seeds and fertilizer. Where data on the *rate* of, or speed of, adoption is available, it appears that there is a slight lag in the subsistence-farmer category but it is not striking.

2. Of greater concern is the evidence in several of the studies that the *level* of application of fertilizer per acre was considerably lower among subsistence farmers than among those who would fall into a surplus category.

3. Where the question was asked. respondents in the small-farmer category were unanimous regarding the difficulties involved in securing supplementary irrigation water.

4. Few of the smaller farmers had applied or even knew anything very concrete about pesticides.

The overall conclusion to be drawn from these surveys and other empirical materials is that the distributive effects of such simple divisible technology as an improved variety will be minor. The effects of somewhat more complicated innovations, such as fertilizer, are currently not due to a lag in adoption but rather in the *level* of use. Thus, it may take appreciable time for the more complicated but still divisible technology, such as pesticides, to filter down. When the technology involves considerable lumpiness as in the case of tractors and tubewells, the adoption rate takes on an additional dimension with which small farmers have difficulty coping. The problems associated with buying water mentioned by most respondents is a case in point.

An Anatomy of the Green Revolution

From the foregoing observations, the following scenario is a plausible reconstruction of agricultural growth during the decade of the sixties.

1. The beginning can be dated somewhere around the turn of the decade. Undoubtedly aided by several good weather years, this period nevertheless marks the use of discernible quantities of fertilizer and the spread of privately installed tubewells. An important growth element was increased acreage under crops and increases in sugarcane, a crop with high water and fertility requirements, which benefited most from these inputs and became the cutting edge of the increased output.[6]

The distributive effect of this period was overwhelmingly in favor of the larger farmers since (a) tubewells are "lumpy" inputs requiring significant capital investments, (b) the percentage of cash crops on large farms unconstrained by subsistence requirements is much larger, and (c) fertilizer stocks were short and adequate supplies required the use of influence and bribery.

2. This initial agricultural growth impetus was interrupted by two drought years, 1965/66 and 1966/67. Although these years saw a significant decrease in output as a result of weather, the impact on the use of inputs was less severe. Indeed, there is undoubtedly a good deal of truth in the argument that the prolonged drought stimulated the installation of tubewells as nothing else could have.

3. The year 1967/68 was the year of Mexipak. The government launched an all-out campaign, sometimes bordering on coercion, to diffuse the Mexican seeds as widely as possible. Good weather, a record off-take of fertilizer, and the water from some 60,000 tubewells boosted wheat output from an average of 3.8 million tons obtained during the first part of the decade to 6.3 million tons, an

increase of 65 percent. Although certain other crops, notably sugarcane, suffered in the process, the net result was a recovery from the slump caused by the drought, plus an increment that reestablished the upward trend in agricultural production begun in the earlier period.

4. The most recent period has witnessed the resurgence of rice, sugarcane, and cotton as the leading growth crops. Due to domestic overvaluation (200 percent above world prices), sugarcane has a comparative advantage over all other crops when supplementary water supplies are available. Growth therefore continues to be the response to a disequilibrium condition that began with the introduction of tubewells. Because of the lack of improved sugarcane technology, it continues to be associated with large increases in sugarcane acreage.

The output of rice has also increased rapidly, particularly in the province of Sind. However, unlike sugarcane, its comparative advantage has been tremendously enhanced by rising productivity. Yields in the past two years have increased by 44 percent over their 1967/68 level.

The increased acreage under wheat, rice, and cotton has come mainly at the expense of other crops. Acreage devoted to oilseeds, gram, jowar, bajra, and so forth, has declined significantly from its 1959/60 level. In general, this reflects a movement away from a risk-oriented, subsistence agriculture toward a higher degree of specialization and commercialization.

The distributive effect during the latter part of the decade tended to be somewhat less in favor of the large farmers simply because they had already adopted many of the improved practices. Small farmers improved their position relatively by "catching up" to what had gone on before.

Future Developments in Pakistani Agriculture

The previous section consisted of some material on the events and statistics of the past few years. Speculation about the future, however, requires that these observed trends be pursued in somewhat greater detail. Such an effort need not involve a model in any formal sense, but there must be some clearly articulated set of questions that probe more deeply into those underlying forces that have shaped the past and will continue to shape the future.

An Outline of the Rural System

In the following paragraphs, a set of four factors is posed whose total is an outline of the *rural system*. Each of the subelements is itself worthy of study; maximum use of the data, however, will require particular attention to the dynamic relationships between them.

The nature of the current and potential agricultural technology. This issue has two basic facets. First, there is the question of technical divisibility. For example, as indicated earlier, seeds and fertilizer are highly divisible, and can in principle be used with equal effectiveness on any size of holding. Tubewells and tractors, on the other hand, are not and will thus exhibit significant economies of scale. Second, it is important to know something about the extent to which the technology embodies a substitution of capital for labor. Historically, lumpy capital inputs that have been profitable only on large farms have also tended to make labor redundant. But an excellent counterexample is the tubewell, which requires both a significant capital investment and yet drastically increases the demand for labor. Indeed, even the tractor, in the use of which the timely application of additional power makes a significant increase in cropping intensity possible, may add to labor requirements. The lesson is obvious; no prognosis of the future structure of agriculture can proceed that is not thoroughly grounded in a detailed analysis of technical production relationships.

With respect to the question of economies of scale, recent farm-management studies in West Pakistan suggest that the optimal size of a farm (1) located in an irrigated area of the Punjab, (2) possessing a single pair of bullocks for power, and (3) using *improved seeds and fertilizer* would lie in the fifteen- to eighteen-acre range. This is somewhat higher than conventional wisdom has indicated and is made possible by slight shifts in the normal cropping pattern to permit bullocks to be used more intensively.

With respect to tubewell water, economic analyses of model

farms, corroborated by field surveys, indicate that the full utilization of a 1-cusec tubewell requires between 60 and 100 acres, depending on the area, the crops grown, and the availability of surface water. Farmers installing tubewells on less land must either sell part of their water or accept higher costs of water per acre. This does not imply, of course, that wells on holdings of even 25 acres are not profitable. But the margin is much less than on the larger holdings. Where possibilities for selling water exist, investments in excess of home farm capacity may actually be turned into a substantial return on capital. Indeed, in some parts of the northern rice tract—Gujranwala and Sialkat—a number of wells have been sunk by townspeople owning no land at all.

To date, the wells that have been sunk in the private sector are virtually all of the 1-cusec, centrifugal-pump type. By being lowered into the ground ten to fifteen feet, they are capable of fairly efficient deliveries where the water table is at a depth of twenty-five to thirty-five feet. However, as the water level declines, as it surely will during the next decade, the type of technology needed to supply supplementary water will be altered significantly. Instead of relying on shallow centrifugal wells, it will be necessary to install deep turbine pumps at a cost of five to ten times that of existing installations. Also to capitalize on the economies of these higher-cost pumps, the capacity of the tubewell will almost surely be larger than the current 1-cusec size.

It is impossible to go into further detail regarding alternatives involved in the choice of water-producing technology as the water table declines. Suffice it to say that if the decision is left completely with farmers in areas where no program for the public installation of tubewells exists, the lumpiness of this technology is likely to have extremely adverse distributive consequences. In an arid area such as West Pakistan, water, not land, is the scarce resource, and control over it will be instrumental in determining the ultimate structure of the farming community.

With respect to the other major facet of mechanical change already available in Pakistani agriculture, namely, tractors, the evidence regarding their impact in the longer run is as yet unclear. Unlike the tubewell, which has shown itself to be both consistently profitable under all conditions and employment creating, tractors and their associated implements, if valued at the higher shadow price of capital, would not be unequivocally profitable. For example, in the areas where the aquifer is saline and supplementary water for irrigation is not available, the ability to prepare a seedbed for the rabi crop with a maximum delay is of marginal value. As indicated above, water, not land, is the binding constraint, and, without the availability of groundwater, mechanization alone is insufficient to increase the cropping intensity. On the other hand, in the areas that have the potential for double cropping, advanced farming systems that incorporate improved seed varieties, fertilizer, tubewells, and mechanization appear to be highly profitable, even where all imported materials are valued at the higher social cost of capital.

The forces that have prompted the rapidity of the initial efforts at mechanization were undoubtedly fueled by the substantial subsidies associated with the importation of capital items and the status enhancement that accompanied the ownership of the equipment. However, as indicated previously, during the recent past an additional force for tractorization is to be found in the form of sporadic tenant and labor militancy. Such activities as refusing to pay the rent to the landlord or striking against the owner-operator need not be widespread to result in what amounts to an increase in the perceived cost of labor by the larger farmers. When the expected private cost of labor exceed its social cost and the private cost of capital is below its social costs, it is little wonder that the demand for tractors, as measured by applications to the Agricultural Development Bank, has been several times the available supply.

Who controls the land? This question must be broken into several parts. First, it is important to ascertain both the absolute size and the size distribution of the holdings. The former is important because of its direct relationship to the earlier question of input divisibility. The latter is significant as a first approximation of the distribution of income and political power.

In addition to the distribution of land, it is important to ascertain the extent of various types of control, that is, the extent to which the land is operated by farmer-owners, by sharecroppers, and so forth. This distinction is particularly important when the potential for the introduction of technology with substantial economies of scale exists. The overall impact of technical change will be significantly affected by the percentage of land that is operated by sharecroppers, and also by the labor requirements of the technology.

Unfortunately, the agricultural census of West Pakistan does not provide the data required to ascertain exactly who controls (i.e., *owns*) the land; only the distribution of *operated* units is presented. However, since all tenants must be the tenants of someone, and since they will undoubtedly be the tenants of large rather than small landowners, it is possible to make some crude calculations regarding the extent of control by holding size. As an example, Table 3 gives the distribution of farming units by operator size for Sahiwal District. Column 4 shows that approximately 27 percent of the land is operated in holding sizes of 25 acres and above. However, after the land reportedly farmed by tenants and owner-cum-tenants is distributed among the ownership categories, a conservative estimate would put approximately 54 percent or over one-half the land in that category. This does not mean, of course, that the land is in contiguous blocks and can readily be farmed in units of that size, for the problem of extensive fragmentation exists in Sahiwal District. However, it does indicate that much of the land is in hands that have command over the resources necessary to utilize modern inputs. Several other size groups of farms emerge from the figures in Table 3. First is the group that will almost certainly require access to nonmarket institutions that can supply resources, information, management help, and the services of otherwise lumpy inputs if they are to participate fully in the increases in productivity that the new technology has made possible. Although any quantitative distinction is somewhat arbitrary, I would include in this category most farmers with less than fifteen acres. Whether it be defined as operator or owner units, in Sahiwal District this would involve on the order of 70 percent of those actively engaged in farming.

A second group, composed of farmers having fifteen to thirty acres, are in a position where a reasonably functioning market mechanism would give them access to most of the divisible inputs needed to increase their output substantially. At least one would not expect that short-run production credit and access to information would present the kind of problem that it poses for subsistence

TABLE 3. Size Distribution of Holdings
in Sahiwal District, by Tenure Status, 1960

	Operated				Owned			
	(1)	*(2)*	*(3)*	*(4)*	*(5)*	*(6)*	*(7)*	*(8)*
Size (acres)	Number (000)	Percent of No.	Area (000)	Percent of Area	Number (000)	Percent of No.	Area (000)	Percent of Area
under 5.0	95	43	184	9	48	43	98	5
5.0–7.5	29	13	164	8	21	19	200	10
7.6–12.5	43	19	399	20	19	17	295	15
12.6–25.0	42	19	693	35	17	15	305	16
25.1–50.0	12	5	364	19	6	5	782	40
50.1 above	2	1	149	8	1	1	273	14
TOTAL	223	100	1953	99	112	100	1953	100

SOURCE: Government of Pakistan (1964).

farmers. The only real difficulty they are likely to encounter is the purchase of water in a situation where they are surrounded by several larger farmers who use virtually all the water from the tubewells they have installed for themselves.

The third group, farmers with over thirty acres, are in a size group that has relatively little need of nonmarket institutions other than those that develop new forms of technology or provide for rural infrastructure in the form of roads, marketing facilities, educational and medical facilities, and so forth.

The magnitude and the distribution of benefits from the institutions that serve farmers.   Here there are several easily quantifiable elements and several that are not so easily measured.[7] The most obvious in the first category are access to information and knowledge; access to capital markets; access of farmers to knowledge about new agricultural technology, marketing opportunities, and so forth; and access to the resources needed to make use of them.

For example, there is a good deal of evidence that the nature of the diffusion curve is a source of income disparity even when the basic technology is perfectly divisible (Figure 3). AA′ is the illustrative diffusion curve of large farmers who learn first about new technology and its use because of their access to the extension-research institutions, and who are able to reach optimum factor combinations by their access to credit. The curve BB′ illustrates farmers who are less likely to come in touch with knowledge, or who are more prone to discount it. They start later, and don't move as far up on the production function. An explanation of *why* this is so is clearly necessary if this essentially descriptive system is to become a policy tool. The result is a basic disparity-creation mechanism that is reinforced by the subsequent dynamics of the system.

Unfortunately, even a casual field trip and some conversations with officials in various government agencies indicate that in Pakistan there is a pervasive bias against the small farmer in almost every institution he confronts. Part of this is due to the ability of the larger farmers to bring their influence to bear on the local officials. However, the handicaps under which government representatives labor are equally important. For example, the Department of Agriculture's extension staff is vastly understaffed and inadequately

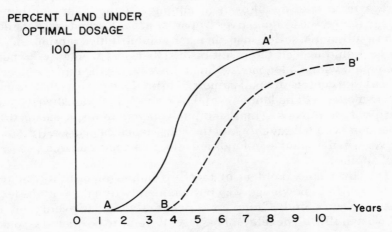

Figure 3. Farm Size and the Distribution of Information and Credit.

equipped. Since there is no way for the field agents to see every-body, it is only natural that they visit those who have the resources necessary to make the recommended changes, and who can pro-vide amenities such as transportation, travel, and so forth. In return, influential farmers receive not only information but services in the form of government-subsidized plant protection.

The biases in the size distribution of institutional credit are equally evident. The Agricultural Development Bank (ADB), which until 1968/69 distributed 30–40 percent of the credit (Table 4), has the responsibility for granting medium-term loans, that is, credits for the purchase of tractors and tubewells. Although there have been several collateral modifications during this period, when coupled with a corruption problem that has not yet been brought under control, the result has invariably been the placement of this subsidized capital on farms of twenty-five acres and larger.

Cooperative loans, although ostensibly designed to provide production credit to poor and subsistence farmers, also have been misused. Again, part of the problem can be traced to the overt actions of larger farmers as they used various methods of exploiting the organization for their own benefit. However, equally important has been the natural tendency of loan officers to look carefully to the repayment rates on all of their lending activities. Through bitter experience, the Cooperatives Department has learned that defaults on a substantial scale can mean harsh administrative reprimand. As one would expect, the result of this "banker's mentality," when coupled with inadequate staffing to investigate the circumstances of a large number of small farmers, is to produce policies that insure that money will be lent only to those who will obviously have the capacity to repay it. Translated into concrete terms, it means that farmers who fall roughly into the subsistence category are passed over when limited loan funds are allocated among a large number of applicants.

The whole problem of the distribution of institutional re-sources and knowledge was put eloquently by former President Ayub Khan's Study Group on Agricultural Policy (Government of Pakistan 1970). The relevant passages deserve to be quoted at some length:

> One of the major elements to be taken into consideration

TABLE 4. Loans Provided to Agriculturalists through Various Institutional Credit Agencies (millions of rupees)

Year	Taccavi	Percent of Total	Coops	Percent of Total	ADB	Percent of Total	Total Loans	Index of Total
1960/61	11.04	7.4	107.28	71.6	31.51	21.0	149.83	100.0
1961/62	10.69	7.2	90.23	61.1	46.91	31.7	147.83	98.7
1962/63	10.34	7.2	92.48	64.4	40.67	28.4	143.49	95.8
1963/64	12.37	7.4	108.83	64.8	46.65	27.8	167.85	112.0
1964/65	21.07	16.3	67.97	52.5	40.47	31.2	129.51	86.4
1965/66	10.74	7.1	71.63	47.7	67.97	45.2	150.34	100.3
1966/67	9.58	4.6	99.24	47.4	100.48	48.0	209.30	139.7
1967/68	12.88	5.0	137.45	53.6	106.25	41.4	256.58	171.2
1968/69	11.16	3.7	200.72	68.3	82.10	28.0	293.98	196.2

SOURCE: Government of Pakistan 1970.

NOTES: *Taccavi* loans are advanced by the government in situations of distress or for agricultural production. ADB is the Agricultural Development Bank.

in the creation of a viable institutional structure of rural credit
is the need to reach the very large number of small farmers
dispersed all over the countryside. In concentrating upon the
small farmer, and emphasize the need for supervised credit,
the terms of reference have got to the heart of the problem.
The big farmer is in little need of further support on the credit
side as in addition to his own resources, a large volume of
non-institutional credit is available to him and he also has full
access to the present credit system. The really important
category of farmers upon whom efforts must be concentrated
is that with economic, subsistence and below subsistence
holdings, that is to say, the medium and small farmer.

Further on:

It is necessary, therefore, that any real effort for provision
of credit in the agricultural sector should consist of major institutional changes so that all loans for the smaller farmer are
in the form of supervised credit. As we have discussed in the
introductory chapter, the major factor in such institutional reorganization is the fact that urban-based bureaucratic institutions cannot reach out to the individual farmers with small
holdings scattered throughout the country. It is only if there
are viable organizations of farmers themselves that this institutional problem can be solved. Cooperation is the only
possible method of organization by which individual ownership can be combined with the benefits of common management and institutions created which are in a position to take
advantage at the appropriate level from the various private
and public sector organizations serving agricultural needs. A
reform and re-direction of the Cooperative Movement in both
wings of the country is, therefore, the fundamental requirement in developing a viable institutional framework for undertaking supervised credit.

However, further on:

. . . we anticipate [subsequent] conclusions here by saying
that in East Pakistan the problem [of organizing cooperatives]
seems to be comparatively less formidable, after the success

of the Comilla experiment and its adaptations in Rangunia and other areas. For West Pakistan, we are not recommending large-scale introduction of cooperatives on a similar pattern until successful models can be developed.... For West Pakistan, therefore, we do not see any short term solution to the problem of supervised credit.

How is the social and political life of the village organized? To a certain extent, of course, the distribution of power will reflect the distribution of land and/or wealth. In traditional societies where the technology was the same across farms, the two were more or less synonymous. One of the significant effects of the green revolution has been to create a mechanism under which, by the intensive application of technology, wealth can be more equitably distributed than land presently is. One would expect that this in turn would produce a redistribution of political power.

But not all power is obtained, at least in the short run, by control over property; there is also the power of status and role. In Western societies, this tends to be minimized, but in traditional communities where the extended family, the kinship lineage, the caste, or the tribe are still basic units of social relationship, this aspect of power must be accounted for as explicitly as possible. In many cases, it is the key to the successful organization of activities at the grass-roots level.

As Hamza Alavi (1971) has pointed out, politics in the Punjab has a distinctly *factional* flavor; that is, individuals in the village do not form groups or allegiances because they have a common goal that their cooperation would serve, but because they are "recruited" by one or another of the local political leaders who offers some sort of transactional relationship. "Recruitment" takes two forms: among those who have a choice in the matter and among those who do not. The latter are epitomized by the sharecroppers and landless laborers whose dependence upon the favor of the landlord for their livelihood predetermines their allegiance.

For others, namely the small and medium landowners, there are certain choices to be made. It is around this group that intense political competition between rival faction leaders takes place. No holds are barred in this struggle: cattle are stolen, buildings are demolished, and so forth. The use of *goondas* or hoodlums as "enforcers" is widespread. Frequently, when two equally powerful individuals are competing for the allegiance of a particular kinship lineage (*biraderi*), composed largely of small landholders, a virtual state of siege may ensue. In some cases, the pressures are such that the kinship group, which is the basic unit of social interaction in Punjabi Muslim villages, may have to divide against itself politically in order to acquire the "protection" of competing leaders.

Obviously, the *vertical* alignment of factions is in direct conflict with the *horizontal* alignment of classes. Where economic dependence is the rule, as in the case of sharecroppers and landless laborers, the latter alignments are virtually impossible. But from Alavai's description, class alignments also would be extremely difficult for small landowners. The necessary conditions would appear to be a *biraderi* that was composed largely of such small farmers, and the physical proximity of the group in a single village or other contiguous area. The latter element is necessary in order that faction members may be able to protect themselves. Unfortunately, such distributions of holding size and kinship characteristics are not the normal pattern in the Punjab. The result is a domination of village life, and the institutions that serve farmers at the local level, by the various faction leaders.

A Scenario for the Future

Solon Barraclough (1971) has distinguished three basic types of national development strategies whose assumptions provide a useful background against which to speculate about the future of the rural areas of Pakistan; they are modernization strategies, reformist strategies, and strategies for deep-seated structural change.

Modernization strategies assume that rural development can be achieved by adopting the technologies of the developed countries without simultaneously reforming social structures. Although there is some acknowledgment that social changes may be required in the future, existing power relationships, current land tenure systems, and class structures are accepted as the starting point for development.

Reformist strategies are characterized by a significant alteration in one particular aspect of the economic environment, say, the distribution of land. However, while the land reform may seriously curtail the incomes and statuses of the agrarian elite, the basic structure of wealth and power in the society remains intact.

Strategies of deep-seated structural change involve profound alterations, not only in the land tenure system, but in the entire social structure. For example, in addition to controlling the land they cultivate, farmers, through their cooperatives and political parties, achieve a dominant voice in all facets of agricultural policy, including those associated with agribusiness.

The current situation in West Pakistan conforms most closely to the first of these three classifications. The green revolution has not—for the most part—involved the development of an indigenous new technology. And, as the answers to the questions on farm size, institutional services, and village organizations imply, the technology is being applied in a situation where almost no attempts to alter the existing social structure have occurred. These elements form the basis of a prognosis that in the short run—say, over the next five years—the forces that have produced past trends will continue to dominate the process of structural change. Some of these will undoubtedly be accelerated. For example, the potentials for utilizing more advanced technology on the larger holdings will certainly continue to produce further land agglomeration. The result, at least in a number of areas, will be to increase further the rate of migration to the urban areas.

Undoubtedly, efforts will be made to dampen the undesirable effects of this dynamic system. Some sort of progressive taxation scheme for agriculture may be implemented during the next decade for example. Such a siphoning off of agricultural profits for general development purposes would both decrease the incentives to invest in expensive labor-displacing technology and more land, and would increase the job potential in the urban areas.

Agricultural prices also are likely to be adjusted and brought more into line with world market prices; the country is too poor to do otherwise. Should surpluses of wheat, rice, and other commodities build up—as they are likely to—Pakistan will have to follow a Canadian-style solution to its surplus problem; that is, the government will operate a storage and marketing program but the returns to farmers will be what the commodity brings on the world market.

With respect to input prices, those subsidies still remaining will be eliminated within a relatively short time. The instrument in bringing both sets of prices in line could well be a devaluation of the rupee in the not-too-distant future.

The question that remains, however, is whether these types of marginal economic policies can offset disparities generated by the market phenomena to the extent necessary to synchronize the pace of change in rural areas with the needs of the nonfarm sector. As Johnston and Cownie have suggested, on the whole, the answer to that question leaves little room for optimism (Johnston and Cownie 1969). Using several alternative assumptions about the rate of mechanization, the type of technology in the nonfarm sector, the marginal savings rate, and so forth, they conclude that extension of recent trends would mean 20–25 percent unemployment by 1985.

As it becomes more apparent that the ingredients of the rural system are such that, left to itself, intolerably high rates of unemployment in both the rural and urban areas will emerge, the government, in the interests of self-preservation, is likely to pursue more vigorously attempts to create institutional answers to the distributive effects of agricultural growth. The most plausible initiatives in Pakistan will involve an attempt to improve the cooperative system. This is based on the hope that the productivity—and hence the political stability—of the small farmer class can be improved.

From the earlier discussion of the politics of the rural areas, it is likely, in my view, that this attempt will fail. The statement made by the Presidential Study Group indicating that there appeared to be no short-run solution to the problem of supervised credit could be reiterated for the long run as well. So long as income and power are distributed as they are, it will be impossible to organize class-based organizations capable of mitigating the cumulative effects of technical change. Indeed, injecting additional institutional resources into the rural areas could be counterproductive, should these larger amounts of subsidized capital go in the hands of those farmers already actively involved in a continuous sequence of innovation.

The combination of rapid increases in the labor force, labor-displacing agricultural growth, and inadequate urban employment opportunities is a nexus of contradictions that the society cannot sustain in the long run. However, it is exceedingly difficult to proceed beyond this point in terms of a scenario. There is a great temptation to join Myrdal:

> What the political repercussions will be if nothing is done in the reform field while the trend toward increasing under-utilization of the labor force is permitted to work for ever greater impoverishment of the masses—somewhat in the perspective of the demographic dictum, when they see a reactivation of the Malthusian checks if population increase is not checked—eludes my power of analysis. (Myrdal 1971:431)

Perhaps all that one can say is that the historical conditions under which revolutions or deep-seated structural changes have occurred are much more stringent than those surrounding reforms. Consequently the possibility that some significant reforms in, say, the distribution of land will occur in the next decades in Pakistan is not to be ruled out.

NOTES

1. This is considerably above the official figures. For a justification, see Gotsch and Timmer (1968).

2. The one person who correctly anticipated the potential for private tubewell installations was the late Ghulam Mohammad of the Pakistan Institute of Development Economics. His calculations are contained in Mohammad (1965).

3. This "naïve" assumption abstracts from the possibility of a completely deteriorating political situation. West Pakistan is not self-sufficient in any of the modern agricultural inputs except perhaps seed. Severe foreign exchange constraints would surely mean significant cutbacks in factor availability—with obvious effects on output. The longer-run outlook is considered later in this article.

4. District-wide production data may be found in Government of Pakistan (1972).

5. Work by Eckert, Hussain, the Punjab Planning and Development Department's Survey Unit, Rochin, and Loudermilk has been summarized in Rochin (1971). For a study that shows the impact of proximity to urban areas on small farmers, see Naseem (1971).

6. Burki presents the thesis in chapter 15 that there is a causal link

between the increased use of modern inputs and the advent of avenues of political participation via the Basic Democracies. While such a hypothesis is admittedly difficult to pin down, it deserves extensive investigation for its implication regarding the future political behavior of innovative groups. See also Burki (1971).

7. The notion of "institutions" used here corresponds to what Gintis has called a "politically integrated decision-making mechanism," i.e., a conscious and articulated apparatus for carrying out the plans and programs of an individual or group of individuals. It is to be contrasted to the use of the word "institutions" when such concepts as "the market" or "private property" are the foci of discussion (Gintis 1970).

BIBLIOGRAPHY

Alavi, Hamza A.
    1971. "The Politics of Dependence: A Village in West Punjab." *South Asian Review* 4(2):111–128.
Barraclough, Solon
    1971. *FAO/SIDA Symposium on Agricultural Institutions for Integrated Rural Development.* Rome: Food and Agriculture Organization.
Burki, Shahid Javed
    1971. "Interest Groups and Agricultural Development." Unpublished. Cambridge, Mass.: Center for International Affairs, Harvard University.
Falcon, Walter P., and Gotsch, Carl H.
    1968. "Agricultural Development in Pakistan, Lessons from the Second Plan Period." In *Development Policy: Theory and Practice,* edited by Gustav F. Papanek, pp. 269–318. Cambridge, Mass.: Harvard University Press.
Gintis, Herbert
    1970. "Towards a Radical Critique of Welfare Economics." Ph.D. dissertation, Harvard University.
Gotsch, Carl H., and Timmer, C. Peter
    1967. "A Consistent Estimate of Livestock Production in West Pakistan." *Pakistan Development Review* 7:485–503.
Government of Pakistan
    1964. *Census of Agriculture, 1960.* vol. 2. West Pakistan Agricultural Census Organization.
    1970. "Report of the Study Group of Agricultural Policy." Rawalpindi: Ministry of Agriculture and Works.
    1972. *Yearbook of Agricultural Statistics.* Islamabad, Pakistan: Ministry of Food, Agriculture and Underdeveloped Areas.

Johnston, Bruce F., and Cownie, John
  1969. "The Seed-Fertilizer Revolution and Labor Force Absorption."
    American Economic Review 59:569–582.
Mohammad, Ghulam
  1965. Unpublished section of the original manuscript for "Private
    Tubewell Development and Cropping Patterns in West Paki-
    stan," which appeared in *Pakistan Development Review*, vol. 5.
Myrdal, Gunnar
  1971. *The Challenge to World Poverty*. New York: Pantheon Books.
Naseem, Mohammad
  1971. "Small Farmers in the Structural Transformation of West Paki-
    stan Agriculture." Ph.D. dissertation, University of California.
Rochin, Refugio I.
  1971. "The Impact of Dwarf Wheats on Farmers with Small Holdings
    in West Pakistan: Excerpts from Recent Studies." Mimeo-
    graphed. Islamabad, Pakistan: Ford Foundation.

Appendix. Trend Rates of Growth by Region and Commodity, 1959/60–1969/70

Crop	West Pakistan			North-West Frontier Province			Punjab			Baluchistan			Sind		
	Rate (%)	R^2	Signifi-cance	Rate (%)	R^2	Signifi-cance	Rate (%)	R^2	Signifi-cance	Rate (%)	R^2	Signifi-cance	Rate (%)	R^2	Signifi-cance
Total Gross Value	5.9	.94	**	5.2	.76	*	6.1	.92	**	7.9	.74		5.8	.95	**
Wheat	6.1	.73	**	1.6	.21	*	6.2	.46	*	7.8	.62	*	7.4	.79	**
Rice	7.9	.86	**	15.0	.81		9.0	.84	**	9.1	.81	*	6.4	.79	**
Barley	-3.2	.39	*	-6.0	.46		2.7	.24		.4	—		7.3	.58	**
Maize	4.7	.79	**	4.2	.75		4.2	.56	**	6.8	.37		14.2	.90	**
Jowar	2.1	.45	*	3.8	.32		2.0	.25		11.1	.84		1.2	.15	*
Bajra	-.1			2.4	.52		.3	-.03					-.9	.01	
Gram	-2.0	.34		-8.9	.26		-3.0	.60	**				3.0	.37	
Tobacco															
Sugarcane (Gur)	7.5	.84	**	5.8	.74		7.3	.82	**				12.5	.68	**
Cotton	6.7	.96	**	2.6	.15		7.3	.93	**				5.1	.66	
Rapeseed & Mustard	-.2			5.8	.40		-.5	-.02					-1.1	.02	

SOURCE: Government of Pakistan 1972.

* Significant at 5% level
** Significant at 1% level

GLOSSARY

AMAN. The summer rice crop in Bangladesh, grown from mid-July through December.

ARZAL. "Lowest of the low"; denotes the lowest status in the traditional South Asian Muslim class hierarchy.

ATRAF. Low class; denotes a grouping of low status in the traditional South Asian Muslim class hierarchy.

AUS. The spring rice crop in Bangladesh, grown from late March through mid-August.

AWANI LEAGUE. The political party, founded in 1953, which led Bangladesh to independence. Presently in power, with Prime Minister Sheikh Mujibur Rahman at its head.

BAJRA. Pearl millet.

BARANI. Land or crops that depend on rainfall for water—nonirrigated.

BARI. Locus (homestead) of an extended peasant family, usually consisting of groups of households.

BASIC DEMOCRAT. An elected union counselor in the Basic Democracies system of government, usually representing a population of about 1,250 (see BASIC DEMOCRACIES).

BASIC DEMOCRACIES. The five-tiered (union, thana, district, division, and province) system of government proclaimed for Pakistan by Ayub Khan in October 1959.

BATAI. On share, as when renting land.

BIRADARI, BIRADERI. Patrilineal descent group and basic institution of kinship in North India and the Pakistani Punjab; emphasizes horizontal ties among contemporaries as well as agnatic descent and can be thought of as a brotherhood.

BORO. The winter rice crop in Bangladesh, grown in the dry season from December through March, usually requiring irrigation.

CHAUKIDARI PANCHAYAT. A village council established in East Bengal in 1870 to finance and supervise village watchmen.

CIRCLE OFFICER. The general administrative officer of a thana, consisting of a circle of grouping of unions. The lowest level of central administration in Bangladesh.

CIVIL SERVICE OF PAKISTAN. A group of officers given major administrative responsibilities in Pakistan, who are selected at a young age by examination. Patterned after the British colonial Indian Civil Service.

CROPPING INTENSITY INDEX. Land area of all crops grown during one year divided by the land area used to grow those crops multiplied by 100; for example, 2 crops on the same land would have a cropping index of 200.

CRORE. 10,000,000 punctuated thus: 1,00,00,000. One hundred lakh.

DESI. Of the country, native or traditional, as in native crops.

DISTRICT. Major governmental administrative unit in Pakistan and Bangladesh, thirty-four in Pakistan and nineteen in Bangladesh.

DEWAN. The finance minister of a province or territory under control of the Mogul empire, responsible especially for land revenue policy.

DOAB. Area of sparcely settled desert land between the rivers and canals in Pakistan, especially in the Punjab.

DUBARI. The general name given winter crops sown in the residual moisture of rice fields.

DWARF WHEAT. New high-yielding strains with short, strong stems, recently introduced into Pakistan and initially developed in Mexico with Rockefeller Foundation support.

DYARCHY. Dual system of government established by the Government of India Act of 1919, which reserved certain administrative functions for the provincial governors and transferred others to elected legislative councils.

GRAM. 1. Any of several leguminous plants grown for their seeds. 2. Bengali word for village.

IZZAT. Honor, status; refers to the perquisites of one's social standing.

JATS. Large landowning caste groups in the Punjab who personally engage in agricultural work.

JOWAR. Any of a number of grain sorghums or millet.

KHARIF. The summer crop season in Pakistan, extending from April/May to October /November.

LAKH. 100,000 punctuated thus: 1,00,000.

LAMBARDAR. An agent appointed by the revenue administration under British colonial rule for the collection of land revenue in a small revenue unit. Sometimes a hereditary office. (See also Numberdar.)

MAHALWARI SYSTEM. A land revenue system of north and northwest India, evolved in the nineteenth century; it lumped land held by patrilineal kin groups into single revenue estates (mahals) and made proprietors individually and collectively responsible for paying the land tax.

MANDI TOWN. Small agricultural market town.

MATABBAR. A traditional village leader in Bangladesh. (See also Sardar.)

MATRICULATE. Secondary school graduate who has completed eleven years of education.

MAUND. A south Asian unit of weight measurement, equivalent to 82.29 pounds.

MAUZA. A village-level revenue unit under the Moguls, still in use today.

MODEL FARMER. In the Comilla cooperative system, a villager designated by the village cooperative to receive training in improved agricultural practices at the thana central cooperative. He has the responsibility to pass on new knowledge to fellow cooperative members in the village.

MOFFUSIL. *n.* Rural areas, provinces; *adj.* provincial.

MONSOON. Heavy, rainy summer season resulting in much flooding in Bangladesh.

MUKHTI BAHINI. Bengali guerillas, "freedom fighters," a term used in the hostilities of 1971; literally 'liberation forces'.

MUSLIM. A believer in Islam, the religion of the Prophet Mohammed.

MUSLIM LEAGUE. A Muslim nationalist political party, which at Partition in 1947 was led by Mohammed Ali Jinnah. The party of Ayub Khan.

MUSTAJIR. A revenue farmer, a collector whose rights were temporary, as opposed to fixed, in the Mogul revenue system in Bengal.

NAWAB. A landed aristocrat, Mogul period especially.

NAZIM. Governor of a province under the Mogul empire.

NUMBERDAR. A revenue-collecting headman found in north and northwest India, including post-1947 Pakistan. (See Also Lambardar)

PAKISTAN PEOPLES' PARTY. The political party of Zulfikar Ali Bhutto, which aided his victory at the polls in December 1970, in West Pakistan.

PANCHAYAT. Traditional village governmental unit.

PARGANA. A Mogul unit of land revenue that covered a number of revenue villages (*mauza*) in Bengal.

PATWARI. Keeper of land records at the village level in Pakistan.

PERMANENT SETTLEMENT. The revenue settlement or arrangements, established in Bengal in 1793 by Lord Cornwallis, fixing "in perpetuity" the amount of land revenue each zamindar would be responsible for collecting; the Permanent Settlement is associated with the establishment of zamindari landlordism in Bengal.

RABI. The winter cropping season in Pakistan and Bangladesh extending from October/November to April/May.

RYOT. Peasant proprietor; cultivator.

RAJ. Literally, 'rule', from Indic words associated with kings, kingdoms;

often used to denote British rule in India, that is, the "British Raj."

REAI, REYAI. A traditional social grouping of homesteads in rural Bangladesh.

RUPEE. Unit of currency in Pakistan. From 1959 to 1971, the official exchange rate was Rs. 4.76 = $1.00 or about $0.21 = R.

SADR. Term denoting official headquarters of a political and administrative area in Mogul Bengal. An area often controlled by one zamindar.

SAHUKAR. Professional village moneylender in nineteenth- and early twentieth-century Punjab, usually of the Bama, Khatri, or Arora castes.

SAMAJ. A multivillage political institution or council of elders traditionally used for the settlement of disputes.

SARDAR. A traditional village leader in Bangladesh. (See also Matabbar.)

SHARIF. High class; denotes a grouping of the highest status in the traditional South Asian Muslim class hierarchy.

SHEIKH. Generally an old man or influential person, head of a tribe. One of the traditionally upper-class groups in Muslim South Asia.

SIKH. Member of a religious and social group (The Sikhs) whose existence dates from the late fifteenth century; an offshoot of the *Bhakti* "devotional" movement fusing elements of Hinduism and Islam. The historical homeland of the Sikhs was the undivided Punjab, but after the Partition of 1947, most Sikhs living in the Pakistani Punjab migrated to India. Few live in Pakistan today.

SYED. A person who claims direct descent from the Prophet Mohammed, through his daughter, Fatima.

TA'ALUQ. A subholding of a zamindari estate, the rights of revenue collection dependent upon a grant of authority from the zamindar.

TA'ALUQDAR. Proprietor and revenue collector of a *ta'aluq*.

TACCAVI LOAN. A loan advanced by government in situations of distress, or for agricultural production.

TARAFDAR. Revenue collector under the Mogul system holding revenue recollection rights to several villages in Bengal.

TEHSIL. A subdivision of a district, smallest major administrative unit in Pakistan (a county).

TEHSILDAR. The revenue official of a *tehsil*.

THANA. The governmental administrative unit next below the subdivisional level in Bangladesh. The lowest level to which government officials are usually posted. Could be compared with a county in the United States. Literally a 'police station'.

UNION. The lowest level of government, under the *thana*, in the Basic Democracies system; amalgamates a number of local villages.

UNION COUNCIL. The group of elected representatives of a union.

V-AID. The village agricultural and industrial development program in the 1950s in Pakistan.

ZAILDAR. A well-to-do farmer, appointed as agent for the collection of revenue from a *zail*, an area of a village or less.

ZAMINDAR. A person given rights to land revenue collection under the Moguls. After the Permanent Settlement in Bengal in 1793, these rights were fixed in perpetuity, which strengthened the landlord class. More generally, landlord.

INDEX

Abbottabad, 275
Abolition Act, 32
Absentee landowners, 204, 336, 337
Academy for Rural Development, 67, 84,
95–128, 165–167; and cooperatives,
84, 99–107, 130–131; and credit problems, 84; educational experiments of,
117–118; environment of, 97; and
family planning, 117; and irrigation
program, 115–116, 146; methods used
in developing programs at, 97–99; and
outside technical knowledge, 102–
103; and pilot irrigation projects, 146;
pilot programs of, 97–99, 146; programs originating at, 88, 95, 97–99,
146; and rural education experiments,
117–118; and rural public works programs, 113–117; and Thana Irrigation
Program, 70, 79, 80, 115–116, 146; and
Thana Training and Development
Center, 107–113; and women's education, 116–117
Agricultural Census of Pakistan, 174–
175, 339
Agricultural Development Bank, 372
Agricultural Development Corporation
(ADC), 45, 74, 75, 115, 117, 275, 276
Agricultural research, 84–86
Agriculture Department: of Bangladesh,
75; and Integrated Rural Develop-
ment Program, 105–106; and prob-
lems of Pakistan, 42–43, 46
Agriculture University, 84, 85
Ahmad, I., 178, 179
Ahmad, M. M., 194, 196, 214–232, 239
Alavi, H., 193, 195, 317–353
Aman crop, 78, 87, 91 n.5, 146, 153
Anderson, J. D., 300
Aquifer, 151, 260
Aristocracy, landed: and Ayub Khan,
343; and control of irrigation, 303, 304;

decline in power of, 304; defined, 301,
338; history of, 299–301; increasing
power of, in 1950s, 301–304
Aurangzeb, 12
Aus crop, 78, 87, 91 n.5, 146, 153
Ayub Khan: and agricultural reforms,
293; and Basic Democracies, 108, 346;
and creation of landed gentry, 49–50;
and economic growth of Pakistan,
189–190; fall of, 190; and landed aristocracy, 343; and middle-class farmers, 6, 307; and political stability of
Pakistan, 189–190; price policy of,
294; and reallotment of land to refugees, 334; reforms of, 46–52, 293, 304,
334; and Study Group on Agricultural
Policy, 372–374. *See also* Basic
Democracies

Bahadur Shah, 12
Baluchistan, 188, 216 map, 328, 356
Bangladesh: agricultural credit in,
82–83; agricultural research in, 85; agricultural zones of, 158; climate of, 3,
73; cooperatives in, 99–107; farm sizes
in, 3–4, 175; and food grain imports,
62, 73; hinterland legacies of, 40; and
irrigation, 80, 86–87, 115–116, 146;
and lack of rural social organization, 5;
land tenure variations in, 178; population of, 3, 4, 158–160; problems of, 6,
40–41, 40–46; rice production in, 73,
81, 97; and rural development problems, 40–46; rural marketing community of, 168–170; social organization and agricultural development in,
157–184; tenant farmers in, 176, 177,
179. *See also* Academy of Rural Development; Bengal; East Bengal;
Comilla Thana; East Pakistan
Barani areas, 270, 271, 321

Bargadars. *See* Sharecropping
Bari, 35, 161
Basic Democracies: and allocations of
funds to councils, 48; and district
councils, 47–48, 221, and emergence
of institutions, 217–218; and governmental organization, 108; and local
government, 221; main significance
of, 346; and middle-class farmers, 6,
307; and rural elite, 49–50; and thana
council, 48, 50, 111
Basic Democracies Department, 114
Basic Democracy Institute, 332
Basic Democrats, 224, 225
Bengal: Agriculture Department of,
42–43; and competition for land,
21–22; delta, 22, 160; homogeneity of,
163; landholding system in, 14–15;
population pressure of, 25; price of
land in, 25; revenue systems in, 12–19
Bengal District Gazetteers, 169
Bertocci, Peter J., 3–8, 32, 157–184
Bhutto, Zulfikar Ali, 190
*Biradari*s (lineages), 204, 206, 376. *See
also* Kinship
Bogra District, 178
Borlaug, Dr. Norman, 238
Boro crop, 69, 77, 87, 146, 153
British: basis for landownership, 199;
and changes made during rule, 25;
early impact of, 198–201; East India
Company, 199; effect of, on agricul-
ture, 200; land revenue systems in
Bengal, 10–19; laws of, 19; rule of East
Bengal, 30–31; and zamindars, 16
Buddhism, 54 n.5
Burdwan, 13, 18
Bureaucracy, civil, 219–225
Bureau of Agricultural Information, 278
Burki, S. J., 192–193, 194, 195, 290–316,
317, 338

Calcutta, 30
Calkins, P. B., 4, 5, 9–28
Canal Colonies: and agricultural debt,
208; and allotment of land to refugees,
322–323; areas of, 321; crops of, 328;
development of projects in, 202–203;
education in, 327; farm size in, 324;
land distribution in, 202; sharecropping in, 324, 325
Canal systems, in Sind, 248–249

Cash crop farming, 3, 325. *See also* Cot-
ton; Jute; Sugarcane
Caste system, 33–34, 54–55 n.8. *See also*
Class systems
Central Bengal (Dacca), 159, 176, 177
Central Cooperative Association, 133,
166
Chaudhari, H. A., 306, 307
Chaukidari panchayats, 38
Chemical fertilizer. *See* Fertilizer
Chickpeas, 249
Chittagong District, 159, 176, 177
Civil service, 46, 218, 219–225
Class systems: and Ayub Khan's re-
forms, 304, 307; changes in, 299–311;
of Comilla Thana, 172–173; of East
Bengal, 33–34; and landed aristoc-
racy, 299–304; and middle-class far-
mers, 307–311
Climate: of Bangladesh, 3, 73; of Lora
Thana, 273; monsoon, 3, 4, 78, 86,
146–147, 273; of Oghi Thana, 273; of
Sind Province, 257; winter, 3. *See also*
Rainfall
Colonialism, legacies of, 29–40
Comilla Kotwali Thana, 147, 148, 149,
153, 166
Comilla rural development programs,
95–128; and agricultural cooperatives, 99–107; and family planning,
117; methods used in developing,
97–99; and rural education experiments, 117–118; and rural public
works program, 113–114; and Thana
Irrigation Program, 115–116; and
Thana Training and Development
Center, 107–113; and women's education, 116–117
Comilla Thana: central cooperative federation in, 101; class systems in, 172–
173; cooperatives, 84, 99–106, 120,
131, 172; experimental developmental programs of, 119; farm sizes in, 129,
172; and green revolution effects, 129;
and improved rice varieties, 134–139,
171; and irrigation, 146, 148; land
ownership in, 129, 131, 180–181 n.4;
population of, 129, 161; social organization in, 161–168. *See also* Academy
for Rural Development; Comilla rural
development programs
Cooperatives, agricultural: in Comilla

Thana, 84, 99–106, 120, 131, 173, 210; economic impact of, 103–104; educational impact of, 106; federation, in Comilla Thana, 101, 104–106; and impact on employment rates, 106–107; and improved rice varieties, 134–135; and irrigation, 133–134; loans of, 101–102, 104–105, 132, 372; membership in, 130–132; number of, in Bangladesh, 101; opposition to, 167; and rural credit, 173–174; and rural development, 43–45; social impact of, 106–107; and stability of cooperative federation, 104–106; technology programs of, 102

Cooperatives Department, 44–45, 46

Cornwallis, Lord, 37, 49

Cotton, 237, 248, 328, 355, 360

Credit, rural, 173–174; in Bangladesh, 82; in Comilla Thana, 181 n.5; and cooperatives, 173–174; in East Pakistan, 82–84; and floods, 113. *See also* Cooperatives; Moneylenders

Crop output: growth of, in Punjab, 296, 297; increase of, by middle-class farmers, 308–310; and irrigation, 77; reporting of, in East Pakistan, 68–69; sources of increased, 295–296. *See also* Yield

Cropping patterns: changes in, 248, 258; and dwarf wheat, 281, 283; effect of, in Pakistan, 361; impact of irrigation on, 293; in Punjab, 245–247; in Sind, 328

Dacca (Central Bengal), 159, 176, 177

Darling, Malcolm, 203, 205, 207

Debts, agricultural, 205; and cooperatives, 210; increase of, in Punjab, 207–209. *See also* Moneylenders

Democracy. *See* Self-government, rural

Democratic values, weakness of, 225–228

Demonstration plots, 280–281

Desi wheats, 282–283

District councils, 38–40, 47, 108–109, 215, 218; and allocation of rural public works funds, 48–49

District road committees, 38

Doabs, 202

Dokri, 257

Dwarf wheat: acreage sown with, 277; adoption of, by *barani* farmers, 271; diffusion of, through mass media, 278–281; greater cropping intensity of, 283; in Hazara District, 275, 276, 282; higher yields of, 282, 283–284; impact of, 283–285; and increased employment, 284; reasons for adopting, 281–283; rejection of, 278

Dyarchy period, 39, 40

East Bengal: agricultural zones of, 158; agriculture of, 5, 6, 30; British rule of, 30–31; class system of, 33–34; description of, 30; ecological zones of, 158; floods of, 70; homogeneity of, 160; institutions of, 30; lack of organized rural groups in, 41; landholdings in, 170, 171; land system of, 5–6; population densities in, 159; problems of, 29; religion in, 34–35; settlement patterns in, 159; State Acquisition and Tenancy Act, 178; village political organizations of, 35–37. *See also* Bangladesh; Bengal; East Pakistan

East Pakistan: Action Program, 113; agricultural planning and development (1955–1969), 60–94; and agricultural research, 84; agricultural sector plan of, 63–64; annual development plans of, 60, 64–66; and cooperatives, 44; and development allocations to agriculture, 61; development expenditures of, 69–70; district administration in, 37–40; and high-yield rice varieties, 63; imports of, 61, 63, 72; irrigation in, 79–80; land laws of, 179–180; money supply of (1963–1968), 72; per capita income of, 72; Planning and Development Department, 66, 67; rice production of, 65, 66, 68, 69; Rice Research Institute, 135; and rural public works programs, 174; and Thana Irrigation Program, 146. *See also* Bangladesh; Bengal; East Bengal

Economic planning, needed improvements in, 66–68

Education: attitudes toward, in Pakistan, 326; Department of, Bangladesh, 118; experiments in, 117–118; extension, 278; and impact of village cooperatives, 106; regional differences in, 326, 327; and relationship to rural de-

Education (*cont.*)
velopment, 327; and Thana Training
and Development Center, 107–113;
women's, 116–117, 118
Elahi, Maryam, 319
Elections, 226; average years between,
in sample district councils, 221; and
landed aristocracy, 302; and middle-
class farmers, 307–308
Elective Bodies (Disqualification) Order, 303
Electoral college, 49, 51
Electricity, 234, 235, 293
Elite, rural, 49–50, 334–337, 349
Elkinton, C. M., 4–5, 6, 60–94
Employment: and growth of opportunities, 240; and impact of cooperative activities, 106–107; increase, and
dwarf wheat, 284; and rural public
works program, 114; and winter crop-
ping, 154
Equipment, farm. *See* Low-lift pumps;
Tractors; Tubewells
Esmay, M. L., 7, 129–145, 170–171
Exchange rate, 237
Extension service and training, 76,
86–87, 220, 222, 285, 371

Faidley, LeVern, 7, 129–145, 170–171
Falcon, W. P., 294
Family: and land ownership, 55 n.11;
patterns, 35; planning, 117
Famines, 199, 200, 201
Farmers. *See* Middle-class farmers;
Large farmers; Small farmers
Farm sizes: in Bangladesh, 3–4, 175; in
Canal Colonies, 324; in Comilla
Thana, 129, 172; and effect of advanced technology, 251; family subsistence and, 324; in Hazara District,
272; and impact of green revolution,
320; and improved varieties, 139–142;
in Lora and Oghi villages, 273; in
Pakistan, 335–336; in Punjab, 301,
323; and relationship to income,
250–256; and surplus crops, 324–325;
technology and, 251, 324; and use of
improved varieties, 139–142
Ferguson, Ben, 165
Fertilizer: production of, in Bangladesh,
74; production of, in Pakistan, 235;

subsidy of, in Pakistan, 239–240; use
of, by Comilla farmers, 103–104,
137–139; use of, in East Pakistan, 65,
73–75; use of, in Pakistan, 235–236,
276, 354
Fisheries Department, 64
Fixed costs, 252–253
Floods, 73, 87–88, 90
Food and Agriculture Commission, 319,
330
Food grains: imports of, in East Paki-
stan, 63; increased production of, in
Bangladesh, 72–73; production of, in
West Pakistan, 62
Food self-sufficiency program, 234, 270
Ford Foundation, 84, 85, 238, 242, 244
Franchise, adult, 215, 218

Gilbert R. B., 114
Goondas, 376
Gotsch, C. H., 192, 193, 195, 196, 242–
269, 295, 296, 320, 354–381
Government: departments of, in Pakistan, 223; of East Pakistan, 37–40; improving rural, 121–123; local, in Pakistan, 219–222; rural development as
process of, 52. *See also* Self-
government, rural
Government of India Act, 346
Gram, 32, 161
Green revolution: and assured water
supplies, 362; defined, 264 n.1, 317–
318; and distribution of incomes,
250–258; effect of, on Comilla farmers,
129; and farm sizes, 320; history of, in
Pakistan, 364–365; indirect effects of,
347–349; and irrigation, 308–309;
maldistribution of benefits of, 174;
and new plant varieties, 242; and optimal allocation of resources, 244–248;
in Pakistan, 357–365; and rural class
structure, 170–174; and rural elite,
349; secondary effects of, 318–319;
and variation in land tenure, 178–180
"Grow More Food" program, 76, 82
Gumti River, 147

Haq, K. A., 7, 146–156
Haripur, 275
Harvard Advisory Group, 60, 66
Hasan, Parvez, 195, 196, 232–241

Hats, 168
Hazara District, 272–278; and diffusion of dwarf wheat and fertilizers, 276; Lora and Oghi villages of, 272–275
High-yielding varieties: and irrigation, 245, 248; in rainfed areas, 250. *See also* Dwarf wheat; Rice; Wheat
Hinduism, 33, 34, 54 n.5
Homes, of Hazara smallholders, 274
Hussain, S. M., 296

Imports: of Bangladesh, 73; of East Pakistan, 61, 63, 72; of fertilizer, 63; of Pakistan, 61, 62; of pesticides, 75; tea, 64
Income: and advanced technology, 251–256; as calculated at domestic prices, 264; disparity of, in Pakistan, 347–348, 361–363; distribution of, and effect of advanced technology, 268; distribution of, and wheat prices, 254; impact of Comilla cooperatives on, 104; increase in, due to new technology, 244–245; and increase of middle-class farmer, 310; levels of Comilla Thana families, 129–130; per capita, in East Pakistan, 72; and relationship to farm size in Punjab, 250–256; of small farmers and advanced technology, 251; and taxes, agricultural, 82, 239
Indian Independence Act, 299
Indus Plains, 201–202, 331
Industry, in East Pakistan, 69
Inflation: and increased incomes of rural elite, 347; and rural works program, 71–72
Inheritance customs, land, 3
Insecticides, 139
Institute of Development Economics, 66, 333
Institutional atomization, 30, 31, 32
Integrated Rural Development Program, 105–106
Interest rates, and cooperative credit, 104
Intermediate council. *See* Thana council
Intermediate revenue collectors, 14–16, 17–18, 20, 23, 24, 25
International Bank for Reconstruction and Development, 79, 325

International Rice Research Institute (IRRI), 62, 63, 76, 78, 85, 86
Irrigation: and Academy for Rural Development, 132–134; in Bangladesh, 80, 86–87, 115–116, 146; and canals, 202–203, 322; control of, by big landlords, 303, 304; and cooperatives, 133–134; and cropping patterns, 293; development of, in Punjab, 201–203; and economic benefits of tubewells, 152–154; in East Pakistan, 79–80; and high-yielding varieties, 245, 248; and increased cropped acreage, 244–245; low-lift pump, 65, 77, 79, 86–87, 102, 115, 133, 147; manual, 77, 79, 133; mechnized, 79, 133, 146, 152–153; in Pakistan, 233–235, 301, 328–334; and sources of water in Indus Plain, 331; training, 86–87; tubewell, 79, 133, 146–156, 233–235, 328–334; winter crop, 79, 87, 115, 133. *See also* Thana Irrigation Program
Islam, 26, 34

Jats, 204, 205, 206
Jhelum, 296
Jinnah, Mohammad Ali, 299–300
Jute, 3, 64, 65, 81–82

Kala Shah Kaku, 257
Khairpur Division, 333
Khan, A. A., 181 n.5
Khan, A. H., 98, 99
Khan, L. A., 300
Kharian Tehsil, 332
Khulna (South Bengal), 159, 176, 177, 178
Kinship, 34, 35, 161. *See also Biradari*

Lahore Division, 321, 326
Lala Musa, 332
Lambardars, 345, 346
Land: Alienation Act, 299, 300; competition for, 20–22, 24, 173–174, 200; concentrated ownership of, in Pakistan, 334; distribution of, in Canal Colonies, 202; increasing market value of, 199–200; laws of East Pakistan, 179–180; legal basis for ownership, under British, 199; mortgages 173, 199, 300; ownership in Bangladesh, 176, 177;

Land (*cont.*)
  ownership in Pakistan, 334; and own-
    ership turnover, 11, 16, 24; price of,
    25, 200, 201; reallotment to refugees,
    334; redistribution, 240, 253; reforms,
    191, 232, 304, 334, 337; tenure pattern,
    4, 174–180, 199–200. *See also* Land-
    holding system; Revenue systems;
    Land
Landed Families of the Punjab, The 302
Landholding system: and agricultural
    families, 130; in Bangladesh, 175; in
    Bengal, 14–15; and changes in, 10–12,
    13; and changes in zamindaris, 19–26;
    in Comilla Thana, 97, 129, 171–172;
    and competition, 21–24; continuity of,
    20; in East Bengal, 170, 171; heredi-
    tary, 3–4, 20; and turnover of rights
    rate, 21
Landless laborers: in Comilla Thana,
    130, 132; and cooperatives, 132;
    defined, 132; improving living stan-
    dard of, 240; incomes of, in Comilla
    Thana, 130; number of, in Pakistan,
    336
Land Reforms Commission, 301, 334,
    338, 343
Large farmers: and advanced technol-
    ogy, 251, 369, 371; and cooperative
    loans, 372; and decline in wheat
    prices, 254, 255; effect of mechaniza-
    tion on, 341; and green revolution,
    171, 364; and modernization, 259;
    percentage of, in Pakistan, 336; politi-
    cal influence of, 173, 259–261, 343–
    344, 371–372; and price supports, 259;
    and private tubewell development,
    333; and public control of aquifer, 260;
    and selective mechanization, 260; and
    sharecroppers, 341–342; and tenant
    evictions, 353; and subsidies, 348;
    wealth of, 259
Lieftinck, Dr. Pieter, 233, 238
Lineages, 204, 206, 376. *See also* Kin-
    ship
Line transplanting, 136
Literacy: in Comilla Thana, 117; in East
    Pakistan, 80
Livestock products, 354
Living costs, 72
Loans, agricultural: and cooperatives,
    101, 104–105, 120, 132, 372; and

Pakistan institutional credit agencies,
    373; *taccavi* type, 105
Local councils, 38–40, 221. *See also* Dis-
    trict councils
Local government. *See* Self-
    government, rural
Local Government College, 217
Lora Thana, 272–285
Low-lift pumps, 65, 77, 79, 86–87, 102,
    115, 133, 147
Luykx, Dr. Nicolaas, 180 n.3
Lyallpur, 202, 203, 208, 296

Machinery agricultural. *See* Low-lift
    pumps; Tractors; Tubewells
Mahalwari system, 300
Maize, 25, 285, 328
Mansehra, 275
Manual for Rural Public Works, 114
Manufacturing, 291
Markets, rural, 168, 169
Marriages, 35, 206
Martial Law Regulation No. 64, 302
Mass media channels, 280
Masud-ul-Hasan, 217
Matabbars, 35, 161
Mauza, 161
Mechanization: effect of, on large and
    small holdings, 339, 341; and land use,
    337; and large farmers, 260; and
    sharecroppers, 338–342; and sub-
    sidies, 368; survey in Pakistan, 332–
    334; and unemployment in Pakistan,
    378
Mexipak-65, 276, 278, 282, 287 n.6, 358,
    364
Middle-class farmers, 6, 307–311, 338
Modernization, 10, 83, 53–54 n.2, 376.
    See also High-yielding varieties; Irri-
    gation; Technology; Tubewells
Moguls, 10–19, 53–54 n.2, 198
Mohammad, Ghulam, 293, 379 n.2
Mohsen, A. K. M., 111–112
Moneylenders, 15–16, 25, 82, 173,
    205–207, 299, 300
Monsoon season, 3, 4, 78, 86, 146–147,
    273
Montgomery, 203, 208, 296
Morris-Jones, W. H., 302
Mortgages, 173, 199, 300
Mosques, 34
Mukherjee, R., 175, 182

Multan, 203, 296, 323
Murshidabad, 18
Murshid Quli Khan, 12–14, 15, 16, 17, 20
Muslim League, 299–300
Muslims, 54 n.5 and 7, 299
Muyeed, Abdul, 129
Mymensingh: Agriculture University, 84; District, 164

Nicholls, W. H., 290
North Bengal, 159, 175, 176, 177
North-West Frontier Province, 188, 216, 250, 272, 301, 328, 356

Oghi Thana, 272–285
Oil seeds, 65

Pakistan: agricultural growth of, 189, 232–241, 290–316; agricultural output of, during 1960s, 232; Agriculture Department of, 46; authoritarian government of, 219; and Ayub Khan government, 108; and Basic Democracies system, 108; crops of, 188, 356, 365, 382; economic development of, 187, 188–189; election commission of, 217; farm sizes in, 335–336; fertilizer use in, 235–236; five-year development plans of, 60; future agricultural developments of, 365–376; geographic regions of, 187–188; green revolution in, 357–365; and high-yielding wheats, 62, 279–289, 354; imports of, 61, 62; industrial development in, 189; Institute of Development Economics, 333; irrigation in, 301, 233, 235, 328–334; land ownership in, 334; People's Party, 190–191, 227; Planning Commission, 66; political development of, 189–191; population of, 187; price support policies of, 236–237; rice production of, 358, 365; and rural bases of political power, 214–232, 343–347; rural economy of, 198–213; rural self-government in, 214–232; size of, 187; subsistence holdings in high-yielding wheats, 62, 279–289; taxation, agricultural, in, 239–240; tubewell development in, 233–235
Panchayats, 215, 217, 344
Papanek, Gustav, 188–189, 293

Partition, 32, 172
Pathans, 62
Patni ta 'aluqs, 18, 19
People's Party, 190–191, 227
Permanent Settlement: and development of *ta'aluqs*, 18; effect of, on rural institutions, 30, 31, 32, 42; and enforcement of revenue demands, 24; and government of Bengal, 30; and increased change in land ownership, 21; and Murshid Quli Khan's land policy, 13; removal of, 32; and revenue collections, 13–14, 24; and zamindars, 11
Peshawar Division, 333
Pesticides, 75, 76, 355
Planning and Development Department, 63, 66
Plant protection, 65, 75–76
Political organization, rural, 32, 35–37, 343–347
Population: control, in Bangladesh, 72; Council, 117
Population density: of Bangladesh, 158–160; of Bengal delta, 22; in Canal Colony Districts, 203; in Comilla Thana, 129; in East Bengal, 159; in Punjab, 203
Potatoes, 65
Prices, agricultural: adjustment of, to world market prices, 261–262, 377; and calculation of farm income, 267; changes in, and new technology, 258; decline of wheat, 254–256; impact of rural works program on, 72; ratio of, to nonfood commodities, 8; support of policies of, 81, 236–237; and yield per acre, 294
"Program Building," 164–165
Public officials, Pakistan, 219–225
Punjab, 216: canal irrigation in, 322; crop productivity growth of, 356; crops of, 328; dryland area of, 355; economic development of, 201–203; farmers and technological change, 257, 362–363; and growth in crop output, 297; higher education in, 326; irrigation development in, 201–203; Land Alienation Act, 205; literacy in, 326; population density of, 203; private tubewells in, 328; prosperity of, 328; representative farm in, 244–248;

Punjab (*cont.*)
    size-pattern of farms in, 301, 323;
    tubewell development in, 332
Punjab Peasant in Prosperity and Debt,
    207

Radio, 279–280
Rainfall: higher areas of, 256–257; of
    Lora Thana, 273; of Oghi Thana, 273;
    of Pakistan, in winter, 115
Rajshahi, 13, 159, 175, 176, 177, 178
Raper, A. F., 113–114
Raulet, Harry M., 191, 193, 198–213
Rawalpindi Division, 322, 323, 325, 326,
    331
Reform: land, 29–39, 191, 232, 304, 334,
    337; strategies, 376–377
Refugee Rehabilitation Policy, 334
Religion: Buddhism, 54 n.5; in East
    Bengal, 34–35; Hinduism, 33, 34, 54
    n.5; Islam, 26, 34; and village life, 34
Rents, Punjab, 304, 305
Research, agricultural: diffusion of,
    306–307; in East Pakistan, 84–86;
    needed economic, 237–238
Reservoir sites, lack of, 87
Revenue system: British changes in,
    10–11; competitiveness of pre-British,
    17; and difficulties in acquiring as-
    sessment information, 15–16; and en-
    forcement of collections, 13–14, 17;
    and intermediate collectors, 14–16,
    17–18, 23; and more efficient adminis-
    trators, 14–19; Murshid Quli Khan's
    reform of, 12–14, 17; similarities be-
    tween Mogul and British, 10–19,
    348–349
Reyai system, 35, 36, 55 n.12, 162
Rice: aman, 78, 87, 97 n.5, 146, 153; areas
    of Sind, 258; aus, 78, 87, 91 n.5, 146,
    153; average minimum price of, in
    East Pakistan, 63; boro, 69, 77, 87, 146,
    153; in Comilla Thana, 97, 103, 134–
    139; errors in estimating production
    of, 68; and floods, 70; high-yield vari-
    eties of, 63, 74, 76–77, 85–86, 129–
    145, 170–171, 257, 354–355; and irri-
    gation, 147, 245; IRRI varieties of, 62;
    prices of, 81; price supports of, 237;
    production of Bangladesh, 73, 81, 97;
    production of East Pakistan, 65, 66,

68–69; production of Pakistan, 358,
    365; research, 84, 85; smuggling of,
    81; sowing of, 136; yield of improved
    varieties, 135–136, 232
Ripon, Lord, 38–40, 214, 215
"Risala-i Zira'at," 14, 15, 23
River management, 87
Road committees, district, 38
Rochin, R. I., 193, 196, 270–289
Rockefeller Foundation, 242
Roy, N. C., 40
Rural development: and Agriculture
    Department problems, 42–43; and
    Ayub's reforms, 46–52; controversies
    in Pakistan's, 196–198; and coopera-
    tives, 43–45; defined, 52; future di-
    lemmas of, 50–52; and relationship to
    education, 327; and rural reconstruc-
    tion, 45–46; and USAID's "Program
    Building" project, 164. *See also*
    Academy for Rural Development
Rural education. *See* Education
Rural public works program, 113–114;
    allotment of funds to, 70; criticism of,
    49; of East Pakistan, 61, 83; and infla-
    tion, 71–72; of Pakistan, 71–72; and
    thana councils, 48, 109

Sahiwal District, 243–244, 369, 370
Sahukars, 205, 206
Salinity Control and Reclamation Pro-
    ject (SCARP), 233, 234
Samaj, 162
Sardars, 35, 161, 162
Schultz, T. W., 4, 194, 292
Seeds, high-yielding, 75, 76–78, 330–
    331; and green revolution, 242; and
    yield effect of, 245. *See also* Dwarf
    wheat; Rice; Wheat
Self-government, rural: and civil
    bureaucracy, 219–225; colonial effort
    toward, 214–215; in the post-
    independence period, 215–218; in-
    troduction of, 214–215; in Pakistan,
    214–232; reasons for slow develop-
    ment of, 218–228; and weak democra-
    tic values, 225–228
"Settlements," 299
Shahpur, 203, 208
Sharecropping: and adverse change in
    rates of sharing, 337; in Bangladesh,
    176, 177, 178; in Canal Colony Dis-

tricts, 324, 325; as cheap source of supplementary labor, 341; and eviction of, 341; and green revolution, 179; and mechanized farming, 338, 341–342; in North Bengal, 175; in Pakistan, 176, 177, 337; in Punjab, 324; reduction in land for, 337; in West Pakistan, 336

Sharif, 33

Shore, John, 14, 15, 16

Sikhs, 198, 204

Sind Province, 188, 216, 249; agricultural incomes in, 258; crops of, 328; growth in crop production, 356; irrigation in, 203; landed aristocracy of, 301–302; and rice production, 257, 258; subsistence economy of, 355; use of new rice varieties in, 362; and wheat production, 328

Skinner, G. W., 169

Small farmers: in Bangladesh, 175; bias against, in Pakistan, 371, 372; and cooperative credit, 174; credit to, 372; and decline in wheat prices, 255; defined, 335; effect of mechanization on, 341; and green revolution, 356; improving living standard of, 240; income of, in Pakistan, 347; and innovations, 369–370; loans to, in Pakistan, 374; and private tubewell development, 333–334; and technology, 251

Smuggling, of rice, 81

Social organization, rural: in Bangladesh, 5, 32, 157–184; in Comilla District, 160–168; of East Pakistan, 32–35; and impact of cooperatives, 106–107

South Asia: and cooperatives, 44; modernization of, 10; governments of, 41–42

South Bengal (Khulna), 159, 176, 177, 178

Stagnation, agricultural, 191, 256

State Acquisition and Tenancy Act, 159

Statistical methods, 66–68

Stevens, R. D., 6, 7, 188–197

Study Group on Agricultural Policy, 372, 374

Subsidies, agricultural: in Bangladesh, 80; in East Pakistan, 80; in Pakistan, 348

Subsistence level: farms in Pakistan,

335–336, 339; income of Comilla Thana family, 129–130

Sugarcane, 65, 237, 261–262, 358, 364, 365

Sutlej Valley, 203

*Ta'aluq*s, 16

Taccavi loans, 105

*Tahsildar*s, 31

Tarbela Dam, 249

Taxation, 82, 239, 377. *See also* Revenue system; Land

Tea, 64, 65

Tebhaga Movement, 179

Technology: ability to adjust to, 256–258; and Academy for Rural Development, 98; and cooperatives, 100, 102; and distribution of incomes, 250–259; distributive effect of, 256–259; and cropping patterns, 246–247, 248; effect of new, 244–245; impact of, on different classes of farmers, 363–364; needed national policy toward, 263; and optimal allocation of resources, 244–248; and political influence, 258–261; problems of new, 171; relationship between prices and income, 242–269; and small farmers, 251. *See also* Fertilizer; Irrigation; Seeds, high-yielding

*Tehsildar*s, 346

Tenant farming: in Bangladesh, 176, 177, 179; in Canal Colony Districts, 324; and eviction, 178, 179, 355; and green revolution, 179; in Lora and Oghi villages, 273–274; in Pakistan, 176, 177, 203–205, 273–274, 324, 336; in Punjab, 203–205. *See also* Sharecropping

Tepper, Elliot L, 6, 29–59

Thana councils, 47, 48, 108; and allocation of rural public works funds, 48–49; and Basic Democracies, 49, 50; and departmental officers' reports, 111–112; and development of rural works programs, 112, 113

Thana Irrigation Program, 70, 79, 80, 115–116, 146

Thana Training and Development Center, 107–113

Thomas, J. W., 114

Threshing, 137

Tilling of land, 137
Timmons, J. F., 178, 179
Tractors, 102, 260, 324, 339, 340, 341, 367–368
Trading Corporation of Pakistan, 237
Tubewells: and Academy for Rural Development, 133; in Comilla Kotwali Thana, 147–151; and cooperatives, 102; development of, in Pakistan, 233–235, 332, 354; economic benefits of, 152–154; experiments with, 115; and farm sizes, in Pakistan, 366–367; hand-dug, 147–151; maintenance of, 151–152, 234; needed improvements in, 154–155; private, 234, 235, 293, 328–334; public, 234, 332, 354; problems involved in public, 234; repair problems of, 151–152; technology and private, 238–334; and wheat production, 245, 248
Tweeten, L. G., 256

Unemployment, 70, 378
Union councils, 40, 47, 56 n.18, 108, 163; and agricultural development, 164–165; under Ayub Khan, 164
United States: Agency for International Development (USAID), 62, 64, 67, 78, 80, 85, 87, 164, 244; export of food grains, 62; Geodetic Survey, 80; Public Law 480, 61, 72
Upper Bari Doab Canal, 202

Vetch, 249
Village-AID, 45, 46, 217
Villages: census of, 161; electrification program of, 293; extension of, 168–170; and meaning of term in Comilla Thana, 161; nondemocratic attitudes of, 227; and nonvillage characteristics, 32, 34; political life of, 35–37, 161–163, 302, 343–344, 375–376; rural markets of, 168; social life of, 161, 375–376; and villagers' concept of, 32–33; and Village Self-Government Act, 39
Village Self-Government Act, 39

Waheed, Zuhra, 222, 223

Water and Power Development Authority (WAPDA), 79, 88, 115, 234, 310
Weeding, 136–137
Western Districts, 321
West Pakistan: agricultural development in, 189; crop production of, by regions, 329; and distribution of land, 368–375; elections in, 220, 221; and food self-sufficiency program, 234; gross value of major crops, 358, 359; industrial development in, 189; land ownership in, 335; money supply of (1963–1968), 72; and optimal farm size, 366; regions of, 319; and rural public works program, 114; and sources of increased crop output, 295. *See also* Pakistan; East Pakistan
Wheat: acreage and yields in West Pakistan (1964–1970), 271; desi, 282–283; domestic trading of, 236; high-yielding varieties of, 62, 270–289, 354; increase in yields in Pakistan, 270, 358–359; irrigation and increased yield, 244–245; in Pakistan, 188, 270, 328, 358–359; prices and distribution of income, 256; price supports of, 236, 237; production in Punjab, 328; production and tubewells, 245, 248; in rainfed areas, 250; and reduction of prices, 254–256; support prices, 259. *See also* Dwarf wheat
Winter growing season: climate, 147; and employment, 154; and improved rice varieties, 134; and increasing planting of crops, 140, 141, 142; and irrigation, 146, 152; water supply for, 115
Women, 116–117, 118
World Bank, 113, 233, 325

Yield: of dwarf wheats, 270, 282, 283–284; effect of increases in crop production, 360; effect of new varieties, 245; and farm size, 142; and improved rice varieties, 103, 135–136, 142, 143, 147, 153; per acre, and higher prices, 294; per acre, and irrigation, 294; of wheat on irrigated lands, 271; of dwarf wheat, 282, 283–284

Zaildars, 345

Zamindars: break up of, 204; bureaucracy of, 30; and British, 16; competition among, 21; and changes in landholding sizes, 19–26; growth of large,
15–16; and institutional weakness, 32;
and local political control, 53–54 n.2;
and Murshid Quli Khan, 12–13; and
Permanent Settlement, 11; removal
of, 20–21; and revenue collections,
12–13, 14, 23–24